Apostle
of
Persuasion

Apostle of Persuasion

Theology and Rhetoric in the Pauline Letters

James W. Thompson

B
Baker Academic
a division of Baker Publishing Group
Grand Rapids, Michigan

Published by Baker Academic
a division of Baker Publishing Group
PO Box 6287, Grand Rapids, MI 49516-6287
www.bakeracademic.com

Printed in the United States of America

Library of Congress Cataloging-in-Publication Data
Names: Thompson, James, 1942– author.
Title: Apostle of persuasion : theology and rhetoric in the Pauline letters / James W. Thompson.
Description: Grand Rapids, Michigan : Baker Academic, a division of Baker Publishing Group, 2020. | Includes bibliographical references and index.
Identifiers: LCCN 2019039574 | ISBN 9780801099724 (cloth)
Subjects: LCSH: Bible. Epistles of Paul—Theology.
Classification: LCC BS2651 .T46 2020 | DDC 227/.06—dc23
LC record available at https://lccn.loc.gov/2019039574

20 21 22 23 24 25 26   7 6 5 4 3 2 1

For Carolyn

Contents

Abbreviations

General

//	parallel (to)	lit.	literally
§(§)	section(s)	LXX	Septuagint
alt.	altered	NASB	New American Standard Bible
AT	author's translation	NIV	New International Version
bis	twice	NRSV	New Revised Standard Version
Eng.	English versification/translation	par(r).	parallel(s)
KJV	King James Version	RSV	Revised Standard Version
LCL	Loeb Classical Library. London: William Heinemann, 1912–. Cambridge, MA: Harvard University Press, 1934–.		

Old Testament

Gen.	Genesis	Neh.	Nehemiah
Exod.	Exodus	Esther	Esther
Lev.	Leviticus	Job	Job
Num.	Numbers	Ps(s).	Psalm(s)
Deut.	Deuteronomy	Prov.	Proverbs
Josh.	Joshua	Eccles.	Ecclesiastes
Judg.	Judges	Song	Song of Songs
Ruth	Ruth	Isa.	Isaiah
1 Sam.	1 Samuel	Jer.	Jeremiah
2 Sam.	2 Samuel	Lam.	Lamentations
1 Kings	1 Kings	Ezek.	Ezekiel
2 Kings	2 Kings	Dan.	Daniel
1 Chron.	1 Chronicles	Hosea	Hosea
2 Chron.	2 Chronicles	Joel	Joel
Ezra	Ezra	Amos	Amos

Obad.	Obadiah	Zeph.	Zephaniah
Jon.	Jonah	Hag.	Haggai
Mic.	Micah	Zech.	Zechariah
Nah.	Nahum	Mal.	Malachi
Hab.	Habakkuk		

New Testament

Matt.	Matthew	1 Tim.	1 Timothy
Mark	Mark	2 Tim.	2 Timothy
Luke	Luke	Titus	Titus
John	John	Philem.	Philemon
Acts	Acts	Heb.	Hebrews
Rom.	Romans	James	James
1 Cor.	1 Corinthians	1 Pet.	1 Peter
2 Cor.	2 Corinthians	2 Pet.	2 Peter
Gal.	Galatians	1 John	1 John
Eph.	Ephesians	2 John	2 John
Phil.	Philippians	3 John	3 John
Col.	Colossians	Jude	Jude
1 Thess.	1 Thessalonians	Rev.	Revelation
2 Thess.	2 Thessalonians		

Old Testament Apocrypha

1–4 Macc.	1–4 Maccabees	Tob.	Tobit
Sir.	Sirach (Ecclesiasticus)	Wis.	Wisdom (of Solomon)

Old Testament Pseudepigrapha

2 Bar.	2 Baruch (Syriac Apocalypse)	Pss. Sol.	Psalms of Solomon
1 En.	1 Enoch (Ethiopic Apocalypse)	Sib. Or.	Sibylline Oracles
		T. Jud.	Testament of Judah
2 En.	2 Enoch (Slavonic Apocalypse)	T. Levi	Testament of Levi
		T. Naph.	Testament of Naphtali
4 Ezra	4 Ezra	T. Sim.	Testament of Simeon
Jub.	Jubilees		

Dead Sea Scrolls

CD	Damascus Document	1QpHab	Pesher Habakkuk
1QH	Thanksgiving Hymns (Hodayot)	1QS	Rule of the Community (Serek Hayaḥad)
1QHª	Thanksgiving Hymns (Hodayotª)	1QSa	Appendix a to 1QS
1QM	War Scroll (Milḥamah)		

Philo

Alleg. Interp.	*Allegorical Interpretation*	*Migration*	*On the Migration of Abraham*
Confusion	*On the Confusion of Tongues*	*Planting*	*On Planting*
Creation	*On the Creation of the World*	*Prelim. Studies*	*On the Preliminary Studies*
Flight	*On Flight and Finding*	*Spec. Laws*	*On the Special Laws*
Good Person	*That Every Good Person Is Free*	*Virtues*	*On the Virtues*
Heir	*Who Is the Heir?*	*Worse*	*That the Worse Attacks the Better*

Josephus

Ant.	*Jewish Antiquities*	*J.W.*	*Jewish War*

Rabbinic Works and Tractates

Avot	*Avot*	*m.*	Mishnah
Deut. Rab.	*Deuteronomy Rabbah*	*Sanh.*	*Sanhedrin*

Classical Authors

ANAXIMENES OF LAMPSACUS

Rhet. Alex. *Rhetoric to Alexander*

ARISTOTLE

Eth. nic. *Ethica nicomachea (Nicomachean Ethics)*
Rhet. *Rhetorica (Rhetoric)*

CICERO

De or. *De oratore (On Oratory)*
Inv. *De inventione rhetorica (On Rhetorical Invention)*
Rab. Post. *Pro Rabirio Postumo*

DEMOSTHENES

Cor. *De corona (On the Crown)*
Or. *Orations*

DIO CHRYSOSTOM

Conc. Apam. *De concordia cum Apamensibus (Or. 40) (On Concord with Apamea)*
4 Regn. *De regno iv (Or. 4) (On Kingship)*

Hom. Socr. *De Homero et Socrate (Or. 55) (On Homer and Socrates)*
Nicom. *Ad Nicomedienses (Or. 38) (To the Nicomedians)*

DIOGENES LAERTIUS

Lives *Lives of Eminent Philosophers*

EPICTETUS

Diatr. *Diatribai/Dissertationes (Informal Talks)*

ISOCRATES

Antid. *Antidosis (Or. 15) (Defense or Autobiography)*

OVID

Metam. *Metamorphoses (Transformations)*

PLATO

Apol. *Apologia (Apology of Socrates)*

Phaed.	Phaedo (On the Soul)
Phaedr.	Phaedrus
Prot.	Protagoras

QUINTILIAN

| Inst. | Institutio oratoria (The Orator's Education) |

SENECA

| Ep. | Epistulae morales (Moral Epistles) |

SUETONIUS

| Claud. | Divine Claudius |

THEOPHRASTUS

| Char. | Characteres |

Secondary Sources

BDAG   W. Bauer, F. W. Danker, W. F. Arndt, and F. W. Gingrich, eds. *A Greek-English Lexicon of the New Testament and Other Early Christian Literature*. 3rd ed. Chicago: University of Chicago Press, 2000.

BDF   F. Blass, A. Debrunner, and R. W. Funk. *A Greek Grammar of the New Testament and Other Early Christian Literature*. Chicago: University of Chicago Press, 1961.

EDNT   *Exegetical Dictionary of the New Testament*. Edited by Horst Balz and Gerhard Schneider. Eng. trans. 3 vols. Grand Rapids: Eerdmans, 1990–93.

NIDB   *New Interpreter's Dictionary of the Bible*. Edited by Katharine Doob Sakenfeld. 5 vols. Nashville: Abingdon, 2006–9.

OTP   *Old Testament Pseudepigrapha*. Edited by James H. Charlesworth. 2 vols. New York: Doubleday, 1983–85.

TDNT   *Theological Dictionary of the New Testament*. Edited by Gerhard Kittel and Gerhard Friedrich. Translated by Geoffrey W. Bromiley. 10 vols. Grand Rapids: Eerdmans, 1964–76.

TLNT   *Theological Lexicon of the New Testament*. By C. Spicq. Translated and edited by J. D. Ernest. 3 vols. Peabody, MA: Hendrickson, 1994.

Introduction

Rhetoric and Theology in Paul

A rthur Koestler once described a children's puzzle from his childhood; the puzzle was a paper with a tangle of very thin blue and red lines. If you just looked at it, you couldn't make out anything. But if you covered it with a piece of transparent red tissue paper, the red lines of the drawing disappeared and the blue lines formed a picture—it was a clown in a circus holding a hoop with a little dog jumping through it. If you covered the same drawing with a blue tissue paper, a roaring lion appeared chasing the clown across the ring. The puzzle is illustrative: you can do the same thing with every mortal, living or dead.[1]

The multilayered drawing is an appropriate metaphor for the study of any figure of the past, as Koestler maintained. It is especially the case with the apostle Paul. N. T. Wright also illustrates the same point, but with different metaphors, recalling that "Water Lilies," Claude Monet's painting, employs layer upon layer and that no interpretation can limit itself to one layer. Wright offers another metaphor, imagining accompanying a song with only two or three strings and suggesting that many interpretations of Paul proceed as though his writings were a one-stringed instrument.[2] He has been described variously as a moral philosopher in the Greek tradition, a mystic, a rabbi, the founder of Christian literature, and a rhetorician.[3] Because of these multiple dimensions of Paul,

---

1. Koestler, *Arrival and Departure*, 17–18. I owe the reference to Plank, *Paul and the Irony of Affliction*, 38.
2. Wright, *Paul and His Recent Interpreters*, 27.
3. Strecker and Nolting, "Der vorchristliche Paulus," 713.

Wayne Meeks describes him as the "Christian Proteus."[4] But as Luke Timothy Johnson says, "Much more difficult is the question of what holds these dimensions together."[5] The task of this book is to examine the relationship between two layers in the Pauline correspondence: his theology and his rhetoric.

Paul the Theologian

Because of the importance of normative doctrine in Western Christianity, interpreters have described Paul as the first Christian theologian.[6] Protestant churches in particular have looked to Paul as the source of timeless truths that can be applied in all ages.[7] According to N. T. Wright, "Paul actually *invents* something that we may call Christian theology."[8] His letters include a discourse that is unprecedented in the Jewish and Greek traditions. He demonstrates an awareness of the rabbinic midrash homily (cf. Rom. 4:1–29; 2 Cor. 3:7–18; Gal. 3:6–29), employing Hillel's rules for interpretation,[9] but he rarely writes in this form. While he presupposes the story of God's saving deeds, he does not write in narrative form. Although his letters—especially in the outer frame—follow the pattern of ancient letter writing, the sustained arguments in his letters have few parallels.[10] Indeed, epistles are well suited for his engagement in a battle of ideas, for Paul can employ this literary form to engage in sustained arguments against his opponents. Like his philosophical contemporaries, he "destroys strongholds," the arguments that are raised up by his opponents against the knowledge of God (2 Cor. 10:4).[11] Thus theologians of later centuries have looked to Paul as their model for theological argumentation and source of Christian doctrine.

If Paul is the first Christian theologian, however, he does not fit the Western understanding of thinkers who organize their thought into neat categories.

4. Meeks, "Christian Proteus."

5. Johnson, "Paul of the Letters," 72.

6. Wrede, *Paulus*, 101. Bultmann, *Theology of the New Testament*, 1:187; Dunn, *Theology of Paul*, 2: "Paul was the first and greatest theologian."

7. Thurén, *Derhetorizing Paul*, 5.

8. Wright, *Paul and the Faithfulness of God*, 1:xvi.

9. See the use of the rabbinic *qal wachomer* in Rom. 5:15, 17; 2 Cor. 3:7–11. The hermeneutic rule *gezera shewa* is employed in the midrash in Rom. 4:3–6. Rabbi Hillel developed seven rules of interpretation, two of which are mentioned here. *Qal wachomer* (lit., "light and heavy") is the argument from the lesser to the greater, from a minor premise to a greater one. *Gezera shewa* (lit., "cut equally") is the interpretation of one verse by a similar one.

10. See Fairweather, "Epistle to the Galatians," 220, 224.

11. For the widespread use of the martial imagery to describe the philosopher's task, cf. Epictetus, *Diatr.* 3.24.31, 34; Seneca, *Ep.* 59.6–8; cf. 64.3–4; 113.27–28; Philo, *Good Person* 15; *Confusion* 128–31. See Malherbe, "Antisthenes and Paul at War."

Instead he writes occasional letters, responding to a variety of questions. His thoughts on Christology and soteriology, for example, are scattered among his letters in his responses to various issues. While he has been our primary source for Christian doctrines, he does not use the terms that later became the categories of dogmatic theology, and he never arranges those thoughts in a systematic way, as if they were discrete topics that could be separated from each other or from the situations in which he expresses himself. Paul, instead, writes letters, often in the heat of battle, over a period of more than a decade.

Obstacles to Writing Pauline Theology

Scholars who attempt to organize Paul's thought in a systematic fashion face at least three major obstacles. First, the fact that his letters are responses to the questions raised in his communities over a period of time limits interpreters' capacity for distilling the essential thought of the apostle. New issues in the churches call for new theological reflection. Topics that are the central focus of one letter are scarcely mentioned in others. The second obstacle is that the interpreter faces the apparent inconsistency in Paul's treatment of the traditional topics. For example, the expectation that "we who are alive . . . will be caught up . . . to meet the Lord . . . in the air" (1 Thess. 4:17) when the day of the Lord comes as "a thief in the night" (1 Thess. 5:2) suggests Paul's expectation of the imminence of Christ's return, while his desire to "depart and be with Christ" (Phil. 1:23; cf. 2 Cor. 5:1–10) appears to assume a return to Christ at death. Indeed, a primary reason that 2 Thessalonians is widely considered pseudonymous is that the extended period of time before the parousia envisioned in 2 Thessalonians conflicts with the imminent expectation in 1 Thessalonians. A comparison of statements about the end-time in Paul's letters will not yield a consistent eschatology.

Scholars have also observed other inconsistencies in Paul. Heikki Räisänen, for example, maintains that there is an inconsistency in Paul's statements about the law. Paul "states in unambiguous terms that the law has been abolished," but he also makes statements that imply that the law is still valid and even appeals to Old Testament commands.[12] Räisänen adds, "While generally holding fast to the divine origin of the law, Paul once in a heated debate also suggests that it was only given by angels and is thus inferior."[13] Additionally, Räisänen and others argue that Paul's view of the destiny of disobedient Israel is inconsistent. In Romans 9, Paul resorts to the extreme explanation of a divine hardening that takes place regardless of human activity (Rom. 9:6–29),

12. Räisänen, *Paul and the Law*, 199.
13. Räisänen, *Paul and the Law*, 200.

whereas in the very next chapter he puts all emphasis on Israel's notorious disobedience. In chapter 11, at last, Paul definitely discards his predestinarian construction and replaces it with the statement that Israel's obduracy is of a temporary nature. But this runs counter to 1 Thessalonians 2:14–16 as well.[14]

The third obstacle faced by interpreters involves the determination of which letters are actually written by Paul. While issues of style and setting play a role in the assessment of Pauline authorship, finding coherence between the theology of the disputed letters and the seven undisputed letters raises the question, What is Pauline theology in actuality?

Approaches to Pauline Theology

In an attempt to overcome these obstacles, interpreters have employed a variety of approaches to the apostle's thought. Since most scholars have approached Paul from a confessional standpoint, the need for a constructive theology has made the discovery of a coherent theology in Paul an indispensable task. From Luther to the present, scholars have assumed a "canon within the canon," a center of Paul's theology. For Luther and his successors, justification by faith is the center of Pauline theology, and Galatians and Romans are the primary focus. But in recent years, alternative proposals have been made. Jürgen Becker argues that the cross is the center of Pauline thought and the presupposition for the doctrine of justification.[15] For Michael Wolter, the center of Pauline thought "is the certainty of Christ-faith, that the God of Israel has acted eschatologically in Jesus Christ for the salvation of all humankind and that this event is made present in the Pauline gospel of salvation for 'everyone who believes' (Rom. 1:16)."[16] James Dunn resists the image of the center but insists that Jesus Christ is the "fulcrum," "pivot point," and criterion by which everything is measured.[17]

While numerous approaches to Pauline theology have treated the apostle's thought without regard to the contingent situation of his letters, J. Christiaan Beker argues for the interplay of the coherence of Paul's thought in the context of the contingent situation, maintaining that the coherent center of Paul's theology is the triumph of God.[18] For Udo Schnelle, "*The eschatological presence of God's salvation in Jesus Christ is the basis and center of Pauline thought.*"[19] Thus the attempt to discover the center has not led to unanimity.

14. Räisänen, *Paul and the Law*, 264.
15. Becker, *Paul*, 289–90.
16. Wolter, *Paul*, 438.
17. Dunn, *Theology of Paul*, 722–23.
18. Beker, *Paul the Apostle*.
19. Schnelle, *Apostle Paul*, 389, Schnelle's emphasis.

Development in Pauline Thought

Because of these obstacles in ascertaining a coherent Pauline theology, scholars have proposed that Paul's thought develops over time, arguing that 1 Thessalonians is a statement of early Pauline theology and that the imminent eschatology of 1 Thessalonians recedes as Paul comes to grips with the delay of the parousia.[20] The absence of the major Pauline themes in the letter, including justification by faith and the problem of the law, is presented as evidence of early Pauline theology.[21] As a result, Romans, commonly regarded as the last among the undisputed letters of Paul, is widely regarded as the mature statement of Paul's theology. Indeed, traditional Protestant scholarship has followed Melanchthon's statement that Romans is the compendium of Pauline theology. Indeed, James Dunn's *Pauline Theology* is based on Romans because it represents Paul's mature thought.[22]

While development in Paul's theology remains a possibility, the capacity of the interpreter to follow the lines of development is less likely. If we consider the span of Paul's life and ministry, 1 Thessalonians, written seventeen years after Paul's conversion, is scarcely early Pauline theology. Indeed, the span of Paul's letter-writing activity is less than that of his life between his conversion/call and the writing of 1 Thessalonians. Furthermore, no consensus exists on the sequence of Paul's letters. The dating of both Galatians and Philippians, for example, is disputed. Furthermore, the tracing of the development of Paul's thought ignores the dialogical nature of his letters as the response to questions that were asked. Therefore, the one-dimensional treatment of Paul as theologian fails to acknowledge the relationship between his theology and his mode of communication.

The Other Layers: Sociology and Rhetoric in the Study of Paul

Attempts to determine the center of Paul's theology treat Paul as a man of ideas, examining only one strand of the total picture of Paul. Wolfgang Stegemann comments on Michael Wolter's *Paul: An Outline of His Theology*, saying that both Paul and his readers appear to be "disembodied" in Wolter's

20. Cf. Söding, "Der erste Thessalonicherbrief," 184. Schnelle, *Apostle Paul*, 190–91.

21. Schnelle, *Apostle Paul*, 188. See Becker, *Paul*, 3: "If we consistently keep the chronological and dialogical position of a letter in view, we will make observations indicating that from his calling until his entry into Rome as a prisoner Paul did not present the same unchanged theology. Rather, with all constancy in a few crucial basic issues, he went through a development that was influenced by his own experiences, by interaction with his churches, and by early Christian history in general."

22. Dunn, *Theology of Paul*.

book: "Their faith has little to do with their bodies and their social reality" but involves especially cognitive contents and problems.[23] A similar critique could be offered of other treatments of Pauline theology that have routinely examined his theology in isolation from the circumstances of his churches, his rhetorical needs, and his own understanding of his task. Major studies of Pauline theology, including those of Ferdinand Hahn,[24] James Dunn,[25] and N. T. Wright,[26] give no attention to the rhetorical dimension in Pauline theology.

In the last generation, scholars have focused on other layers of Paul's letters,[27] moving beyond the traditional confessional issues to explore, among other topics, Paul's relationship to the empire,[28] ethnicity,[29] and gender[30]—the questions that reflect our own intellectual climate. But the rise of sociological and rhetorical criticism has raised the question of the relationship between Paul's theology and his strategies for persuasion—two layers in the study of Paul. Krister Stendahl argues that the doctrine of justification by faith is not the center but is instead a means of defending the gentile mission: "The doctrine of justification by faith was hammered out by Paul for the very specific and limited purpose of defending the rights of Gentile converts to be full and genuine heirs to the promise of God to Israel."[31] Some have argued that Paul employs strategies of community building and rhetoric to advance his theology, while others reduce his theology to strategy. For example, Francis Watson argues that "Pauline texts become much more readily comprehensible when one abandons this overtly theological approach."[32] He claims that Paul first preached to the gentiles as a result of the failure of his mission to the Jews: "Paul protests that his reasons for dispensing with the law are strictly theological ([Gal.] 2:15–5:11), but his own words in 1 Corinthians 9:21 and 10:32–33 prove that the setting aside of parts of the law was originally not a matter of theological principle but of practical expediency." He adds, "To prevent their bitter experience of almost total rejection being repeated, they set aside some of the requirements of the law which would be most offensive

23. Stegemann, "Wie wörtlich?," 196.
24. Hahn, *Theologie des Neuen Testaments*.
25. Dunn, *Theology of Paul*.
26. Wright, *Paul and the Faithfulness of God*, 2 vols.
27. See the surveys in Zetterholm, *Approaches to Paul*, and in Wright, *Paul and His Recent Interpreters*.
28. Cf. Horsley, *Paul and Empire*.
29. Cf. Hodge, *If Sons, Then Heirs*.
30. Cf. Ehrensperger, *That We May Be Mutually Encouraged*.
31. Stendahl, *Paul among Jews and Gentiles*, 2. The departure from the traditional Lutheran and evangelical view of justification as the center of Pauline theology was anticipated by Schweitzer, *Mysticism of Paul the Apostle*, and Wrede, *Paul*.
32. F. Watson, *Paul, Judaism, and the Gentiles*, ix–x.

to Gentiles, and so ensured the success of their preaching. Paul's theological discussions about the law are therefore attempts to justify this essentially non-theological decision."[33] Employing the sociological categories of sectarian groups, Watson insists that the maintenance of the community as a distinct religious body requires an ideology legitimating its identity—that is, "a theoretical justification for its existence."[34] Theology becomes strategy.

The rise of rhetorical criticism has also raised questions about the relationship between Paul's theology and his strategy. Scholars have increasingly acknowledged that Paul is not merely the source of disembodied ideas; his goal is to persuade the audience and affect their behavior. In the past generation, this relationship between theology and rhetoric has been a question of continuing concern.

The debate about Paul's rhetoric and theology begins with an examination of Paul's initial interaction with his churches. As one devoted to public speaking, he was naturally compared to the orators of his time by his converts, some of whom judged him "untrained in speech" (*idōtēs tō logō*, 2 Cor. 11:6; cf. 10:10). With his insistence that he did not employ "persuasive words of wisdom" (2 Cor. 2:4; cf. Gal. 1:10), he disavowed the practice that was the heart of ancient rhetoric.[35] Similarly, his denial that he employed flattery (cf. 1 Thess. 2:5) or attempted to please his audience (Gal. 1:10; 1 Thess. 2:4) distinguished him from the common perception of the rhetoricians.[36] His claim not to be among those who "peddle" (*kapēleuontes*) God's word (2 Cor. 2:17) echoes the criticism of the Sophists, who went about "hawking [*kapēleuō*] their doctrines to any odd purchaser who desire[d] them" (Plato, *Prot.* 313d). Indeed, Paul consistently refers to his public speaking in terms that are "decidedly nonrhetorical; rhetoricians did not use such verbs as *euangelizein*, *kēryssein*, and *katangelein* to describe their practice."[37]

Despite these disclaimers, Paul declares, "We persuade others" (2 Cor. 5:11). Indeed, this declaration introduces a dense argumentative section (2 Cor. 5:11–6:2) that is intended to persuade the Corinthians to "be reconciled to God" (2 Cor. 5:20). Thus persuasion plays a role in the letters. Paul develops theological arguments to state the implications of the gospel while

---

33. F. Watson, *Paul, Judaism, and the Gentiles*, 36.

34. F. Watson, *Paul, Judaism, and the Gentiles*, 20.

35. See Litfin, *Paul's Theology of Proclamation*, 262: "It was πείθειν, the calling forth of some particular judgment or verdict or conviction from the audience, that fired classical rhetoric." See further discussion of persuasion (πείθειν) in chap. 2 of this study.

36. Cf. Seneca's Votienus Montanus in Seneca the Elder, *Controversiae*. "If you prepare a declamation beforehand, you write not to win but to please. . . . Your aim is to win approval for yourself rather than for the case." Cited in Litfin, *Paul's Theology of Proclamation*, 86.

37. Litfin, *Paul's Theology of Proclamation*, 184.

providing his community with arguments that they can then employ against opponents (cf. 2 Cor. 5:12). While his original preaching is an announcement of the good news, the letters both restate the original message and develop arguments consistent with his ultimate goal for his churches.

As interpreters since Augustine have noted, Paul argues with rhetorical competence. While we know little about his rhetorical training,[38] we recognize abundant evidence that his letters were not "boxes full of theology."[39] As his opponents conceded, "His letters are weighty and strong" (2 Cor. 10:10). Scholars have examined both his arrangement and his style, demonstrating the coherence of his arguments and classifying stylistic features into rhetorical categories. Lauri Thurén has pointed out that Paul's statements are not always to be taken at face value, for he speaks with irony (cf. 1 Cor. 4:8–9; 2 Cor. 11:20), frequently exaggerates,[40] and employs praise as a means of ethical persuasion. Paul's task is not only to inform or to educate but also to affect the readers and to shape their behavior. Consequently, contradictory statements may be accounted for by differing persuasive tasks.[41] Thus the relationship between Paul's theology and rhetoric is a persistent issue in Pauline scholarship.

The traditional model approaches theology and rhetoric as separate disciplines. Many treat rhetoric and theology as rooted in the classic distinction between form and content, *res* and *verba*. One can change the form without changing the content.[42] Johannes Weiss, who offered an extensive treatment of Paul's rhetorical style, suggests that one should discern between rhetorical devices in a text and the "doctrine that is already fixed and pronounced."[43] Rudolf Bultmann, who wrote both a study of Pauline rhetoric and the classic *New Testament Theology*,[44] assumed that theology was the content and

38. Cf. Hübner, *Theologie des Neuen Testaments*, 2:27. The question of Paul's rhetorical education has been a center of debate. Porter, "Ancient Literate Culture," 103, suggests that Paul went through Greek grammar school in Tarsus. Vegge, *Paulus und das antike Schulwesen*, 462, maintains that Paul was taught the *progymnasmata* by a teacher of rhetoric.

39. The expression is from Hartman, "Galatians 3:15–4:11," 127.

40. Cf. Rom. 1:8, "Your faith is made known throughout the world" (AT); "You that abhor idols, do you rob temples?" (Rom. 2:23 AT). See other examples in Thurén, *Derhetorizing Paul*, 33–34. See also Cosby, "Galatians," 296–300: "When Paul equates living under the law with slavery in Galatians 3–4, his stark assertions overstate his true attitude toward the law. Does the former Pharisee, who in another rhetorical context proudly claims that his righteousness under the law was blameless (Phil. 3:6), literally believe that living under the law is living under a curse?"

41. Thurén, *Derhetorizing Paul*, 181.

42. Lampe, "Theology and Rhetoric," 90–91.

43. Weiss, *Beiträge zur paulinische Rhetorik*, 6.

44. Cf. Bultmann, *Der Stil der paulinischen Predigt*; Bultmann, *Theology of the New Testament*.

rhetoric was the form. Unfortunately, most studies of Pauline theology do not engage in rhetorical analysis.

According to another model, Paul maintains a coherent set of convictions, but rhetoric and theology are interwoven in various ways. Paul is not an opportunist who changes positions to please his audience but one who employs rhetoric to defend the truth of the gospel. According to Jürgen Becker, Paul employs rhetoric primarily in polemical texts such as Galatians, where the needs of polemic prevent Paul from giving a well-balanced view of the law and faith.[45] Indeed, "Whoever wants to understand Paul must distinguish between his serious concerns and his polemical attacks."[46] Similarly, J. Christiaan Beker, in distinguishing between the coherence and the contingency of Paul's argument, maintains that Paul is a coherent thinker who holds a firm set of convictions while employing rhetorical devices to fit specific contexts: "Without a coherent center, Paul [would] degenerate into a purely opportunistic theologian, who, with the help of various rhetorical skills, adapts the gospel to whatever the sociological situation demands."[47]

Lauri Thurén recognizes the rhetorical dimension but argues that the interpreter's task is to distinguish between the theology and the rhetoric of Paul's letters. Taking Galatians as his example, he argues that the purpose of Galatians is not theoretical; it is to persuade the community to follow Paul, not the other teachers.[48] Consequently, Paul does not record all of his thoughts but presents a one-sided view for rhetorical effect.[49] The interpreter's task, therefore, is to "derhetorize"—to separate the theological statements from the exaggeration and pathos that have a rhetorical effect.

By analyzing Paul's letters in chronological order and by applying rhetorical analysis to each letter, Hans Hübner tries to illuminate the dynamic character of Paul's theology. According to Hübner, theological thinking for Paul is theological arguing. Argumentation is the development of thought about theological questions, and in his argumentation, the apostle shows rhetorical competence.[50] "Theology is a process of developing convincing arguments in a specific rhetorical situation in which content of theological thought and contingent rhetoric are intertwined. Only the convictional core—the proclamation of the gospel of justification, for example—is not touched by rhetoric."[51]

45. Becker, *Paul*, 303.
46. Becker, *Paul*, 304.
47. Beker, "Paul's Theology," 367–68.
48. Thurén, *Derhetorizing Paul*, 92–94.
49. Thurén, *Derhetorizing Paul*, 92.
50. Hübner, *Theologie das Neuen Testaments*, 2:26–27.
51. Lampe, "Theology and Rhetoric," 94. See Hübner, "Die Rhetorik und die Theologie," 168–69.

According to another model, theology and rhetoric do not relate as content and form. Rather, the theological content is part of the rhetorical means in persuading the audience.[52] In examining the theology of Ephesians, Andrew T. Lincoln insists that the letter is not primarily focused on communicating coherent ideas. It is a letter written for pastoral purposes: "It achieves its purposes by rhetorical means, by adopting a strategy of persuasion. In his attempt to persuade, the writer constructs a symbolic universe, which the readers are expected to share to a large extent."[53]

Johan S. Vos recalls the ancient debates between the Platonists and the rhetoricians, comparing them with the contemporary discussion on the relationship between theology and rhetoric in Paul. According to the Platonists, truth exists apart from human opinions and the means by which truth is expressed. Platonists, then, distinguished between the *res* (the conceptual content) and the *verba* (the words) used to communicate the *res*.[54]

According to the (neo)-sophistic view, truth is contingent, something the orator creates. Truth is "what communities are persuaded of at any particular time."[55] Some scholars interpret Paul in Platonic terms, ignoring the rhetorical dimension of his arguments. Other scholars take a neo-sophistic view, interpreting theology as a form of strategy.

Paul, Persuasion, and the Goals of the Orator

For ancient orators, all strategies of persuasion were determined by the orator's goal of gaining the appropriate result from the listeners: the acceptance of the argument. In the search for the center of Pauline theology, little attention has been given to Paul's understanding of God's telos for the world and humankind. With the exception of Philemon, all the undisputed letters, as well as Colossians and Ephesians, declare God's ultimate purpose. Missing from the discussion of rhetoric and theology in Paul, however, is the apostle's own understanding of himself and his goals, which he states on numerous occasions. Paul consistently announces the aims that govern his persuasion, both in summary statements of his ultimate ambition and in his prayers for the congregations. The telos of his ministry aligns with God's telos, for he has been called to be God's servant. The letters are not theological essays but his means of persuading the readers to reach that goal.

52. Lampe, "Theology and Rhetoric," 95.
53. Lincoln, "Theology of Ephesians," 76.
54. Vos, "Rhetoric and Theology in the Letters," 172.
55. Guthrie, *Sophists*, 51.

Telos in Paul's Prayer Reports

The introductory thanksgivings, or prayer reports, provide an important indicator of the central concerns and telos of Pauline thought. Unlike the rare thanksgivings in Hellenistic letters,[56] Paul's prayer reports express gratitude for the community's moral progress from the time of their conversion until Paul writes ("from the first day until now," Phil. 1:5; cf. 1 Thess. 1:5–10; Philem. 3–5). Paul Schubert observes that an eschatological climax also appears frequently in the thanksgivings,[57] as Paul looks toward the end, reflecting his understanding of a community that is in the middle of a corporate narrative that stands between the past and the future under the power of God.[58]

In his prayer reports, Paul describes the end of the narrative as "the day of our Lord Jesus" (1 Cor. 1:8), "the day of Christ Jesus" (Phil. 1:6), "the day of Christ" (Phil. 1:10), and the parousia (1 Thess. 3:13). Elsewhere in his letters, he speaks of "the day of the Lord" (1 Cor. 5:5; 2 Cor. 1:14; 1 Thess. 5:2), "the day of wrath" (Rom. 2:5), "the day when . . . God judges the secrets of the heart" (Rom. 2:16), "the day of Christ" (Phil. 2:16), or simply "the day" (Rom. 13:12; 1 Cor. 3:13), adapting the prophetic expectation of the day of the Lord to the hope of believers for the return of Christ. For Paul, the Lord is the exalted Christ, who will descend from heaven (1 Thess. 4:16; cf. Phil. 3:20; 1 Thess. 1:10). Living between the past of God's saving acts and the future day of the Lord, the community waits for the ultimate redemption (1 Cor. 1:7; Gal. 5:5; Phil. 3:20; 1 Thess. 1:10). Thus the church stands in the middle of a corporate narrative.

This interim period is a time of moral transformation, for Paul consistently expresses confidence (1 Cor. 1:8) or prays that his communities will be morally formed at the day of Christ. Paul uses a variety of synonyms, frequently terms with the alpha privative, to describe this transformed community.

Speaking to a deeply flawed community in Corinth, Paul expresses the confidence that God "will strengthen [the Corinthians], so that [they] are blameless [*anenklētos*] until the end at the day of the Lord" (1 Cor. 1:8). *Anenklētos*, a term used in the Septuagint only in 3 Maccabees 5:31, is a judicial image describing one against whom no one can bring charges (cf. Rom.

---

56. Contrary to the widespread belief that the thanksgiving was common at the beginning of Hellenistic letters, Peter Arzt has demonstrated that the thanksgiving was not a common component of the Hellenistic letter. See Artz, "'Epistolary Introductory Thanksgiving' in the Papyri and in Paul."

57. Schubert, *Form and Function of the Pauline Thanksgivings*, 4–9; cf. Pao, "Constraints of an Epistolary Form," 123.

58. Pao, "Constraints of an Epistolary Form," 125.

8:33, "Who can bring charges against God's elect?").[59] In Colossians 1:22, it is used synonymously with "holy [*hagios*] and unblemished [*amōmos*]" (AT), and in the Pastoral Epistles, the term is used for the requirements for Christian leaders (cf. 1 Tim. 3:10; Titus 1:6–7). Paul emphasizes that it is God who is at work to transform a morally deficient community into one that is irreproachable at the end (1 Cor. 1:8).

In Philippians, Paul adds a petition to his introductory thanksgiving (Phil. 1:9–11), praying that the community will be "sincere [*eilikrinēs*] and faultless [*aproskopos*] at the day of Christ" (Phil. 1:10). *Eilikrinēs*, literally "unmixed, without alloy,"[60] signifies the sincerity and purity of motive (1 Cor. 5:8; Plato, *Phaed.* 66) that Paul claims for himself (cf. 2 Cor. 2:17). With *aproskopos*, literally "without giving offense,"[61] Paul elaborates on the meaning of these terms, indicating that the faultless behavior involves love that grows increasingly in full knowledge and discernment (Phil. 1:9), the capacity to discern the better things (Phil. 1:10), and a life that demonstrates "the fruit of righteousness" (Phil. 1:11 NIV). Indeed, as in 1 Corinthians, Paul is confident that the God who began a good work among the Philippians will bring it to completion at the day of Christ (Phil. 1:6) in a transformed community.

In 1 Thessalonians, Paul offers thanksgiving for the community's moral progress in 1:2–10 and later prays to God that the Lord will cause them to "increase and abound in love for one another and for all" and that they will be "blameless [*amemptos*] in holiness [*hagiōsynē*] before our God and Father at the parousia" (1 Thess. 3:12–13). *Amemptos* is a common term in the Old Testament for the righteous person (cf. Gen. 17:1 LXX) and is especially prominent in the Wisdom of Solomon and Job. According to Wisdom 10:5, it is synonymous with *righteousness* (cf. Luke 1:6), and in Wisdom 10:15, it is synonymous with *holy*. Job was "blameless and upright" (Job 1:1, 8), unlike anyone else on earth. His blamelessness is a constant thread throughout the drama of the book (cf. Job 4:17; 9:20; 11:4; 12:4; 15:14; 33:9). Paul, prior to his conversion, was also *amemptos* in keeping the law (Phil. 3:6).

In the concluding benediction in 1 Thessalonians (5:23), Paul reinforces the prayer of 3:11–13, praying that God will sanctify the community wholly, that their "spirit and soul and body" will be "blameless" (*amemptos*) at the parousia. Thus, while they are incomplete in their faith at the moment (cf. 3:8), Paul prays that God will act to sanctify them in preparation for the end.

59. W. Grundmann, "ἀνέγκλητος," *TDNT* 1:357.
60. BDAG 282.
61. BDAG 125.

As the two prayer reports in 1 Thessalonians indicate (3:11–13; 5:23), the moral formation that Paul describes is the process of sanctification. *Hagiōsynē* signifies holiness as a completed process (cf. 2 Cor. 7:1), the work that God has brought "to completion by the day of Jesus Christ" (Phil. 1:6), while the verb *hagiasai* (1 Thess. 5:23) points to the continuing process in which God is at work. This process is especially evident in the prayer that the Thessalonians "increase and abound in love for one another and for all" (1 Thess. 3:12) and in the instruction that the Thessalonians' sanctification (*hagiasmos*) involves an appropriate sexual ethic (1 Thess. 4:3, 7). Thus just as God called Israel to be holy as God is holy (Lev. 19:2), Paul envisions a process in which the church, which lives in continuity with Israel, becomes what God intended Israel to be before the end.

Paul's prayers probably also reflect Israel's hope that a flawed people would ultimately stand before God as a restored and righteous community.[62] Trito-Isaiah looks forward to the return from exile when the people will be righteous (*dikaios*, Isa. 60:21). Zechariah promises a restored Israel in which the people will "speak truth to one another," "render . . . judgments that are true and make for peace," and "love no false oaths" (Zech. 8:16–17). Jeremiah anticipates a new covenant in which the law is written on the hearts of the people (Jer. 31:31–34), and Ezekiel anticipates a time when God will intervene to cleanse Israel and make them follow his statutes (Ezek. 36:25–27). Similarly, *1 Enoch* 10:21 anticipates the time when "the children of the earth will become righteous, and all nations shall worship and bless [the Lord]." Like the prophets, Paul looks forward to the end of Israel's narrative and the restoration of a righteous people from all the nations of the earth. In describing the telos of moral formation for his communities, Paul also encourages his communities indirectly to be shaped by his ethical vision.

Telos in Paul's Pastoral Goals

Paul consistently announces his own pastoral goals, indicating that he is not only the herald who preaches where Christ has not been named (Rom. 15:19–20) but also the servant who anticipates presenting a sanctified people to God at the day of the Lord. He is God's instrument for bringing God's purpose for humanity to completion, and his goals align with the purposes of God. This alignment is evident in 1 Thessalonians, his earliest letter. Not only does he pray for a blameless people at the parousia, but he also expresses his mission to establish their moral formation. Using parental imagery (1 Thess.

62. See Chester, *Future Hope and Present Reality*, 1:325.

2:17; cf. 2:7–8), he declares that the church is his "hope or joy or crown of boasting" (1 Thess. 2:19) at the parousia and his "glory and joy!" (1 Thess. 2:20). This "crown of boasting" is apparently their blamelessness and holiness at the day of Christ (cf. 1 Thess. 3:13).

In Philippians, Paul prays for the moral formation of the community in 1:9–11 and then declares that his goal is that the community be "blameless [amōmoi] and pure [akeraioi] in a crooked and perverse generation" (Phil. 2:15 AT) and his "boast [kauchēma] on the day of Christ" (Phil. 2:16). Amōmos, which can be used for those who have no physical or moral defects,[63] is a term the Septuagint frequently employs for those who keep God's commands. The psalmist speaks of those who "walk blamelessly" (Ps. 15:2 [14:2 LXX]; cf. 18:23 [17:23 LXX]; 19:13 [18:13 LXX]; 37:18 [36:18 LXX]; 119:1, 80 [118:1, 80 LXX]), and the wisdom literature speaks of those who are morally blameless (Prov. 11:20; Sir. 40:19; Eccles. 11:9). The term can be used synonymously with righteous(ness) (cf. Prov. 11:5; 20:7; Isa. 33:15). According to Ephesians (1:4), God's plan from the beginning was a people that would be "holy [hagios] and blameless [amōmos]"; and Christ, as a result of his death (Eph. 5:27; cf. Col. 1:22), will present to himself a church that is holy (hagia) and blameless (amōmos).

Paul adds to amōmos in Philippians 2:15 the synonymous word "innocent" (akeraios), a term that was used for "that which is still in its original state of intactness" in reference to a country, city, or walls but then became used metaphorically for the moral purity[64] that should characterize his communities at the end (cf. Rom. 16:19, "guileless in what is evil").

As in 1 Thessalonians (3:13; 5:23), Paul associates the final outcome of his churches with sanctification. In summarizing his purpose in writing Romans as the apologetic for his ministry (Rom. 15:14–21), he describes himself in priestly terms, declaring that he is a servant (leitourgos) doing priestly service (hierourgounta) "so that the offering of the Gentiles may be acceptable, sanctified in the Spirit" (Rom. 15:16). Sanctification is the completed process that began with the gentile community's baptism (cf. Rom. 6:1–21; 1 Cor. 6:11) and continued as converts yielded themselves to hagiasmos (Rom. 6:19, 22). His calling for the "obedience of . . . the Gentiles," mentioned at the beginning and end of Romans (1:5; 15:18), is complete when Paul offers the gentiles as a sacrifice to God at the completion of his work.

Paul's presentation of a blameless church is also suggested by his use of paristēmi (to present someone), which can be either a technical term for

---

63. Cf. Hauck, "ἄμωμος," TDNT 4:830–31. In the Septuagint, it is most often used for physical perfection in a cultic sense—i.e., for the offering or the priest who is qualified to sacrifice.
64. Kittel, "ἀκέραιος," TDNT 1:209.

presenting a sacrifice (cf. Rom. 12:1) or a legal term for presenting someone to a judge.[65] According to 2 Corinthians, "The one who raised the Lord Jesus will raise us also and present ["bring into his presence," NRSV] us with you" (2 Cor. 4:14 AT) in the future. Paul is the father of the bride who betrothed his daughter and now protects his daughter in order that he may present her as a pure virgin to Christ (2 Cor. 11:2). Thus the final day is a time when a pure church will be presented to Christ.

Paul describes this completed task as his "boast" (*kauchēsis*, Rom. 15:17), a term that he employs frequently in describing his mission, along with the related term *kauchēma*, which is used for describing what one is "proud of." In 2 Corinthians, his boast (*kauchēsis*) is that he has acted with integrity and sincerity (2 Cor. 1:12), and his goal is that the church will be his boast (*kauchēma*) and he will be theirs at the day of Christ (2 Cor. 1:14). Similarly, when he declares in Philippians his goal that the church be "blameless" and "without blemish" (Phil. 2:15 AT), he adds, "It is by your holding fast to the word of life that I can boast on the day of Christ that I did not run or labor in vain" (Phil. 2:16). This boasting is the equivalent of exultation and joy (Rom. 5:1, 10–11; 2 Cor. 7:4; 1 Thess. 2:19; cf. Phil. 4:1), especially the pride one takes in others. Paul boasts about his converts in the present (2 Cor. 7:4, 14–15, 16; 9:2), and he hopes that they will be his pride and joy at the end.

Despite Paul's hope that God will complete his work at the end (Phil. 1:6) and that his community will be his "boast" at the day of Christ, he considers the possibility that he will have "run . . . in vain" (Phil. 2:16), a concern that he expresses frequently in the letters (cf. Gal. 2:2; 4:11; 1 Thess. 3:5). He therefore challenges the Corinthians not to "receive the grace of God in vain" (2 Cor. 6:1 NASB). Paul's language echoes the words of the servant in Isaiah 49:4, who says, "I have labored in vain." Thus, when Paul declares, "I fear that I have labored in vain" (Gal. 4:11 AT) and "I can boast . . . that I did not run in vain" (Phil. 2:16), he identifies with the servant, who has been called to restore the fortunes of Israel and be "a light to the nations" (Isa. 49:6). As Philippians 2:16 indicates, either Paul is the servant who will have a transformed and blameless community as his pride and joy (cf. 1 Thess. 2:19) or he will have run in vain. Elsewhere, using imagery from family life, he describes himself as the pregnant mother in the pangs of childbirth until the infant is "formed" in his churches (Gal. 4:19).

The consistent feature of Paul's letters is ethical exhortation, which is anticipated in the thanksgivings and developed in the correspondence. He gives thanks for the Romans' faith (Rom. 1:8), for the Thessalonians' "work

65. BDAG 778.

of faith and labor of love and steadfastness of hope" (1 Thess. 1:3), and for
Philemon's love and faith (Philem. 5); and he prays for the moral progress of
the Philippians (Phil. 1:9–11) and Thessalonians (1 Thess. 3:11–13). In his
initial catechetical instruction, Paul is like a father, "urging and encouraging . . . and pleading" that his converts conduct themselves worthily of the
God who calls them "into his own kingdom and glory" (1 Thess. 2:12). His
correspondence is a continuation of his appeal for the community's moral
formation in preparation for the parousia (1 Thess. 2:19). The telos of Paul's
ministry determines his persuasive task, and theology and rhetoric are instruments for reaching that goal.

Theology and Rhetoric and Paul's Persuasive Task

Because an understanding of Paul comes only when one can see more than
one layer at a time, this book will demonstrate that theology and rhetoric
are not alternative approaches to Paul but inseparable parts of his persuasion
of others. While Paul's knowledge of ancient rhetoric is a matter of debate,
the analytical tools of classical rhetoric are useful means for examining his
arguments.[66] Of the five dimensions of rhetoric (invention, arrangement,
style, memory, delivery), I shall focus primarily on arrangement and invention (argumentation), the choice of arguments that support the basic thesis
of the communication. This type of argumentation begins with the common
ground shared by the speaker and listener in order to modify or confirm what
the listener already believes. As one dimension of argumentation, persuasion
involves changing the behavior of the listeners. According to Lauri Thurén,
"In order to persuade, the author usually needs to give reasons for the change;
to give such reasons and to justify them so that the recipients' opinions are
affected is called argument. It becomes persuasion if the goal is to create in
the recipients a volition to act in some way."[67]

Paul engages in persuasion to shape the behavior of the listeners. He is
not an opportunist but one who holds convictions for which he is willing
to die. He articulates these convictions in fulfilling the telos of his work:
the presentation of a transformed people to God. He elaborates on these
convictions in a dialogue with his converts in response to their questions or
misunderstandings of his message. Paul states these convictions in all of the

66. See Kennedy, *Interpretation through Rhetorical Criticism*, 10. See also Schellenberg,
Rethinking Paul's Rhetorical Education, 185–99. Schellenberg analyzes a speech of Red Jacket,
a Native American, describing his eloquence and demonstrating the use of rhetorical means of
persuasion identified by the classical rhetoricians.
67. Thurén, "On Studying Ethical Argumentation and Persuasion," 468.

letters as the foundation for his pastoral instructions. Indeed, theology is a dimension of persuasion as it serves Paul's pastoral purposes.[68]

In chapter 1, I shall explore the nature of Paul's rhetoric, demonstrating that Paul both employs the rhetoric of his time and creates a new prophetic rhetoric. As an educated man, he is familiar with both ancient letter writing and oratory, yet his arguments and authority distinguish his communication from that of his contemporaries. Indeed, he created a new rhetoric.

Paul's arguments are based on premises that distinguish his persuasion. Consistent with his Pharisaic upbringing, he continues to hold to the basic narrative of the one God who chose Israel and promised to rectify the world's lost condition in a new covenant when God vindicates the faithful and punishes the wicked. These are convictions that he did not abandon. In chapter 2, I will explore these premises to his argument.

Paul also inherited premises from Jesus and the early church. From Jesus, he inherited the conviction that the new age has dawned and that the people of God live between the time of the coming of the kingdom and its ultimate realization. He inherited from the early church the basic christological and soteriological confessions that also became premises to his arguments. Chapter 3 is an examination of the premises that Paul inherited from Jesus and the early church.

In chapter 4, I shall explore the transforming event that reshaped Paul's most basic convictions and separated him from the Jewish community. He argues autobiographically and with a prophetic rhetoric that is rooted in the transformative event in his life. Like the ancient orators, he appeals to his own ethos, but it is an ethos that is shaped by the gospel. His understanding of himself is an important basis for his theology.

Paul's letters consist of theological argumentation as he reflects on the basic premises in dialogue with his communities. New rhetorical situations call for theological elaboration on various themes. In chapter 5, I will explore Paul's first letter (1 Thessalonians), noting the categories that Paul inherited and transformed in Christ. This letter is an appropriate place to begin not only because it is Paul's first letter but also because it is most clearly the continuation of his earlier catechesis. It does not offer an extended development of the major theological themes but alludes to all of the major theological categories as part of his catechetical work. He is apparently not arguing against misunderstandings but is employing theological categories as part of his effort at community formation. As the shape of the letter indicates, Paul employs theology as the foundation for persuading the community to

68. See Wischmeyer, "Themes in Pauline Theology," 285.

maintain appropriate behavior. I do not assume that 1 Thessalonians is an early stage in a developing theology but believe, rather, that it is an example of theology as catechesis. Subsequent chapters will demonstrate the process of theologizing in response to the issues in the churches.

In 1 Thessalonians, Paul assumes the christological confession that Jesus is the Son of God and Lord, placing Jesus Christ alongside God, but he does not develop the subject. While he never offers a detailed discussion of Christology, he elaborates on the subject most in Philippians, where the christological hymn is the premise of his effort at moral formation, and in the Corinthian correspondence, where it is the basis of moral instruction. Chapter 6 will explore the persuasive nature of Paul's christological claims.

The Corinthian correspondence responds to new issues, calling forth Paul's most extensive elaboration on the meaning of the cross and of Christian community. Paul has introduced creedal statements interpreting the death of Jesus (cf. 1 Thess. 4:14; 5:10) but has not developed them at length. Chapter 7 will treat the Corinthian correspondence as a window into Paul's soteriology and ecclesiology. Paul makes major theological arguments before describing the significance of theology for ethics.

From the beginning of Paul's ministry, he has welcomed gentiles but has not offered a theological explanation. Under the pressure of opponents, Paul offers the explanation in Galatians. Here for the first time he elaborates on justification by faith, a topic that he has introduced earlier but now develops extensively. Chapter 8 is an initial examination of both the conditions that led to Paul's articulation of justification by faith and the issues to which he responds as he persuades the community to reject life under the law and to maintain a life governed by the Spirit.

Romans is a further elaboration on justification by faith. Paul repeats some of the argument of Galatians and corrects misunderstandings of his earlier argument in a new situation. New questions arising from Galatians require Paul to articulate his anthropology, elaborate on the doctrine of the Spirit, and offer a theological discussion of the hope of Israel. This is the subject of chapter 9.

Most Pauline theologies treat only the undisputed letters of Paul. Chapter 10 will demonstrate the continuity between these letters and Paul in Ephesians and Colossians, and chapter 11 will examine the continuity between Paul's persuasive aims in the Pastoral Epistles and those in the undisputed letters. The conclusion will contain reflections on the place of rhetoric and theology in Paul's persuasive task, indicating that Pauline theology is a reflection on his basic premises in dialogue with the rhetorical situation.

1

The Rhetoric of Paul's Letters

Although the letter is a common means of overcoming the distance between the sender and the recipient in both Greco-Roman and Jewish literature, Paul is the one who made the letter the primary mode of communication. In the presence of his converts, he is a man of the spoken word, but in his absence, he writes letters (cf. 2 Cor. 10:10–11). While letters are embedded in the narrative, prophetic, and apocalyptic works in the Old Testament and Jewish literature, with Paul they become a new form of literature and a model for both canonical writings and the Christian literature of subsequent generations. Paul dictates letters, assuming that they will be read orally to an assembled congregation, maintain contact with his converts, reiterate earlier teaching, correct misunderstandings, and shape the behavior of his community. As the substitute for Paul's presence and the continuation of his earlier instruction, the letters play a vital role in his goal of presenting a blameless people to God at the parousia. This goal requires that he demonstrate his affection for his readers and respond to danger, often with extended theological arguments.

Interpreters have agreed with the author of 2 Peter, however, that Paul's letters are "hard to understand" (2 Pet. 3:16; cf. 2 Cor. 1:13). In the past century, scholars have recognized that a key to the interpretation of Paul's letters is the identification of the genre in which he speaks. While both Paul and his opponents identify his communications as epistles (cf. 2 Cor. 7:8; 10:9–10), the unresolved question is the relationship between Paul's epistles and the literary conventions of his time. Today scholars debate whether Paul's letters conform to the conventions of ancient epistles or of ancient rhetoric.

Epistolography and the Letters of Paul

A new era in the study of Paul's letters began with the publication of two books by Adolf Deissmann, *Bible Studies* and *Light from the Ancient East*.[1] Deissmann examines ancient papyrus letters and demonstrates that Paul's letters conformed to conventions of his time. The identification of the author and sender at the beginning of the letters is parallel to the beginning of a Hellenistic letter, and the expression of grace (*charis*) is a Christian adaptation of the customary greeting (*chairein*). Deissmann and others suggest that the introductory thanksgivings also conformed to ancient letter writing.[2] Like Paul's correspondence, ancient letters also concluded with greetings from acquaintances.

While Deissmann's discoveries demonstrate parallels between the frame of Paul's letters and the letter-writing conventions of his time, they do not provide significant insight into the body of the letters. In the 1970s, scholars examined other papyrus letters further in order to determine the generic characteristics of the body of the Pauline letter, observing other conventions in ancient correspondence.[3] The disclosure form ("I want you to know"; "I do not want you to be ignorant") at the beginning of the body of Paul's letters (cf. Rom. 1:13; 2 Cor. 1:8; Phil. 1:12) also marked the beginning of the body of some ancient letters. Ancient letters also commonly included a request introduced by *parakalō* ("I appeal to you"), which consistently appears in Paul's letters.[4] Besides these characteristics, however, scholars were unable to draw significant parallels between the body of the ancient papyrus letter and the body of the Pauline letter.[5] Recent studies have also shown that the thanksgiving at the beginning of the letter was rare among ancient letters,[6] and none involved gratitude for the readers' moral formation. Unlike Paul's letters, the papyrus letters were brief and private, not instruments for teaching and moral formation.

Since the 1980s, scholars have examined the ancient literary theorists and the model letters they provided, comparing them to Paul's letters. A handbook on letter writing, *De elocutione*, written between the third and first centuries BCE and falsely attributed to Demetrius of Phalerum,[7] offers

---

1. Deissmann, *Bible Studies*; Deissmann, *Light from the Ancient East*.
2. Cf. Deissmann, *Light from the Ancient East*, 168; Schubert, *Form and Function of the Pauline Thanksgivings*, 180.
3. See White, *Form and Function of the Body of the Greek Letter*, 1.
4. Stowers, *Letter Writing in Greco-Roman Antiquity*, 24.
5. See Classen, "Theory of Rhetoric," 27–36.
6. Arzt-Grabner, "Paul's Letter Thanksgiving," 143.
7. Malherbe, *Ancient Epistolary Theorists*, 2.

an excursus on writing in the "plain style." The handbook then lists twenty-one types of letters, giving an example of each.[8] Centuries later (between the fourth and sixth centuries CE), a handbook attributed to Libanius (*Epistolary Styles*) defines the letter as a written conversation with someone who is absent and lists forty-one types of letters. Scholars have identified several of these letter types with Pauline letters. Pseudo-Demetrius's model of a friendly letter, for example, expresses the kind of intimacy with the recipient that is common in Paul's letters. The model of a commendatory letter recalls recommendations in Paul's letters (cf. Rom. 16:1–2). The consoling type also has points of contact with Pauline letters (cf. 1 Thess. 4:13–5:11). The apologetic type has been proposed as the letter type of Galatians, and Libanius mentions the paraenetic letter, which Abraham Malherbe proposes as the literary genre of 1 Thessalonians.[9] However, while Paul's letters have points of contact with these epistolary types, they cannot be identified with any of them, for Paul's letters are much longer than the ancient examples. Indeed, several of these epistolary types appear in single Pauline letters, making the identification of the Pauline letter with any of them problematic.[10]

Paul's letters have points of contact with other types of letters as well. Official letters, like Paul's correspondence, were written by an authoritative person to a community and intended for wider dissemination. As in Paul's letters, the senders indicated their authority, adding the title and position of responsibility, and often provided the names of cosenders. The authors issued directives, made announcements, and indicated that the message was intended for a distinct audience, all of whom were responsible to comply with the instructions.[11]

The philosophical letter also offers some parallels. In the first century CE, philosophers employed the letter as an instrument for philosophical instruction. The letters of Plato and Aristotle were significant models. Letters were a means for philosophers to maintain contact with, and disseminate their teachings to, followers in distant places.[12] Several of the letters of Epicurus have survived in which the philosopher presented his philosophy. Preserved in Diogenes Laertius are letters epitomizing his philosophy (to Herodotus), summarizing his meteorology and his morality (Diogenes Laertius, *Lives*

8. Malherbe, *Ancient Epistolary Theorists*, 2.
9. Malherbe, *Letters to the Thessalonians*, 83.
10. Martin, "Investigating the Pauline Letter Body," 195.
11. Stirewalt, *Paul, the Letter Writer*, 45–46; Aune, *New Testament in Its Literary Environment*, 164–65; Adams, "Paul's Letter Opening and Greek Epistolography," 37.
12. Eckstein, *Gemeinde, Brief und Heilsbotschaft*, 92.

10.34–83). A letter could include personal communications, teaching, or responses to attacks.[13]

Scholars have also shown parallels between Pauline correspondence and Seneca's letters to Lucilius. These letters contain Seneca's philosophy and consist of philosophical teaching followed by moral exhortation. Seneca presents his moral progress as an example for his pupil to follow.

While one may observe the parallels between Paul's correspondence and ancient letters, his letters do not fit into any category.[14] They contain the personal warmth of the friendly letter, the authoritative quality of the official letter to multiple recipients, the extended presentation of his teaching comparable to the philosophical letter, and the hortatory dimension of the paraenetic letter. Within his letters are commendations (Rom. 16:1–2), expressions of consolation (1 Thess. 4:13–18), and mediation (Philemon), all of which have points of contact with ancient letters. These are only partial parallels, however. Nothing in ancient letter writing corresponds to the authoritative voice of Paul, who speaks not only for himself but also for God. He not only offers moral advice, like that of Seneca to Lucilius, but also declares the will of God (cf. 1 Thess. 4:3). In the letters in which he needs to assert his authority, he identifies himself as an apostle sent by God.[15]

Letters that respond to the questions and crises of the community are also unparalleled.[16] Paul writes to the churches that he founded in a process of interaction over the issues facing the church. In some instances, he writes to reaffirm and encourage, and in other instances, he writes in response to crises that threaten his work. He writes with "anxiety for all the churches" (2 Cor. 11:28) and the goal of ensuring their ultimate transformation. In contrast, we know little about the interlocutors in ancient philosophical letters.

The most distinguishing feature of Paul's letters is their length. While the sample letters prove useful for understanding specific sections of Pauline letter bodies, they do not provide a convincing parallel to the body of the Pauline letter. We have found no parallels to a letter written to a community and containing extended teaching and paraenesis. Indeed, Pseudo-Demetrius forbids letters that are overly didactic, maintaining that neither moral exhortation nor philosophizing is fitting in a letter: "If anybody should write of logical subtleties or questions of natural history in a letter, he writes indeed,

13. Eckstein, *Gemeinde, Brief und Heilsbotschaft*, 93.
14. Adams, "Paul's Letter Opening and Greek Epistolography," 38.
15. See Tite, "How to Begin, and Why?," 66, 75.
16. Cf. Pitts, "Philosophical and Epistolary Contexts," 277: "Seneca's correspondent, Lucilius, is referenced very little and, given the immense amount of material written to this young philosopher, one can gather only a few details regarding his life and situation."

but not a letter."[17] Nor do we find the personal engagement and interaction with a community that we find in Paul's letters. "Within these conventional structures, variously modified, Paul stretches the letter form almost to the breaking point. He writes elaborate theological arguments, personal appeals, denunciations, and ethical paraenesis, all designed to be delivered in speech to the assemblies of his converts."[18] According to Ryan Schellenberg, "Clearly, if Paul knew anything about conventional epistolary style, he flagrantly violated its strictures."[19] One cannot find ancient letters with corresponding length, genre, function, and communicative conventions.[20]

Rhetoric and the Letters of Paul

Both Paul and his opponents insist that he is not a rhetorician (cf. 2 Cor. 10:10; 11:6). His denial that he persuades (1 Cor. 2:4; Gal. 1:10) or pleases others (Gal. 1:10; 1 Thess. 2:4) indicates his refusal to be classified among the rhetoricians. When he denies that he attempts to please (*areskein*) others, he assures his readers that he does not employ the tactics of the rhetoricians. In Galatians 1:10, he initiates the argument for his apostolic authority, asking, "Do I please people or God?" (AT). In a series of sharp contrasts between his proclamation and that of the wandering preachers in 1 Thessalonians, he insists that he does not attempt to please his listeners (1 Thess. 2:4) or flatter them as "a pretext for greed" (1 Thess. 2:5), a practice often identified with the Sophists.[21] In denying that he pleases or flatters others for gain, Paul echoes the ancient debate between the Platonists and the Sophists. In Plato's *Gorgias* (462b3–465e6), Socrates draws a sharp distinction between the skills or arts (*technai*) that aim at excellence and those that are meant mainly to please.[22] Paul's insistence that he does not "persuade people" also recalls the ancient criticisms of the Sophists. According to Socrates, "Then the case

17. *De elocutione* 232. See Schellenberg, *Rethinking Paul's Rhetorical Education*, 260.
18. Forbes, "Ancient Rhetoric and Ancient Letters," 159.
19. Schellenberg, *Rethinking Paul's Rhetorical Education*, 260.
20. Thurén, "Rhetoric and Epistolography," 145.
21. Cf. the speech by C. Claudius in Dionysius of Halicarnassus, *Roman Antiquities* 11.9.1: "I ask this, Appius, of you men who are at the head of the commonwealth and are in duty bound to consult the common interest of all rather than your private advantage, that if I speak some truths with frankness instead of trying to please you, you will not be offended on that account, when you consider that I shall not make my remarks with any intent to abuse and insult your magistracy, but in order to show in how great a sea the affairs of the commonwealth are tossed and to point out what will be both their safety and their reformation." Cited in Fairweather, "Galatians and Classical Rhetoric," 214.
22. Krentz, *Logos* or *Sophia*, 285.

is the same in all the other arts for the orator and his rhetoric: there is no need to know the truth of the actual matters, but one merely needs to have discovered some device of persuasion which will make one appear to those who do not know to know better than those who know" (459C [LCL]). That is, he rejects the claim, later made by Aristotle, that rhetoric is "the faculty of discovering the possible means of persuasion in reference to any subject whatever" (*Rhet.* 1.1.1).[23]

Despite Paul's claim that he is not a rhetorician, interpreters from Augustine to Johannes Weiss have analyzed Paul's letters with the categories of ancient rhetoric.[24] Eduard Norden's critique of Paul's rhetoric in *Antike Kunstprosa* marked the end of the application of rhetorical criticism to Paul's letters until the 1980s, when Hans Dieter Betz examined Galatians with the categories of Greco-Roman rhetoric.[25] Following Betz's lead, interpreters have examined every letter in the Pauline corpus, using Aristotelian rhetoric.

Many scholars, noting that Paul dictated his letters for oral presentation, maintain that Paul argued his case with the tools of Aristotelian rhetoric. Because Paul's letters are completely atypical in size, content, and style and are intended for oral presentation to an assembled group, they function as speeches. Thus many interpreters in the last generation have abandoned the attempt to classify Paul's letters with any of the types suggested by ancient epistolary theorists and have focused on the categories of Greco-Roman rhetoric as the lens for reading them, thus identifying the species of the presentation and the analysis of the five categories of ancient rhetoric: invention, arrangement, style, memory, and delivery.

Aristotle identified three species of speeches (*Rhet.* 1.2.3). The judicial speech was intended for the law court and involved an assessment of an event in the past. The deliberative speech was intended for the democratic assembly and involved exhortation or dissuasion about a future decision.[26] The epideictic speech, concerned with praise or blame, was intended for the

23. Dio Chrysostom draws a distinction between the rhetoric of flatterers, who titillate the masses with mere demagoguery (*Nicom.* 38.1–3), and his own rhetoric. Cf. Theophrastus, *Char.* 2.13: "You will see the flatterer say and do things that he hopes will ingratiate him." Aristotle, *Eth. nic.* 4.6.1: "In society and in common life and intercourse of conversation and business, some men are considered to be obsequious [*areskoi*, lit., "pleasers"]." Cf. also 2.7.13: "In respect of general pleasantness in life, the man who is pleasant in the proper manner is friendly, and the observance of the mean is friendliness; he that exceeds, if from no interested motive, is obsequious [*areskos*], if for his own advantage, a flatterer."
24. On Augustine, cf. book 4 of *De doctrina christiana*; cf. Weiss, *Beiträge zur paulinische Rhetorik*.
25. Norden, *Die antike Kunstprosa*; Betz, *Galatians*.
26. Olbricht, "Rhetorical Analysis of 1 Thessalonians," 224–27.

ceremonial occasion. While scholars apply these categories to Paul's letters, they have reached no consensus. Indeed, as in ancient rhetoric, more than one kind of rhetoric may be present in the same letter.

Rhetorical criticism of Paul's letters includes analyses of the rhetorical species, arrangement, style, and invention (argumentation). While these categories are derived from classical rhetoric, they can be applied to all speech, as George Kennedy maintains.[27] Thus we may apply Aristotelian analysis without assuming that Paul had formally studied rhetoric.

Identification of the species. Scholars have reached no consensus on the species of Paul's rhetoric. As Thomas Olbricht has demonstrated, the audience of Paul's letters bears no resemblance to the ancient law court, assembly, or public ceremony. Olbricht suggests that Paul's speech belongs to a separate category of "church rhetoric."[28] Ancient speeches have nothing parallel to the extended ethical exhortations in Paul's letters.[29] However, all of Paul's letters call for future action and attempt to persuade and dissuade; thus they have some functional similarity to deliberative rhetoric.

Arrangement. Rhetorical studies have given the most attention to the arrangement of Paul's letters, comparing them to the arrangement often proposed in the rhetorical handbooks. Rhetorical theorists suggest that the effective speech was composed of *exordium, narratio, propositio, probatio,* and *peroratio.* These categories are useful in the analysis of Paul's letters, although they cannot be pressed too far. Inasmuch as the thanksgivings at the beginning of Paul's letters introduce the topic and make the audience favorably disposed, they function as the exordium. The survey of recent events that frequently follows the thanksgiving has a functional similarity to the narratio. Paul then frequently follows with a thesis statement that will guide the argument (cf. Rom. 1:16–17; 1 Cor. 1:10–13; 2 Cor. 1:14; Phil. 1:27–30); this thesis statement functions as the propositio. The argument that follows functions as the probatio.[30] The peroratio, which concludes the speech with an emotional appeal and summation of the argument, has only "vague similarities" to the closing of a Pauline letter.[31]

While the presence of functional similarities among the parts of the ancient speech does not demonstrate Paul's conscious use of Aristotelian rhetoric,

27. Kennedy, *Interpretation through Rhetorical Criticism,* 9–10.
28. Olbricht, "Aristotelian Rhetorical Analysis," 224–27. On the imprecision of these categories, see Forbes, *Ancient Rhetoric and Ancient Letters,* 145–46.
29. See Classen, *Rhetorical Criticism of the New Testament,* 23.
30. See Porter, "Popular Rhetorical Knowledge," 110.
31. Porter, "Popular Rhetorical Knowledge," 110. The paraenetic sections of Paul's letters are unparalleled in ancient rhetoric.

they are useful categories for observing the progression and coherence in Paul's written communication.[32] They have also offered alternative explanations to the theories of displacement in Paul's letters.[33] Attention to arrangement was an advance over the atomizing tendencies of form criticism and the search for the history behind the text. However, Paul's arguments do not always fit the parts of the ancient speech, and they should not be forced into these categories.[34]

Style. From the ancient exegetes John Chrysostom, Jerome, and Augustine to contemporary scholars, readers have analyzed the style of the Pauline letters with the categories of ancient rhetoric, observing both the Greco-Roman and Hebrew features in his writings and classifying them with Aristotelian categories. This classification includes specific figures, tropes, and entire writings.[35] Scholars agree that, of the three styles in Greco-Roman classification—the grand, the middle, and the plain—Paul writes primarily in the middle style, although he occasionally approaches the grand style (cf. Rom. 8:31–39; 1 Cor. 13). Hebrew writings employ metaphor, parallelism, antithesis, and chiasm.[36] Contemporary scholars have identified Paul's use of metaphor, parallelism, antithesis, chiasm, irony, apostrophe, rhetorical questions, personification, hyperbole, *prosopopoia*,[37] and numerous other categories listed in the handbooks.[38] These stylistic features are not mere ornamentation but actually advance the argument.

Invention. Invention involves finding the best available means of persuasion. Aristotle describes these arguments as proofs (*pisteis*) and distinguishes between the artificial and inartificial proofs. The latter are those that require no argument but depend on the contracts, oaths, and testimony of witnesses. Artificial proofs are those that require logical argument. These arguments have been limited to ethos, pathos, and logos. Scholars have analyzed Paul's arguments, pointing to parallels with ancient argumentation.

The argument from ethos appeals to the speaker's credibility. One of the most consistent features in Paul's argument is his argument from ethos. He

32. Porter, "Popular Rhetorical Knowledge," 110. Classen, "Theory of Rhetoric," 36–37.

33. Rhetorical critics have demonstrated the importance of the *digressio* in ancient argumentation. Thus passages such as 1 Cor. 9 and 1 Cor. 13, which interrupt the flow of the argument, are not evidence of displacement but of the *digressio*, the insertion of an independent section into a text that is thematically related to the subject (Cicero, *De or.* 3.53.203).

34. Cf. Classen, "Theory of Rhetoric," 35: "The classical orators follow a structure consisting of *prooemiium, propositio, narratio, argumentatio* (*confirmatio* and *refutatio*) and *peroratio* when it suits their purposes, but only then."

35. D. Watson, "Style in the Pauline Epistles," 119.

36. For Paul's use of the characteristic Hebrew features of parallelism and antithesis, see the extended discussion in Weiss, *Beiträge zur paulinischen Rhetorik*, 6–40.

37. D. Watson, "Style in the Pauline Epistles," 133.

38. See the extensive catalog of figures in Porter, "Paul of Tarsus and His Letters."

regularly establishes his credibility before he challenges his readers to adopt his way of life (cf. 1 Cor. 2:1–5; 4:1–13; Gal. 1:10–2:21; Phil. 1:12–26; 1 Thess. 2:1–12). Indeed, 2 Corinthians is dominated by the argument from Paul's character, which has been occasioned by criticisms of his ministry (see chap. 4 below).

The argument from pathos is an appeal to emotion. Aristotle indicates that this is an effective argument (*Rhet.* 1.2.5). Paul regularly indicates his own emotions (cf. 2 Cor. 1:3–7; 2:1–4; 11:11; Phil. 3:18; 1 Thess. 2:17) and appeals to the emotions of his churches (cf. 2 Cor. 6:11–7:1).

According to the rhetoricians, the appeal to logos includes the use of logical deduction, including the enthymeme and the use of *exempla* (Latin for "examples"). According to the *Rhetoric to Alexander*, which is attributed to Aristotle, one delivering a deliberative speech should prove that the courses to follow are just (*dikaia*), lawful (*nomima*), expedient (*sympheronta*), honorable (*kala*), pleasant (*hēdea*), and easily practicable (*radia parachthēnai*). Failing this, the orator should show that they are feasible (*dynata*) and unavoidable (*anankaia*).[39] Paul makes logical deductions, frequently using enthymemes, the argument from the lesser to the greater, and the argument from expediency. He also argues from exempla (*paradeigmata*), appealing to his own personal example, the example of others, and the exempla from Scripture. In Romans (4:1–25) and Galatians (3:6–29), he appeals to the example of Abraham. In 1 Corinthians, he recalls the example of ancient Israel (1 Cor. 10:1–13). He draws examples from law (Rom. 7:1–4), sports (1 Cor. 9:24–27; Phil. 3:12–16), agriculture (1 Cor. 3:1–9; 9:10), the military (1 Cor. 9:7), and the Roman victory processional (2 Cor. 2:14). Nevertheless, Paul's arguments would have been scarcely persuasive to an ancient audience, for they are credible only to the subculture that accepts his authority.[40] While he offers rational arguments, his appeal to divinely sanctioned apostolic authority and revelation set him apart from the orator of the Greek *polis*, who appealed primarily to the standards of rationality.[41] The premises for his arguments belong to the subculture of his communities.[42] He appeals to what only this subculture knows (cf. Rom. 2:2; 5:3; 6:3; 8:22; 1 Cor. 6:2–3, 9, 15), indicating that he shares premises with the community that would

---

39. Anaximenes, *Rhet. Alex.* 1421b. Cited in Fairweather, "Galatians and Classical Rhetoric," 221. Cf. Philo in *Worse*: "Sophists . . . make our ears ache with their demonstrations of the social character of righteousness, the advantageous nature of moderation, the nobility of self-control, the great benefits conferred by piety, the power of every kind of virtue to bring health and safety."

40. Fenske, *Die Argumentation des Paulus*, 26.

41. Fairweather, "Galatians and Classical Rhetoric," 222.

42. Fairweather, "Galatians and Classical Rhetoric," 236.

not have been acceptable to others.[43] Janet Fairweather speaks of this as "Christ-based logic."[44]

The foundation of Paul's arguments is frequently derived from the Jewish tradition (cf. Rom. 2:2; 5:3; 1 Cor. 6:2–3). In other instances, the premises for his arguments are to be found in the early Christian kerygma (cf. 1 Cor. 15:3–58; 2 Cor. 5:14–21; 1 Thess. 4:14). Eschatology, Christology, ecclesiology, and other theological categories form the premises for his reasoning. Thus while ancient literary and rhetorical conventions provide helpful categories for analyzing Paul's letters, they offer no parallel to Paul's persona as the speaker and to the argument that he makes.

Although Paul has rhetorical competence, one cannot be certain where he learned his rhetorical skills, for his youth and his education are *terra incognita* for us.[45] No consensus exists as to whether Paul studied with Gamaliel, as Acts 22:3 suggests. While some maintain that the letters exhibit evidence of Paul's formal rhetorical training, others argue that they reflect only a natural rhetoric that any educated person in the ancient cities would have absorbed.

Paul's Authoritative Rhetoric

Paul speaks with a voice that is unparalleled in ancient texts. Unlike ancient orators, he addresses the assemblies that he has founded and nurtured. He speaks consistently with the tenderness and authoritative voice of a parent. His arguments are not frequently those of the Greek orator but of the apostle who speaks for God. Indeed, Paul identifies himself with the prophets, offering divine mysteries and demanding the obedience of his listeners.

Paul as Parent

At the conclusion of his extended theological response to Corinthian factionalism, Paul says, "I do not write this to shame you, but to admonish you as beloved children" (1 Cor. 4:14 AT). This passage suggests three dimensions of ancient fatherhood in Paul's voice. First, Paul indicates the intimacy of a parent with a child. The readers are "beloved children" (*agapēta tekna*, 1 Cor. 4:14), whom Paul "fathered" (1 Cor. 4:15). Paul emphasizes the intimacy of the parent-child relationship (cf. 2 Cor. 6:11–13: "I speak as to children. My

43. Fenske, *Die Argumentation des Paulus*, 65.
44. Fairweather, "Galatians and Classical Rhetoric," 236.
45. Hübner, *Theologie des Neuen Testaments*, 2:27.

heart is wide open to you. . . . Open your hearts to us" [AT]) and commonly speaks to his communities as "beloved" (agapētoi).

The second paternal role evident in Paul's writings is that of admonishing (nouthetōn) the children (cf. Eph. 6:4). While this verb is used to mean "instruct" or "lecture,"[46] it frequently means "reprimand," as in the obligation of parents.[47] Elsewhere Paul describes himself as a new father, "urging, encouraging and witnessing to [them] to walk worthily of the God who calls [them]" (1 Thess. 2:12 AT). That is, the role of the father is to provide moral instruction.

The third parental role is to punish—to come with the rod (cf. 1 Cor. 4:21 RSV). Paul will come either with the rod or with a spirit of meekness. Thus the parental role involves both authority and intimacy. He expects obedience from his children (cf. 2 Cor. 7:15; 10:6; Philem. 21), and he threatens to punish those who do not obey (cf. 2 Cor. 13:1–2).

The parent was also the object of imitation, as Paul indicates in 1 Corinthians 4:16. This was a common command of Paul (cf. 1 Cor. 11:1; Phil. 3:17; 4:9), and his frequent autobiographical sections offer models for imitation.

Paul uses this parental image also in two passages where he considers the parent's role in ensuring that the child comes to maturity. In Galatians 4:19, he is a mother in birth pangs "until Christ is formed among [them]" (AT). According to 2 Corinthians 11:2, he is the father of the bride and thus responsible for the bride's purity until her wedding. According to 1 Thessalonians 2:12, his paternal instruction is intended to encourage the converts to "walk worthily of the one who called [them] into his kingdom" (AT).

Paul as Apostle

Ancient letter writers frequently identified themselves with a title. Of the thirteen letters attributed to Paul, eleven identify Paul as an apostle.[48] While the term "apostle" in antiquity simply referred to a messenger, for Paul it had a special meaning. He was called by God to be an apostle (Rom. 1:1, 5; 1 Cor. 1:1; Gal. 1:1); thus he identifies himself regularly as an "apostle of Jesus Christ" (1 Cor. 1:1; 2 Cor. 1:1; cf. Gal. 1:1; Eph. 1:1; Col. 1:1; 1 Tim. 1:1; 2 Tim. 1:1; Titus 1:1). While others are also apostles (cf. Rom. 16:7; 2 Cor.

46. Spicq, "νουθεσία," TLNT 2:548.

47. Eli is blamed for not having rebuked his sons, who have cursed God (1 Sam. 3:13). Cf. Philo, Spec. Laws 2.232: "Fathers have the right to admonish their children severely." Josephus, Ant. 4.260: parents are the first to admonish children verbally. Spicq, "νουθεσία," TLNT 2:550.

48. The exceptions are 1 Thessalonians and Philippians. In 1 Thessalonians, he does not identify himself as an apostle in the salutation but speaks of his right as an apostle in 1 Thess. 2:7.

8:23), Paul belongs in the special circle alongside the Twelve. Like them, he has seen the Lord (cf. 1 Cor. 9:1; 15:7–8).

At the beginning of his communication, Paul's claim to be sent by God anticipates the nature of his rhetoric: he is a spokesman for God. That he speaks for God is a constant feature of his rhetoric. He has been "entrusted with the . . . gospel" (1 Thess. 2:4), and he is a steward (*oikonomos*) "of the mysteries of God" (1 Cor. 4:1 RSV). He speaks in Jesus Christ (2 Cor. 12:19). When he distances himself from the rhetoricians by claiming that he did not use persuasive words of wisdom (1 Cor. 2:1–2), he claims that his word came with power (1 Cor. 2:4–5; 1 Thess. 1:5). Indeed, the Thessalonians receive his words as the very words of God (1 Thess. 2:13).

Paul's authoritative voice comes to clearest expression when his leadership is challenged. In 2 Corinthians 10–13, Paul's response to those who challenge his authority reaches its culmination. In response to those who charge him with lacking boldness (10:1–2) and who say that "his bodily presence is weak and his speech is of no account" (10:10 AT), Paul claims an authority (*exousia*) given to him by the Lord (10:8). The opening statement, "I ask not to need to show boldness by daring to oppose those who suppose that we conduct ourselves in a worldly way [*kata sarka*]" (10:2 AT), forms an *inclusio* with the conclusion of the argument, when Paul indicates that he is writing "so that I may not be severe in using the authority that the Lord has given me for building up and not tearing down" (13:10 AT). That is, although he spared the Corinthian opposition on an earlier visit (1:23), he will not spare them when he returns (13:2). Echoing some of the philosophical discussion, he describes himself as a participant in a war in which he tears down fortresses, which are the arguments that are raised against the knowledge of God (10:5).[49] In this role, he will "take every thought captive to obey Christ" as he is prepared to punish disobedience (10:5–6).

Paul has received this authority for building up and not for tearing down from Christ. This imagery recalls the mission of Jeremiah, whom God called "to build and to plant" (Jer. 1:10). Indeed, the imagery of building and planting is a major theme in Jeremiah. God will "pluck up and break down and

---

49. Antisthenes applied the image of the fortified city to the sage's soul. "Virtue is a weapon that cannot be taken away" (Diogenes Laertius, *Lives* 6.11). "Prudence is a most secure stronghold, for it does not crumble nor is it betrayed. We must build walls of defense with our own impregnable reasonings" (Diogenes Laertius, *Lives* 6.13). Malherbe, "Antisthenes and Paul at War," 151: "Here for the first time we have Paul's imagery in which the reasoning faculties function in the inner fortification of a person." Seneca: "Life is a battle" (*Ep.* 96.5). Epictetus: "The philosopher's thoughts are his protection" (*Diatr.* 4.16.14). "His authority to censure does not derive from weapons and bodyguards, but from his conscience and a purified mind" (*Diatr.* 3.22.13–19).

destroy" unrighteous kingdoms (18:7), but God will also "build and plant" a nation (18:9). God will bring the exiles back from Chaldea to "build them up, and not tear them down; . . . will plant them, and not pluck them up" (24:6). Jeremiah also declares, "And just as I have watched over them to pluck up and break down, to overthrow, destroy, and bring evil, so I will watch over them to build and to plant, says the LORD" (31:28). According to 33:7, God promises, "I will restore the fortunes . . . of Israel, and rebuild them as at first." He promises, "If you . . . remain in this land, then I will build you up and not pull you down; I will plant you, and not pluck you up" (42:10).[50]

Paul had already evoked the message of Jeremiah earlier in the Corinthian correspondence—in his conflict with opponents who boast in their wisdom—by paraphrasing Jeremiah's words, "Let those who boast, boast in the Lord" (1 Cor. 1:31 AT; cf. Jer. 9:23–24). He cites the message again in words against those who boast (2 Cor. 10:17). In 1 Corinthians 3:6–17, he develops the images of planting and building, identifying himself as a planter and builder. When he defends his ministry in 2 Corinthians 3, he compares himself to Moses, claiming to be a minister of the new covenant promised by Jeremiah (2 Cor. 3:6) and a figure comparable to Moses. His community is the new covenant people promised by Jeremiah who have received God's Spirit. Thus his appeal to the building and planting metaphor in 2 Corinthians 10:8–9 is a prophetic claim. At his call, he was given the authority to build and not to tear down. He claims that "everything is for your edification" (2 Cor. 12:19 AT). He is both the parent who punishes the disobedient child (1 Cor. 4:21) and the prophetic figure who has been given the authority both to build and not to tear down, to act severely toward those who are disobedient.

Paul as Apocalyptic Seer

In other words, Paul speaks as an apocalyptic seer. When he distinguishes himself from the rhetoricians, he describes his ministry of speaking "wisdom in a mystery that had been hidden" (1 Cor. 2:7 AT; cf. 2:1) and inaccessible to human reasoning but which God revealed (*apekalypsen*) through the Spirit (1 Cor. 2:10). Both *mystērion* and forms of *apokalyptō* are terms from Jewish apocalyptic literature. As one who knows the mysteries (1 Cor. 4:1), Paul announces a mystery about the future destiny of the gentiles (Rom. 11:25) and about the eschatological destiny of all (1 Cor. 15:51). The language of mystery is especially pronounced in Ephesians and Colossians, but the language of *apokalypsis* is commonplace in Paul. He announces that the righteousness of

---

50. Cf. Jer. 45:4: "Thus says the LORD: I am going to break down what I have built, and pluck up what I have planted—that is, the whole land."

God is being revealed (Rom. 1:17–18); that God revealed his Son so that Paul might proclaim him (Gal. 1:15–16); that Paul has an abundance of revelations (2 Cor. 12:7); and that his gospel is a revelation (Gal. 1:12).

Paul's speech is also prophetic rhetoric. Klaus Berger has demonstrated the background of prophetic letters in Paul's literary work.[51] Jeremiah's letter to the exiles (Jer. 29:1–31), for example, established the precedent for a divine revelation mediated in a letter.[52] This letter also inspired the later Epistle of Jeremiah, which purports to be an additional letter of the prophet. Elijah's letter to Jehoram (2 Chron. 21:12–15), condemning him for his wicked rule, also influenced Paul's work. Letters also play a role in apocalyptic literature, as the epistolary form of Revelation indicates. The seer of *1 Enoch*, for example, refers to his apocalypse as a letter (*1 En.* 100:6 Greek version). *Second Baruch*, as another example, is a revelation of God containing an interpretation of recent events (*2 Bar.* 79:1–80:7) and a consolation over the fate of Zion (*2 Bar.* 81:1; 82:1). The concluding chapters contain an extended letter to the exiles that is modeled after Jeremiah's letter (Jer. 29:1–31), and the letter begins with the formula "grace and peace be with you" (*2 Bar.* 78:3), a formula found elsewhere only in Paul's letters. At the end, the author encourages the readers to ensure that the letter is read to all of the assemblies (*2 Bar.* 86:1). Thus authoritative official letters had become commonplace in the Jewish tradition and would have been known to Paul.[53] These letters, which are presented as prophetic speech intended to be read in assemblies as the word of God, have significant analogies to the Pauline letters.

Paul's Authority

While one may find parallels between Paul's letters and ancient rhetoric in arrangement, style, and invention, the letters have a dimension that is indebted to prophetic speech inasmuch as Paul speaks for God. In his earliest letter, Paul distinguishes himself from the orators, indicating that his gospel was entrusted to him (1 Thess. 2:4), and he declares that his gospel is not the word of human beings but of God (1 Thess. 2:13). When he gives moral instructions, he speaks "through the Lord Jesus" (1 Thess. 4:2) and speaks of the authority (*exousia*) that he has been given by God as an apostle (1 Cor. 9:4–6, 12, 18; 2 Cor. 10:8; 13:10; 2 Thess. 3:9).

This authority is evident in the terms with which Paul addresses his communities. In several instances, he uses the language of command (*diatassō*,

51. Berger, "Apostelbrief and apostolische Rede," 216.
52. See Taatz, *Frühjüdische Briefe*, 105–9.
53. Taatz, *Frühjüdische Briefe*, 111.

diatagē). When he instructs the Corinthians on marriage, he says, "This is what I command [*diatassō*] in all of the churches" (1 Cor. 7:17 AT). When he gives instructions on the Lord's Supper, he concludes, "I will command [*diataxomai*] you about the other matters when I come" (1 Cor. 11:34 AT). He also commands the churches of Macedonia to participate in the collection (1 Cor. 16:1). Thus while Paul at times appeals to what "the Lord commanded" (1 Cor. 9:14; cf. 7:10), he also commands his churches. Even when Paul indicates that he is not giving a command (*epitagē*, 1 Cor. 7:6, 25; 2 Cor. 8:8; *epitassein*, Philem. 8), he implies that he has the right to do so.[54]

Closely related to *diatassein* (or *epitassein*, *epitagē*) is the authoritative character of forms of *parangellein*, which can mean either "make an announcement" or "command."[55] Both the noun (*parangelia*) and the verb (*parangellein*) designate the action in which a person in authority commands an activity.[56] Paul speaks of the instructions (*parangelia*) he gave the Thessalonians, indicating that they were "the will of God" (1 Thess. 4:2) in recalling his command to abstain from sexual immorality (1 Thess. 4:3–8), concluding that anyone who rejects the command also rejects God (1 Thess. 4:8). When he writes (in 1 Cor. 7:10), "To the married I give this command [*parangellō*]— not I but the Lord—that the wife should not separate from her husband," he suggests that he in other instances does command the church.[57]

Paul's request to Philemon, "Although I am bold in Christ to command [*epitassein*] you to do what is right, because of love I appeal [*parakalō*] to you" (Philem. 8–9 AT), offers an important insight into Paul's relationship to his churches. While he commands in some instances, he most frequently appeals (*parakalei*) to them. As the distinction between "command" and "appeal" indicates, *parakalein* is a gentler term for a request. In Philemon, it is combined with love (8) and implies a special relationship (17). At the end of Philemon, Paul expresses confidence in Philemon's obedience (21). According to 1 Thessalonians 2:12, it is the term for the father who appeals to the children to behave appropriately.

Parakalō, implying both intimacy and authority, frequently introduces Paul's ethical advice. He appeals to his congregations through "the mercies of God" (Rom. 12:1), through "the name of our Lord Jesus Christ" (1 Cor. 1:10), through "the meekness and gentleness of Christ" (2 Cor. 10:1), and "in the Lord Jesus" (1 Thess. 4:1). As Paul's appeal to the Corinthians indicates, it is God who makes his appeal through Paul (*hōs tou theou parakalountos di'*

---

54. Eckstein, *Gemeinde, Brief und Heilsbotschaft*, 226.
55. BDAG 760.
56. Radl, "παραγγέλλω," *EDNT* 3:16.
57. Eckstein, *Gemeinde, Brief und Heilsbotschaft*, 226.

hēmōn), God's ambassador (2 Cor. 5:20). Thus he says, "Working together with him, we appeal [*parakaloumen*] to you not to receive the grace of God in vain" (2 Cor. 6:1 AT).[58] As he declares to a community that he did not establish, he writes "because of the grace of God given to [him]" (Rom. 15:15 AT).

In both Corinthian letters, Paul contrasts himself with the orators who are admired by the listeners, recalling that he speaks wisdom that is not of this age, a wisdom unintelligible to ordinary rationality; he speaks wisdom in a mystery that had been hidden (1 Cor. 2:7) but that has now been revealed through the Spirit (1 Cor. 2:10). This language of the mystery and revelation belongs to Jewish apocalyptic. Paul's speech is not the rational argument of the rhetorical tradition. The idea of the hidden mystery that has now been made known is already present in the Gospel tradition and continues in the announcement in Colossians and Ephesians that the Christian message is the revelation of a mystery that had been hidden with God. One finds this claim in the apocalypses. Daniel interprets the mystery (Dan. 2:18) of the king's dreams about coming events, declaring that "there is a God in heaven who reveals mysteries, and he has disclosed to King Nebuchadnezzar what will happen at the end of days" (2:28–30). In the apocalypses, God is the one who knows what will happen at the end of time, and God reveals coming events to those who fear him (*2 Bar.* 54:1–4; cf. *1 En.* 38:3; 103:2; *4 Ezra* 10:59; 12:36–39; 14:5–6). Only the seer is capable of interpreting the mystery. Similarly, the hidden mystery is a common theme in the Dead Sea Scrolls (cf. 1QS 11.18).[59] Thus Paul's language in 1 Corinthians 2:6–17 is drawn from apocalyptic literature. Like the apocalyptic visionary, Paul proclaims a hidden wisdom that is not intelligible to human rationality.[60]

Conclusion: Paul's New Rhetoric

Although Paul insists that he does not use the "persuasive words of wisdom" (1 Cor. 2:4 NASB; cf. Gal. 1:20) associated with ancient rhetoric, he nevertheless declares that his mission is to "persuade others" (*anthrōpous peithomen*, 2 Cor. 5:11), appealing to them to "be reconciled to God" (2 Cor. 5:20). While we know his oral presentation only from his frequent references to his evangelistic preaching (cf. Rom. 10:5–21; 1 Cor. 1:18–25; 1 Thess. 1:2–10), we know his pastoral communication through the letters, the continuation of his ministry of forming churches. In his evangelistic preaching, he is a herald

58. Eckstein, *Gemeinde, Brief und Heilsbotschaft*, 227.
59. Krämer, "μυστήριον," *EDNT* 2:447.
60. Selby, "Paul the Seer," 367.

announcing the good news and summoning hearers to obey. Confidence in divine power rather than persuasion to bring about the desired results distinguished Paul from the rhetoricians.[61] His letters continue his ministry of "encouraging, consoling, and witnessing" (1 Thess. 2:12 AT); thus they are exercises in persuasion. They have points of contact with ancient literary conventions, and they may be analyzed with the categories of ancient communication. However, the ancient literary conventions do not explain their persuasive power. As Amos Wilder maintained, the gospel creates a new kind of rhetoric.[62] As the prominence of ethical exhortation in his letters indicates, Paul's goal of moral formation of his communities determines the nature of his rhetoric.

61. Litfin, *Paul's Theology of Preaching*, 177.
62. Wilder, *Early Christian Rhetoric*, 10–25.

2

Paul and the Pharisaic Tradition

In Paul's most thorough autobiographical statement (Phil. 3:4–7), he offers information about his background and early life that he gives nowhere else, describing himself as the epitome of the faithful Jew. Having listed credentials that include his role as a Hebrew of Hebrews and a Pharisee whose zeal had led him to persecute the church (3:5–6), he concludes, "Whatever gains I had, these I have come to regard as loss" (3:7). Indeed, he is so emphatic in this claim that he states it in three tenses (3:7–8): "I have come to regard [hēgēmai] these things as loss [zēmia, perfect tense]" (AT); "I count [hēgoumai] all things as loss because of Christ, for whose sake I suffered loss [ezēmiōthēn, aorist]"; and "I count all things as garbage [present]" (AT). The repetition signifies the radical change in Paul's life.

He makes a similar claim in the autobiographical section of Galatians, speaking of his "former life in Judaism" (Gal. 1:13 RSV). Paul divides his life into two stages: his past in Judaism and the period after the life-changing moment that marked the new direction in his life. His claim "I have become a Jew to the Jews, in order that I might gain the Jews" (1 Cor. 9:20 AT) also suggests a major change in Paul's identity from the one who had once been a Hebrew of Hebrews.

According to a long tradition of Protestant scholarship, these passages depict Paul's abandonment of the law and Judaism. Thus Adolf von Harnack declared, Paul "delivered the Christian religion from Judaism."[1] In his classic

---

1. Harnack, *What Is Christianity?*, 176. Cf. Wilckens, *Rechtfertigung als Freiheit*, 7: "Paul was an unreconciled adversary of any 'Judaism' in Christianity." See the discussion in Bird, *Anomalous Jew*, 33.

Theology of the New Testament, Rudolf Bultmann maintained that Paul "surrendered his previous understanding of himself; that is, he surrendered what had till then been the norm and meaning of his life, he sacrificed what had hitherto been his pride and joy (Phil. 3:4–7)."[2] Following the views of Wilhelm Bousset, Bultmann argued that Paul's conversion brought him into contact with the Hellenistic church in Antioch, a community that had already abandoned many elements of the Jewish tradition and adopted features from Gnosticism and the mystery religions.[3] In this environment, according to Bousset, the church adopted the title "lord" (*kyrios*) to describe Jesus and established a Christ cult analogous to Hellenistic religions.[4] According to Bultmann, Paul's theological framework was indebted to the Hellenistic church at Antioch, not to Judaism or the Jerusalem church: "Standing within the frame of Hellenistic Christianity, he raised the theological motifs that were at work in the proclamation of the Hellenistic Church to the clarity of theological thinking; he called to attention the problems latent in the Hellenistic proclamation and brought them to a decision; and thus—so far as our sources permit an opinion on the matter—became the founder of Christian theology."[5]

Until recently, major works on Pauline theology gave scant attention to Paul's Jewish background, assuming that Paul counted as loss the entire Pharisaic tradition.[6] More recent scholarship, however, has demonstrated Paul's indebtedness to the Jewish tradition.[7] In this chapter, I will explore some questions: What did Paul count as loss? To what extent is Paul's Jewish heritage the foundation of his theology? I will argue that Paul's Jewish heritage formed the substructure of his theology, an important premise in his theologizing.

The Pharisees and "Common Judaism"

The Pharisees

The fact that Paul is the first person on record to identify himself as a Pharisee is an indication of the challenge of delineating Pharisaic beliefs.

2. Bultmann, *Theology of the New Testament*, 1:188.
3. See Schnelle, *Apostle Paul*, 116.
4. Bousset, *Kyrios Christos*, 146.
5. Bultmann, *Theology of the New Testament*, 1:187.
6. See Becker, *Paul, Apostle to the Gentiles*, 33: "In Paul's letters the Jewish portion of his life is not presented at all for its own sake. It only serves here and there, sporadically and typified by a few narrowly limited statements, as dark background and as harshly drawn contrast to the beginning of his second, real life."
7. See esp. Sanders, *Paul and Palestinian Judaism*; Wright, *Paul and the Faithfulness of God*; Boccaccini, Segovia, and Doody, *Paul the Jew*.

According to Philippians (3:5) and Acts (23:6; 26:5), Paul was educated as a Pharisee, the primary antagonists of Jesus in the Gospels and of the early church in Acts (Acts 5:34; 15:5; 23:8–9). However, because the portrayal of the Pharisees in most instances is determined by the polemical situation, we do not find a comprehensive statement of their beliefs in these sources, though rabbinic sources after 70 CE provide more information about them.[8] Scholars have also maintained that the *Psalms of Solomon* and *4 Ezra* are derived from the Pharisees,[9] and some references in the Dead Sea Scrolls probably also allude to the Pharisees.[10] Thus while our knowledge of the Pharisees is limited, the sources we have indicate their most characteristic beliefs.

At the end of the first century, Josephus recalls the activities of the Pharisees from the first century BCE to his own time. According to the *Antiquities*, they were one of the three schools of thought in Judaism (*Ant.* 13.172; cf. *J.W.* 2.119) and were distinguished by their belief in fate (*Ant.* 18.1–10). Additionally, Josephus gives considerable attention to the their influence on both the masses and the rulers (*Ant.* 13.288, 292–95, 408–10, 423).

Although the Gospels' portrayal of the Pharisees reflects polemical engagement with them, it nevertheless offers insights to basic Pharisaic beliefs, especially when the information corresponds to what we learn from Josephus and the rabbinic tradition. The basic beliefs include the following.

Adherence to the law and oral tradition. The consistent portrait in the Gospels is that the Pharisees gave special attention to matters of *halakah*: the Sabbath (Matt. 12:1–8 // Mark 2:23–28), divorce (Matt. 5:31–32; 19:3–12), ritual purity (Matt. 15:1–11; 23:23–24), oaths (Matt. 5:33–37; 23:16–22), and tithing (Matt. 23:24). They insisted on keeping not only the laws laid down in the Pentateuch but also the "tradition of the elders" (cf. Matt. 15:2). This description corresponds to the evidence from Josephus, who speaks favorably of the Pharisees as those who adhere to regulations not in the Torah "in accordance with the tradition of the fathers" (*Ant.* 13.296–97; 408). According to Josephus (*Ant.* 18.11–23), the Pharisees had their own traditions in addition to the holy Scriptures, while the Sadducees accepted the authority only of biblical laws. Josephus says that the Pharisees considered themselves

8. See Neusner, "Rabbinic Traditions about the Pharisees before 70 CE."

9. Cf. Lührmann, "Paul and the Pharisaic Tradition," 88: "The *Psalms of Solomon*, I think, bring us nearer to Paul than do the other sources of Pharisaism discussed earlier. They can show us some of Paul's presuppositions, options and questions or even solutions and can lead us to understand what it meant to be a Pharisee in his day."

10. Polemic against the Pharisees appears in CD 1.13–17. Teachers are mentioned who "sought after smooth things." They "chose deceits, kept watch with a view to lawless deeds," and "justified the wicked and condemned the righteous." Their deeds were "uncleanness before God." See Lührmann, "Paul and the Pharisaic Tradition," 78.

more pious than others and that they interpreted the Torah more accurately than others (*J.W.* 1.110; 2.162). This description corresponds also to the views recorded in rabbinic writings, which address the numerous concerns mentioned in the Gospels, relying on both Scripture and tradition. According to *Pirqe Avot*, "Moses received Torah from Sinai and delivered it to Joshua, and Joshua to the Elders, and the Elders to the Prophets, and the Prophets delivered it to the men of the Great Synagogue" (*Pirqe Avot* 1:1). Their task was to "be deliberate in judgment; and raise up many disciples; and make a fence around the Torah" (*Pirqe Avot* 1:1). While the topics discussed in the Gospels are only a small sampling of the issues discussed among the teachers of the law, they indicate the Pharisees' major concerns.

A basic dimension in the Pharisees' concern for the precise keeping of the law was the concern for purity, as Jesus's numerous encounters with the Pharisees suggest (cf. Mark 7:1–15). This concern expressed the commitment not only to personal purity but also to Israel's separation from the nations.[11] The concern also distinguished Pharisees from other Jews who did not maintain strict adherence to the purity laws.

When Paul attributes his earlier persecution of the church to "zeal" for the law (Phil. 3:6) and recalls that he was "zealous for the tradition of the fathers" (cf. Gal. 1:14 RSV), he identifies his conduct in terms that were associated with at least one segment of the Pharisees: those whose "zeal for the law" motivated them to engage in violent activities for the sake of the law. The tradition of "zeal for the law" was associated with Elijah (2 Kings 2:9–12) and Phinehas (cf. Num. 25:6–9), both of whom used violence in defense of righteousness. "Zeal for the law" also motivated the Maccabees in their struggle for independence (1 Macc. 2:52–58) and later became the motivation for the Zealots in the time of Jesus (cf. Luke 6:15; Acts 1:13).

Belief in the resurrection and final judgment. The description of the Sadducees as those who do not believe in the resurrection (Mark 12:18; cf. Acts 23:6–8) suggests that their views differ from those of the Pharisees and other groups. Paul's claim that he is a Pharisee being judged for his belief in the resurrection of the dead (Acts 23:6) also indicates this Pharisaic belief. This view is confirmed by Josephus's description of the Pharisees: they "hold that every soul is immortal, but that only the souls of the virtuous pass on into another body, while those of the wicked are punished with an everlasting judgment" (*J.W.* 2.163). According to the *Antiquities*, "They believe that souls have power to survive death and that there are rewards and punishments under the earth for those who have led lives of virtue or vice: eternal imprisonment

---

11. See Wright, *Paul and the Faithfulness of God*, 1:83.

is the lot of evil souls, while the good souls receive an easy passage to a new life" (*Ant.* 18.13–14).

This view is confirmed in the *Psalms of Solomon* and other sources from the period of the Second Temple. According to the *Psalms of Solomon*, destruction is the destiny of sinners, while "those who fear the Lord will find mercy" (*Pss. Sol.* 6:12). Similar views are expressed in the Maccabean literature. As the brothers in 2 Maccabees go to their deaths, they express their confidence in the resurrection to their torturers.[12] The second brother says, "You cursed wretch, you dismiss us from this present life, but the King of the universe will raise us up to an everlasting renewal of life, because we have died for his laws" (2 Macc. 7:9 AT). The third brother says, "I got [the tongue and the hands] from Heaven, and because of his laws I disdain them, and from him I hope to get them back again" (2 Macc. 7:11 AT). Their mother encouraged each of them, saying, "The Creator of the world, who shaped the beginning of humankind and devised the origin of all things, will in his mercy give life and breath back to you again" (2 Macc. 7:23 AT). Belief in the resurrection became the common expectation not only of the Pharisees but also of other groups in the period of the Second Temple.[13]

They also believed that in the final judgment, God will judge the people according to their works. The constant theme of the *Psalms of Solomon* is God's righteous judgment, which God has demonstrated in the past and will demonstrate in the future. Writing in the period of oppression when the sons of Jerusalem have profaned the sanctuary (*Pss. Sol.* 2:3) and Roman conquerors have polluted Jerusalem (cf. *Pss. Sol.* 2:1–2), the writer affirms God's justice (*dikaiosynē*). The author writes to show that God is righteous (*Pss. Sol.* 2:15, *egō dikaiōsō se*; cf. 10:5), that in his judgments there is righteousness (2:15). "God is a righteous judge who will not be impressed by appearances" (*Pss. Sol.* 2:18; cf. Rom. 2:11). He calls on the rulers of the earth to see the judgments of the Lord, that he is a great and righteous king (*Pss. Sol.* 2:32). When God judges the world in righteousness (*dikaiosynē*, *Pss. Sol.* 8:24; 9:2; 10:5), God will separate the sinners from the faithful, rendering to sinners the punishment according to their works (2:16–17, 34; 3:11–12; 15:8–12), but will have mercy on the righteous ones (2:34) who fear God (8:28, 32), cleansing them from their sins (9:6–7).[14]

The coming messiah and the promises of God. Scholars have maintained that the *Psalms of Solomon*, written in the first century BCE, is a Pharisaic

---

12. See Wright, *Resurrection of the Son of God*, 151.

13. See Wright, *Paul and the Faithfulness of God*, 1:83. While the Maccabean literature is not, strictly speaking, Pharisaic, it reflects the agenda and aspirations shared by the Pharisees.

14. For the pervasiveness of the concepts of reward and punishment in Second Temple Judaism, see Gathercole, *Where Is Boasting?*, 37–111.

document. Although the specific Pharisaic origins of this work are now debated, they remain "as close as we can get to a Pharisaic document."[15] The author believes that Israel's redemption will occur when a descendant of David arises. He recalls that God chose David to be king over Israel and swore that his descendants would be kings forever and that his kingdom would never fall (*Pss. Sol.* 17:3; cf. 2 Sam. 7:13, 16). He prays, "Raise up for them their king, the son of David, to rule over your servant Israel" (*Pss. Sol.* 17:21). The Pharisees therefore believed a descendant of David would destroy the enemies, purify Jerusalem, and gather a holy people, whom he would lead in righteousness (*Pss. Sol.* 17:26).

Common Judaism

These beliefs were not held by the Pharisees alone. The larger context for the study of Paul is the wider current of Second Temple Judaism, which included the Greek-speaking communities of the diaspora, the sectarians at Qumran, and the communities that produced the apocalypses.[16] While Judaism was diverse in some respects,[17] most groups and the population at large shared the belief that the creator God had chosen Israel to be his people, giving Israel the Torah and the land. God had given Israel a covenant, promising fidelity to the people and obligating them to be a holy people, set apart from the nations. Because God's covenant with Israel was irrevocable, the people could trust that God's justice would be established throughout the world.[18] These beliefs would later be summarized with the categories of theology, covenant, election, and eschatology.[19]

As the literature of the period of the Second Temple indicates, the promises for the reign of God had not yet become a reality. God's justice had not prevailed, Israel was not in possession of the land, and the prophetic promises remained unfulfilled. Writers distinguished between this age, the time when the promises remained unfulfilled, and the age to come, when God would restore the land and renew the covenant. Apocalyptic literature, which may reflect the views of most Pharisees,[20] consistently portrayed the age to come

---

15. Wright, *Paul and the Faithfulness of God*, 1:127.

16. See Charlesworth, "Paul, the Jewish Apocalypses, and Apocalyptic Eschatology," 90–95.

17. Jacob Neusner rejects the concept of "common Judaism," preferring to speak of "Judaisms." See Neusner, "From Judaism to Judaisms."

18. Wright, *New Testament and the People of God*, 279.

19. Wright, *New Testament and the People of God*, 279.

20. See Deines, "The Pharisees," 1:499. Although some scholars in the past distinguished between Pharisaism and apocalyptic, evidence suggests that apocalyptic groups maintained Pharisaic halakah and shared Pharisaic expectations. Indeed, the Zealots may be viewed as one of these Pharisaic groups.

(cf. *4 Ezra* 8:1–3; *m. Sanh.* 10:1).[21] In this new era, people with renewed hearts would keep the Torah perfectly (cf. Jer. 31:31–34), and God would vindicate the righteous and punish sinners. While the literature of the period depicted this new age with a variety of images, most Jews looked forward to the ultimate reign of God.

While for some writers God's ultimate justice would involve the destruction of gentiles, an important conviction of others was the inclusion of gentiles and the restoration of a united humanity. This theme has an important place in the Old Testament as well (cf. 1 Kings 8:41–43; Isa. 2:2–4; Mic. 4:1–5). Deutero-Isaiah, for example, gives special focus to the reunification of Jews and gentiles in the coming age (Isa. 42:1, 4, 6; 43:9; 45:20–22; 49:1–8; 52:10, 15; 55:4–5; 56:7; 60:3–5; 61:11; 62:2; 65:1; 66:18–21). This theme continues in the literature of the Second Temple. According to Tobit (14:5–7), when Israel returns from exile, "then the nations in the whole world will all be converted and worship God in truth," and "in righteousness they will praise the eternal God" (Tob. 14:6–7; cf. *1 En.* 10:16–22; *Sib. Or.* 3:772–75).[22]

Paul is also "an anomalous diaspora Jew,"[23] a witness to the fact that Hellenistic Judaism and Pharisaic Judaism were not separated by walls. Indeed, the wisdom tradition provided basic assumptions in Paul's thought. His analysis of idolatry and its consequences in Romans 1:18–32 indicates a familiarity with Wisdom of Solomon 12–14. The description of Christ as the image of God (2 Cor. 3:18; 4:4; cf. Col. 1:15) and his reformulation of the Shema, describing Christ as the one "through whom are all things and through whom we exist" (1 Cor. 8:6 AT), employ the language of wisdom (cf. Wis. 7:22–26) and Philo's Logos (cf. Philo, *Confusion* 97, 147; *Flight* 101). Paul's claim that God sent his Son (Rom. 8:3; Gal. 4:4) also echoes Jewish themes about the God who sent wisdom into the world (cf. Sir. 24:1, 3, 6–10, 23).[24]

Scholars have also pointed to parallels between Paul and Philo, Paul's near contemporary. While Paul is not dependent on Philo, that they are drawing on similar traditions appears to be evident in some places,[25] although the writers use those traditions for different purposes. Paul's comparison of the "first" and "second" man (1 Cor. 15:45–50) and his description of the "heavenly person" and "earthly person" employ identical terminology with that of Philo

21. Cf. *4 Ezra* 7:50: "The most high has not made one age, but two." Cf. *1 En.* 71:115; *2 Bar.* 14:13; *m. Avot* 4:1. See Wright, *New Testament and the People of God*, 252–54, 299–300; Wright, *Paul and the Faithfulness of God*, 2:1059.

22. Sherwood, *Paul and the Restoration of Humanity*, 152, 75.

23. Barclay, *Jews in the Mediterranean Diaspora*, 381–95.

24. Wright, *Paul and the Faithfulness of God*, 671.

25. Cf. Chadwick, "St. Paul and Philo of Alexandria," 292: "Both men fished in the same pool."

(cf. *Creation* 136, 140, 142, 145, 148; *Alleg. Interp.* 1.31, 37).[26] Both Philo and Paul share the polemic against those who exalt themselves and ignore that all they have comes from God (cf. 1 Cor. 1:18–31; 2 Cor. 10:1–18), and both employ the image of the arrogant whose ideas are bulwarks raised against God (cf. *Prelim. Studies* 128–30; *Worse* 32–34; *Confusion* 122–33).[27]

Paul and the Jewish Tradition

Paul's Jewish Identity

In addition to the autobiographical reflection in Philippians 3:4–6, Paul offers his Jewish credentials in three other instances (Rom. 11:1; 2 Cor. 11:22–25; Gal. 1:11–17). His role as a persecutor places him among the strictest sect of the Pharisees.[28] His zeal for the traditions of the fathers (Gal. 1:14; cf. Phil. 3:6) led him to follow the traditions of the Maccabees, whose "zeal for the law" (cf. 1 Macc. 2:58) motivated them to protect the integrity of Judaism. This movement was active only in Judea.

Unlike most other Pharisees, however, Paul was at home in the diaspora. His letters are written in good but not polished Greek.[29] According to Acts, he was a citizen of Tarsus in Cilicia (Acts 21:39), born in that city and educated in Jerusalem (22:3). Neither Acts nor the letters indicate at what age Paul went to Jerusalem, and he gives no indication of advanced literary or rhetorical training. Consequently, scholars debate the extent of the influence of diaspora Judaism and Pharisaic Judaism on Paul's theology.[30]

The fact that he speaks of his Jewish identity twice in the present tense (Rom. 11:1; 2 Cor. 11:22–25) and twice in the past tense (Gal. 1:11–17; Phil. 3:4–7) reflects his dialectical relationship to his Jewish heritage. When he describes the radical change in his life (Gal. 1:11–17), he speaks of his past "in Judaism" (Gal. 1:13) or of his past life as a Pharisee (Phil. 3:3–7). Nevertheless, as his use of the present tense indicates (Rom. 11:1; 2 Cor. 11:22–25), he continues to be an Israelite (Rom. 11:1) and a Hebrew (2 Cor. 11:22; Phil. 3:5), and he insists that his gentile converts are the children of Abraham

26. See Hultgren, "Doctrine of the Two Adams," 344.
27. See G. Holtz, "Von Alexandrien nach Jerusalem," 244; Noack, "Haben oder Empfangen."
28. See Wright, *What St. Paul Really Said*; Wright, *Paul and the Faithfulness of God*.
29. Barclay, *Jews in the Mediterranean Diaspora*, 383; cf. Frey, "Jewishness of Paul," 67.
30. Paul also demonstrates some familiarity with Greek intellectual traditions, particularly Stoic ideas, as his arguments from nature (Rom. 1:18–24; 1 Cor. 11:14) and use of Greek categories (e.g., "sufficiency" in Phil. 4:11) indicate. His familiarity with popular religious thought may be mediated through the literature of diaspora Judaism (e.g., Wisdom of Solomon, 4 Maccabees, Philo of Alexandria), which reflects significant engagement with popular philosophy.

(Rom. 4:1–23; Gal. 3:6–29) and descendants of the Israelites (1 Cor. 10:1–2). Although the forty lashes less one that he received multiple times from "the Jews" (2 Cor. 11:24) and the constant danger from his own countrymen (2 Cor. 11:26) indicate that his compatriots considered him an apostate, he remains an Israelite who believes that God's promises have become a reality in Christ (2 Cor. 1:20).

Both Paul's previous life as a persecutor of believers and the hostility that he later incurred from the Jews indicate that his contemporaries saw in his work a practice that could not be tolerated. In his mission to gentiles, he treated the most important badges of Israelite identity—circumcision, food laws, and the Sabbath—as adiaphora. Although Jewish freedom fighters died for these badges of identity two centuries earlier, Paul converted gentiles without requiring these fundamental boundary markers.

Paul's Basic Jewish Beliefs

Although Paul did not require these boundary markers for his converts, he continued to consider himself an Israelite and his gentile converts as the heirs of ancient Israel. The basic Jewish beliefs continued to play a role in his theology, although they were transformed by his new experience. He continues his belief in the God of Israel, the Scriptures, judgment according to deeds, and God's righteousness and wrath.

God. Paul held to the Jewish doctrine of God. He continued to recite the Shema (cf. 1 Cor. 8:6) and made it the foundation of his argument (Rom. 3:29–30; Gal. 3:19–20). The Shema defined the most basic Jewish conviction over against the polytheism of pagans, and it contained fighting words among Jews.[31] It was recited twice daily at Qumran (1QS 10.10), as well as in the rabbinic tradition, as the Tannaitic literature indicates.[32] In fact, Rabbi Akiba died reciting these words, and in the subsequent interpretive tradition, the Shema is associated with the call to martyrdom.[33]

With the Jews of the period, Paul referred to God as the "living God" in contrast to the idols (2 Cor. 3:3; 1 Thess. 1:9–10; cf. 1 Tim. 3:15; 4:10). God is the creator (Rom. 1:20; 1 Cor. 8:6; 2 Cor. 4:6) and father (Rom. 8:14; Gal. 4:6) who, because of his love, elected a people. Paul's frequent references to the power of God (2 Cor. 4:7; 6:7; 13:4; Phil. 2:13) are consistent with the Old Testament tradition (cf. Exod. 12:41; Josh. 4:24; 1 Chron. 29:11; Job 12:13).

---

31. See Wright, *New Testament and the People of God*, 199; cf. Nanos, "Paul and the Jewish Tradition," 64.
32. See Schiffman, "Shema," *NIDB* 5:225.
33. Nanos, "Paul and the Jewish Tradition," 63.

Scripture. Paul did not count as loss his devotion to Scripture as the Word of God, who has spoken through the prophets, promising the coming of the Davidic son (Rom. 1:2–3) and the election of "a people who are no people" (Rom. 9:25). Indeed, Paul appeals to authoritative Scripture, most frequently introducing citations with "it is written" (*gegraptai*; cf. Rom. 1:17; 3:10; 12:19; 1 Cor. 1:19; 9:9; 2 Cor. 8:15) or "Scripture [*graphē*] says" (Rom. 4:3; 9:17). He appeals to Scripture to support his arguments, maintaining that Scripture is "written for our instruction" (Rom. 15:4; cf. 1 Cor. 9:10), giving an eschatological interpretation of the passages.

The Jewish presuppositions of Paul's theology are evident in the way he uses Scripture. He employs the argument from the lesser to the greater (*qal wachomer*) in the Adam-Christ typology (Rom. 5:15, 17) and in the contrast between the glory of the old covenant and the glory of the new covenant (2 Cor. 3:7–11; cf. Rom. 11:12).[34] He employs the argument from analogy, according to which two passages containing the same word interpret each other (*gezera shewa*). This method is employed in Romans 4:3, 7 when Paul employs two passages that have the word "reckon" (*logizesthai*) to equate the forgiveness of sins (Rom. 4:7; cf. Ps. 31:2 LXX) with the reckoning of righteousness to Abraham. These two rules of interpretation are rules established by Rabbi Hillel.[35]

Paul's reliance on Scripture cannot be measured, however, in the number of citations in the letters. Indeed, three of the undisputed letters (Philippians, Philemon, 1 Thessalonians) contain no explicit citations. However, every letter reflects a belief in an implicit scriptural narrative in which the participants find themselves.[36] He refers to Adam as the founder of humanity (Rom. 5:14; 1 Cor. 15:22, 45; cf. 1 Tim. 2:13), to the incursion of sin (Rom. 5:12; cf. 7:7–25; 2 Cor. 11:2–4), to Abraham as the new beginning of the narrative, and to Moses and the wilderness. He speaks of the Israelites in the wilderness as "our ancestors" (1 Cor. 10:1). While he refers explicitly to major figures and events only rarely, the scriptural narrative is implicit in all of the letters.

Scripture is a narrative that consists of the anticipation of the fulfillment of God's promises in which God will bless the world (cf. Rom. 1:2; 4:11–14, 20–21; 15:8; 2 Cor. 9:5; Gal. 3:14–19). Thus Paul, like the prophets before him, anticipated a day when God would set things right. Almost every letter refers to the final day, the end of the narrative. With others in Second Temple Judaism, Paul recognizes the call and promise to Abraham as the promise

---

34. See Strecker and Nolting, "Der vorchristliche Paulus," 736.
35. Strecker and Nolting, "Der vorchristliche Paulus," 736.
36. Wright, *New Testament and the People of God*, 405.

awaiting fulfillment. In 1 and 2 Corinthians, he recalls Moses and the exodus as formative moments (1 Cor. 10:1–12; 2 Cor. 3:7–18). In Romans, Paul offers the full panorama of the narrative that is implicit elsewhere. It extends from creation and the fall to the restoration of God's creation. Paul's community here, as elsewhere, lives between the times—between the coming of the good news and the end.

The story was thus incomplete. With Jews of the Second Temple period, Paul believed in the two ages: this age and the age to come. The age to come has already become a reality. This is especially evident in Paul's use of the term "gospel." Paul had believed in the promise of the good news of the return from exile, like others who had looked forward to a new covenant and the outpouring of the Spirit, a time when Israel would be faithful. Thus Deuteronomy 30 probably played a role.[37] Similarly, the promises of Jeremiah and Ezekiel played a role.

No section of Scripture was as formative for Paul as Isaiah 40–66. Paul had believed in a time when the herald would declare the good news of the return from exile (Isa. 52:7) and the gentiles would be incorporated into the people of God (cf. 49:6; 56:6–8). As a result of his call, he understands that he is the herald of the good news for the nations (Gal. 1:15). Like the prophet, he was "set apart" from his "mother's womb" (cf. Isa. 49:1; Gal. 1:15) for his mission, hoping that his work is not "in vain" (2 Cor. 6:2; Gal. 4:11; Phil. 2:16). With the prophet, he asks despairingly, "Who has believed our message?" (Rom. 10:16; cf. Isa. 53:1), and he applies to the conversion of the gentiles the prophet's words, "I was found by those who did not seek me" (Rom. 10:20; cf. Isa. 65:1). Nevertheless, despite Israel's current disbelief, Paul shares the hope of the prophet that "a deliverer will come from Zion, who will turn ungodliness from Jacob" (Rom. 11:26 AT; Isa. 59:20). He assumes a narrative of the gentile mission, Israel's disobedience, and ultimate restoration for all on the basis of his reading of Isaiah 40–66. Paul probably shared with his contemporaries the conviction that the exile was the result of Israel's sin, that God would restore Israel, and that Israel would keep the commandments. God would establish a covenant in the heart and place God's Spirit within the people.

Although Paul admitted gentiles into the church without requiring the traditional boundary markers, he initiated them into the Jewish identity and continued to divide between "Jews and Greeks" (Rom. 1:16; 2:9–10; 3:9; 10:12; 1 Cor. 1:22, 24; 10:32; 12:13; Gal. 3:28), with the latter often referred to as the uncircumcised (akrobystia, Rom. 2:27; 3:30; cf. Eph. 2:11) or "gentile sinners"

---

37. See Wright, "Israel's Scriptures in Paul's Narrative Theology," 552.

(Gal. 2:15).[38] His gentile converts no longer belong in that category, however, for they were *formerly* gentiles (1 Cor. 12:2). Consequently, they should no longer behave like "the Gentiles who do not know God" (1 Thess. 4:5; cf. 1 Cor. 5:1).[39] In continuity with ancient Israel, they are the elect, the holy, the "Israel of God" (Gal. 6:16). Thus his theology is shaped by traditional Jewish categories.

Judgment according to deeds. A consistent feature of Paul's letters is the anticipation of the coming wrath of God, a topic that appears in both the earliest and the latest undisputed letters (1 Thess. 1:10; 2:16; 5:9; Rom. 1:18; 2:5; 5:9) and extends to Colossians and Ephesians. Gentile believers were once "children of wrath" (Eph. 2:3) like the rest of humankind but have now been saved (Eph. 2:8) in Christ. The wrath of God comes on the children of disobedience (Eph. 5:6; Col. 3:6), while the faithful have a hope laid up in the heavens (Col. 1:5; cf.1:27).

The coming wrath described in 1 Thessalonians 1:10 is associated with "the day of the Lord" (1 Thess. 5:2), when the Savior will rescue the faithful (Rom. 5:9; 1 Thess. 5:10), and the disobedient will not escape (1 Thess. 5:3; cf. Rom. 2:3). This is a common theme in Paul's letters. Paul holds to the traditional views of a day of wrath and final judgment according to deeds. He consistently speaks of the final day. It will be a "day of wrath" (Rom. 2:5) when God judges the world (Rom. 2:16). It is imminent (Rom. 13:12) and comes as a thief in the night (1 Thess. 5:2). He describes it simply as "the day" (1 Cor. 3:13; 1 Thess. 5:4), "the day of the Lord" (1 Cor. 1:8; 5:5; 2 Cor. 1:14; 1 Thess. 5:2; 2 Thess. 2:2), and "the day of Christ" (Phil. 1:6, 10; 2:16). While this day is a day of wrath for some (Rom. 2:5; cf. 1 Thess. 1:10), Paul prays that believers will be blameless at the day of the Lord (1 Cor. 1:8; Phil. 2:15; cf. 1 Thess. 3:13). The day of the Lord is the same as the parousia (1 Cor. 15:23; 1 Thess. 2:19; 3:13; 4:15; 5:23). Paul anticipates that his churches will be his boast at the day of the Lord (2 Cor. 1:14; Phil. 1:26; 2:16; cf. 2 Cor. 11:2).

That God judges those who practice specific vices is a frequent theme in Paul. Those who practice these vices will not inherit the kingdom of God (1 Cor. 6:19; Gal. 5:21). The end of those who do not conform to the will of God will be destruction (2 Cor. 11:15; Phil. 3:19; cf. 1 Thess. 2:16). "We all will stand before the judgment seat of God" (Rom. 14:10) to give an account of our deeds (2 Cor. 5:10).

God's righteousness and wrath in Romans. The first four chapters of Romans have played a major role in the insistence of Protestant theologians

38. Barclay, *Jews in the Mediterranean World*, 388.
39. Barclay, *Jews in the Mediterranean World*, 388.

that Paul counted Judaism "as loss." In the thesis statement of Romans, Paul announces that "the righteousness of God is being revealed" and that "the righteous will live by faith" (1:17), a theme he reiterates throughout the letter (cf. 3:25, 27–30; 4:3–23; 5:1; 10:6, 8, 17; 11:20). In contrast to traditional Jewish thinking, Paul regards faith (*pistis*) as the opposite of works of the law (3:20, 27–28; 4:1–8; 9:12, 32), a phrase that Paul abbreviates to "the law" (4:13; cf. 5:1; 9:30–10:4; 10:9–13). As the appropriate response to the gospel, *pistis* rather than the law can be the response of both Jews and gentiles (Rom. 4) and the basis for a church not divided by the traditional Jewish boundary markers of circumcision, the Sabbath, and the dietary laws. The insistence that God's righteousness is being revealed (1:17, or "has been manifested," 3:21 AT) forms part of the thesis statement of the letter and is expanded in 3:21–26 and illustrated in the midrash on Abraham in Romans 4.

The claim that God's righteousness is known in the death of Jesus was "a stumbling block to Jews" (1 Cor. 1:23) that separated Paul from his heritage (cf. Rom. 9:1–5). The alternative between faithfulness (*pistis*) and works of the law was unprecedented in the Jewish tradition, for whom faithfulness was demonstrated by keeping the law. For Paul, the fact that "Abraham believed God, and it was reckoned to him as righteousness" (Gen. 15:6; Rom. 4:3) precluded works (Rom. 4:3–9), while Jewish tradition insisted that Abraham's belief included faithfulness to the law (1 Macc. 2:52; cf. Sir. 44:20). For Paul, Abraham was counted faithful before he was circumcised; thus he became the father of believing gentiles, while traditional Jewish interpretation claimed Abraham as the father of national Israel. Although Paul argues from Scripture, his differences from the Pharisaic tradition inevitably created a separation.

Maintaining that justification by faith is the central focus of Romans, scholars have been puzzled by the place in the argument of 1:18–3:20, especially 2:1–29. Little is said in this section that is not in full agreement with Jewish tradition. While scholars generally agree that the focus on the sinfulness of all humanity in this section (cf. 3:9) corresponds to the announcement of the revelation of God's righteousness for all humanity, this section contains statements that do not appear to cohere with the rest of Paul's argument. The indictment of idolaters in 1:18–32 parallels closely Wisdom of Solomon 12–14. The description of those who "hold the truth in ungodliness" in Romans 1:18–32 (AT) echoes the indictment in the Wisdom of Solomon against those "who were unable from the good things that are seen to know the one who exists" (Wis. 13:1; cf. Rom. 1:20). The claim that the making of idols is the beginning of fornication (Wis. 14:12) anticipates Paul's description of the sexual vices that are the result of idolatry (Rom. 1:24–26). Like the author of Wisdom (13:8), Paul claims that those who commit these vices are without excuse (Rom. 1:20; 2:1), for they do not use the knowledge that they have. The claim that "the doers of the law . . . will be justified" (Rom. 2:13) appears to conflict with the later statement that "no one will be justified by works of the law" (3:20 AT). The focus on judgment according to one's deeds (2:1–11) stands in tension with the later announcement that believers are justified by faith (cf. 3:22; 4:1–6; 5:1) rather than works of the law (cf. 3:20). The claim that gentiles do what the Lord requires (2:14–15) appears to contradict the indictment of gentiles in 1:18–32. Thus 1:18–2:29, according to numerous scholars, is too Jewish to cohere with Pauline theology. Paul parts from the Jewish tradition only in his claim that both Jews and Greeks are under the power of sin (cf. 3:9).[40]

According to E. P. Sanders, "Not all the material actually lends itself to the desired conclusion, and there are substantial ways in which parts of it conflict with positions Paul elsewhere adopts."[41] Sanders indicates that Paul "takes over to an unusual degree homiletical material from Diaspora Judaism, that he alters it in only insubstantial ways," and that Paul's treatment of the law in Romans 2 cannot be harmonized with what Paul says about the law elsewhere.[42] Heikki Räisänen argues that Romans 2 is evidence that Paul is not a coherent thinker.[43] Other scholars have argued that what Paul says about obedience to the law is hypothetical; that is, only perfect obedience would gain righteousness, and such obedience is impossible.[44] These studies assume that Romans 2 is anomalous in Paul and at least marginal in his theology. I shall explore the chapter in order to see its place in Paul's theology.

While Wisdom 12–14 distinguishes between the righteous, whom God judges with mildness and forbearance (Wis. 12:18), and their enemies, whom God punishes "ten thousand times more" (Wis. 12:22), Paul's address to the imaginary interlocutor (Rom. 2:1–29) indicates no such distinction. The one who judges those who are guilty of idolatry and the multiple vices in 1:18–32 is also without excuse (2:1), for the one who judges is guilty of the "same things" (2:1). That is, all are under the power of sin (3:9). Unlike Wisdom

40. See the discussion in Barclay, "Believer and the 'Last Judgment' in Paul." A conundrum in scholarship has been the apparent conflict in Paul's letters between the theology of grace and judgment according to deeds. Most attempts at resolution involve "privileging of one of the two principles over the other" (Barclay, "Believer and the 'Last Judgment' in Paul," 198). Barclay insists that interpreters reconsider their understanding of grace, inasmuch as gifts in the ancient world entailed expectations and obligations.
41. Sanders, *Paul, the Law, and the Jewish People*, 123.
42. Sanders, *Paul, the Law, and the Jewish People*, 123.
43. Sanders, *Paul, the Law, and the Jewish People*, 123, 129; Räisänen, *Paul and the Law*, 106–8.
44. Schreiner, "Did Paul Believe in Justification by Works?," 136.

12–14 and the *Psalms of Solomon* (3:9–10), Romans does not distinguish between the sinners and the righteous but concludes that those who judge the unrighteous are also without excuse, for they do the same things (Rom. 2:1).

Paul elaborates on judgment in Romans 2:1–11, appealing first to common knowledge among Jews: "We know that the judgment of God is according to truth on those who do these things" (2:2 AT). He frequently appeals to what "we know" (cf. "Do you not know?") as a basis for argument. What "we know" may be based on Scripture (3:19; 8:22; 11:2), common Jewish tradition (1 Cor. 5:6; 6:2–3, 9–10; 9:13; 1 Thess. 4:2; 5:2), logical inference (Rom. 6:19; 8:1, 4), or Christian catechetical teaching (1 Cor. 3:16). In this instance, what "we know" is the Jewish expectation of judgment on sinners (cf. *Pss. Sol.* 2:16–17, 34; 3:11–12; 15:8–12), which Paul shares.[45] In the two rhetorical questions that follow, Paul turns from the general expectation to the interlocutor, who would expect to escape God's judgment. The two rhetorical questions (Rom. 2:3–5) indicate that God's judgment is not only on the idolaters (1:18–32) but also on the law-keeping interlocutor (2:3–5). In the first rhetorical question, Paul suggests that those who judge sinners—presumably the Jewish interlocutor—will not escape God's wrath, applying to him the general truth about others who will not escape God's wrath (*Pss. Sol.* 15:8). In the question "Are you ignorant that the kindness of God leads to repentance?" (Rom. 2:4 AT), Paul appeals once more to Jewish assumptions that the interlocutor should know (cf. Wis. 11:23; *4 Ezra* 9:12): that the kindness of God leads to repentance. That the interlocutor needs to repent is indicated in the statement "you store up wrath for the day of wrath and the revelation of the righteous judgment of God" (Rom. 2:5 AT). Paul appeals to the Jewish conviction that one stores up either good works or evil deeds before the final day (cf. *Pss. Sol.* 9:5; *1 En.* 38:2; *4 Ezra* 6:5; 7:77; 8:33; *2 Bar.* 14:12; 24:1; *2 En.* 50:5).[46]

In speaking of the interlocutor's hard heart, Paul applies to him the term that was commonly used for Israel (Deut. 10:16; Prov. 17:20; Jer. 4:4; Ezek. 3:7; Sir. 16:10). The "righteous judgment of God" (Rom. 2:5 AT) is a familiar theme of the *Psalms of Solomon*, which declares that God's judgments are just (*Pss. Sol.* 2:10, 18; 8:24; 9:2; 10:5) and that God will act in the future to demonstrate justice in the separation of the good from the evil (2:34), demonstrating mercy on those who fear God (2:34; 8:28, 32). In turning once more from the interlocutor to the general principle that God "renders to each according to each one's works" (*Pss. Sol.* 2:6 AT), Paul once more appeals

---

45. Cf. Becker, *Paul*, 47.
46. See Zeller, "θησαυρός," *EDNT* 2:150.

to a common Jewish expectation (*Pss. Sol.* 2:16–17, 34; 3:11–12; 15:8–12) of the righteous judgment of God, citing Psalm 62:12 and echoing numerous passages about God's final judgment. Thus Paul appeals to basic Jewish assumptions about the final judgment based on one's deeds.

The chiastic arrangement in Romans 2:7–10 reiterates the nature of the judgment on both Jews and Greeks according to their deeds.[47] There will be eternal life for those who have done good deeds and wrath for those whose deeds were evil. Unlike his contemporaries, Paul insists that God is the impartial judge, whose impartiality extends to both Jew and Greek.

The expectation of a day of judgment and wrath is consistent not only with the Pharisaic tradition but with the entire prophetic tradition. The day of the Lord is a frequent theme among the prophets, for whom the day of the Lord is the time when the righteous will be rewarded and the wicked will be punished. For the righteous, this will be the time for the restoration of Israel. According to Joel, "In those days [I, God, will] . . . restore the fortunes of Judah and Jerusalem" (Joel 3:1) and "gather all the nations and bring them down to the valley of Jehoshaphat, and I will enter into judgment with them there, on account of my people and my heritage Israel" (3:2). "In that day the mountains shall drip sweet wine, the hills shall flow with milk, and all the stream beds of Judah shall flow with water" (3:18).

For the unrighteous, that day is a time of punishment. According to Amos, the day of the Lord is darkness and not light (Amos 5:18; Joel 2:1–2; 3:14 [4:14 LXX]). It is a day of the Lord against all the nations (Obad. 1:15), a time to punish corrupt officials (Zeph. 1:7–8), a time of destruction (Isa. 13:6) and wrath (Isa. 13:9; Ezek. 7:10), and a day of punishment on Israel. It is the day when the Lord comes (Ezek. 13:5); the day of the Lord will be a day of wrath (Zeph. 1:10–15; cf. Mal. 4:3, "on the day when I act," the wicked will be punished).

Paul elaborates on the impartiality of God's judgment in Romans 2:12–16, as the conjunction *gar* indicates (2:12). The distinction between those who sin with or without the law (2:12) and the doers of the law (2:13) reiterates the earlier distinction between the judgment given to those who do evil (2:9) and that given to those who do good (2:10) in Paul's first reference to the law in the argument. That both will be judged follows from God's impartiality in judging Jews and gentiles (2:11). The statement that the doers of the law will be justified (2:13) is parallel to the eternal life mentioned for those who do the good in 2:7, 10 and is a contrast to those who will be judged (2:13). Paul anticipates this event as the ultimate scene of judgment.

47. Schreiner, "Did Paul Believe in Justification by Works?," 132.

That the "doers of the law" include gentiles becomes evident in the clarifying statement in 2:14–16. In view of the categorical judgment on gentiles in 1:18–32, Paul's statement is surprising. Thus scholars have debated whether the gentiles of 2:14–16 are non-Christian or Christ-believing gentiles. The fact that they have the law "written on their hearts" (2:15) indicates that Paul is not speaking of the gentiles mentioned in 1:18–32 but of those who have come to faith. The "law written on their hearts" is the new covenant described by the exilic prophets. Ezekiel speaks of the new heart (Ezek. 11:19) of flesh and the new Spirit, which will empower Israel to keep the commandments (Ezek. 11:20). For those who do not obey, God will bring their deeds upon their heads (cf. Ezek. 11:21). Jeremiah speaks of the covenant written on hearts (Jer. 31:33). In Deuteronomy (10:16), the circumcision of the foreskin of the heart results in the keeping of the commandments (Deut. 10:19–11:12). Paul anticipates this in Romans 8, according to which the just requirement of the law is fulfilled by those who walk according to the Spirit (Rom. 8:4). According to 2 Corinthians, believers are Paul's letters of recommendation, written on hearts (2 Cor. 3:2–3).

Paul again contrasts those who do not keep the law (Rom. 2:17–24) with those who do (2:25–29), beginning once more with the indictment of the interlocutor (2:17–24; cf. 2:2–5) before proceeding to a general principle. The criticism of the interlocutor is not aimed at a specific person who calls himself a Jew (2:17) but is a restatement of the prophetic critique on Israel, which broke God's covenant. This indictment provides the contrast with those who keep the law (2:25–29). Mentioning circumcision for the first time (2:25), Paul's claim that circumcision becomes uncircumcision for those who do not keep the law, Paul summarizes his case about those who sin with the law (2:12, 17–24). On the other hand, he offers the general principle of the uncircumcision, those who, unlike the gentiles of 1:32, actually keep the just requirements of the law (2:27). This obedience "will be reckoned" (*logisthēsetai*, 2:26) as circumcision. The verb anticipates the later claim that Abraham's faith was "reckoned" as righteousness (4:3–4, 6, 10–11, 24). The passive voice indicates the divine action of declaring someone to be among the people of God.[48]

Paul concludes the comparison in Romans 2:25–29. In 2:26, he again mentions the uncircumcised who "keep the just requirements of the law" (AT). He knows a "circumcision of the heart in the Spirit and not the letter" (2:29 AT). This claim about the righteous gentile appears within the larger unit that declares that all are under the power of sin. Thus although Paul echoes

---

48. Wright, "Law in Romans 2," 136; Wright, *Paul and the Faithfulness of God*, 1029.

the idea of natural law by using Stoic and Hellenistic-Jewish language,[49] he is not making the case that gentiles are not under God's judgment. He is stating a general principle and anticipating the later argument. He recalls Jeremiah's promise that God will take unrighteous Israel and write the law on their hearts (Jer. 31:33; cf. Rom. 2:15), and they will keep the commandments. God will circumcise the hearts of the people (Deut. 30:6; cf. 30:10, 16; Rom. 2:26–29) and place his Spirit within them (Ezek. 11:19; 36:27). The community that went into exile because of its disobedience to the law will return from exile and keep the law that God will write on their hearts. Thus having spoken earlier of gentiles who do not do the good that they learn from nature (Rom. 1:18–24), Paul does not reverse himself in Romans 2 but anticipates the later argument that, in the new situation, some gentiles "keep the just requirement of the law" (Rom. 8:4 AT). Paul's statements about the gentiles who keep the law is only a general principle that becomes a reality in Christ.

One may compare Paul's claim in Philippians that "we are the circumcision, those who serve God in the Spirit and boast in Christ Jesus and do not place confidence in the flesh" (Phil. 3:3 AT) and his claim that "neither circumcision nor uncircumcision matters, but keeping the commandments" (1 Cor. 7:19 AT; cf. Gal. 6:15). These statements clearly indicate that the commandments continue to be obligatory for Christian believers.

Paul elaborates on the themes of wrath and judgment in Romans, repeating the claim in 1 Thessalonians (1:10) that believers will be saved from the coming wrath (Rom. 5:9). This claim comes after Paul has laid out the foundation of the argument in Romans 1–4, claiming that both the righteousness and the wrath of God "are being revealed" (Rom. 1:17–18 AT) with the proclamation of the gospel.

In the Jewish tradition, the day of the Lord was the conclusion of a narrative of God's covenant with the people. Like other Jews, Paul had expected the end to the narrative that would conclude with the demonstration of God's justice, when the good would be rewarded and the evil would be punished. Paul had learned the distinction between this age and the age to come.

Although scholars have regarded this statement as "un-Pauline," it is consistent with numerous comments in the Pauline literature. His statement that believers will be saved from God's wrath appears in the first and the last of the undisputed letters (1 Thess. 1:10; Rom. 5:10). That all people, including believers, will stand before the judgment seat of God is a statement that appears to appeal to common knowledge (Rom. 14:10; 2 Cor. 5:10). Thus this is neither a marginal theme in Pauline theology nor contradictory to Paul's

---

49. Cf. Martens, "Romans 2:14–16: A Stoic Reading."

theology of grace. Paul looks to the end of exile, a time when gentiles will be accepted on the basis of the foreskin of their hearts being removed.

The major focus of Romans 1:18–3:20 is that both Jews and Greeks hold the truth in ungodliness and unrighteousness (1:18) and are all under the power of sin (3:9), a claim that does not conform to traditional Jewish views. Neither the gentiles nor the Jews make use of their available knowledge, for the gentiles know the righteous judgments of God and do not keep them (1:32), and the Jews know the law but do not keep it (2:1, 17–24).

Romans 1:18–3:20 is an elaboration of the declaration that "the wrath of God is being revealed against all ungodliness and unrighteousness of those who hold the truth in unrighteousness" (1:18 AT). As the developing argument indicates, "those who hold the truth in unrighteousness" include both Jews and Greeks (2:10 AT; cf. 3:9)—those who have the law and those who do not. The announcement that "the wrath of God is being revealed" (1:18 AT) is parallel to the declaration that "the righteousness of God is being revealed" (1:17 AT) through the faith of Jesus Christ "for all who believe" (3:21–26 AT). Paul assumes the Jewish expectation of the eschatological revelation, when God's righteous judgments become evident in reward for the faithful and wrath for the wicked. While the announcement of the revelation of God's righteousness and wrath corresponds to Jewish expectation, Paul departs from Jewish expectation by holding that this event has already occurred in the death of Jesus Christ (3:21–26).

Conclusion: The Jewish Substructure of Paul's Theology

Paul stands firmly within the Jewish tradition, maintaining the convictions of his Pharisaic heritage and the wider streams of Second Temple Judaism. While he maintains his essential Jewishness, Paul was set apart from his Jewish contemporaries due to his convictions that in the death of Jesus Christ the turn of the ages had come and set him apart from his Jewish contemporaries. The Jewish narrative of creation, humankind under God's wrath, and ultimate reconciliation continues as the substructure of Paul's theology. He continues to believe in a day of judgment when the "doers of the law" will be justified (Rom. 2:13). As Romans 2 and the larger context of Romans indicate (cf. 8:1–11), the "just requirement of the law" (AT) will be fulfilled in the community of the new age. Paul consistently expresses these convictions throughout his correspondence, and they form one dimension of the premises of his argumentation.

3

Where Christian Theology Began

Jesus and the Early Church

Is Antioch the place where Christian theology began?" ask Martin Hengel and Anna Maria Schwemer.[1] According to a major tradition of Pauline scholarship, Paul was the first Christian theologian, but his theology was heavily dependent on the church at Antioch. Here, according to Michael Wolter, Paul spent many years as a member of the Antioch church, which had already separated from the synagogue, welcomed gentiles, and practiced a law-free gospel.[2] Over a century ago, Wilhelm Bousset argued that Hellenistic Christianity came into being in Antioch.[3] The young Christian movement applied the term *kyrios* (Lord) to Jesus and maintained few ties to Judaism, Jesus, and the Jerusalem church (see chap. 2 above). Here Christianity came into contact with the mystery cults and developed a syncretism that incorporated elements from Hellenistic culture and laid the foundation for a universal religion. Under the influence of Bousset, Rudolf Bultmann maintained that Paul first developed "the clarity of theological thinking."[4]

Interpreters have continued to posit the Antioch church as the source of Pauline theology and of the universal mission. Jürgen Becker argues that

1. Hengel and Schwemer, *Paul between Damascus and Antioch*, 279.
2. Wolter, *Paul*, 31–50.
3. Bousset, *Kyrios Christos*, 136–52.
4. Bultmann, *Theology of the New Testament*, 1:187.

the basic insights of Pauline thought originated in the Antioch church.[5] The church at Antioch "entered church history because the community separated itself from the synagogue and formed a law-free fellowship based on Christ alone. That is, it surrendered the previously undisputed, natural conception of the Christian faith as an intra-Jewish group and understood Christianity as a new kind of phenomenon defining itself solely on its own terms."[6]

Becker adds that the Antioch church marked the first step "from a Jewish faction to a 'world religion.'"[7] Here the Antiochian theology had already determined the presence of the Spirit outside Judaism and practiced a law-free gospel. Pre-Pauline traditions, including christological formulas (i.e., Jesus is Lord) and soteriological confessions (i.e., Christ died "for us," "for our sins," cf. Rom. 5:8; 1 Cor. 15:3), probably existed in Antioch, where Paul inherited them.[8]

Michael Wolter summarizes the beliefs of the Antioch church prior to Paul, indicating that the Antioch church believed (1) that God raised Jesus from the dead and exalted him to heaven, (2) that the exalted Lord would return, and (3) that Christ would judge the world, saving only those who belonged to him. Wolter also maintains that the believers assembled regularly, practiced baptism as a rite of entry, and experienced the Holy Spirit. Membership was open to all who called on the name of Jesus as Lord.[9] For Wolter and others, Antioch, the place of the confrontation with Cephas (Gal. 2:11–14), was also the place where Paul separated from Jerusalem believers and began his mission among the gentiles.[10] The corollary to this view is that Paul was influenced little by the Jewish tradition, Jesus, or the Jerusalem church. According to Bousset, the connections between Paul and the Jerusalem church are scant.[11]

Despite the place that scholars have given to Antioch, Paul offers no evidence of his indebtedness to the Antioch church. While Acts depicts Antioch as the place where Paul lived and from which he began his missionary journeys, he mentions the city only once in the entire corpus of his writings. When he recalls his travels in Galatians 1:10–2:10, he does not mention Antioch specifically,

---

5. Becker, *Paul*, 103–4.
6. Becker, *Paul*, 102.
7. Becker, *Paul*, 102.
8. Becker, *Paul*, 111–12.
9. Becker, *Paul*, 36–38.
10. Schnelle, *Apostle Paul*, 138.
11. Bousset, *Kyrios Christos*, 119. Cf. Becker, *Paul*, 374: "Pauline theology is not to be comprehended as the attempt to understand the Christian confession of the history of Old Testament-Jewish tradition, so that this history is carried forward and still written under the dominant viewpoint of continuity. . . . Paul's first concern is not how he might successfully extend Old Testament-Jewish religion into the Christian, or even whether he does justice to the Jewish self-understanding. His pressing concern is how he can let the Christ who is near in the gospel determine and value everything."

although he probably includes it in the report of his travels in Syria and Cilicia (Gal. 1:21). According to Acts, he spent an extended time there, but he gives no indication in the letters of its influence on his theology—nor can one verify the influence of Hellenistic religiosity on the thought of Paul or the Antioch church.[12] Moreover, the multiple interactions between the churches of Jerusalem and Antioch (Acts 11:27–30; 14:25–15:2, 22; Gal. 2:11–14) indicate that the church at Antioch maintained a relationship with the church in Jerusalem.

In the previous chapter, I indicated the foundation of Paul's theology in the Old Testament and Jewish tradition. In this chapter, I will explore the convictions that Paul inherited from those who went before him in the movement inaugurated by Jesus. These convictions remained with Paul as he articulated the meaning of the Christian faith in changing situations.

Paul and Jesus

To say that Pauline theology is the articulation of Antiochian theology is to deny the importance of Jesus in Pauline thought. William Wrede's description of Paul as "the second founder of Christianity" reflects this perceived discontinuity between Jesus and Paul.[13] Rudolf Bultmann's claim that Paul had no interest in the historical Jesus has also been influential in Pauline studies.[14] In fact, many treatments of Pauline theology give little attention to the possibility of Paul's dependence on the Jesus traditions in the shaping of his theology.[15]

The dependence of Paul on Jesus is not self-evident, however. Paul cites Jesus explicitly only three times in the undisputed letters (1 Cor. 7:10; 9:14; 11:23–26), and he tells us next to nothing about the life and ministry of Jesus apart from its climactic finale.[16] The focus of his preaching is not on the words and deeds of Jesus but on the death and resurrection of Jesus. Though numerous texts may be allusions to the words of Jesus (e.g., Rom. 12:9–21; 1 Cor. 13:2), Paul does not indicate the origin of the words.[17] Jesus preaches

12. See Hengel and Schwemer, *Paul between Damascus and Antioch*, 279–310.

13. Wrede, *Paul*, 179.

14. Bultmann, *Theology of the New Testament*, 1:188: "All that is important for [Paul] in the story of Jesus is the fact that Jesus was born and lived under the law (Gal. 4:4) and that he had been crucified (Gal. 3:1; 1 Cor. 2:2; Phil. 2:5ff)."

15. Besides Bultmann, who devoted thirty pages of *Theology of the New Testament* to the message of Jesus, cf. Becker, *Paul*, whose index lists no entry for Jesus.

16. Dunn, *Theology of Paul*, 184.

17. Other texts have been identified: allusions to Jesus's words (Rom. 12:14, 20 to Luke 6:27–28, 35 // Matt. 5:44; Rom. 14:14 to Mark 7:15; 1 Cor. 1:2 to Mark 11:23; 1 Thess. 5:2, 6 to Luke 12:39 // Matt. 24:43 // Mark 13:35). Wolter, *Paul*, 451; Riesner, "Paulus und die Jesus-Überlieferung," 360.

the kingdom, while Paul mentions it only rarely (Rom. 14:17; 1 Cor. 4:20; 6:9; 15:24, 50; Gal. 5:21; 1 Thess. 2:12; cf. Eph. 5:5; Col. 1:13)and instead preaches the gospel (*euangelion*; cf. Rom. 1:16; 1 Cor. 15:1; Gal. 1:11), the content of which he describes in various ways: "Christ crucified" (1 Cor. 1:23; 2:2); "Jesus Christ as Lord" (2 Cor. 4:5); "that Christ died for our sins" (1 Cor. 15:1–3).

The discontinuity between Jesus and Paul is also evident in the nature of their respective missions. Jesus was sent to the lost sheep of the house of Israel (Matt. 15:24), to which he also sends his disciples (Matt. 10:6), while Paul has been sent (cf. Rom. 10:15; 1 Cor. 1:17) to the nations (cf. Rom. 1:5, 14–15; 15:18; Gal. 1:16). This difference corresponds to their respective places in salvation history. Paul lives in the post-Easter situation, sharing the convictions of the early church that the new era called forth a new mission.[18]

Despite the areas of discontinuity, Paul undoubtedly shaped his theology with a knowledge of the message of Jesus. "It would be astonishing indeed if a movement which focused so intensively on Jesus Christ . . . was uninterested in this Jesus."[19] As James Dunn argues, the Epistles are the middle of a conversation, and a prior explanation about the man Jesus is probable in Paul's mission preaching and catechesis. Paul undoubtedly knew more about Jesus than he mentions explicitly in the letters.[20] One cannot imagine the frequent references to the name "Jesus" without reflection on the course of Jesus's life prior to the crucifixion. To preach that "Jesus Christ is Lord" (2 Cor. 4:5) and that "Christ is raised from the dead" (Rom. 6:9 AT) is to assume a knowledge of the man Jesus. Paul had a definite perception of the character of Jesus, speaking of the "meekness and gentleness of Christ" (2 Cor. 10:1) and recalling that Christ "did not please himself" (Rom. 15:3). Thus Paul believed that Jesus was unselfish, meek, and humble, and he challenged his churches to imitate him as he imitates Christ (1 Cor. 11:1). He gained this impression from hearing the narratives about Jesus (Mark 14:22–25, 43–49, 60–61, 65; 15:16–32).[21] "Thus there is no doubt that his message points back to the historical Jesus and his work and message."[22]

The Coming of the Kingdom and the Turn of the Ages

We look for the foundations of Pauline theology not only in isolated sayings and in the pattern of Jesus's life but also in the major themes of Paul

---

18. See Kümmel, *Die Theologie des Neuen Testaments*, 220.
19. See Dunn, *Theology of Paul*, 185.
20. Riesner, "Paulus und die Jesus-Überlieferung," 359; Häußer, *Christusbekenntnis und Jesusüberlieferung*, 352.
21. Allison, *Constructing Jesus*, 406.
22. Kümmel, *Die Theologie des Neuen Testaments*, 219.

and Jesus. The major theme of Jesus's proclamation, as the Gospel of Mark indicates, is "The time has been fulfilled; the kingdom of God is at hand" (Mark 1:14–15 AT). This theme appears in every layer of the synoptic tradition.[23] Jesus takes up the Jewish hope for the time when God's reign will be established in all of the earth (cf. Dan. 2:44; Zech. 14:3–9) and applies it to his own activity. The anticipated battle over the forces of evil that will result in God's triumph, for example, is taking place in the exorcisms (Mark 3:23–27; Luke 10:18).[24] Jesus responds to the inquiry of John the Baptist about his identity, pointing to his actions: "The blind see, the lame walk, the lepers are cleansed, the deaf hear, the dead are raised, and the poor have good news preached to them" (Matt. 11:5 AT // Luke 7:22), alluding to several passages from the book of Isaiah (Isa. 26:19; 29:18; 35:5–6; 61:1) that describe Israel's expectation for the reign of God. His table fellowship with sinners, a defining characteristic of Jesus's ministry, was probably a proleptic demonstration of the eschatological banquet (cf. Isa. 25:6).

These events are the fulfillment of Scripture (cf. Luke 4:21). Thus Jesus's announcement of the coming of the kingdom signified the realization of Israel's hopes as they are described in Scripture. Jesus's appeals to Scripture suggest that he taught his disciples the eschatological reading of Scripture that was practiced among other groups in Second Temple Judaism. Indeed, his announcement of "good news for the poor" (Luke 4:18 AT; cf. Isa. 61:1) was probably the origin of the term "gospel" (*euangelion*) among Paul and other early Christian writers.[25] The prophet's announcement "Your God reigns" (Isa. 52:7) lies behind Jesus's announcement of the kingdom. Similarly, Deutero- and Trito-Isaiah played the decisive role in Paul's theology, as I argued in the previous chapter. Moreover, Paul repeatedly argues on the basis of the eschatological reading of Scripture (cf. Rom. 15:3; 1 Cor. 9:10; 10:11).

While Jesus taught that the kingdom was among them already (Luke 17:21), he also taught his disciples to pray "Thy kingdom come," and he spoke frequently of the future kingdom. Those who received the message of the kingdom became a community of disciples that was distinct from the people of Israel. He challenged them to believe (*pisteuein*) in his message (Mark 1:15). He healed in response to faith (Matt. 8:10; 9:2, 22; Mark 5:36), and he called for faith as a continuing response of his disciples (Matt. 17:20; 21:21; Mark 11:23). Similarly, Paul gathered a community of those who believed his

23. Wolter, *Paul*, 451.
24. See Schnelle, *Theology of the New Testament*, 58, for major texts on the Jewish tradition of holy war.
25. Dunn, *Theology of Paul*, 190.

proclamation of the good news and called for faith as a response to the good news (cf. Rom. 10:9–10, 17; 2 Cor. 5:7; Gal. 3:7–9).

The coming of the kingdom is also a time for judgment. For Jesus, the impending triumph of God is also the occasion for the outpouring of God's wrath on those who do not repent (cf. Matt. 11:20–24; Luke 13:1–5; 21:23). Paul shared this expectation of both the triumph of God's kingdom (1 Cor. 15:21–28) and the impending wrath on those who do not receive the message (1 Thess. 1:9–10; 2:16; 5:9).

While Paul did not speak frequently of the kingdom, he undoubtedly shared with Jesus the conviction that the turn of the ages is both a present and a future reality. Paul's gospel is the message prophesied in Scripture (Rom. 1:2), especially in Deutero-Isaiah (cf. Isa. 52:7); the manifestation of the righteousness of God, long anticipated in Jewish literature, has become a reality (cf. Rom. 3:21). Both the new covenant anticipated by Jeremiah (Jer. 31:31–34) and the new creation promised in the book of Isaiah (Isa. 65:17; 66:22) have become a reality. Indeed, the end of the ages has come for the community (cf. 1 Cor. 10:11), which has been "rescued from the present evil age" (Gal. 1:4 AT).

Paul's statements about those who "will not inherit the kingdom" (1 Cor. 6:9–10; 15:50; Gal. 5:21) are parallel to Jesus's comments about those who "will not enter into the kingdom" (Matt. 5:20 AT; 7:21; 18:3; 19:17, 23). For Paul, as for Jesus, the coming of the kingdom will involve the triumph over cosmic powers (1 Cor. 15:23–25) and wrath for unbelievers (1 Thess. 1:9–10). Thus he shares with Jesus the view that the community lives between the times.

Jesus, Paul, and the Law

Jesus and Paul shared the Jewish expectation that those who do the will of God will enter the kingdom. However, while Jesus was faithful to the Torah, he distinguished himself from the Pharisaic obedience to Torah (Matt. 5:17–20), calling for a radical obedience that surpassed the demands of the Torah (Mark 10:2–9, 17–22) but that was more relaxed toward the Pharisaic laws on purity (Mark 7:1–16). Thus the table fellowship with sinners, a common practice in Jesus's ministry, was a violation of the Pharisaic interpretation of the law.

Jesus's relationship to the laws of purity anticipated Paul's view of the law. Like Jesus, Paul frequently appealed to the law as an expression of the divine norm of conduct (cf. Rom. 15:3; 1 Cor. 9:9; 14:34; 2 Cor. 6:2; 9:9); he did not require the traditional boundary markers of Judaism for his converts. Indeed, his statement that "nothing is common or unclean" (Rom. 14:14 AT) may be an echo of Jesus's earlier statements on the laws of purity (cf. Mark

7:1–15). Jesus's table fellowship with sinners, a violation of Pharisaic purity laws, anticipated Paul's insistence that Jews and gentiles share common meals in violation of traditional Pharisaic practice (cf. Gal. 2:11–14). The coming of the kingdom in Jesus's message is "good news for the poor" and acceptance of "tax collectors and sinners," as the parables indicate. For Paul, the revelation in Christ is justification of the godless and the acceptance of all who have faith in the message (Rom. 10:9–10). Both Jesus and Paul outraged their contemporaries with their practices related to the Torah, particularly its laws on ceremonial purity.

The Law and the Love Command

A further point of continuity between Jesus and Paul is the central place of love as the summation of the law, which is based on the command in Leviticus, "You shall love your neighbor as yourself" (Lev. 19:18). This connection is especially noteworthy in view of the paucity of references to Leviticus 19:18 in Jewish literature.[26] In the Synoptic Gospels, references to Leviticus 19:18 occur in several instances. In the antithesis of the Sermon on the Mount, the citation is modified to "You shall love your neighbor," to which Jesus adds the common interpretation "and hate your enemy" (Matt. 5:43) before he offers his alternative: "love your enemies" (Matt. 5:44). In contrast to common interpretation in Judaism that the neighbor is the fellow Israelite, Matthew's Jesus extends the command to the enemy. In the dialogue with the young ruler, Jesus places Leviticus 19:18 alongside the Decalogue as a summary of the law (Matt. 19:18–19). In response to questions about the great commandment, he combines the two passages that have *agapēseis* ("You shall love"), linking love for God with love for the neighbor. According to Mark's version, these two commandments are "greater than all of the burnt offerings and sacrifices" (Mark 12:33 AT), while in Matthew's version, the law and the prophets "hang" on these two commands (Matt. 22:40). In Luke, the parable of the good Samaritan then elaborates on the meaning of the neighbor beyond traditional limits.

Paul differs from both his Jewish and his Greek contemporaries in the primacy he gives to love. In Romans 12:9–13:10, the extended ethical appeal appears within the inclusio defined by love and is followed by a concrete instance in 14:1–15:13. This love extends not only to those in the family of God (12:9–16) but also to enemies (12:17–21). At the end of the ethical instructions,

26. Wischmeyer, "Das Gebot der Nächstenliebe bei Paulus," 163–64. While citations of Lev. 19:18 are rare in Judaism, echoes of the passage are commonplace. Cf. *Jub.* 20:2; 36:4; 36:8; Sir. 13:15.

Paul's statement that the one who loves others has fulfilled the law recalls the earlier comment that "the just requirement of the law is fulfilled in us, who walk . . . according to the Spirit" (8:4 AT). He indicates that the law is "summed up" in the words "You shall love your neighbor as yourself" and that love is the fulfillment of the law (13:9–10). He elaborates in 14:1–15:13, insisting that the neighbor is the "other" within the church (15:1–2).

Similarly, in Galatians, after Paul has insisted that believers are not under the law, he introduces the ethical requirements for a community that does not observe the boundary markers of the law with the command to "serve one another" (Gal. 5:13 NIV), adding that the whole law is fulfilled in one word, "You shall love your neighbor as yourself" (5:14).

Inasmuch as Leviticus 19:18 did not play a major role in Jewish summations of the law, the important place of the love command as the summation or the fulfillment of the law in both Jesus and Paul suggests that Paul inherited this view from the Jesus tradition. For both Paul and Jesus, the love command is the summary of the law.

Christology, Soteriology, and Ecclesiology

As the sign on the cross, "King of the Jews," indicates (Matt. 27:37; cf. 27:11, 29 parr.), Roman authorities identified Jesus as a potential political threat. Jesus's announcement of the coming of the kingdom undoubtedly implied his role in bringing in the kingdom and "fanned the flames" of messianic hopes.[27] While the entire synoptic tradition regularly speaks in a veiled manner about Jesus's identity, Jesus speaks with an authority throughout that indicates that he is more than a teacher or prophet. His self-description as the Son of Man, a title not used in the early church after Easter, indicates that Jesus identifies himself with the apocalyptic figure of Second Temple Judaism (cf. 1 En. 48:10; 52:4; 4 Ezra 12:32). While the term Christos is used sparingly in the Synoptic Gospels,[28] Jesus's authority, his sovereign call to discipleship, and his freedom with regard to the Torah are consistent with Jesus's use of that title. Thus he laid the foundations for the later christological reflections by the early church and Paul.

All four Gospels indicate that Jesus's authoritative claims led to conflict with both Jewish and Roman authorities, ultimately leading to his death. His confrontations with the authorities and his final trip to Jerusalem were

27. Schnelle, Theology of the New Testament, 154.
28. Schnelle, Theology of the New Testament, 154. The title appears seven times in Mark, of which the two most significant examples are in Mark 8:29 ("You are the Christ," RSV) and 14:61–62 ("Are you the Christ?," RSV). The other Synoptic Gospels follow Mark's usage.

undoubtedly a challenge that would result in the ultimate conflict. Although the Gospels preserve few sayings in which Jesus interpreted his death, he undoubtedly anticipated his death. In the clearest expression of Jesus's interpretation of his death, he assures the disciples that he offers "the blood of the covenant [shed] . . . for many" (Mark 14:24 AT parr.; cf. 10:45). This echo of Isaiah 53 indicates that his life is for others. He fulfills the destiny of the suffering servant, and this interpretation continued in the early church.

Paul and the Jerusalem Church

While we know little about Christian theology in Antioch, we can ascertain more about the church in Jerusalem, where the followers of Jesus remained after the death of Jesus, who died as a supposed messianic pretender (Matt. 27:37; Mark 15:26; Luke 23:38; John 19:19). The first seven chapters of Acts continue the closing narrative of the Gospels, describing the loyalty of the disciples to their teacher and the continued hostility toward them from the leaders who had condemned Jesus to death. Paul is introduced for the first time in Acts 7:58 as one who participated in the persecution of Christ-believers, having concluded that the new movement was a threat to Jewish traditions (cf. Acts 9:1–2).

Paul and Early Christian Worship

The loyalty of the disciples to Jesus did not preclude their active participation in Jewish institutions. They observed Jewish fasts, attended temple, and observed hours of prayer (Acts 3:1; 5:21; 10:9).[29] At the same time, they developed their own worship forms in gatherings in private homes (Acts 2:46; 5:42) as a separate community (Acts 1:14; 2:42; 4:23–31; 12:12). Luke offers a programmatic statement of their emerging identity in Acts 2:42: they "continued steadfastly in the apostles' teaching and fellowship, the breaking of bread and prayer" (AT). The teaching of the apostles was, perhaps, the passing on and recollection of the words of Jesus. In the breaking of bread, they continued the fellowship inaugurated by Jesus.[30] These gatherings marked the beginning of a separate identity of the Christ-believers.

Paul, for example, mentions the practice of the Lord's Supper, accompanied by Jesus's words of institution that he "received" (1 Cor. 11:23) and passed on to the Corinthians. While the tradition known to Paul is not identical to

29. Dunn, *Theology of Paul*, 127.
30. Cf. Stuhlmacher, *Theologie des Neuen Testaments*, 1:206–9.

the one in Mark, the presence of the tradition in multiple strands of early Christian tradition (cf. Matt. 26:28–29; Luke 22:15–22) indicates that it belonged to the earliest Jerusalem traditions and would have been known to Paul's companions, Silvanus and Barnabas, who came from Jerusalem.[31] The repetition of the Lord's Supper, including words interpreting the bread and wine, probably derives from members of the Jerusalem church, who served as a bridge between Jesus and Paul.

The practice of baptism, which was evidently the common initiatory rite in Paul's churches (cf. 1 Cor. 12:12–13; Gal. 3:27; Col. 2:12–13) as well as other communities (cf. Rom. 6:1–11; 1 Pet. 3:21), was the means of incorporation into the community in Jerusalem as an expression of repentance and faith (cf. Acts 2:37; 3:19) and was associated from the beginning with the reception of the Holy Spirit (Acts 2:38). While the Synoptic Gospels are silent about the practice among Jesus and his disciples, they are unanimous that John the Baptist initiated this practice as a sign of repentance. For the first believers, baptism was "in the name of Jesus" and promised forgiveness of sins (Acts 2:38).[32] It thus clearly demarcated the Christ-believers from other groups and united believers with one another. Like the baptism of John the Baptist, it offered forgiveness of sins outside the normal Jewish institutions.

Baptism in the name of Jesus also reflected an explicit Christology (Acts 2:38; 10:48). Peter's announcement that Jesus has become "Lord and Christ" (Acts 2:36 RSV) indicates the christological reflection at the beginning. *Christos*, the Greek translation of the Hebrew *messiah*, was the royal figure of Jewish expectation. In the Psalms, it is the term for the king, the Lord's anointed (cf. Pss. 2:2; 18:50; 89:38), and in Second Temple Judaism, it was the term used for a wide variety of messianic hopes.[33] What was implicit in the message of Jesus becomes explicit in the faith of the disciples after the resurrection and in the common confession of the early church. For Paul, Jesus Christ (or Christ Jesus) has become a proper name.

Preceding the theological reflection were the disciples' experiences. One hears echoes of their worship service in the Aramaic cry "Maranatha," which is also known to Paul's Greek-speaking churches (1 Cor. 16:22 KJV). Similarly, the cry "Abba Father," which is known to Paul's churches in the Aramaic form (cf. Rom. 8:15; Gal. 4:6), is derived from the Jerusalem church and ultimately from Jesus (cf. Mark 14:36). With the confession that Jesus is Lord (*kyrios*), the early believers employed the term that is regularly used for God

31. Hengel and Schwemer, *Paul between Damascus and Antioch*, 288.
32. Stuhlmacher, *Theologie des Neuen Testaments*, 217.
33. Schnelle, *Theology of the New Testament*, 153.

in the Old Testament. For Paul, this confession becomes the defining mark of those who will be saved (Rom. 10:9–10). Thus Paul's proclamation that Jesus is Lord (2 Cor. 4:5) and his claim that "every tongue will confess that Jesus is Lord" (Phil. 2:11 AT) attest to a Christology that originated in the Jerusalem church.

Theological Reflection and the Interpretation of Scripture

With the experience of the Spirit, as the narrative indicates, the disciples engaged in a period of reflection on the meaning of the events that had taken place. The resurrection appearances demonstrated to them that Jesus's death on the cross was not the sign of failure but the vindication by God. The outpouring of the Spirit set in motion a new understanding of the events.[34] Because Jewish expectation had no place for a messiah who was rejected by his own people and the victim of a violent death, early believers reread Scripture to articulate their beliefs.

Reflection on Scripture was their means of christological reflection. Believers appealed especially to the Psalms to understand the significance of Jesus. The enthronement psalms 2 and 110 provided the terms for designating Jesus. Like the Davidic king, Jesus is the Son of God (Ps. 2:7), God's anointed (Christos), whom Gsod has installed as king (Ps. 2:7), and the Lord who sits at God's right hand (Ps. 110:1). Consistent with the conviction of Jesus's resurrection, the claim that Christ sits at God's right hand takes on a new meaning. He is now the exalted Lord who is above all angelic beings (cf. 1 Cor. 15:21–28; 1 Pet. 3:22) and cosmic forces (cf. Phil. 2:9–11). This view of the messiah was unprecedented in Jewish expectation.

Reflection on Scripture also provided the means for interpreting the death of Jesus. As the conversation of the resurrected Jesus with the two on the road to Emmaus suggests (Luke 24:13–27), the crucifixion was the negation of the hope that Jesus was the one who would redeem Israel (Luke 24:21). While the messiah was described in various ways in Second Temple Judaism, no one expected the messiah to suffer and die. Through the rereading of Scripture, early believers determined that it was "necessary for the Christ to suffer and enter into his glory" (Luke 24:26 AT), a claim that was unprecedented in Second Temple Judaism.[35] In the earliest days of the movement, believers reinterpreted the Psalms, identifying Christ with the suffering righteous one of Psalms 16, 22, 69, and 116.[36]

---

34. Hengel, Between Jesus and Paul, 44.
35. Hurtado, "Paul's Messianic Christology."
36. Hengel, Between Jesus and Paul, 46.

In 1 Corinthians, Paul indicates that he has delivered to this community what he had received, "that Christ died for our sins according to the Scriptures, that he was buried, and that he was raised on the third day according to the Scriptures" (1 Cor. 15:3–4 AT). Paul's claim that this was the gospel that both he and the other apostles preached (1 Cor. 15:11) indicates that he received this interpretation of Jesus's death from the Jerusalem church. "For our sins" associates Jesus with the suffering servant of Isaiah 53:5–12. Thus Paul learned from those who went before him that "Christ died for our sins according to the Scriptures" (1 Cor. 15:3 AT). His statement that he preaches the same message as the original disciples indicates that the Jerusalem church interpreted the death of Jesus as "for our sins." Thus the death on the cross was not the scandal of Jewish interpretation but the saving event. Jesus was the servant of Isaiah 53.

When Paul recalls that he received the words "he was raised on the third day according to the Scriptures" (1 Cor. 15:3 AT), he does not indicate what passages of Scripture provided support for this claim. Indeed, just as no one had expected a suffering messiah, no one anticipated the resurrection of the messiah in advance of the resurrection of others. Nevertheless, they supported their own experience of the resurrected Lord with a claim that the death and resurrection of Jesus fulfilled a divine plan that was promised in Scripture.

Appealing once more to Scripture, believers in the Jerusalem church also concluded from the recent events that the resurrected Lord would come again. According to the earliest preaching, which proclaimed the death and resurrection, the final chapter in the story of Jesus was his return to earth.[37] Paul was not the first to offer a christological reinterpretation of Jewish eschatology. Indeed, Jesus had probably applied to himself the depictions of the Son of Man who comes with the clouds (Matt. 24:30 par.; 26:64; Dan. 7:13). The Jerusalem church probably appropriated the Jewish expectations of "the day of the Lord" and the day of judgment, anticipating Paul's frequent references to "the day of Christ" (cf. 1 Cor. 1:8; 5:5; 2 Cor. 1:14; Phil. 1:10).

As the words "according to the Scriptures" indicate, theological reflection involved the interpretation of Scripture. The Jerusalem church continued Jesus's eschatological interpretation of Scripture, reading the Scripture in light of the events that had taken place. Paul inherited from the Jerusalem church not only the practices of baptism and the Lord's Supper but also their christological and soteriological convictions that were developed from their reading of Scripture.

37. Cf. C. H. Dodd, *Apostolic Preaching and Its Developments*, 17.

The Self-Understanding of the Jerusalem Church

The believers designated themselves the *ekklēsia tou theou*—the assembly of God.[38] While Jesus gathered a community to live under God's reign, *ekklēsia* was a term first applied to the community by the post-Easter church.[39] This term identified the community with ancient Israel, the *ekklēsia kyriou* (Hebrew *qahal 'el*; cf. Deut. 23:2–4; 1 Chron. 28:8; Neh. 13:1), and distinguished the Christ-believers from the synagogue.[40] Paul inherited this designation from the early church.

Conclusion: Paul's Inheritance from Jesus and the Early Church

At Paul's conversion, he inherited the theological reflection that began with Jesus and continued with the early church. The one who died as a supposed messianic pretender was none other than the Son of God. The death of Jesus on a cross was not only the curse mentioned in Deuteronomy 21:22–23 but the death "for our sins." Those who responded in faith and baptism were the *ekklēsia* of God, the heirs of ancient Israel. While they did not abandon the synagogue, their convictions set the stage for conflict with the larger Jewish community, including Paul. While his conversion transformed his convictions about the place of Jesus in the Jewish tradition, he also inherited specific traditions from the Jerusalem church. Thus the premises for Paul's theologizing included not only the legacy of Pharisaic Judaism but also the reinterpretation of that tradition by Jesus and the early church. Paul inherited from Jesus and the early church the eschatological reading of Scripture and the early christological and soteriological reflection that became the premises of his theological arguments.

As I will argue in the next chapter, Paul's theology was not merely a restatement of the theology of the Jerusalem church but also a reflection based on his prophetic calling. In the formation of churches, Paul appealed to his prophetic consciousness as a further foundation for his theologizing. He is the inspired interpreter of the traditions as he works toward his goal of presenting a transformed people to God at the end.

38. For other terms designating the first Christ-believers in Jerusalem, see Dunn, *Beginning from Jerusalem*, 13–17.
39. Thompson, *Church according to Paul*, 32.
40. Although *synagōgē* is used synonymously with *ekklēsia* in the LXX, those who believed in Christ appear to have avoided the former term because it designated Jewish communities not associated with the Jesus movement. Only in James 2:2 is it used for the Christian gathering. Cf. Trebilco, "Why Did the Early Christians Call Themselves ἡ ἐκκλησία?"

4

Paul's Ethos and His Theology

While Paul's heritage in Judaism (chap. 2 above) and the message of Jesus and the early church (chap. 3) shaped Paul's fundamental convictions and the premises for his theologizing, this background does not account for his authority and mission. In his letters, he frequently establishes his authority with the claim that he has been called to be an apostle (Rom. 1:1; 1 Cor. 1:1; 2 Cor. 1:1; Gal. 1:1–4), pointing to a decisive moment in his life as the basis of his claim to speak for God. This call becomes an additional premise in Paul's theology.

Only in Acts (9:1–22; 22:3–21; 26:1–23) does the reader learn of the location of Paul's call (the Damascus Road), the voice from heaven, and his baptism in Damascus. In the letters, Paul recalls the story only in the context of theological debate, never in detail. In 1 Corinthians, he offers his credentials, saying, "Am I not an apostle? Have I not seen Jesus our Lord?" (1 Cor. 9:1). Later in the same letter, he responds to the Corinthian denial of Jesus's resurrection, recalling the appearance of Jesus to the apostles and major pillars of the church, adding, "Last of all, he appeared to me, one who was untimely born" (1 Cor. 15:8 AT). In 2 Corinthians, he speaks of the light that "shone in our hearts for the revelation of the glory of God in the face of Jesus Christ" (2 Cor. 4:6), who is the image of God. In Philippians, he speaks of that decisive moment when he counted all things loss (Phil. 3:7) and was grasped (3:12) by Christ (3:7). In each case, he names this event as the defining moment of his life and ministry.

While Paul does not describe the event in detail, he leaves no doubt about its lasting significance. When he says that the risen Lord appeared (ōphthē, 1 Cor. 15:8), he uses the terminology of a theophany. The Lord "appeared" to him, just as God had appeared (ōphthē LXX) to Abraham (Gen. 12:7; 17:1) and Solomon (1 Kings 3:5), the glory of the Lord to the people (Exod. 16:10; Lev. 9:23; Num. 14:10), and an angel of the Lord to Moses (Exod. 3:2), Gideon (Judg. 6:12), and Tobit (Tob. 12:22).[1] In Galatians, Paul describes the event as a revelation (apokalypsis, Gal. 1:12; cf. 1:16; 2:2) of the Son.

The event was decisive for Paul's theology and self-understanding. Paul recalls this event frequently as the moment not of abandoning his inherited beliefs but of reframing his theology and self-understanding. The close relationship between Paul's new self-understanding and his theology becomes especially evident in his autobiographical reflections, which frequently compose the first stage in his argument (cf. 1 Cor. 1–4; 9; Gal. 1:10–2:14; Phil. 1:12–26; 3:2–21; 1 Thess. 2:1–12) but can appear throughout his letters. Indeed, 2 Corinthians is composed almost entirely of autobiographical reflection.

The Argument from Ethos in Antiquity

Autobiography had a variety of functions in antiquity. In some instances, writers appealed to their own narrative to defend themselves against accusations, while in other instances, writers employed autobiography as an example for their readers to emulate. In 2 Corinthians, Paul's most thoroughly autobiographical letter, his first-person narrative is a defense against accusations against his ministry. While scholars debate whether his autobiography in Galatians, 1 Thessalonians, and Philippians is a defense against attacks or a call for imitation, they agree that Paul's argument serves a rhetorical purpose. The rhetorical theorists would call this an argument from ethos.

Plato maintained that the honorable orator should be of good character and be knowledgeable, alert, and able to adapt the argument to the audience (Phaedr. 261a, 270b, 271d). Aristotle was the first, however, to include the speaker's character (ethos) as a distinct form of proof.[2] He included it as one of the three artificial proofs alongside logos (argument) and pathos (emotion).[3] The three proofs together were what later rhetorical theorists

1. See Wolter, Paul, 25–26.
2. See Aune, "Ēthos," 169.
3. Cicero, Inv. 5.11.1–2; Aristotle, Rhet. 1.2.2–6 (13556a). The inartificial proofs included witnesses, tortures, and contracts—evidence that was already in existence, and not supplied by the orator. Cf. Cicero, De or. 2.114–15.

called *inventio*, the discovery of arguments. According to Aristotle, "The orator persuades by moral character when his speech is delivered in such a manner as to render him worthy of confidence; for we feel confidence in a greater degree and more readily in persons of worth in regard to everything in general, but where there is no certainty and there is room for doubt, our confidence is absolute" (*Rhet.* 1.2.4 [1356a LCL]). While Aristotle maintains that confidence in the speaker must emerge from the speech itself and not from any preconceived ideas about the speaker's character, others argued that the good name of the speaker was also a determining factor in the argument of ethos. For example, Isocrates declares that the speaker "will not be negligent as to the question of character. On the contrary, he will apply himself above all to establishing a most honorable name among his fellow citizens; for who does not know that words carry greater conviction when spoken by men of good repute than when spoken by men who are under a cloud, and that the argument that is made by a man's life is of more weight than what is furnished by words" (*Antid.* 278 [LCL]).

The good character of the orator involves the demonstration of the virtues that were praised in Greek and Roman society. According to Aristotle, the speaker needs to demonstrate good judgment (*phronēsis*), virtue (*aretē*), and goodwill (*eunoia*; *Rhet.* 2.1.5). According to Quintilian, the ideal orator is "a good man, skilled in speaking," a phrase attributed to Marcus Cato (*Inst.* 12.1.1 [LCL]).[4] The ideal orator should devote his attention to the formation of moral character; have a good understanding of all that is just and honorable; have much to say about justice, fortitude, abstinence, self-control, and piety; and exhibit these personal characteristics (*Inst.* 12.2.17).

Examples accompany precepts; the speaker's conduct leads to a virtuous life.[5] According to Seneca, the student must be given a pattern to imitate and must be shown people who exemplify the point of the lesson.[6] Thus Seneca consistently employs autobiographical references alongside the precepts that he offers (cf. *Ep.* 6.3–5). He calls attention to his own moral progress and offers himself as an example of striving toward the ideal, indicating that his life verifies his teaching.[7]

Some of the orators speak extensively of their own moral character.[8] Demosthenes is a prominent example. In his famous speech *De corona*, Demosthenes demonstrates the importance of ethos in persuading an audience.

---

4. Olbricht, "Foundations of the Ēthos in Paul," 149.
5. See Fiore, *Function of Personal Example*, 65.
6. Seneca, *Ep.* 94.73–74. See Fiore, *Function of Personal Example*, 94.
7. Seneca, *Ep.* 71.7. Fiore, *Function of Personal Example*, 88.
8. Cf. Dio Chrysostom, *Hom. Socr.* 55.4–5; 18.21; Epictetus, *Diatr.* 3.21.1–6.

The argument from ethos was especially critical in this instance because he had to defend himself against the charges against his character, which could have resulted in severe penalties. Throughout his career, he had dedicated himself to "the honor, the power, and the glory" of his native land (*Cor.* 322); thus he had earned the gratitude of the populace, not its condemnation (*Cor.* 268–69, 316).[9] Demosthenes recognized that self-praise could be offensive to the audience but insisted that he had been forced to recall his many contributions to the state in order to clear his name. Interpreters have recognized parallels between Demosthenes's argument in self-defense and Paul's similar argument in 2 Corinthians 10–13.[10]

Ethos and Theology in the Pauline Letters

Galatians

Because Galatians 1–2 presents autobiographical details that are unavailable in Paul's other letters, interpreters have examined this section primarily for historical details, comparing it with the conversion stories in Acts, but less attention has been given to the role of these chapters in the argument of the letter. Indeed, while scholars commonly divide Galatians into three sections (autobiography [chaps. 1–2], argument from Scripture [chaps. 3–4], exhortation [chaps. 5–6]), they have reached little consensus on how these three sections form a coherent letter;[11] thus 1:10–2:21 is commonly divorced from its theological argument. Consequently, the role of autobiography in Galatians remains a debated question.[12]

The Issue in the Galatian Churches

While interpreters debate the coherence of Galatians and the function of Paul's autobiography, no one doubts that Galatians is a response to one of the major challenges to his mission. Paul's opponents have insisted that the Galatians' conversion is incomplete; thus Paul fears that his work among them is in vain (Gal. 4:11). Although the opponents have been commonly labeled as Judaizers, Paul mentions no names but describes them as "some who trouble you" (1:7 RSV; 5:10), "those who unsettle you" (5:12 RSV), and "those who

9. See DiCicco, *Paul's Use of Ēthos*, 65–71.
10. DiCicco, *Paul's Use of Ēthos*, 79–80.
11. Hans Dieter Betz, for example, describes Galatians as an apologetic letter, interpreting the letter as judicial rhetoric. The hortatory section in 5:1–6:10, however, has no place in either the apologetic letter or judicial rhetoric. See Betz, *Galatians*, 14–23.
12. See Gaventa, "Galatians 1 and 2," 310.

want to make a good showing in the flesh" (6:12). Behind Paul's heated rhetoric, one can make reasonable assumptions about the opponents' point of view. They probably acknowledged that Jesus is Israel's messiah but maintained the traditional Jewish understanding of the law, according to which circumcision was the means by which gentiles were incorporated into the people of God. Indeed, they may have shared the view that gentiles would stream into Zion in the messianic age (cf. Isa. 56:6–8) and keep the law. For the opponents, therefore, Paul has, by admitting gentiles into the community without circumcision, unilaterally violated the scriptural injunctions that have maintained the identity of Israel and preserved it from assimilating into the larger society.

Paul insists that the opponents' teaching is both "another gospel" (Gal. 1:6 RSV) and a distortion of the gospel (1:7), and he pronounces an anathema on those who preach anything other than the gospel that he preaches (1:9). The number of times that Paul uses the noun "gospel" (*euangelion*) and the verb "proclaim the gospel" (*euangelizesthai*) in 1:6–9 indicates that what is at stake is the message that Paul preaches. In the argument that follows, Paul attempts to convince his converts of the truth of his gospel (1:6–5:10) and to conduct themselves accordingly (chaps. 5–6). As a call for a specific course of action in the future (5:11–6:10), Galatians approximates deliberative rhetoric. Paul is like a mother in birth pangs "until Christ is formed" among the Galatians (4:19). Only the truth of the gospel results in the moral formation of believers, which Paul describes in 5:11–6:10. Thus Paul argues the case for his gospel, laying the foundation for the imperatives in the latter part of the book (4:12; 5:1, 13, 16; 6:1–6; cf. 5:25–26), which describes the conduct that is the alternative to the obedience to the law commended by the opponents. The exhortations, therefore, are not the appendix to the letter but the culmination of the argument.

THEOLOGY AND ETHOS

Hans Dieter Betz has argued that Galatians is an apologetic letter and that 1:10–2:14 is a defense against attacks on Paul's apostleship.[13] However, Paul never indicates that he is responding to charges against him.[14] Moreover, inasmuch as the exhortations that extend from 4:12 to 6:10 are integral to the argument, the focus of Galatians is not apologetic but hortatory. The autobiography is thus a vital part of Paul's argument for the moral formation of his converts—that Christ may be "formed among" the Galatians (4:19).

13. Betz, *Galatians*, 14.
14. Cf. Hardin, "Galatians 1 and 2 without a Mirror," 286: "The view that Paul is defending himself is purely in the eye of the beholder."

Like the narratio of an ancient speech, 1:10–2:14 describes the history of the issue that stands before the listeners. As the Greek word *gar* (1:10) indicates, the autobiography is the confirmation that Paul's gospel is the only alternative to the "other gospel" (1:6 AT) that some Galatians have accepted. The rhetorical questions "Do I now persuade people or God?" and "Do I seek to please people?" (1:10 AT) anticipate a negative answer as Paul distinguishes himself from the Sophists and charlatans, who persuade others for their own benefit.[15] Such persuasion is incompatible with Paul's role as a slave of Christ (1:10). That is, Paul is no ordinary rhetor. As a slave of Christ (cf. Rom. 1:1; 2 Cor. 4:5) whose message is not his own, he has been compelled to speak (cf. 1 Cor. 9:15–18). Thus the initial argument for Paul's gospel (Gal. 1:10–2:14) is an appeal to his ethos as one who speaks for God.

The rhetorical questions in 1:10 do not indicate that the autobiography is a defense against accusations of rhetorical deceit. Indeed, the antithesis in 1:10–12 between human instruction and revelation is the thesis statement for the autobiography in 1:10–2:14.[16] His gospel is not merely human (*kata anthrōpon*)—that is, a message intended to persuade or please (cf. 1:10)—inasmuch as it is neither of human origin (*para anthrōpou*) nor from human instruction. It is the only gospel (1:6–9) because it came by revelation (*apokalypsis*). Paul elaborates on this revelation, recalling the event when "it pleased God to reveal [*apokalypsai*] his Son in me" (1:16). The narrative of his call appears in a dependent clause (the main clause is "I did not consult with flesh and blood"; AT). The sequence of events recalled in 1:17–24, with the repeated negative statements (1:16b–17, 19, 22), indicates that his ministry was determined by revelation rather than by human instruction. Having been in Jerusalem only briefly after his call, he has had minimal contact with the Jerusalem leaders. When he finally went to Jerusalem seventeen years after his call (2:1), he went by revelation (*apokalypsis*, 2:2). He did not consult the leaders but set before them the gospel that he preached among the gentiles. In the two incidents that he recalls in 2:1–14—the conflict over circumcision (2:1–10) and table fellowship between Jews and gentiles (2:11–14)—"the truth of the gospel" was maintained (2:5, 14). The good news promised in Isaiah 52:7 has become a reality in the death and resurrection of Christ, and Paul is the herald of that news. By divine revelation, gentiles were full members among the people of God without keeping the law (cf. Isa. 49:6).

While Galatians 1:10–2:14 is an argument from ethos, scholars debate the precise rhetorical function of Paul's autobiography. Paul is not answering

15. On rhetoric as the art of persuasion, see chap. 2 above.
16. Hunn, "Pleasing God or Pleasing People?," 34.

charges leveled against him but is giving the initial argument in a hortatory letter. He makes the case for the legitimacy of his gospel, indicating the inseparability between his life and his message. He offers himself as an example for the way of life that he commends in 4:12–6:10. Indeed, the argument from ethos extends to 2:19–21 in his claim that he has "died to the law" in order to live for Christ. He concludes, "I have been crucified with Christ; and it is no longer I who live, but it is Christ who lives in me. And the life I now live in the flesh I live by faith in the Son of God, who loved me and gave himself for me" (2:19–20).

Paul's ethos is not that of the ancient orator, therefore, for his autobiography has been determined by his gospel. As a result of his call, he now embodies a new understanding of the relationship between the law and faith in Christ. Consequently, he has a new Christology and soteriology that determine his ethos as he exemplifies the moral life that he commends in chapters 5 and 6. He does not abandon the scriptural narrative, but he now sees it from a new perspective.

PAUL'S GOSPEL AND HIS IDENTITY

The autobiography establishes not only the truth of Paul's gospel but also his role as the proclaimer called by God. "When it pleased God, who separated [aphorisas] me from my mother's womb and called [kalesas] me by God's grace" (Gal. 1:15 AT) evokes the memory of Jeremiah (Jer. 1:5, 10; 24:6) and the servant of Deutero-Isaiah (Isa. 49:1). "When it pleased God" (eudokēsen ho theos) is probably an allusion to the servant of Isaiah 42:1, in whom God is pleased.[17] Later in the letter, when he expresses the fear that he has "labored in vain" (Gal. 4:11), he identifies with the servant of Deutero-Isaiah (Isa. 49:4).[18]

In the other letters, Paul consistently identifies himself in prophetic terms. He identifies himself in Romans 1:1 as "separated [aphōrismenos] for the gospel of God" (AT), using a term (aphorizein) commonly employed for a holy requisition by God (Lev. 20:26)[19] and parallel to the verb exelexamēn in God's statement to the servant in Isaiah 41:9, "I have chosen [exelexamēn] you" (AT).

---

17. See S. Kim, *Paul and the New Perspective*.

18. Gibson, "Paul the Missionary," 56–59, demonstrates that "labored in vain" is evidence that Paul identified himself with the servant's mission (2 Cor. 6:2; Phil. 2:16). This constellation of ideas is consistent with Paul's use of a quotation from the fourth servant song of Isaiah in Rom. 15:21, where Paul cites Isa. 52:15 (LXX): "Those who have never been told of him shall see, and those who have never heard of him shall understand."

19. Kellermann, "ἀφορίζω," *EDNT* 1:184.

As a result of this event when God called him by his grace (Gal. 1:15), Paul refers to himself regularly as "called [*klētos*] to be an apostle" (Rom. 1:1; 1 Cor. 1:1). One may compare Galatians 1:1: "Paul an apostle—not from men nor through man, but through Jesus Christ and God the Father" (RSV). Elsewhere he is an apostle "by the will of God" (2 Cor. 1:1; cf. Eph. 1:1; Col. 1:1). He also describes himself regularly as an apostle by the grace of God (Rom. 1:5; 12:3; 15:15; 1 Cor. 3:10; 15:10). Only in Philippians, 1 Thessalonians, and Philemon does he not indicate his apostolic credentials. This prophetic call determines the nature of Paul's rhetoric. He is not the orator who pleases others but the prophet who speaks for God. As a result of his call, he sees his mission and convictions in new ways: with a new Christology, a new mission, a new reading of Scripture, and a new gospel for the nations.

A new Christology. Paul describes the content of the vision at his call in various ways, consistently indicating that he saw the exalted one, whom he describes as God's Son (Gal. 1:16), the Lord (1 Cor. 9:1), Christ (1 Cor. 15:3, 8), and "the light of the knowledge of God in the face of Jesus Christ," who is the image of God (2 Cor. 4:6). Thus the Christology that is a constant feature in the letters began with this vision. The man Jesus, whom Paul may have seen at an earlier time in Jerusalem, was now the exalted Son. The one who was condemned to die by both Jewish and Roman leaders was raised from the dead and was both the messiah of Jewish expectation and the cosmic Lord (cf. Phil. 2:9–11). Undoubtedly, this event resulted in a transformed identity. While Israel's narrative remained a reality for Paul, his vision gave him a view of Israel's messiah that was unprecedented in Jewish thought—a messiah who was both crucified and exalted.

In the episodes that he recalls in Galatians 2:1–14, Paul demonstrates behavior that is in keeping with the truth of the gospel as an example for the Galatians, who face a situation similar to Paul's. His autobiographical section concludes with a turn from the past to the present. After stating that Cephas, Barnabas, and others violated "the truth of the gospel" (2:14) when they separated from the gentiles, Paul states the general principle that "no one will be justified by works of the law" (2:16) before he returns to autobiographical reflection. The three tenses indicate the lasting significance of Paul's conversion. The aorist ("I died [*apethanon*] to the law," 2:19) describes a moment in the past, and the perfect tense ("I have been crucified [*synestaurōmai*] with Christ," 20) describes the lasting consequences of the radical change in his life. In the present tense ("It is no longer I who live, but Christ who lives in me," 2:20), Paul describes the continuing reality of his life. In dying to the law in order to live for Christ, Paul is the model for the Galatians, who have been taught by Paul's opponents to combine Christ and the law. Just as he had stood for "the truth of the gospel" (2:5, 14), they should follow his example in their own situation. Like Paul, the community should "die to the law" and live for Christ. Thus Paul offers an example of the power of the gospel to transform lives, anticipating the argument for the Galatians' conduct in chapters 5–6.[20]

A new mission. The vision of the risen Lord was accompanied by a mission. Like the prophets, Paul is sent to speak for God: "In order that I may proclaim him among the Gentiles" (*euangelizōmai auton en tois ethnesin,* Gal. 1:16). Paul's primary task, therefore, is to "proclaim [*euangelisasthai*] him"—the Son who revealed himself to Paul. He describes this activity with different verbs, including *euangelizein, kēryssein,* and *katangellein,* indicating his mission to proclaim the good news (*euanglisasthai*) on numerous occasions.

My desire to proclaim [*euangelisasthai*] the good news to you in Rome. (Rom. 1:15 AT)

How beautiful on the mountains are the feet of the one who proclaims the good news [*euangelizomenēn*]. (Rom. 10:15 AT)

My desire to proclaim the good news [*euangelizesthai*] where Christ has not been named. (Rom. 15:20 AT)

Christ sent me not to baptize but to proclaim the good news [*euangelizesthai*]. (1 Cor. 1:17 AT)

Woe to me if I do not proclaim the good news [*euangelisōmai*]. (1 Cor. 9:16 AT)

The good news [*euangelion*] that I proclaimed [*euangelisamēn*] to you. (1 Cor. 15:1)

So that we may proclaim the good news [*euangelisasthai*] in lands beyond you. (2 Cor. 10:16)

I proclaimed God's good news [*euangelion euēngelisamēn*] free of charge. (2 Cor. 11:7 AT)

He also describes his mission to preach (*kēryssein*).

We preach [*kēryssomen*] not ourselves, but Jesus Christ as Lord. (2 Cor. 4:5 AT)

20. See Gaventa, "Galatians 1 and 2," 319.

For the Son of God, Jesus Christ, whom we proclaimed [*kērychtheis*] among you. (2 Cor. 1:19)

We preached [*ekēryxamen*] to you the gospel of God. (1 Thess. 2:9 AT)

That is, the word of faith that we preach [*ho kēryssomen*]. (Rom. 10:8 AT)

He sometimes uses alternative terminology to describe the preaching.

I did not come proclaiming [*katangellōn*] the mystery of God in lofty words of wisdom. (1 Cor. 2:1 AT)

Christ is preached [*Christos katangelletai*]. (Phil. 1:18)

To declare [*lalēsai*] the gospel of God [*euangelion*] in the midst of much opposition. (1 Thess. 2:2 AT)

[Christ,] whom we preach [*hon hēmeis katangellomen*]. (Col. 1:28 AT)

Like Jeremiah, Paul has been appointed to proclaim to the nations (Gal. 1:15–16; cf. Jer. 1:5). Paul's statements that "necessity" (*anankē*) compels him (1 Cor. 9:16) and "woe to me if I do not proclaim" evoke the language of Moses and the prophets, all of whom were called to speak for God (cf. Exod. 3:11; 4:10–11; Jer. 1:5; 20:9; Ezek. 3:17; Amos 3:8; *Sib. Or.* 3:25–29).[21] In other words, Paul frequently speaks of the content of his proclamation but never the same way twice.

According to Galatians 1:16, he received the call to preach him (i.e., the Son), which is the equivalent of preaching the gospel (*euangelion*, 1:11). He proclaims the gospel of God (Rom. 1:1; 15:16; 2 Cor. 11:7; 1 Thess. 2:2, 8–9), the gospel of Christ (Rom. 15:19; 1 Cor. 9:12; 2 Cor. 2:12; 9:13; 10:14; Gal. 1:7; Phil. 1:27; 1 Thess. 3:2; cf. Rom. 1:9, "gospel of his Son"), and the gospel of the glory of Christ (2 Cor. 4:4). He also frequently abbreviates the phrases, describing the content of his message as "the gospel" (Rom. 1:16; 10:16; 11:28; 1 Cor. 4:15; 9:14, 18, 23; 15:1; 2 Cor. 8:18; Gal. 1:11; 2:2, 5, 14; Phil. 1:5, 7, 12, 16, 27; 2:22; 4:3, 15; Philem. 13) or "my/our gospel" (Rom. 2:16; 2 Cor. 4:3; 1 Thess. 1:5). He sometimes also refers to the gospel in summary statements. He preaches "Christ crucified" (1 Cor. 1:18; 2:2 AT). He proclaims "the gospel of God, . . . concerning his Son, who was born from the seed of David according to the flesh and designated Son of God in power according to

---

21. Schrage, *Der erste Brief an die Korinther*, 2:280.

the Spirit of holiness from the resurrection of the dead, Jesus Christ" (Rom. 1:1–4 AT). He reminds the Corinthians of his gospel, "that Christ died for our sins, according to the Scriptures, . . . was buried, and . . . was raised on the third day according to the Scriptures" (1 Cor. 15:3–4).

While Paul summarizes his gospel with a variety of terms, he recognizes only one gospel (Gal. 1:6–9). The reception of his message determines those who are being saved and those who are perishing (1 Cor. 1:18; 2 Cor. 2:15). Because he has received the gospel as a trust (cf. Gal. 2:7; 1 Thess. 2:4), he distinguishes himself from those who peddle (2 Cor. 2:17) or tamper with God's word (2 Cor. 4:2). He is not like the rhetoricians who speak to please others (Gal. 1:10; 1 Thess. 2:4) or engage in persuasive speech (1 Cor. 2:4; 2 Cor. 5:11), for he speaks only the word of God (1 Thess. 2:13), the mystery that has come by revelation (1 Cor. 2:6–16).

A new reading of Scripture. The frequent references to the Scriptures indicate that the content of the gospel was the culmination of prophetic hopes for the coming eschatological age, which has been inaugurated by Christ.[22] The term "gospel," then, serves as a sort of shorthand for the eschatological message of salvation promised in Deutero-Isaiah.[23] Thus Paul explains his gospel with allusions to specific passages or to Scripture as an organic whole.[24] According to Romans 1:2–3, the gospel was "promised beforehand through his prophets in the holy scriptures." According to Romans 1:16–17, "The righteousness of God is being revealed" (AT) in the gospel, confirming the words of Habakkuk, "The righteous shall live by faith" (Hab. 2:4 AT; Rom. 1:17). This righteousness is witnessed by the law and the prophets (Rom. 3:21). In Romans 10:8, he explains "the word of faith" that he preaches with the confession that Jesus is Lord (10:9–10), supporting his claim with an appeal to Scripture (10:11–13). His description of the gospel (*euangelion*) in Romans 10:16 is supported by several texts of Scripture in 10:6–21 (cf. Deut. 30:14, 21; 32:21; Ps. 19:4; Isa. 52:7; 53:1; 65:1–2; Joel 2:32). In 1 Corinthians 15:1–3, his gospel of the death, burial, and resurrection of Christ is "according to the Scriptures" (AT).[25]

While *euangelizesthai* and *euangelion* were commonplace in Greco-Roman literature, they have a particular resonance in the Septuagint. In the Psalms, *euangelizesthai* refers to the announcement of God's saving deeds (Pss. 67:12 LXX; 95:2 LXX), and in the prophets, it also refers to God's saving deeds (Joel 3:5 LXX; Nah. 2:1 LXX [1:15]). Paul's task of proclaiming to the nations (Gal.

22. Ciampa, "Paul's Theology of the Gospel," 181.
23. Cf. Koch, *Die Schrift als Zeuge des Evangeliums*, 327–29.
24. Koch, *Die Schrift als Zeuge des Evangeliums*, 327–29.
25. Koch, *Die Schrift als Zeuge des Evangeliums*, 327–29.

1:16) specifically echoes Deutero-Isaiah. Paul uses both the noun *euangelion* to speak of the content of his message and the verb *euangelizesthai* for the act of proclaiming. The language is especially prominent in Deutero-Isaiah for the announcement of the return from exile. The prophet proclaims, "Get up to a high mountain, O Zion, herald of good tidings [*ho euangelizomenos*], lift up your voice with strength, O Jerusalem, herald of good tidings [*ho euange-lizomenos*]" (Isa. 40:9 LXX). Later the prophet announces, "How beautiful . . . are the feet of the one who spreads good news [*euangelizomenos agatha*]" (Isa. 52:7 LXX). Even foreigners will come and announce the salvation of the Lord (Isa. 60:6 LXX). The herald announces, "The Spirit of the Lord is upon me to announce good news [*euangelisasthai*] to the poor" (Isa. 61:1 LXX).

A new gospel for the nations. Paul's task is not just to proclaim Christ but specifically to "proclaim him among the nations" (Gal. 1:16 AT). He has received "grace and apostleship for the obedience of faith among all the na-tions" (Rom. 1:5 AT). He describes himself in priestly terms as the minister (*leitourgos*) of Christ to the gentiles in priestly service, who offers the sacrifice of the nations (Rom. 15:16). Just as the good news is the fulfillment of the promise of Deutero-Isaiah (Isa. 52:7), Paul is the herald who announces the saving news to the nations. He probably saw his apostolic commission in the work of the servant of Isaiah 61:1–3, whom Yahweh "anoints" (*echrisen*) with the Spirit and "sends" to "preach the gospel" (LXX).[26] That Paul saw his apostolic commission in terms of Isaiah 61:1–3 is further supported by his echoes of the text in his description of his apostolic commitment (cf. 1 Cor. 1:17). Thus he identifies himself with the servant of Isaiah 49:1–6, who is chosen from his mother's womb (Isa. 49:1) and brings "light to the nations" (Isa. 49:6; cf. 42:6–12). When he expresses the fear that he has "run in vain" (Gal. 4:11 AT), he identifies himself with the servant of Isaiah, who says, "I have labored in vain" (Isa. 49:4).[27] Thus in describing his task of proclamation with the language of Isaiah 49:1–8, he places himself at the center of Jewish hopes for the redemption of Israel.[28]

Other texts from the Old Testament also shaped Paul's understanding of a mission to the gentiles and God's redemptive plans for them. According to common expectation, the gentiles will stream into Zion (cf. Isa. 2:2–4; 11:10) and enjoy the future blessings that God has promised (Isa. 25:6–10; 55:3–5; 56:6–8; 60:1–5; 66:18–21). In the last days, the gentiles will worship

26. S. Kim, "Paul as an Eschatological Herald," 14.

27. Gibson, "Paul the Missionary," 56.

28. Ciampa, "Paul's Theology of the Gospel," 181. See Wagner, *Heralds of the Good News*. Wagner demonstrates that Paul's consistent use of Isaianic texts reveals that Isaiah 51–55 exer-cised a formative influence on Paul's conception of his apostolic ministry.

Yahweh and participate in his salvation (cf. also Jer. 3:17; Mic. 4:1–3; Zeph. 3:8–10; Zech. 2:8–12; 8:20–23). This hope is also expressed frequently in Second Temple Jewish literature (e.g., Tob. 13:11; 14:5–7; *1 En.* 48:4–5; 90:33; *T. Sim.* 7:2; *T. Levi* 18:2–9; *T. Jud.* 24:6; 25:5; *T. Naph.* 8:3–4; *2 Bar.* 68:5; *Sib. Or.* 3:710–30).[29]

A Reexamination of His Identity

Paul's experience undoubtedly led him to reexamine his identity and convictions.[30] However, he does not indicate the extent to which the major themes of his theology, including his critique of the law and his doctrine of justification by faith, were immediately evident to him. One may assume that major themes of Paul's theology were at least implicit in Paul's thought at his call.[31] Since the preaching of Christ placed Paul on the side of those whom he had persecuted, he concluded that the Christ-believers were the people of God. The cross was no longer a cursed death but the prelude to the resurrection. As a Pharisee who anticipated the general resurrection of the faithful, Paul probably also concluded that the resurrection of Christ was the beginning of the general resurrection. This revelation placed the Torah in a new light, and the experience inevitably challenged Paul's previous understanding of soteriology and the people of God. If Jesus is Lord, those whom Paul had been persecuting belonged to the people of God.

His apostleship includes not only a commission to proclaim the good news to the nations but also an authority over the converts. With his statement of apostolic credentials, he indicates that his authority comes from God. As an apostle, he has the right to make demands on his converts (1 Thess. 2:7) and has authority (*exousia*) over his converts (1 Cor. 9:4–6, 10, 12). When his authority is questioned, he indicates that he is engaged in warfare, not on fleshly terms but with the means that are mighty for the tearing down of strongholds, destroying arguments, and taking every thought captive to Christ, being ready to punish all disobedience, "when your obedience is complete" (2 Cor. 10:6; cf. 1 Cor. 4:21).

29. Wagner, *Heralds of the Good News*, 15.
30. Schnelle, *Apostle Paul*, 101.
31. Cf. Schnelle, *Apostle Paul*, 99: "There can be no dispute . . . that Damascus must have had an effect on the Pauline understanding of the law/Torah and justification and on Paul's thought as a whole." Michael Wolter also considers the significance of the Damascus Road experience for Paul's theology, maintaining that Paul immediately recognized the significance of the event. He recognized not only that Christ was the way to salvation but also that the way was open for the gentiles to participate in God's holiness without being circumcised or keeping the law (Wolter, *Paul*, 9–30).

Paul's task is not only to preach where Christ has not been named (Rom. 15:20) but also to present a blameless people to God at the eschaton. According to Romans 15:16, he is the priest who offers the sacrifice of the gentiles who are sanctified in the Holy Spirit. He is the father urging his children to live worthily of the God who calls them into his kingdom (1 Thess. 2:12), the pregnant woman in labor for the unborn child as it is being formed (Gal. 4:19), and the father who desires to present his daughter to her husband (2 Cor. 11:1–4). Thus his repeated desire is that his communities be "blameless" at the day of Christ (Phil. 1:10 AT; 2:15). If his churches do not reach that goal, he will have "run in vain" (Gal. 2:2; Phil. 2:16; cf. Gal. 4:11, "labored in vain"). Consequently, he urges the Corinthians not to receive the grace of God "in vain" (2 Cor. 6:1), adding words from Isaiah 49:8, "At the acceptable time I gave attention to you, and in the day of salvation I helped you" (AT).

First Thessalonians

In 1 Thessalonians, as in the other letters (cf. 1 Cor. 1:18–2:5; 2 Cor. 3:1–6; Gal. 3:1–5; Phil. 1:6–11), Paul recalls his original preaching ministry and the community's response (1 Thess. 1:5–2:12) as he writes to confirm his original catechetical instruction (cf. 4:1–2, 6, 9; 5:1–2). Having urged the Thessalonians while he was there to "conduct [themselves] worthily" of God's call (2:12 AT), he writes to instruct the new converts to continue doing what they have been doing (4:1–2) and gives specific instructions in chapters 4–5. Before stating the basic thesis in 4:1–2, he builds his case by expressing gratitude for their moral progress (1:2–10). Like the thanksgiving sections of Paul's other letters, this functions as the exordium, making the audience favorably disposed and introducing the topic: the Thessalonians' conversion (1:9–10) and their "work of faith, labor of love, and steadfastness of hope" (1:3 AT). The reminder of his past relationship with the Thessalonians (2:1–3:10) functions as the narratio, building the case for the prayer in 3:11–13 and the thesis statement (propositio) in 4:1–2. Having earlier urged the readers to live a life "worthy of the God who called [them]" (2:12), Paul gives specific instructions for this moral conduct in 4:3–5:15.

The autobiographical section in 2:1–12 is part of the narratio that recalls past events and anticipates the instructions that follow. Paul introduced the topic of his welcome (*eisodos*) among them in 1:9 and elaborates on that brief period in 2:1–12. Having recalled the coming of the gospel and their reception of it in the thanksgiving (1:5–10), he now focuses on his own character as the speaker. Paul gives no indication that he is defending himself against accusations but opens the autobiographical section with the assurance that his coming (*eisodos*) was "not in vain" (*ou kenē*, 2:1). The antithetical comments in 2:2 elaborate on this claim. Despite the abuse he had received in Philippi, he was bold (*eparrēsametha*) "to speak the gospel of God in much conflict [*en pollō agōni*]" (AT). He spoke openly (*eparrhēsiasametha*), unlike the charlatans, and this open proclamation resulted in much opposition (*en pollō agōni*, 2:2).[32]

As Paul will demonstrate in subsequent letters, his preaching ministry involved suffering (cf. 1 Cor. 4:9–13; 2 Cor. 4:7–12; 6:4–11; Gal. 6:17; Col. 1:24–29). Indeed, the athletic image of the *agōn* (cf. Phil. 1:30; Col. 2:1), a term used for the struggle of the Maccabean martyrs (cf. 4 Macc. 9:23–24; 17:11–16), indicates Paul's total investment in the gospel. It was a term used for a fight or a race (Heb. 12:1)[33] and was widely used in antiquity for a struggle that involved pain and self-denial.

Regardless, Paul had fulfilled his mission to "proclaim him [Christ] among the nations" (Gal. 1:16 AT) in Thessalonica, despite the opposition that he had incurred. The response of the community and its continued existence (cf. 1 Thess. 2:13) are evidence that his labor was not "in vain." Indeed, the Thessalonians received his message in the context of affliction (1 Thess. 1:6), which had become a continuing reality for them (3:3). Paul speaks elsewhere of his concern that his labor could be "in vain" (cf. 1 Thess. 3:5). This is in contrast to his fear in Galatians that he has "labored in vain" (Gal. 4:11 AT). According to Philippians 2:16, he hopes that the community will be his boast at the day of Christ; otherwise, he will have "run in vain" (AT). The image evokes the voice of the servant of Isaiah 49:4, who cries out, "I have labored in vain" (AT).

The transition from the proclamation of the gospel (1 Thess. 2:2) to the exhortation (*paraklēsis*, 2:3) indicates the inseparability of proclamation and the appeal to respond. Verses 3–12, which are framed by *paraklēsis* (2:3) and *parakalountes* (2:12), elaborate on Paul's demeanor as he has proclaimed the gospel, and 2:13–14 describes the Thessalonians' response. In a series of antithetical statements (2:3–8), Paul distinguishes his speech from that of the charlatans. In the first contrast, he distinguishes the deceit (*planē*), impure motives (*akatharsia*), and cunning (*dolos*) practiced by others from his own speech, declaring that he has been "found worthy" (*dedokimasmetha*) by God to be entrusted with the gospel. Thus he is not like the orator who makes the worse argument appear the better but is one who is faithful to a trust (2:4). His claim is similar to claims in the other letters. He describes himself in

32. T. Holtz, *Der erste Brief an die Thessalonicher*, 70.
33. BDAG 17.

1 Corinthians 9:16–17 as one who preaches not of his own volition but as one who is under compulsion and entrusted with a commission. He thus appeals to his call to proclaim the gospel as the occasion when he was entrusted with the gospel. Because the gospel is a trust, he does not speak to please human beings but the God who tests the hearts (cf. Gal. 1:10).

In the second antithesis (1 Thess. 2:5–8), Paul contrasts his own demeanor with the one who comes with flattery (*kolakeia*) and greed (*pleonexia*) and seeks glory from people. Indeed, although as an apostle he could have insisted on his own importance (*dynamenoi en barei*), he chose to be "gentle as a nurse" (2:7 AT). That is, while Paul does not insist on his apostolic authority in the salutation, he writes with authority. Where his authority is challenged, he insists on the right to build and tear down and even to punish. However, where his authority is not challenged, as in Thessalonica, he is a nurse taking care of her own children (2:7). Paul focuses on his selfless behavior and total devotion to his community as he shares not only the gospel but also his entire being (2:8).

He recalls the circumstances of his preaching (1 Thess. 2:9–12) as an example of his selfless conduct. He "preached the gospel of God" (2:9 AT), carrying out his commission to proclaim to the nations (Gal. 1:16). He embodied his message when he urged his listeners to live worthily of the God who calls people into his kingdom. Paul's original preaching was a call to moral formation. Those who live worthily of the God who calls people into his kingdom are a moral community. In 1 Thessalonians 4–5, Paul offers specific instructions that reiterate that original teaching.

Paul's focus in the autobiography is his role as model for the new converts. They have already imitated him and the Lord (1 Thess. 1:6). He has, like a father, urged the listeners to live worthily of the God who called them into the kingdom (2:12), but he has also modeled the transformation of the community. The absence of the terms "uncleanness" (*akatharsia*) and "greed" (*pleonexia*) anticipates his instructions to them to behave without these vices (4:4, 7; cf. 4:6). His total devotion to them anticipates his prayer for their familial love (3:12) and his instructions to practice familial love (4:9–12). In conducting himself blamelessly (*amemptōs*, 2:10), he is a model for the blameless existence he desires for them at the parousia (3:13). In working with his hands (2:9–10), he is an example for the Thessalonians (4:11).

Paul's gospel is inseparable from his way of life. He is a model of the transformed existence that he urges on his readers. Not only does he pray for their transformation (3:11–13), but he also demonstrates the transformation that he expects from his people. He has offered a model of faithfulness in persecution (2:1–2) that he wants them to follow (3:1–5), and he has displayed the character that he instructs his community to acquire. Thus his argument from ethos is defined by his theological convictions.

The Corinthian Correspondence

First Corinthians. Autobiography plays a significant role in the Corinthian correspondence. In both Corinthian letters, Paul states his credentials as "called to be an apostle" (1 Cor. 1:1; cf. 2 Cor. 1:1, "apostle . . . by the will of God"), recalling the original call (cf. Gal. 1:15) as the basis for his authority. After the opening thanksgiving in 1 Corinthians (1:4–9) introduces the topics of the letter ("grace," 1:4; "gift," 1:7; "enriched," 1:5; "word" and "knowledge," 1:5) and indicates the ultimate goal of a people "blameless at the day of Christ" (1:8 AT), Paul confronts the challenges posed by readers who divide the community over partisan politics (1:10–11), quarreling over their allegiance to leaders and boasting of superior wisdom (1:29, 31). The claim to superior wisdom has resulted in a lack of concern for others, as the specific examples in 5:1–11:1 indicate. Paul speaks to the fundamental issue in chapters 1–4 before addressing the specific examples of Corinthian behavior in 5:1–11:1, including their insistence on personal freedom (cf. 6:12; 8:9; 10:23), the anticommunal tendencies in corporate worship (11:2–14:40), and their denial of the resurrection (chap. 15). Despite the eighteen months that Paul had spent in Corinth, these issues continued.

At two critical points in the argument of 1:10–11:1, Paul indicates that his autobiographical reflections are invitations to follow his example (4:16; 11:1). The first challenge to imitate Paul comes near the conclusion of the opening argument (1:10–4:21) after Paul has offered the alternative to the rivalry over church leaders.

In 1 Corinthians 1:18–2:5, he recalls his own preaching ministry, in which he not only proclaimed the cross (1:18–25) but also, in contrast to the orators' "persuasive words of wisdom" (2:4 AT), embodied the weakness of the cross. He maintains that what is foolishness to the Greeks (1:18–25) is God's wisdom, which the world cannot understand (2:6–16). The Corinthians' quarreling over leaders is an indication that they, like the world around them, have not grasped the wisdom of the cross (3:1–5). By judging leaders according to the standards of human wisdom and eloquence, they are still children, people of the flesh.

Against those who maintain secular values, Paul presents his own self-understanding as their leader. He did not come "with persuasive words of wisdom" but "in weakness and in fear and trembling" (2:2–3 AT). Although he is an apostle, both he and Apollos are only *diakonoi*—servants at the disposal of their master (3:5). Paul describes his service with two images. He planted (3:6), and by the grace given to him, he laid a foundation (3:10). The combination of these images recalls the role of Jeremiah, whom God appointed "to build and to plant" (Jer. 1:10). The church, like Israel, is God's vineyard and God's house, and Paul is only God's instrument.

Paul's servant role is further indicated in 1 Corinthians 4:1–2, where he describes himself and others as "helpers [hypēretas] of Christ and stewards [oikonomoi] of God's mysteries" (AT), whose task is to be faithful to their master. Over against those who judge their leaders, Paul draws a sharp contrast. In contrast to those who claim to rule (4:8),[34] Paul presents himself as one "sentenced to death" (epithanatios, 4:9), a spectacle (theatron) to the world. In the catalog of sufferings in 4:11–13, he presents himself as one who accepts suffering, refuses patronage, and accepts abuse. As a parent, he is the model for their imitation (4:16).

The arrogance of the Corinthians described in chapters 1–4 manifests itself in the behavior that Paul describes in 5:1–11:1 and stands in sharp contrast to Paul's example. Paul confronts the Corinthian slogan "all things are lawful for me" (panta moi exestin), which serves as their claim to freedom to engage in sexual offenses (6:12–20) and to eat meat offered to idols (10:23). Chapter 9 is an extended autobiographical section, a digression that serves a strategic role in the argument. It is an exemplum intended to argue the case, continuing the first-person reference in 8:13.[35] The four rhetorical questions, all assuming an affirmative answer, suggest the close relationship between them. "Am I not free?" connects with the Corinthians' claim to authority (exousia, 8:9). The foundation of Paul's freedom is that he is an apostle, qualified by the fact that he has seen the Lord. He is especially an apostle to the Corinthians.

In 9:4–18, Paul establishes his authority (exousia) but claims that he did not use it (9:12). He amplifies the argument, adding once more that he did not use his rights (9:15), but a shift in the thought occurs in the incomplete sentence of 9:15. Paul says, "I would rather die than that—no one will deprive me of my boast [kauchēma]." This boast is not the negative response that Paul describes in relationship to salvation by works. His boast is the fulfillment of his mission (cf. Rom. 15:17; 2 Cor. 1:14; Phil. 2:16).

Paul elaborates on this boast in 1 Corinthians 9:16–18, as the sequence introduced by gar indicates. "If I proclaim the good news" is not the boast. Paul explains, "For necessity [ananke] has been laid upon me" (AT). The negative

34. See B. Dodd, Paul's Paradigmatic "I," 59–60.
35. Schrage, Der erste Brief an die Korinther, 2:280.

side is "Woe to me if I do not proclaim the good news" (9:16 AT). *Anankē*, which in other contexts refers to the power of fate,[36] is here a reference to the power of God and the divine summons to proclaim. Paul's expression is comparable to that of Old Testament prophets, who are also compelled to speak for God (cf. Exod. 4:10–17 [cf. Philo, *Virtues* 63]; Jer. 1:5–6; 20:9; Ezek. 3:1–2; Amos 3:8; Jon. 1:2).

Paul elaborates in 1 Corinthians 9:17, contrasting service that is *hekōn* (willing) with service that is *akōn* (unwilling), a familiar distinction. As one whose service is not of his own will, he is entrusted with a task (*oikonomia*); that is, he is the trusted slave who administers the master's possessions (cf. *oikonomos* in 4:1). Paul's reward is the equivalent of his *kauchēma* (boast): to proclaim the gospel free of charge. Thus he does not make use of his authority (9:18). In 9:19–23, Paul expands further on his freedom, which he established in 9:1–15, maintaining that his freedom consists of slavery (9:19). His description of his preaching activity is not a statement of his flexibility but of the "winning" of others. He has subordinated himself to the gospel.

The autobiographical reflection in chapter 9 is a response to the Corinthians' insistence on their own authority (*exousia*, 8:9). Paul presents himself as one who did not use his rights. Indeed, he became a slave to all (9:19) and a model for the Corinthians (cf. 10:33–11:1). Thus he challenges the Corinthians to follow his example in confronting all of the issues that he has mentioned in 5:1–11:1.[37] As the selfless one who defines his identity by the cross, Paul offers the countercultural example that is necessary for the moral formation for which he prays (1:8).

Second Corinthians. Because Paul's apostleship continues to be challenged after the writing of 1 Corinthians, he elaborates further on the meaning of his ministry in 2 Corinthians, his most autobiographical letter. As in 1 Corinthians (cf. 1 Cor. 1:10–17), the community must now judge between Paul and other leaders, whom he calls "false apostles" (2 Cor. 11:13) and "super-apostles" (2 Cor. 11:5; 12:11), who have apparently come to Corinth after the writing of 1 Corinthians and presented letters of recommendation (2 Cor. 3:1). They boast of their achievements (2 Cor. 5:12; 11:12, 16, 18) and compare themselves with others (2 Cor. 10:12). Claiming to be "ministers of Christ" (2 Cor. 11:23), they maintain that Paul lacks the qualifications for leadership. He is "humble" (*tapeinos*) in their presence (2 Cor. 10:1), and "his bodily presence is weak and his speech is of no account" (2 Cor. 10:10 AT). Because Paul has been forced into professional boasting, he answers the charges against

36. BDAG 61.
37. B. Dodd, *Paul's Paradigmatic "I,"* 113.

him by giving his most extended statement of the theological foundations of his ministry.[38]

Paul begins the defense in the exordium (2 Cor. 1:3–7), a blessing that introduces the topic of his suffering. After recalling his recent suffering in the narratio (1:8–11), Paul presents the thesis that he argues in the letter. He has conducted himself with sincerity and purity of motive (1:12); thus his desire is that "we are your boast and you are ours at the day of Christ" (1:14 AT). In the defense in chapters 1–9, he repeatedly declares his boasting on their behalf (7:4, 14; 8:24; 9:2–3), and in chapters 10–13, he boasts on his own behalf because the Corinthians have forced him to do so (cf. 12:11). He writes to establish the reciprocity of boasting that he describes in 1:14. His "boast" (*kauchēma*) is the fulfillment of his mission (cf. 1 Cor. 9:15; Phil. 2:16; 1 Thess. 2:19), a community that is blameless at the parousia (2 Cor. 1:14).

After the initial response to complaints that he is vacillating, he insists that his behavior conforms to his message (2 Cor. 1:15–23) as he writes with anguish for his congregation (2:1–4). In 2:14–7:4, he proceeds from the past tense of recent events to the present tense, now speaking in the first-person plural but referring primarily to himself. In response to those who criticize him for the ineffectiveness of his ministry, he describes himself as a participant in a victory processional (2:14). That is, despite the appearances and despite his suffering, he is engaged in a victory processional in his work of proclamation.

In the initial part of the defense in 2:14–7:4, he focuses on his task of proclamation (2:14–4:6). The argument for his ministry in 2:14–4:6 is a tightly woven unit in which he demonstrates the glory of his ministry and his confidence in his role as God's minister. The structure of the argument provides insights into Paul's message. He introduces his case (2:14–3:6) and concludes it (4:1–6) with the same themes.[39] The concluding section in 4:1–6 also summarizes the themes from the middle section (3:7–18): the unbelievers' inability to see because of the veil on their eyes (3:14; 4:4).

Paul's apologia resonates with Old Testament echoes, presenting him as a prophetic figure. When he asks, after recalling the cosmic nature of his ministry, "Who is sufficient for these things?" (2 Cor. 2:16), he echoes Moses's response to the divine call, "I am not sufficient [*hikanos*]" (Exod. 4:10 LXX).

---

38. Although 2 Corinthians is widely held to be a composite document, the thematic unity in the letter suggests that Paul is facing the same issues throughout the letter, though chaps. 10–13 have a more intense tone. Paul is on the defensive throughout the letter against those who "commend themselves" (cf. 3:1–2; 5:11–13; 10:12), and he responds with his own self-commendation (6:4; 11:23–30).

39. According to 2:17, he does not peddle (*kapēleuein*) God's word; according to 4:2, he does not adulterate (*doloun*) God's word.

He also describes the Corinthian church as his letter, "written on your hearts"[40] and "ministered [*diakonētheisa*] by us, written not with ink but with the Spirit of the living God, not in stone tablets, but in fleshy hearts" (2 Cor. 3:2–3 AT). Thus he compares his ministry to that of Moses and indicates that he has inaugurated the new covenant promised by Ezekiel and Jeremiah through his proclamation. Indeed, he is the "minister of the new covenant" promised by Jeremiah (2 Cor. 3:6 AT). In his midrash on Exodus 34:29–35, he declares that his ministry is more glorious than the covenant inaugurated by Moses (2 Cor. 3:7–11), comparing himself to Moses and insisting that he possesses the boldness that Moses did not have (2 Cor. 3:12). He beholds the glory of the Lord with an unveiled face and declares that the whole community ("we all") gazes at the glory of the Lord and is being transformed into the image of the Son. He preaches Jesus Christ as Lord (2 Cor. 4:5) rather than distorting God's word (2 Cor. 4:2), even if his gospel is veiled. The glory of his ministry is apparent in the fact that the community, unlike Israel, can behold the glory of the Lord and be transformed into his image (2 Cor. 3:18).

In 2 Corinthians 4:7–5:10, he proceeds from the proclamation (2:14–4:6) to a description of the sufferings that accompany the proclamation. He responds to the charge of weakness, declaring, "We hold this treasure in earthen vessels so that the surpassing power may be God's and not ours" (4:7 AT), introducing the first among several catalogs of sufferings in the letter (cf. 6:4–10; 11:23–33; 12:11). He is "always carrying around the dying of Jesus" (4:10 AT) and is handed over (*paradidometha*) to death (4:11) so that the life of Jesus may be manifested in his body. That God's power is present in human weakness is a consistent theme of the letter (cf. 1:8; 6:7; 8:3; 12:9, 12; 13:4), suggesting that the new covenant is the time for the outpouring of the empowering Spirit. As Paul said in the exordium, the sufferings of Christ overflow in him.

Having indicated in 2:14–4:6 that he is a prophetic figure, Paul identifies his suffering with that of the servant of Deutero-Isaiah, who was "handed over to death" (Isa. 53:12 AT; cf. 2 Cor. 4:10). As the one who proclaims good news, Paul is the herald of Deutero-Isaiah (Isa. 52:7). Thus Paul not only preaches the cross but also participates in the suffering of the cross.

Paul's explanation in 2 Corinthians 5:11–6:2 that he "persuades others" is the centerpiece of the defense of his preaching ministry, which began with the thesis statement of the letter in 1:12–14 and according to which Paul writes the letter to explain his conduct (1:12) and to restore the reciprocity of boasting that once existed between him and this church that he had founded (1:14). "We persuade men" (5:11 KJV) refers to his preaching ministry, which includes

---

40. "Your hearts" is the reading of Codex Sinaiticus, which I prefer.

both the announcement of God's saving deeds and the appeal for response (cf. 5:20–6:2). Paul echoes the letter's propositio, introducing the theological explanation by affirming that he is now giving them the means for boasting on his behalf (5:12). The introductory statement "If we are out of our mind, it is for God, if we are in our right mind, it is for you" (5:13 AT) indicates that his ministry is on their behalf (cf. 2:4; 4:15). Paul is actually summarizing his ministerial existence as being "for you," suggesting his sacrificial life for the Corinthians and his desire for their reciprocity of boasting (cf. 4:12, 15). He begins the defense, "The love of Christ compels us" (5:14 AT); "love of Christ" is a subjective genitive that recalls the Old Testament claims that the saving events were expressions of God's love (cf. Rom. 5:8), which for Paul is interchangeable with Christ's own love (cf. Rom. 8; Gal. 2:20). The language of compulsion (*synechei hēmas*, "urges us on," 2 Cor. 5:14) suggests that Paul is not his own master, and the phrase recalls his description of himself as God's captive in the victorious processional (2 Cor. 2:14) and as the recipient of a prophetic call (cf. 1 Cor. 9:15–18; Gal. 1:15). The continuing reality of Paul's ministry is the power of the past event that has taken over his life (Phil. 3:12).

The phrase "because we are convinced" (*krinantas touto*, 2 Cor. 5:14) introduces the basis for Paul's selfless ministry: "One died for all." He does not, like the rhetoricians, build his argument on an appeal to what is "just" and "appropriate" but on the Christian creed, the tradition the Corinthians have received.[41] Just as Paul speaks of the one "who loved me and gave himself for me" (Gal. 2:20), he recalls the foundational story as the ultimate expression of God's love. "One died for all" is an abbreviated form of the gospel that Paul first preached to the Corinthians: "Christ died for our sins" (1 Cor. 15:3; cf. Rom. 4:25; 5:7–8; 8:32). The love of Christ that continues to impel Paul is rooted in an event of the past. Whereas Paul has earlier explained his sacrificial existence in terms of the continuing reality of the cross in his life (2 Cor. 1:5; 4:10–15), here his existence for others is based on the death of Jesus as a past event. Paul defends his ministry by appealing to the church's fundamental convictions. In the phrase "one died for all," he offers a variant of the words he first preached to the Corinthians: that "Christ died for our sins according to the Scriptures" (cf. 1 Cor. 15:3). Now, in the middle of a debate about the nature of his ministry, he returns to the words that the Corinthians will remember, the common ground that they share.

By adapting the confessional statement "one died for all," Paul prepares the way for his interpretation of the foundational story in 2 Corinthians 5:14c–15.

---

41. See Eriksson, *Traditions as Rhetorical Proof*, 84–130, for Paul's use of pre-Pauline traditions as rhetorical proof.

His argument suggests that the "all" of the creed is the believing community, for which Paul serves as a model. Paul offers an initial interpretation in 5:14c ("therefore all died") before repeating the creed in 5:15a and offering a second interpretation in 5:15b ("in order that they no longer live for themselves," AT). In the phrase "therefore all died" (5:14c), Paul speaks in the past tense to show that others are caught up in God's grand narrative. In contrast to earlier passages in which Paul has described his own experience as involving the sharing of the suffering of Christ (1:3–7; 4:10), here he extends his own experience to that of others to indicate the general principle that "all died." That is, "all"—the entire believing community—share the narrative of Christ. As Paul says in Romans, "We were buried with him" (6:2) and "our old self was crucified with him" (6:6), here he says that with Christ "all have died." Their own personal stories are subordinated to the big story.

In the second interpretation of the cross for the life of the church ("those who live no longer live for themselves, but for him," 5:15 AT), Paul again describes why his ministry is actually for others. The selfless act of Christ "for all" is not merely an event of the past but the defining quality of Christian existence. This abandonment of egoism is the basis for Paul's ethical exhortation in Romans 14:7–9, where he instructs the members of the Christian community to welcome each other without despising the other, recognizing that our existence is determined by the power of the cross as a continuing reality within the community.

The consequence of the Christ event—and the structural center of 2 Corinthians 5:11–6:2—is Paul's conclusion in 5:16–17. The twofold *hōste* in verses 16–17 ("therefore" in v. 16; "so" in v. 17) indicates that Paul is drawing the consequences of his statement for his own ministry, moving from his own story (v. 16) to the story of the entire Christian community ("anyone," v. 17). The contrast signaled by "from now on," "once," and "no longer" (5:16) reflects Paul's own narrative and the determining influence of the Christ event on his life. Paul describes a change in epistemology, from the old existence when he knew Christ "from a human point of view" (*kata sarka*) to the new existence when he knows no one "from a human point of view." Unlike his opponents, who boast "according to human standards" (*kata sarka*, 11:18) and accuse Paul of behaving "according to human standards" (*kata sarka*, 10:2), he has a changed existence that conforms to the general statement in 5:17, which describes "anyone . . . in Christ." In the reference to the "new creation," Paul recalls Israel's story, again referring to Israel's postexilic hope. According to Isaiah 65:17,

> I am about to create
>   new heavens and a new earth;

the former things shall not be remembered
or come to mind.

No longer will he *know* ("regard," NRSV) anyone from a human point of view, even if he once *knew* Christ from a human point of view. The context indicates that the NRSV has correctly rendered the sentence, "If anyone is in Christ, *there is* a new creation" (2 Cor. 5:17). That is, Paul is describing his new way of knowing. The believer who has been shaped by the Christ event sees the world in an entirely new way. The hope expressed in the Old Testament for a "new heaven and new earth" (Isa. 65:17; 66:22 AT) has become a reality for those who share the cross of Christ. If Paul's ministry does not measure up to the standards of his opposition, it is because his opponents have not recognized the reality of the "new creation." Thus he challenges the readers to recognize that this ministry that has occasioned criticism from his opponents is rooted in the Christian story.

Paul explains this "new creation" in the grand confessional statement of 2 Corinthians 5:18–19. As in 5:14, he appeals to the church's fundamental conviction as the basis for his ministry. The claim that God was "reconciling us to himself through Christ" is equivalent to the statement in 5:14 that "one died for all." In the parallel statements of 5:18–19, Paul summarizes the Christian story, emphasizing that God is the initiator of the cosmic drama of reconciliation. Whereas other texts of the period expressed the hope that God would become reconciled to the people (2 Macc. 1:5; 5:20), Paul speaks of God's initiative in reconciling humanity. Christ's death for human sin (2 Cor. 5:14–15, 21) has removed the condition of separation between God and sinful people. In the "new creation" and "reconciliation" in Christ, God has fulfilled Israel's hope for a new world in which the nation would be restored to a peaceful relationship with Yahweh.[42]

The parallel statements in 5:18–19 indicate that the God who acted at the cross also called Paul to service as the proclaimer of this good news. God has "given [Paul] the ministry of reconciliation" (5:18) and "the word of reconciliation" (5:19 AT). Paul responds to the criticism of his ministry with the bold claim that this ministry is from God. Indeed, in the appeal to the Corinthians in 5:20 and 6:1–2, Paul acts as God's ambassador, appealing to the Corinthians to be reconciled to God. He implies that alienation from Paul is also alienation from God. Thus the end of this unit corresponds to the beginning. To reciprocate Paul's devotion to the Corinthians is nothing less than to be reconciled to God.

42. Eriksson, *Traditions as Rhetorical Proof*, 558.

The narrative of God's reconciling activity is incomplete, for the Corinthians remain unreconciled to God. In 5:20–6:2, Paul returns to his present role in the unfinished narrative to describe his role of persuasion (cf. 5:11) and to challenge the readers to respond to God's deed of reconciliation. As God's ambassador, he does not speak for himself; instead, he says, "God is making his appeal through us" (5:20 AT). In 5:20b and 6:1–2, Paul makes an appeal to the Corinthians for reconciliation. That it is God who makes the appeal through Paul is reminiscent of the relationship between Yahweh and the servant in Isaiah 40–66, where God is the one who "comforts" (*ho parakalōn*) Israel (40:1–2, 11; 41:27; 49:10, 13; 51:3, 12, 18–19; 54:11; 57:5, 18; 61:2, 13), and the servant is God's spokesman.[43]

The appeal "not to receive the grace of God in vain" (2 Cor. 6:1 AT) echoes the cry of the servant, "I have labored in vain" (Isa. 49:4). Like the exilic prophet, who agonizes over Israel's failure to respond to his message (Isa. 43:22), Paul recognizes that the Corinthian community, despite their original acceptance of the gospel, is in danger of receiving the message in vain. In 2 Corinthians 6:2, Paul supports his appeal with the words of Isaiah 49:8, thus identifying with the servant and calling for a response.

In sum, the argument from ethos in 2 Corinthians is both a defense against criticism and a call for imitation as Paul distinguishes himself from the rhetoricians who peddle their message (2 Cor. 2:17) and boast of their achievements. As the frequent catalogs of suffering indicate (2 Cor. 4:7–10; 6:4–10; 11:23–33), Paul's boast in his weakness is contrary to the values of ancient society. His ethos has been determined not by the secular values of his time but by his theology. Paul's ethos is shaped by the message of the cross, which he not only proclaims but also embodies. He identifies with both Jeremiah (Jer. 1:5; cf. 2 Cor. 10:6–10) and the suffering servant, who gives himself for others. As a result of his work, the whole community is transformed into the image of Christ (2 Cor. 3:18).

Philippians

Philippians is "Paul's most egocentric letter," according to Robert Fortna,[44] who observed the apostle's pervasive appeal to his autobiography in the argument of Philippians. Paul's autobiography, however, is only one of several exempla in a letter that makes no explicit argument from Scripture but intersperses a series of examples (Phil. 2:6–11, 19–30; 3:2–21; 4:10–20) with exhortations for behavior that is worthy of the gospel (1:27). The centerpiece of the

---

43. See Thompson, "Reading the Letters as Narrative," 105.
44. Fortna, "Philippians," 220–34.

exempla is that of the preexistent Christ, who "emptied himself" and took on the form of a slave (2:6–11). As the predominance of *phron-* in Philippians indicates, this behavior grows out of a distinctive *phronēsis* among the believers.

But to speak of Philippians as "egocentric" is to miss Paul's ultimate aim in the letter. As the exhortations indicate, he writes to ensure that the church will ultimately be "pure and blameless " at the day of Christ (1:10; 2:15), and he offers ethical instructions to guide them. His concern for their moral formation is evident in the opening thanksgiving (1:3–11), which functions as the exordium to the letter, in which he appeals to his own ethos and pathos, speaking of his imprisonment (1:7) and of his deep desire to see the community (1:8). The church stands in the middle of a corporate narrative between the beginning of the community and the telos at the day of Christ (1:6, 11). His prayer that they will "love more and more" and "approve the better things" (1:9–10 AT) anticipates the moral instruction that distinguishes the letter, indicating that the telos of the church is their moral formation, which guides Paul's persuasive task.

Paul builds the case in his first autobiographical statement (1:12–26), which functions as the narratio of the letter. The autobiographical statement in 1:12–26 is not only a report on his recent imprisonment but also a description of his own state of mind. Despite his imprisonment by the Romans and the hostile behavior among believers, he is confident in the advance of the gospel (1:12) and joyful that Christ is preached (1:18a). He is also confident that events will result in salvation (1:18) and that "Christ will be magnified, either in life or death" (1:20 AT). He elaborates on the reference to life or death, declaring, "For me, to live is Christ, and to die is gain" (1:21 RSV). That is, if he lives, Christ is the center of his existence; if he dies, he will be "with Christ" (1:23). In life, Christ is the point of orientation. While death is preferable for him, he selflessly hopes to be reunited with this community (1:25–26). "To live is Christ" is thus to care for others.

In this deeply introspective section, Paul exhibits the *phronēsis* that he encourages the Philippians to adopt as both he and the Philippians face the consequences of confessing in Caesar's empire that Jesus is Lord. He is now in prison for his proclamation (1:12–13), and they, as a minority group, face adversaries (1:28) in the local society, suffering in the same struggle along with Paul (1:30). Thus Paul introduces the argument with his example of one who, despite current conditions, is confident of the advance of the gospel (1:12, 25), joyful in suffering (1:18), and hopeful when death is imminent (1:21–26). His statement of hope (1:18b–25) is not a discussion of eschatology but of the assurance that he commends for the Philippians. Thus he is the example of the *phronēsis* for living in a hostile society.

This tenuous situation offered the temptation for believers to assimilate to the values of the dominant culture. Paul, however, encourages the community to live "worthily of the gospel" (1:27 AT) in the letter's propositio (1:27–30). This existence involves a countercultural conduct and a united front against the adversaries (1:28–30). In the argument (probatio, 2:1–4:1), he elaborates on the specific conduct in the exhortations that appear throughout the letter (1:27–30; 2:1–5, 12–18; 4:2–9) as he insists on a life of humility in which members count others better than themselves (2:1–4) and a *phronēsis* that is contrary to the values of Philippian society (2:3–4).[45] The community can face the hostile populace only if the members "think the same thing" (2:2; 4:2), are of one mind, and stand together in one spirit. As the imperatives indicate (1:27–30; 2:11–18; 4:1–9), Paul writes to encourage the readers to share a common *phronēsis* (cf. 2:2–5) as a basis for their moral transformation.

The centerpiece of the argument and the primary example of this *phronēsis* is the narrative of the descent and ascent of the one whom they call Lord (2:6–11). In his self-emptying (2:7–8), Christ exemplified values contrary to the Hellenistic emphasis on self-aggrandizement, and his death on the cross, the nadir of his descent, was the epitome of shame in the Roman world.[46] Thus Jesus—the opposite of Hellenistic rulers, who exploited their power— exemplified the countercultural *phronēsis* that is present for believers who are in Christ (2:5). Paul challenges the readers to put this mind-set into practice as they "work out [their] own salvation" (2:12). In their countercultural existence, they will be lights in the world (2:15) and Paul's boast at the day of Christ (2:16).

After presenting Christ as the ultimate example (2:6–11) and his coworkers as exemplary followers of the ultimate example (2:19–30), Paul presents his own example in 3:2–21. This extended section is neither an interpolation nor a polemic against false teachers but an argument from Paul's own example. Typical of Paul's use of sharp contrasts in Philippians (cf. 1:12–18; 2:21), his autobiography is the central section (3:4–17) in a passage that is framed by negative examples (3:2, 18–19) of those who exemplify "boasting in the flesh" (3:3–4a AT) and a mind set on earthly things (3:19). Paul's list of achievements in 3:4–6 is parallel to the common topics for "boasting in the flesh." He describes a radical change in values in 3:7, using the accounting terminology of profit and loss: "Whatever gains I had, I have come to count as loss" (AT). Just as his Lord "emptied himself" of divine prerogatives (2:7), Paul "counted

---

45. See Thompson and Longenecker, *Philippians and Philemon*, 100–101.
46. Cf. Cicero, *Rab. Post.* 5.16: the word *cross* should be far removed from the "thoughts, eyes, and ears" of Roman citizens.

as loss" the achievements that he had gained before his conversion (3:7). The verb (from *hēgeomai*) suggests a parallel to the preexistent Christ, who did not count (*hēgēsato*) equality with God a thing to be grasped (2:6), and the transference of gain to loss recalls the self-emptying of Christ (2:7).[47] The change of tenses indicates the lasting significance of the event. Paul employs the perfect tense in 3:7 to describe a point in the past that remains the reality in his life, while in 3:8, he uses the present tense of *hēgeomai* (I regard as loss; I regard as rubbish) and the aorist tense of *zēmioō* (suffered loss) to speak of his conversion and its lasting significance.

The image of profit and loss provides the sharp dichotomy that Paul employs. He regards all things as loss "because of Christ" (3:7), "because of the surpassing quality of the knowledge of Christ" (3:8 AT), in order that he might "gain Christ." One may compare the dichotomies elsewhere: "I through the law died to the law, that I might live to . . . Christ" (Gal. 2:19 AT). As Paul declared earlier, "To live is Christ, and to die is gain" (Phil. 1:21 KJV).

Philippians 3:8–11 is a lengthy sentence elaborating on the profit and loss mentioned in 3:7. Paul clarifies the meaning of gaining Christ (3:8), speaking again in dichotomies: "to be found in him, not having a righteousness of my own, but a righteousness from the faith in Christ, the righteousness by faith" (AT). That is, the loss described in 3:7 is his own righteousness, described in 3:4–6, which has been replaced by the gain: a new kind of righteousness based on "faith in Christ."[48]

While Paul has not abandoned the Torah, the Torah now plays a different place in his life. He mentions in 3:9 that the law is not the basis of his righteousness. As Paul says, he has been "grasped" by Christ (3:12), with permanent consequences. Like his community, he is in the middle of a corporate narrative, hoping to reach the goal (3:12–16).

Paul then elaborates on the significance of gaining Christ in 3:9–10. Again speaking in dichotomies, he indicates that the faithfulness of Christ is the alternative to his own righteousness (3:9). In 3:10, he discusses the righteousness by faith in the chiasm that follows. To live in faith (3:9) is to know Christ (3:10)—Paul writes more on the meaning of knowing Christ.

The purpose clause in 3:10–11 elaborates further on the life of faith. "To know him" is the life of faith. Thus the appropriate translation is "to know him,

---

47. Thompson and Longenecker, *Philippians and Philemon*, 108.

48. Michael Wolter correctly notes that the interpreter is not limited to the alternatives of subjective and objective genitive in the interpretation of *pistis christou* (faith of Christ or faith in Christ). Wolter suggests that *pistis christou* may be rendered as a genitive of quality ("Christ faith"), with the emphasis on the content of the faith—the destiny of Jesus Christ in his death and resurrection. Wolter, *Paul*, 75–77.

that is, the power of his resurrection and the sharing of his sufferings" (AT).[49] And then the meaning of knowing Christ is expressed in a chiasm (3:10–11).

A   Both the power [*dynamin*] of his resurrection [*anastaseōs*]

B   And the sharing [*koinōnian*] of his sufferings [*pathēmatōn*]

B′ Being conformed [*symmorphizomenos*] to his death

A′ If somehow I will attain to the resurrection of the dead.[50]

As the chiasm in 3:10–11 indicates, the power of the resurrection is present in the life of believers both now and in the future. Paul maintains elsewhere that it is present as he shares in the suffering of Christ, and in the frailty of the earthen vessel, the power belongs to God (2 Cor. 4:7–10). The result is the resurrection. As Paul says in Romans, "If we suffer with him, we shall be glorified with him" (Rom. 8:17 AT).

Paul concludes the autobiography by indicating that his perspective is the *phronēsis* that he desires for his listeners (Phil. 3:15). In their own suffering (1:29), they imitate him. He encourages them to imitate him (3:17) rather than the enemies of the cross (3:18–19). Those who imitate him can anticipate that they will be conformed to the body of Christ's glory "according to the power that is able to subject all things" (3:20–21).

Conclusion: An Ethos of Suffering with Christ

A consistent feature in Paul's argument from ethos is his differentiation from the orators. He does not set out to please people (Gal. 1:10; 1 Thess. 2:4), use persuasive words of wisdom (1 Cor. 2:2), or peddle his message (cf. 2 Cor. 2:17)—as the orators do. Nor does he establish his ethos by claiming that he embodies Hellenistic values. His ethos is determined by the prophetic call that compels him to speak and his claim that he speaks for God. As the herald of the good news promised in Isaiah 52:7, he has taken over the role of the servant, the "light to the nations" (Isa. 49:6), who fears his work is "in vain" (Isa. 49:4; cf. 2 Cor. 6:1; Gal. 2:2; 4:11; Phil. 2:16; 1 Thess. 2:2; 3:5). He consistently establishes his ethos by insisting that he participates in the sufferings of Christ, and he challenges his readers to imitate his example. Just as he exhibits a countercultural ethos, he challenges his communities to join him in a countercultural existence that is shaped by the cross of Christ.

49. Fee, *Pauline Christology*, 328.
50. Thompson and Longenecker, *Philippians and Philemon*, 109.

5

First Thessalonians

A Template for Theological Reflection

irst Thessalonians has played a minor role in the literature on Pauline theology because in this letter Paul does not develop the themes that become the central theological categories associated with his thought. Because he does not explicitly mention justification by faith or the law, scholars debate whether these topics belong to a later period of Pauline thought. Additionally, the imminent eschatology of 1 Thessalonians has suggested to many interpreters that the letter is an example of the early stages in Pauline theology, in contrast to the mature theological arguments in the major letters.[1]

As our earliest preserved example of Christian literature, 1 Thessalonians is of special importance. As Helmut Koester argued, 1 Thessalonians is a communication that was sui generis in the first century. While it has the form of a letter, it does not conform fully to any of the types of letters identified by epistolary theorists.[2] Many scholars have maintained that it, like the other letters, is a speech, but they have reached no consensus on the type of speech it is.[3] It fits neither the audience nor the content described by ancient rhetorical

---

1. Cf. Schnelle, *Apostle Paul*, 191; Söding, "Der erste Thessalonicherbrief."
2. Koester, "1 Thessalonians—Experiment in Christian Writing."
3. Robert Jewett and Wilhelm Wuellner conclude that 1 Thessalonians is a letter of praise containing features of epideictic rhetoric. See Jewett, *Thessalonian Correspondence*, 71–72; Wuellner, "Argumentative Structure of 1 Thessalonians," 126. Hans Hübner maintains that it contains both epideictic and deliberative elements (*Theologie des Neuen Testaments*,

theorists,[4] but it is an exercise in persuasion that points toward future conduct and bears some similarities to deliberative rhetoric.[5] The theological
convictions that Paul develops in the later correspondence are introduced in
1 Thessalonians. These theological categories play an important role in Paul's
persuasive task of boasting in his blameless community at the parousia (cf.
2:19).

The Rhetorical Situation of 1 Thessalonians

While our sources do not provide the full details of the historical context
of 1 Thessalonians, we can discern from the letter the rhetorical situation
as perceived by Paul.[6] The letter is a continuation of the instruction that
Paul gave on his founding visit, in which the Thessalonians had "received
the word in the midst of affliction [*thlipsis*] with the joy of the Holy Spirit"
(1 Thess. 1:6) and continued to be shaped by Paul's exercise in community formation. He describes his earlier instruction as *paraklēsis* (1 Thess.
2:3), a term that has the connotations of comfort (2 Cor. 1:3–7), entreaty,
challenge, and encouragement.[7] He recalls that, prior to his premature
departure, he had, like a father, continued "encouraging [*parakalountos*],
consoling [*paramythoumenoi*], and bearing witness [*martyromenoi*] that
[they] walk worthily of the God who calls" them into his kingdom (1 Thess.
2:12 AT).

Because the affliction (*thlipsis*) that the Thessalonians encountered at
their conversion was a continuing reality after Paul left the city (3:3), he
sent Timothy to "strengthen" (*stērixai*) and encourage (*parakalesai*) their
faithfulness (*pistis*, 3:2). After receiving Timothy's positive report of the
Thessalonians' faithfulness (*pistis*) and love (*agapē*), Paul writes to continue
the conversation (3:6). He probably also addresses questions that the Thessalonians have asked about those who have died, recalling Paul's words that
they were all "waiting for his Son from heaven" (1:10). When Paul writes,
"I ask you and encourage [*parakalō*] you . . . to conduct yourselves as it is
necessary and please God" (4:1), he continues his earlier work of encouraging

---

2:41–43). George A. Kennedy maintains that the letter is deliberative (*Interpretation through
Rhetorical Criticism*, 142).

4. See Olbricht, "Rhetorical Analysis of 1 Thessalonians," 225–26.

5. Kennedy, *Interpretation through Rhetorical Criticism*, 142.

6. The rhetorical situation is to be distinguished from the historical situation. As Dennis L.
Stamps has argued, the rhetorical situation is the situation that is embedded in the text. Stamps,
"Rethinking the Rhetorical Situation."

7. Grabner-Haider, *Paraklese und Eschatologie in Paulus*, 7.

(*parakalountes*) his children to walk worthily of the kingdom (2:12). The letter is, therefore, *paraklēsis*, a distinct form of rhetoric, and it contains the two primary dimensions of *paraklēsis*: consolation (cf. 4:13–18) and encouragement (4:1–12; 5:1–22) for a community that has suffered disappointment over the death of loved ones and discouragement over continuing hostility from others. The movement of the argument from the past (1:3–3:10) to the future conduct of the Thessalonians (3:11–5:22) indicates Paul's singular purpose in writing: to ensure that converts who began as idolaters (1:9–10) would ultimately be "blameless in holiness" at the end (3:13; 5:23–25). Echoing the prophet in Isaiah 49:4, Paul hopes that his work is not "in vain" (1 Thess. 3:5; cf. 2:1).

Invention, Arrangement, and Theology

Although 1 Thessalonians does not conform fully to one of the species of ancient rhetoric, Aristotelian categories provide a helpful lens for analyzing the arrangement of Paul's argument.[8] The thanksgiving (1 Thess. 1:2–10), like the introductory thanksgivings in the other letters, introduces the topic and makes the audience favorably disposed, thus functioning as the exordium.[9] Paul expresses gratitude for his converts' "work of faith, labor of love, and steadfastness of hope" (1:3), the themes that he develops throughout the letter (see below). The recollection that conversion involves waiting for the Son from heaven (1:10) introduces the future expectation that becomes a constant refrain of the letter (cf. 2:16, 19; 3:13; 4:13–5:11).

Paul is also thankful that, after turning to God from idols (1 Thess. 1:9) and imitating the Lord, the community has become the model for others in Macedonia and Achaia (1:7). This thanksgiving is both a statement of gratitude and a motivation for the continued moral progress of the church. In expressing gratitude for the Thessalonians' faithfulness, Paul signals the

8. See Kennedy, *Interpretation through Rhetorical Criticism*, 10: "Though rhetoric is colored by the traditions and conventions of the society in which it is applied, it is also a universal phenomenon which is conditioned by basic workings of the human mind and heart and by the nature of all human society. . . . It is perfectly possible to utilize the categories of Aristotelian rhetoric to study speech in China, India, Africa, and elsewhere in the world." He adds that "what is unique about Greek rhetoric, and what makes it useful for criticism, is the degree to which it was conceptualized. The Greeks gave names to rhetorical techniques, many of which are found all over the world." See also Schellenberg, *Rethinking Paul's Rhetorical Education*, 251–52: "Most people acquire rhetorical competency the same way they do most of their learning—through social interaction."

9. On the functions of the exordium, see Quintilian, *Inst.* 3.8.6; Cicero, *Inv.* 1.15.20; cf. Aristotle, *Rhet.* 3.14.75.

priority that motivates his ministry—the moral formation of the community—
and prepares the community to maintain the values that he mentions in the
thanksgiving.[10]

The praise of both the Thessalonians' moral progress and their endurance
in the midst of persecution (*thlipsis*, 1:6) introduces pathos into the argument
as Paul anticipates his comments on the continuing *thlipsis* endured by the
community (3:3). The memory of the Thessalonians' past sufferings is an
encouragement for them to continue to demonstrate faithfulness and hope
in the context of the hostility from their neighbors. Their reception of the
message "in the joy of the Holy Spirit" (1:6) is a reminder of the range of
emotions experienced by the Thessalonians at their conversion.

In 2:1–3:10, Paul recalls his past history with the Thessalonians as a
prelude to his requests in chapters 4–5. This history of their relationship
functions as the narratio of the argument, as Paul builds his case, and is
an expression of ethos and pathos, as Paul first recalls his conduct among
the new converts. In establishing that he is unlike the orators who enrich
themselves, he argues from ethos (2:1–12),[11] offering himself as an exemplum
of moral formation.[12] Indeed, his "blameless" behavior (2:10) and his work
with his hands (2:9) serve as a model for the Thessalonians (3:13; 4:9). As an
example of appropriate conduct, he is also engaged in "urging, encouraging, and pleading" with the community to "walk worthily of the God who
calls [them] into his kingdom and glory" (2:12), anticipating the content of
chapters 4 and 5.[13]

Paul appeals to pathos in describing his relationship to the church. In
preaching in spite of opposition (*agōn*, 2:2), he shares their afflictions (cf.
3:3). He also appeals to pathos in both his paternal and his maternal relationship to the church. He is like a nurse caring for the children (2:7) and a
father who devotes himself totally to the community (2:8). When he is not
present with them, he feels "orphaned" (*aporphanisthentes*, 2:17). Thus he
hopes to see them in the future, for they are his crown of boasting at the
parousia (2:19–20).

---

10. Cf. Selby, *Not with Wisdom of Words*, 106. Cf. D. Watson, "Paul's Appropriation of
Apocalyptic Discourse," 65–66.

11. See Morgan, *Roman Faith and Christian Faith*, 244: "In a world where attitudes to
rhetoric, as we have seen, are profoundly conflicted, and where orators are both lionized and
constantly criticized as sycophants, twisters, moneygrubbers, and publicity hounds, it is routine
for an orator to try to capture the favour of his audience by claiming that he has not flattered
or manipulated it."

12. For the importance of exempla in ancient rhetoric, see chap. 1 above. On the argument
from ethos in 1 Thessalonians, see chap. 4.

13. See Hübner, *Theologie des Neuen Testaments*, 2:43.

The exordium (1:2–12) and narratio (2:1–3:10) build the case for the argument that Paul makes in chapters 4–5. The prayer in 3:11–13 is the *transitus* that introduces the ethical instructions that follow,[14] including the call to sanctification at the end (cf. 4:3, 7; 5:23) and to love one another (cf. 4:9–12), before the propositio in 4:1–2. Having expressed his desire that the community will be his "hope or joy or crown of boasting" before the Lord at the parousia (2:19), he prays that God will make them blameless at the parousia (3:13). Like the opening thanksgiving, this prayer invites the Thessalonians to embody the values expressed in it, while the propositio in 4:1–2 states the case that will be argued.

Paraklēsis—both consolation and encouragement—requires a theological foundation to motivate the community to meet the challenge of living in the midst of conflict with the surrounding world. Paul provides the basis for the Thessalonians' moral formation that will be complete at the parousia of Christ. In the instructions that follow, Paul does not employ Aristotelian proofs but appeals to his own authority (4:2), the will of God as known from Israel's Scriptures (4:1–11), the community's tradition (4:14; 5:2–3), and his prophetic insight into the future events (4:13–5:11).

The Thessalonians' Narrative Existence

The Beginning of the Narrative: Election and the Coming of the Gospel

Paul introduces theological vocabulary in the exordium and narratio and develops it in the main argument (1 Thess. 4–5). These terms include *ekklēsia*, *kyrios Jesus*, *euangelion*, *eklogē*, *dikaiosynē* and *orgē*, and *pneuma*. Although the terms are common in Greek, Paul employs them in a way that would have been new to gentile converts, for Paul's usage is rooted in Israel's narrative. His challenge is to create a shared identity and symbolic world among converts from various backgrounds in order to establish the common ethos that he describes in chapters 4–5.[15]

Ekklēsia. With the address to "the church of the Thessalonians in God the Father and the Lord Jesus Christ" (1:1), Paul establishes the identity of the converts, including them in Israel's narrative. While *ekklēsia* among Greeks referred to any assembly, the identification of the community as "the church of the Thessalonians in God the Father and the Lord Jesus Christ" indicates

---

14. See D. Watson, "Paul's Appropriation of Apocalyptic Discourse," 71: "A *transitus* is one way of concluding the narration, summarizing its themes and introducing themes of the probatio, the main part of the rhetorical piece that develops the propositions."

15. See Thompson, *Moral Formation according to Paul*, 44.

the Thessalonian Christians' place in Israel's narrative, for this *ekklēsia* is to be distinguished from both the synagogue and the other gatherings (*ekklēsiai*) in Thessalonica. In the Septuagint, "the church of God" is a translation of the Hebrew *qahal 'el* (cf. Deut. 23:2, 4; 1 Chron. 28:8; Neh. 13:1). The phrase is frequently used in the apocalyptic literature for the eschatological people of God.[16] In other words, Paul employs a term that has already been used in the Jerusalem church to designate the true Israel (cf. chap. 3 above). This term—along with the synonyms "brothers and sisters" (*adelphoi*), "children of light" (1 Thess. 5:4–5), "believers" (1:7; 2:10), and "the elect" (1:4)—suggests that the community is the eschatological people of God,[17] an assembly demarcated from other assemblies and separated from the rest of the Thessalonians (cf. 4:12–13) by its response to Jesus Christ.

Kyrios Jesus. Paul transforms Israel's narrative with the phrase "the Lord Jesus Christ" (1:1), anticipating his numerous references to the Lord (*kyrios*) in 1 Thessalonians (cf. 1:6; 3:12; 4:6, 15; 5:27). Jesus is both *kyrios* and the Son of God (1:10), titles that originated in the earliest Jerusalem church. Because Christology is not a topic of debate, Paul does not elaborate on the relationship between God the Father and the Lord Jesus Christ. He only says that God raised Jesus from the dead (1:10) and that God will bring believers through Jesus to be with him (4:14). In the prayer in 3:11–13, he prays that God will lead him back to the Thessalonians (3:11) and that the Lord (*kyrios*) will increase their love (3:12–13). He also says that the Lord (*kyrios*) is an avenger (4:6), as well as the one who sanctifies, while in 5:23, it is God who sanctifies. The community's task is to be well-pleasing to God and do the will of God (4:3), who called them into his kingdom and glory (2:12). The Lord will return, and "we will always be with the Lord" (4:16–17). While Paul does not mention the exaltation, his references to the Lord's return from heaven presuppose it.

Euangelion. The Thessalonians have their own narrative within Israel's larger narrative. In 1 Thessalonians, as in Paul's other letters, Paul recalls the community's narrative, which began when the gospel (*euangelion*) came to the Thessalonians (cf. 1:5). He commonly refers to the beginning of a community's narrative, which is the culmination of Israel's narrative (cf. 1 Cor. 1:18–2:5; Gal. 3:1–6).[18] In 1 Thessalonians, Paul declared (*lalēsai*, 1 Thess.

16. Thompson, *Church according to Paul*, 31.

17. See Thompson, *Church according to Paul*, 31. This is a rendering of *qahal 'el*, a term in the Second Temple period for the true Israel.

18. The significant meaning of the beginning is evident in the way Paul consistently reminds the readers of their beginning (e.g., 1 Cor. 2:1–5; 3:1–2, 5–10; 4:15; 15:1–3; Gal. 3:1–2; 4:13–14; Phil. 1:5; 4:15; 1 Thess. 1:5–10; 2:1–13; 4:2).

2:2), preached (*ekēryxamen*, 2:9; cf. Gal. 2:2), and shared (*metadounai*) the gospel (1 Thess. 2:8) at the beginning of their narrative. This gospel is not ordinary rhetoric but the word of God (1 Thess. 1:6; cf. 1 Cor. 14:36; 2 Cor. 2:17; 4:2; Phil. 1:14; 1 Thess. 2:13). Thus it came with "power, the Holy Spirit, and full assurance" (1 Thess. 1:5).

Paul elaborates on the content of his preaching here in subsequent letters. In 1 Corinthians, he declares that the word of the cross is "the power of God" (1 Cor. 1:18) and that his words were not persuasive words of wisdom but "the demonstration of the Spirit and power" (1 Cor. 2:4). He speaks of the gospel as "the power of God to salvation" (Rom. 1:16). Indeed, his entire ministry is a demonstration of the power of God in the context of his own weakness. Paul is a prophetic figure who speaks the word of God.

Eklogē. The coming of the gospel was the election (*eklogē*) of the community (1 Thess. 1:4), the divine initiative by which this gentile community was incorporated into Israel. The God who once chose Israel (cf. Deut. 7:7–11) has also chosen this gentile community, which, like Israel, is "beloved of God" (1 Thess. 1:4; cf. Deut. 7:8). God has called the community into his kingdom and glory (1 Thess. 2:12) and to holiness (1 Thess. 4:7). Paul extends this image throughout the letters, regularly mentioning their call (Rom. 1:7; 8:28; 1 Cor. 1:24, 26; 7:20). This description of the community as the elect culminates in Romans 9:6–29, when Paul applies the election traditions to the gentile church (see below).

The coming of the gospel involves both the proclamation and the content of the message. Paul never summarizes his gospel the same way twice.[19] In 1 Thessalonians 1:9–10, Paul's memory of the Thessalonians' response to the message probably also includes a summary of his missionary preaching to gentiles.[20] Paul had challenged the listeners to "turn to God from idols, to serve a true and living God and wait for his Son from heaven, whom he raised from the dead." The phrase "his Son, . . . whom he raised from the dead" is probably a summary of his gospel. In 4:14, the phrase "since we believe that Jesus died and arose" appeals to what the Thessalonians already believed. One may also compare the phrase "Christ, who died for us" (1 Thess. 5:10), as a summary of Paul's message. Paul does not elaborate on the *hyper* formula, which he apparently inherited from the Jerusalem church (cf. 1 Cor. 15:3). He will elaborate in later letters.

Summaries of the gospel appear frequently in Paul as the basis for his argumentation. In 1 Corinthians 15:3–4, the gospel is the message of the death,

19. Ciampa, "Paul's Theology of the Gospel," 184.
20. Wolter, *Paul*, 63–64.

burial, and resurrection of Christ. His message is the "word of the cross" (1 Cor. 1:18 AT) and "Christ crucified" (1 Cor. 2:2 AT). In 2 Corinthians 5:14, "One has died for all" is the basis for further argumentation; Paul preaches "Jesus Christ as Lord" (2 Cor. 4:5). According to Romans 1:3–4, the content of the gospel is "his Son, born from the seed of David according to the flesh, designated Son of God in power according to the spirit of holiness from the resurrection of the dead, Jesus Christ our Lord." According to Philippians, the gospel advances when Christ is preached (Phil. 1:15, 17–18). Thus while Paul summarizes the gospel in a variety of ways, the subject is always Jesus Christ, the one who died, was raised, and will come again. The return from exile announced by Deutero-Isaiah has occurred in the Christ event.

The coming of the gospel was accompanied by the Thessalonians' response. At the beginning of its narrative, the community received the message (1 Thess. 1:6), turned to God from idols (1:9), and "believed that Jesus died and arose" (4:14), becoming a model for others (1:7). This was the moment when God called them to holiness (4:7). Paul considered the church of the Thessalonians to be the true people of God, the renewed community anticipated by the prophets. This is the common designation for the community elsewhere in the New Testament.

Dikaiosynē and orgē. The good news is also that "we shall be saved from God's wrath" (1:10 AT). Thus without the good news, humanity stands under the wrath of God and in need of the good news. The coming wrath is a familiar theme in the prophets. It presupposes the just judgments of God, according to which the righteous will be justified (cf. Rom. 2:13). This wrath has already come upon some (1 Thess. 2:16; cf. Rom. 1:18). God is the one who punishes according to his justice (cf. *ekdikos*, 1 Thess. 4:6).[21] One may compare Paul's references in Romans to "the day of wrath and the revelation of the righteous judgment of God" (Rom. 2:5 AT; cf. 2:8–9). God's righteousness (*dikaiosynē*) and wrath (*orgē*) are related eschatological events, signifying the event when God will vindicate the righteous and pour out wrath on the unrighteous. Indeed, the prophet prays, "Lord, in view of your righteousness [*dikaiosynē*], turn away your anger and wrath" (Dan. 9:16 LXX). In Deutero-Isaiah, God has poured out his wrath on Israel (Isa. 42:25; 58:13–14; 59:18–19; 60:10; 63:6) but will now vindicate them in his righteousness (Isa. 41:10; 42:6; 45:19; 46:13; 47:3; 51:5–8; 53:11; cf. 61:8–11).

What is implicit in 1 Thessalonians becomes explicit in 2 Thessalonians. It is just (*dikaion*) for God to render punishment to those who persecute believers.

---

21. *Ekdikos* is related to *ekdikeō*, which means either to grant justice (cf. Luke 18:3, 7) or to punish (cf. 2 Cor. 10:6). BDAG 301.

God will give justice (*ekdikēsis*) to those who do not know God and do not obey the gospel (2 Thess. 1:8). This anticipates Paul's view in Romans. Thus it can be assumed that already in 1 Thessalonians a concept of justification is present, which then is developed in Galatians.[22] According to Martin Hengel, Paul's statements about election, saving faith, and salvation from God's wrath are unintelligible without the background of the righteousness of God.[23]

Pneuma. The Spirit (*pneuma*) was not only present in the proclamation but also present for those who received the message. The reception of the Spirit is an indication that the readers live in the new age. Paul recalls the prophecy of Ezekiel 36:27 that God would place the Spirit within the people and make them follow God's statutes (cf. Ezek. 37:14). The good news is not only a message but also a power (1 Thess. 1:5) that was not only present in the preaching of the word but also continues to be active in the community (1 Thess. 2:13; 4:8). The continuing theological significance of Ezekiel 36 and 37 for Paul's theology is evident in Paul's appeal to the passage in 2 Corinthians (3:1–6) and Romans (8:1–17).[24]

The power of the Spirit is a continuing theme in Paul's letters. The community is the temple of the Holy Spirit, the place of God's dwelling (1 Cor. 3:16). The Spirit is the power into which the community was baptized (1 Cor. 12:13) and the power for ethical living (Gal. 5:22–29). At the beginning of Romans, Paul speaks of the power of the gospel (Rom. 1:16), and at the end, he speaks of the power of the Holy Spirit (Rom. 15:13). In one of his most extended discussions of the Holy Spirit (Rom. 8:1–17), Paul describes him as the power that enables the community to do the will of God.

In describing the beginning of the Thessalonians' narrative, Paul introduces the theological themes that will remain consistent in all of his letters. These themes, taken primarily from Israel's narrative, have an important rhetorical function in the argument. Paul provides a marginalized community with an identity as the elect, eschatological people of God. Thus he legitimizes their minority status, reminding them of the identity that will be the basis for their future conduct as the eschatological Israel. He appeals to both ethos and pathos in establishing the basis for this persuasion.

The Completion of the Narrative and the Apocalyptic Vision

The end of the narrative is of special importance in 1 Thessalonians. The congregation learned at the beginning that they "wait for a Son from heaven,

---

22. Schließer, "Paulustheologien im Vergleich," 64.
23. Hengel, "Die Stellung des Apostels Paulus zum Gesetz," 214.
24. Hübner, *Theologie des Neuen Testaments*, 2:50.

. . . who will save [them] from the coming wrath" (1 Thess. 1:10 AT). Paul's repeated references to the parousia (2:19; 3:13) remind the readers of the hope that sustains them in a time of crisis. In 4:13–5:11, he develops this theme at length. Both the appearance of this section under the heading of moral behavior (4:1–2) and the frame of this section (4:13; 5:11; cf. 4:18) indicate that Paul's primary focus is not a detailed description of the end but encouragement for a distressed community. When he addresses the problem of "those who are asleep" (4:13 AT), indicating that hope is the quality that distinguishes the Thessalonians from their neighbors, he offers a pastoral word for those who are in danger of losing hope. His assurances suggest that the Thessalonians, having been taught that they are "waiting for the Son from heaven" (1:10 AT), are now disoriented by the deaths of some in the congregation.

Paul first responds by appealing to the creed that they first accepted at their conversion: "We believe that Jesus died and arose" (1 Thess. 4:14 AT). Forms of this creed are common in the Pauline literature (cf. 1 Cor. 15:3; 2 Cor. 5:14) and function as the premise of his argument.[25] The logical conclusion to this creed is "so also God will bring with him those who are asleep" (1 Thess. 4:14 AT). That the resurrection of believers follows naturally from the resurrection of Jesus is a common affirmation in the New Testament (1 Cor. 6:14; 2 Cor. 4:14), an argument Paul develops at length in 1 Corinthians 15:20–28. The specific wording indicates that Paul is not giving a general statement on eschatology but is answering the question that the Thessalonians are asking. The repetition of "with him" (1 Thess. 4:14) and "with the Lord" (1 Thess. 4:17) suggests that the Thessalonians are concerned about the absence of those who are "dead in Christ" (1 Thess. 4:17) and their separation from those who are left. Paul's thesis will develop around this.

Paul proceeds from the premise based on the Christian creed (1 Thess. 4:14) to a prophetic announcement, appealing to a word of the Lord as an additional premise to the argument, assuring the readers that "we who are left . . . will not precede those who have died" (4:15 AT). Thus the focus is on the sequence of events and the relationship between "those who are left" and those who are "dead in Christ." Verses 16–17 confirm the sequence with traditional apocalyptic images. The exalted Lord (*kyrios*) will come down with a cry of command (*keleusma*). This recalls Daniel's vision of the "son of man" coming "with the clouds" (Dan. 7:13 RSV) and other references to the coming of the one who sits at God's right hand (cf. Mark 13:26; 14:62; Acts 1:11). Paul employs the traditional apocalyptic images of the voice of

25. Hübner, *Theologie des Neuen Testaments*, 2:46; Eriksson, *Traditions as Rhetorical Proof*, 73–134.

the archangel (1 Thess. 4:16; cf. Jude 9; *4 Ezra* 4:36) and the sound of the trumpet (cf. 1 Cor. 15:52; Rev. 15:2; cf. Zech. 9:14; *4 Ezra* 6:23), but his focus is on the reunion with those who have died: we will not precede them; they will precede us. They will be "with us" as we meet Christ in the air. The final result is that "we"—both those who have died and those who remain alive—"will be with the Lord" (1 Thess. 4:17).

The certainty of the Lord's return stamps the life of believers in the present, and Paul encourages believers to "comfort one another" (4:18 RSV). In 5:1–11, he gives further indication of how faith in the return of Christ shapes present existence. "The day of the Lord" of Old Testament expectation is the equivalent of the descent of the Son (1:10; 4:16). One cannot speculate on times and seasons (5:1); one only knows that it will come as a thief in the night (5:2). The focus is not on the details of the event but on the separation that will take place between believers and those who have no hope (cf. 4:13). This event will be a time of judgment, a day of wrath (1:10). Thus Paul's argument is based on apocalyptic traditions that have become the shared assumptions of this gentile subculture. The task of believers is to recognize that they already live in the new aeon as children of light and children of the day and to recognize that hope gives urgency to their moral behavior.

Paul is not merely offering information to the Thessalonians. He is providing a vision of the reality unknown to the majority culture, a reality that will sustain the Thessalonians in their time of affliction. Only they are "children of light," while others in the local society are people of the darkness (5:5). The sharp demarcation between the readers and "the rest" (4:13; 5:6) reaffirms the identity of the marginalized community. The description of the end is not aimed at merely giving facts but at offering an emotion of hopefulness.[26] This vision will sustain their "endurance of hope" (1:3 AT), provide the basis for readers to encourage one another (4:18), and give urgency to their moral behavior (5:5–9).

The Present as a Time of Moral Formation

To "wait for his Son from heaven" (1:10) is to live between the coming of the gospel and the return of the Savior. Thus the God who calls the community is still at work (2:13), and the community "called . . . into his kingdom and glory" (2:12) has not reached the goal. Living between the times, they are already "children of light" and "children of the day" (5:5). The members belong already to the heavenly world, and God's salvation is already present.[27]

---

26. Selby, *Not with Wisdom of Words*, 41; Hester, "Creating the Future," 196.
27. Wolter, *Paul*, 119–200.

The new age anticipated by the prophets has come to them, but they still wait for the return of the Son. They live amid sufferings (*thlipseis*), which they have experienced from the beginning (1:6; 3:3–4), and with the endurance of suffering, they imitate the Lord (1:6). As Paul indicates (3:3), suffering is the destiny of the community, the prelude to the ultimate salvation. This claim is based on premises common in apocalyptic expectation.[28]

Thlipsis, according to Jewish literature, is the prelude to the final victory (cf. Matt. 24:9, 29; John 16:2; Rev. 1:9; 2:9–10, 22; 7:14). This is a major theme in Pauline literature. According to 2 Corinthians, Paul and the community share in the suffering, which is nothing other than the participation in the suffering of Christ (1 Thess. 1:3–7). One may compare this to "the time of tribulation" in apocalyptic literature (cf. *4 Ezra* 13:16–19; *2 Bar.* 25:1–4; *Sib. Or.* 2:154–70; 8:85). Thus Jewish apocalyptic literature provides the basic knowledge that Paul has given to the Thessalonians already (1 Thess. 3:3). The suffering in 1 Thessalonians is participation in the sufferings of Christ and in the tribulation, which is a common expectation in Jewish apocalyptic literature. According to Philippians 1:28, it is a gift at the present time. Paul's appeal is based on the knowledge that is known only to the subculture in which he lives.[29]

The present, in other words, is the time for moral formation. The opening and closing of the letter indicate the nature of this response. At the beginning, Paul expresses gratitude for their work of faith, labor of love, and steadfastness of hope. Near the end he urges them to put on the breastplate of faith and love and a helmet of hope of salvation (1 Thess. 5:8). The triad of faith, hope, and love plays an important part in Pauline ethics, indicating a complementary relationship between them. For example, "Faith, hope, and love abide" (1 Cor. 13:13). According to Galatians, "We by the Spirit await the hope of righteousness" (Gal. 5:5 AT), as faith is active through love (Gal. 5:6). Thus faith, hope, and love are the continuing responses of a community under duress and are a comprehensive description of Christian existence.[30]

Paul also mentions two of the three in the triad in 1 Thessalonians: the "labor of love" is closely associated with the "work of faith" (1 Thess. 1:3). He writes after Timothy has brought good news of their faith and love (1 Thess. 3:6). This duality is present elsewhere in the letter and is commonplace in Paul's other letters as well, in both the undisputed and the disputed letters. Faith is at work through love (Gal. 5:6). Paul expresses gratitude for Philemon's love and faith (Philem. 4–5). He gives thanks for the Colossians' faith

28. For the premises in Paul's arguments, see Fenske, *Die Argumentation des Paulus*, 65.
29. Cf. Fenske, *Die Argumentation des Paulus*, 65.
30. Söding, "Der erste Thessalonicherbrief," 196.

in Christ and their love for the saints (Col. 1:4; cf. Eph. 1:15). He gives thanks for the Thessalonians' growing faith and their increasing love (2 Thess. 1:3). Indeed, faith and love frequently appear together as inseparable concepts (cf. Gal. 5:6; Eph. 1:15; 3:17; 6:23; Col. 1:4; 1 Thess. 3:6; 5:8; 2 Thess. 1:3; 1 Tim. 1:14; 2:15; 2 Tim. 1:13).[31]

Additionally, Paul refers separately to the Thessalonians' work of faith (1 Thess. 3:2, 5, 7), labor of love (3:12; 4:9–12), and steadfastness of hope (4:13).

Work of faith. At the beginning of their corporate narrative, the Thessalonians believed "Jesus died and arose" (4:14 AT), received the proclamation (1:6), and turned to God from idols (1:9). This response is so fundamental that Paul describes members of the community as "those who believe" (*hoi pisteuontes*, 1:7; 2:10).[32] Faith is not, however, limited to the initial experience, for Paul's gratitude for their work of faith indicates that faith is a continuing response to the gospel.[33] Indeed, Paul sent Timothy to strengthen and encourage the Thessalonians on behalf of their faith (3:2) so that they would not be shaken by the suffering that was a consequence of their conversion, and he hopes to come to restore what is lacking in their faith (3:10). Faith is the opposite of being shaken (3:3) and the equivalent of standing firm in the Lord (3:8) in the midst of duress.

Paul most frequently uses the term "faith" without an object in 1 Thessalonians. This usage is commonplace in the subsequent letters. He encourages the communities to "stand firm in [their] faith" (1 Cor. 16:13), live in faith (2 Cor. 13:5; Gal. 2:20), and take a firm stand in faith (Rom. 11:20; 2 Cor. 1:24). He speaks of those who overflow in faith (2 Cor. 8:7), grow in faith (2 Cor. 10:15; cf. Phil. 1:25), lack faith (1 Thess. 3:10), or are weak in faith (Rom. 14:1). Faith is the consistent response to the gospel in all of the letters (cf. Rom. 1:8, 12; 2 Cor. 1:24; 8:7; 10:15; 13:5; Phil. 1:25; 2:17), and the work of faith is the equivalent of the obedience of faith (Rom. 1:5; cf. 6:12, 17; 10:16; 15:18), the continuing response to the gospel. Paul's subsequent letters will elaborate on the christological aspect.

While *pistis* plays a major role in 1 Thessalonians, Paul never speaks of believing in Christ or of the faithfulness of Christ (*pistis christou*). He speaks, however, of the Thessalonians' faith in God (1:8) and their faith that "Jesus died and arose" (4:14 AT). Faith in God and faith in Christ are not two different aspects of faith but the same thing. The faith that Jesus is raised (4:14)

---

31. Wolter, *Paul*, 325–26.
32. See Morgan, *Roman Faith and Christian Faith*, 238–41.
33. Wolter, *Paul*, 81–82.

is only possible as faith that "[God] raised him from the dead" (1:10 AT; cf. Rom. 4:24; 10:9).[34] Faith becomes the constant term for the human response throughout Paul's letters as Paul employs the term to face a variety of issues.

Labor of love. The labor of love (*kopos tou agapēs*, 1 Thess. 1:3) is also a continuing response to the gospel; it is the dominant ethical category in Paul's letters. Paul is grateful for the Thessalonians' labor of love, and he prays that the Lord will make them increase in love to one another and to all (3:12) and then instructs the readers to continue to practice love (4:9–12). The primary object of love is "one another" (3:12; 4:9), but it also extends to all people (3:12). With the frequent use of "one another," Paul indicates the dimensions of love within the community. They respect their leaders with love (5:12), and they encourage one another (4:18), build one another up (5:11), and pursue the good for one another (5:15).

Steadfastness of hope. Just as faith and love stand in a complementary relationship to each other, faith and hope also stand together as the continuing response to the gospel. Indeed, Abraham is the model of one who believed while "hoping against hope" (Rom. 4:18). Love "believes all things, hopes all things" (1 Cor. 13:7). Hope gives endurance and steadfastness (cf. Rom. 5:1–5; 12:13). Hope is the response of those who know that they will be saved from the coming wrath (1 Thess. 1:10) and a response that demarcates the church from those "who have no hope" (1 Thess. 4:13). It is the response of those who have been called into God's kingdom and glory (1 Thess. 2:12). A consistent focus of 1 Thessalonians regarding hope is the parousia of the Lord (1 Thess. 1:10; 2:19; 3:13; 4:13–5:11; 5:23).

Sanctification

While the first three chapters recall the Thessalonians' continuing response to the coming of the gospel and their election, chapters 4 and 5 focus on the end of the narrative and elaborate on the steadfastness of hope (1:3), which Paul has anticipated in the frequent references to the parousia (1:10; 2:19). The prayer in 3:11–13 is the transition to the instructions that follow. The inclusio marked by "holiness" (*hagiōsynē*, 3:13) and "sanctify" (*hagiasai*, 5:23), both in the form of petitions, indicates that it is God who sanctifies the community (cf. 2:13). The petition in 5:23 suggests that sanctification is a process, while *hagiōsynē* in 3:13 describes the final result, when the community is "blameless . . . in holiness" (AT) at the parousia. Indeed, the petition that the Lord may cause the Thessalonians "to increase and abound

34. Wolter, *Paul*, 75.

in love" (3:12) indicates that sanctification is a continuing process. Sanctification is thus a process that occurs as their love increases for one another and for all. The end result (*eis to stērixai*, 3:13) is that they will be blameless in holiness at the parousia.

Sanctification takes on concrete form in the instructions that follow in chapters 4–5. Paul does not employ common rhetorical arguments but declares that his instructions are "the will of God" (4:3). These instructions indicate that sanctification is not only the work of God but also the united response of the community. Paul first elaborates on the nature of sanctification with the instruction that "[their] sanctification" (*hagiasmos*) is "to abstain from sexual immorality [*porneia*]" (4:3 AT), which forms an inclusio with 4:7, "God has not called you to uncleanness [*akatharsia*], but in holiness [*en hagiasmō*]" (AT). The alternative to sexual immorality is to "take a vessel in holiness and in honor" (4:4 AT).[35] That is, the sanctification of "spirit, soul, and body" (5:23 AT) is not limited to special places or events but extends to all of life.[36] Nor is sexual conduct a private matter but the behavior that is expected for the whole community.

Holiness involves believers who conduct themselves "not like the gentiles who do not know God" (4:5 AT). The holy community recognizes boundaries between insiders and outsiders—between the family of believers and "the rest" (4:13 NIV), believers and those who are outside (4:12). Thus holiness involves separation from the world.

Paul's argument assumes that the church lives in continuity with ancient Israel. To be holy in ancient Israel was to separate from the nations and their practices (Lev. 18:2–5). For example, holiness involved the maintenance of a sexual ethic that distinguished Israel from its neighbors (cf. Lev. 18:6–30). For Paul, "your sanctification" involves the adoption of a sexual ethic that is "not . . . like the gentiles" (1 Thess. 4:3, 5). The basis of the argument is the will of God (1 Thess. 4:3), the knowledge that "God is the one who punishes" (1 Thess. 4:6 AT). Paul does not employ the Hellenistic rational arguments but premises drawn from the Jewish tradition.

In subsequent letters, Paul elaborates on the sexual dimension of sanctification. After a vice list that includes sexual matters, he concludes, "You were washed, you were sanctified, you were justified" (1 Cor. 6:11). Sanctification is both a past event and a continuing process. He challenges his readers to present their bodies to righteousness for sanctification (Rom. 6:19, 22).

---

35. The translation of "vessel" (*skeuos*) is disputed. The metaphor can be used for the body (cf. 2 Cor. 4:7) or for a wife (1 Pet. 3:7; BDAG 928). The elaboration of 4:4 in 1 Cor. 7:2 suggests that the alternative to sexual immorality in 1 Thess. 4:4 is "to take a wife."

36. Schrage, "Heiligung als Prozess bei Paulus," 212.

Familial love (1 Thess. 4:9–12) is another dimension of sanctification, as Paul has indicated in 3:12. Paul has expressed gratitude for their labor of love (1:3), but he recognizes that this attribute is a continuing process. Thus he prays that the Lord will make them increase and abound in love to one another and to all (3:12), and he repeats earlier instruction on familial love (4:9–12). The end result of this increase in familial love is that the community will be blameless in holiness at the parousia.

The instruction on familial love after instructions on sexuality may reflect Paul's continuing use of the holiness code, which demanded that the Israelites "not do as they do in the land of Egypt" (Lev. 18:3). God's demand "You shall be holy as I . . . am holy" (Lev. 19:2 AT) included the demand "Love your neighbor as yourself" (Lev. 19:18), which introduces specific instructions for behavior that distinguishes Israel from the nations. Paul interprets the demand primarily as love within the community, indicating that they have been taught to "love one another" (1 Thess. 4:9). This demand is consistent with Paul's repeated references to the Thessalonians as family.

Paul consistently appropriates the language of sanctification to describe his churches. They are "sanctified [hēgiasmenoi], . . . called to be saints [hagioi]" (1 Cor. 1:2). As the perfect tense indicates, sanctification is not only the end result of the community's narrative but also an event of the past and a continuing process. Paul indicates the radical separation of the community from its previous existence and from its surrounding culture, describing the vices that once characterized their conduct, and then concludes with the aorist tense, "You were washed, you were sanctified, you were justified" (1 Cor. 6:11), indicating that both justification and sanctification occurred at baptism. Similarly, in Romans 6:1–11, he speaks of baptism as the entrance into the new aeon and the occasion of justification (cf. Rom. 6:7). The declaration that the believer is dead to sin (Rom. 6:11) is the basis for the imperative "Do not let sin reign in your mortal bodies, to obey its desires" (Rom. 6:12 AT) and the image of the competing powers of sin and righteousness (Rom. 6:12–23). The imperatives reflect the believers' response to what God has done. Paul instructs the readers to "present [their] members as slaves to righteousness" (Rom. 6:19 AT) and to God (Rom. 6:22) "for sanctification" (eis hagiasmon). The twofold mention of "for sanctification" (Rom. 6:19, 22) indicates that sanctification is a process that occurs when the members present themselves to righteousness. As in 1 Thessalonians 4:4, the process occurs when the members deny the desires of the flesh. The end result of the process is eternal life (Rom. 6:22). At the end of the letter, Paul declares that his pastoral ambition is to present the gentiles sanctified (hēgiasmenē) in Christ (Rom. 15:16).

The transition from familial love (1 Thess. 4:9–12) to concerns about the end (4:13–5:11) elaborates on the earlier connection between the labor of love and the steadfastness of hope (1:3). This extended section is probably a response to questions in Thessalonica that undermined the community's hope. Indeed, Timothy's report of their faith and their love (3:6) does not mention their hope. As the outer frame of 4:13–5:11 indicates, Paul's task is not to give a complete essay on eschatology but to reassure the community and challenge the listeners to engage in continued pastoral care for one another. Paul challenges them to comfort one another (4:13) and build one another up (5:11) in order to meet his goal of a blameless people at the parousia (2:19).

First Thessalonians as the Anticipation of Future Correspondence

In 1 Thessalonians, as in all of Paul's correspondence, Paul writes to gentile converts. The shape of 1 Thessalonians indicates that Paul's primary aim is the moral transformation of the community. Indeed, the constant presence of moral exhortation in all of the letters indicates that Paul's ultimate aim is a community that is blameless at the parousia, the end of Israel's narrative. Paul employs theological categories that he will develop in subsequent letters, maintaining the same categories for reflection and elaborating when he is under attack.

Although Paul neither cites Scripture nor mentions the law in 1 Thessalonians, he assumes that gentile converts have been incorporated into Israel's narrative without the traditional badges of Israel's identity—circumcision, Sabbath, and food laws. Living between the turn of the ages and the consummation of Israel's story, they define their existence with the categories drawn from Israel's Scriptures. Paul's letters consistently presuppose that the turn of the ages has come and that the gentile church is participating in Israel's story as it awaits its completion. Paul's focus on the end of Israel's story is a consistent feature, and he expects to see the parousia in the believers' lifetime. It will come as a thief in the night, according to 1 Thessalonians (5:2), while according to Romans, "salvation is nearer . . . than when we believed" (Rom. 13:11) and "the night is almost gone, and the day is at hand" (Rom. 13:12 AT). This consistency of eschatological urgency suggests that one cannot trace a development in Paul's eschatology and the loss of the imminent expectation of the end.

Because of Paul's conviction that Jesus is Lord, he transforms Israel's narrative. He holds to the Pharisaic belief in the resurrection of the faithful, but he maintains that the resurrection of Christ is the firstfruits of the later resurrection of believers. He believes in the one God, but he places the exalted Christ along-side God (cf. 1 Thess. 1:1; 3:12–13; 1 Cor. 8:6). He maintains the apocalyptic expectation of the one who "comes with the clouds" (Dan. 7:13 AT). But for him, the *kyrios* who comes with the clouds is the exalted Lord (1 Thess. 4:17), and those who will arise are the "dead in Christ" (1 Thess. 4:16).

Paul's gospel includes the basic creed that he inherited from the early church that Christ died (1 Thess. 4:14) "for us" (5:10), but he does not de-velop the subject of soteriology. He assumes a Christology that places the exalted Jesus alongside God (1:1; 3:12–13), but he does not develop it. Only in subsequent letters, when these topics are misunderstood or under dispute, does he develop these themes.

Although Paul writes to a gentile church, he distinguishes the listeners from "the Gentiles who do not know God" (4:5), initiating them into Israel's narrative. While he never cites Scripture explicitly in the letter, he initiates the converts into Israel's narrative, establishing an identity, an ethos, and a theo-logical vocabulary that has been shaped by the Old Testament. This identity is the consistent feature in all of the letters.

Paul not only initiates readers into Israel's narrative world but also in-troduces the categories that will be consistent features in all of the letters. Consequently, 1 Thessalonians is a template for development in subsequent letters. All of the following terms are taken from Israel's narrative world.

Election. The Thessalonians' conversion is their election (*eklogē*, 1:4), the occasion when God called the new converts into the kingdom (2:12; 4:7). Paul appeals to the doctrine of election not only in 1 Thessalonians but also in both the undisputed and the disputed letters. God's call is both a call to Paul's apostolic service (Rom. 1:1; 1 Cor. 1:1; Gal. 1:15) and the election of the gentile communities, whom God calls the elect (*eklektoi*, Rom. 8:33; 16:13) and the called (Rom. 1:6–7; 8:28; 1 Cor. 1:24). Their conversion was their calling (*klēsis*, 1 Cor. 1:26; 7:20; *eklektoi*, Col. 3:12), and they are called (*klētoi*) of Jesus Christ (Rom. 1:6). God called the community into the fel-lowship of the Son (1 Cor. 1:9) by grace (Gal. 1:6), which was also a call to freedom (Gal. 5:13).

According to Ephesians, the gentile community was elected from the foun-dation of the world (Eph. 1:4). When Paul explains the presence of gentiles and the absence of Jews in the community of Christ-believers, he transforms the Jewish election tradition. Consistent with the Jewish election tradition, he recalls Israel's history, observing that God chose Isaac rather than Ish-mael (Rom. 9:6–9) and Jacob rather than Esau (Rom. 9:10–13), continuing with other examples of God's sovereign choice. Those chosen, however, are not the Jews alone but Jews and gentiles (Rom. 9:24). Appealing to familiar passages, Paul argues that the "not my people" whom God called to be "my people" (Rom. 9:25) are the gentiles. The election of gentiles does not negate the election of Israel, however, for a remnant remains, according to election (Rom. 11:5–7).

Sanctification. Election is inseparable from sanctification, for God has called the people to holiness (*hagiasmos*, 1 Thess. 4:6–7), and Paul prays that his readers will be fully sanctified at the parousia (1 Thess. 3:13; 5:23). In other letters, believers are "called to be saints" (Rom. 1:7; 1 Cor. 1:2; 2 Cor. 1:1), a term in common use in Second Temple Judaism for the eschatological people of God.[37] But holiness is not only an event of the past but also a continuing process. Paul speaks of holiness as a goal, and believers become slaves of righteousness "for sanctification" (Rom. 6:19, 22).[38] Hence a favorite term for believers is *hagioi*. Paul describes sanctification as an event occurring at baptism (1 Cor. 6:11) and as a continuing process that takes place until the end (1 Thess. 3:13), an important process because Paul's pastoral ambition is to offer the gentiles as a sanctified people and sacrifice to God (Rom. 15:16; cf. 6:19, 22).

Just as Israel's call to be a holy people was expressed with laws on marriage and love for others (Lev. 18–19), sanctification is expressed by sexual behavior that is not like that of the gentiles (1 Thess. 4:5) and by the familial love within the community. Similarly, in Paul's other letters, the moral life is an expression of sanctification (cf. Rom. 6:19; 1 Cor. 6:11), and the final goal is a sanctified people (Rom. 15:16) who are "blameless" at the end (1 Cor. 1:8; 1 Thess. 3:13; cf. Phil. 1:10; 2:15).

The parousia. The parousia of the Lord is the topic in each chapter of 1 Thessalonians (1:10; 2:19; 3:13), culminating in the extended discussion in 4:13–5:11, a description of the end of Israel's narrative as now transformed by the exalted Lord. This topic is a theme in all of the Pauline correspondence, including the disputed letters (cf. Eph. 4:30; 5:5–6; Col. 1:27; 3:6, 8; 2 Thess. 1–2; 1 Tim. 6:14; Titus 1:2; 2:13; 3:7). The community now awaits (cf. Rom. 8:19, 23, 25; 1 Cor. 1:7; Gal. 5:5; Phil. 3:20) the conclusion of the narrative, which includes the resurrection of believers (1 Cor. 15; 2 Cor. 4:14; 5:1–10; Phil. 3:20–21; 1 Thess. 4:14), the return of Christ (Phil. 3:20–21; cf. Rom. 8:23–24; 11:26; 13:11–13), and final judgment (Rom. 14:10; 2 Cor. 5:10; cf. Rom. 2:6–11).

---

37. Balz, "ἅγιος κτλ," *EDNT* 1:18. In late texts, (*hoi*) *hagioi* designates those who belong to God: Dan. 7:21; Tob. 8:15; 12:15; 1 Macc. 1:46. The Qumran community in particular designates itself as "Community of the Holy Ones" (1QSb 1.5) or as "saints of [God's] people" (1QM 6.6; cf. also 1QS 5.18, 20; 11.8).

38. Balz, "ἅγιος κτλ," *EDNT* 1:17.

The judgment. In keeping with the Jewish tradition, Paul anticipates "the day of the Lord" (1 Thess. 5:2, 4; cf. Rom. 2:5, 16; 13:12; 1 Cor. 1:8; 5:5; 2 Cor. 1:14; Phil. 1:6, 10), when God will set the world right by rewarding the faithful and punishing the wicked (cf. Rom. 2:2–16; 14:10; 2 Cor. 5:10). The references to God's justice not only inform the readers but also have a rhetorical function that shapes their behavior.[39] The certainty of God's judgment may have the function of reassuring the church that they will escape God's wrath (Rom. 5:9; 1 Thess. 1:10). This is especially the case in 2 Thessalonians, where God's judgment results in the destruction of those who threaten the community. This judgment is also the occasion when believers will receive a reward (1 Cor. 3:6–8, 12–15; 4:4–5; 2 Cor. 5:9–10).

In other instances, Paul refers to the judgment in paraenetic contexts in which he warns believers that they will stand before God. Believers should not judge others because they themselves will stand before the judgment seat of God (Rom. 14:10). Those who are guilty of vices will not inherit the kingdom of God (1 Cor. 6:9; Gal. 5:21) and will reap what they sow (Gal. 6:6–7). If anyone destroys God's temple, the church, God will destroy that person (1 Cor. 3:17).

Rhetoric and the Development of Paul's Eschatology

While the apocalyptic images are present throughout Paul's letters, the apostle never brings them together into a coherent vision. Consequently, interpreters have attempted to account for the tensions between the different apocalyptic scenarios in the Pauline letters. A common explanation is that one can trace the development of Paul's eschatology from the expectation of an imminent return of Christ in 1 Thessalonians to the focus expressed in Paul's desire "to depart and be with Christ" (Phil. 1:23) and an emphasis on realized eschatology. According to Udo Schnelle, the various eschatological statements in Paul point to the progress in his thinking.[40] The question of the development of Paul's eschatology reflects the larger issue of the development of the apostle's theological vision.[41]

The eschatological vision of 1 Thessalonians, as I argued above, has a decidedly pastoral and rhetorical function. As the inclusio in 4:13 with 5:11 indicates, Paul's task is to give comfort and assurance to a community disoriented by persecution (3:2–5) and the death of some community members

39. Wolter, *Paul*, 217–18.
40. Schnelle, *Wandlungen im paulinischen Denken*, 48.
41. Cf. Landmesser, "Die Entwicklung der paulinischen Theologie," 173–74.

(4:13–18). He gives no comprehensive treatment of the end but focuses on the assurance that the readers will be with Christ (4:14, 17) and with those who have died (4:17), answering the question that is being asked. He also employs eschatological images to restore hope among disoriented believers.[42]

In 1 Corinthians, Paul responds to a new set of questions as he offers details about the end. In this instance, he does not answer a grieving community but responds to those who say that there is no resurrection (1 Cor. 15:12, 16–17). The questions "But how are the dead raised? With what kind of body will they come?" (15:35 AT) and Paul's extended answer (15:35–49) suggest that he is responding here to those who maintain the absurdity of the resuscitation of the body.[43] This denial was inevitable for those who were unfamiliar with Pharisaic eschatology. The Corinthians' questions reflected their dualistic distinction between body and soul, a distinction common in Hellenistic anthropology,[44] leading them to reject the idea of resurrection because of its association with the body. Having earlier confronted Corinthian views of the body (6:12–20), Paul again responds to readers who apparently accept the immortality of the soul but reject the resurrection of the body.

Numerous interpreters have observed that 1 Corinthians 15 is a complete rhetorical unit that may be analyzed with the instruments of Aristotelian rhetoric.[45] As the inclusio at the beginning and end of the chapter indicates, Paul's response is not merely a treatise on the resurrection, for the larger issue is whether the Corinthians have "believed in vain" (*eikē*, 15:2) or labor in vain (*kenos*, 15:58). The repetition of this theme in the chapter reinforces the focus on whether their faith is in vain. According to 15:14, "If Christ has not been raised, our preaching is in vain [*kenon*]" and "your faith is in vain [*kenē*]" (AT). Paul reiterates the claim in 15:17: "If Christ has not been raised, your faith is empty [*mataia*]" (AT). This concern is at the heart of Paul's ministry, as he indicates in recalling that God's grace was not "in vain," adding that he had labored more than anyone (15:10). This echo of the servant's claim "I have labored in vain" (Isa. 49:4) indicates what is at stake for Paul. Belief in the resurrection is the foundation for Paul's ultimate goal: a community that is blameless (1 Cor. 1:8) at the parousia. If the Corinthians reject the resurrection, they are "still in [their] sins" (15:17), and those who have died will have perished (15:18). Indeed, the resurrection of the dead is Paul's driving

---

42. Landmesser, "Die Entwicklung der paulinischen Theologie," 181.
43. See Wegener, "Rhetorical Strategy of 1 Corinthians 15," 438.
44. Wolter, *Paul*, 208.
45. Wegener, "Rhetorical Strategy of 1 Corinthians 15"; see Mack, *Rhetoric and the New Testament*; D. Watson, "Paul's Rhetorical Strategy in 1 Corinthians 15"; Saw, *Paul's Rhetoric in 1 Corinthians 15*.

motivation for ministry (15:30–32) and the Corinthians' motivation for moral living (15:32–33, 58).

In response to the Corinthians' rejection of the bodily nature of resurrection, Paul offers an illustration from nature (15:35–49) before concluding the argument in the peroratio in 15:50–58. He speaks as a prophetic seer, introducing a mystery (cf. Rom. 11:25; 1 Cor. 2:1, 7; 4:1). Paul assumes, as in 1 Thessalonians, that "we shall not all sleep." The new dimension that he describes is that "we shall all be changed" (1 Cor. 15:51 AT). Paul meets the Corinthians' objection with the proposal of a transformed body, omitting features of the eschatological expectation from 1 Corinthians that he had included in 1 Thessalonians: the descent of the Lord and the meeting with him in the air. But he also introduces new dimensions that are not mentioned in 1 Thessalonians. While the transformed body is introduced here, it is not incompatible with the view of meeting Christ in the air.

As the impassioned rhetoric of 15:50–58 indicates, Paul's eschatological language is not a detailed description of the end but an assurance that their "labor is not in vain" (15:58). This peroratio, therefore, combines Paul's prophetic speech with an argument from pathos, as Paul presents an eschatological vision of victory that is designed to encourage the community to maintain its labor in the Lord.

Paul continues this eschatological vision in 2 Corinthians. Interpreters have suggested that the eschatological section in 2 Corinthians 5:1–10 represents a significant shift in Paul's eschatology, for he now declares, "We know that if this earthly house is destroyed, we have a building from God, . . . eternal in the heavens" (2 Cor. 5:1), but he says nothing about the end-time. Udo Schnelle maintains that Paul reckons with his own death before the parousia and has now individualized Christian hope, anticipating a home in heaven before the parousia.[46] This passage must be seen, however, within the context of its rhetorical function. In this instance, the question Paul is answering involves the legitimacy of his ministry. While the integrity of 2 Corinthians is a disputed matter, all sections focus on this central issue. Paul first answers the question with an eschatological claim in the letter's propositio: he anticipates "the day of Christ" (2 Cor. 1:14; cf. Rom. 2:5, 16; 13:12; 1 Cor. 1:8; Phil. 1:6, 10; 1 Thess. 5:2, 4) and hopes that the community will be his boast. In the defense in 2 Corinthians 2:14–7:4, he speaks in the first-person plural, claiming that God's power is present in his weakness (cf. 2 Cor. 4:7–15) and declaring that he has been given over to death (2 Cor. 4:11). Although death and resurrection are present realities (2 Cor. 4:7–11), Paul looks forward to

46. Schnelle, *Apostle Paul*, 249.

the resurrection, paraphrasing the claims of 1 Corinthians and 1 Thessalonians and arguing on the basis of Christian tradition: "Knowing that the one who raised the Lord Jesus from the dead will raise us from the dead and present us with you" (2 Cor. 4:14 AT). The distinction between "we" and "you" indicates that Paul speaks of himself, indicating that he will share the resurrection with the Corinthians.

Paul elaborates in 2 Corinthians 4:16–5:10, first continuing the theme of God's empowerment in his frail body (4:16–18) before speaking of his death in 5:1–10. The tent is the frail human body described in 4:16–18, which may be destroyed (*katalythē*, 5:1) at death but will be replaced by the permanent dwelling, the transformed body. Paul may be thinking of being clothed with the spiritual body (*sōma pneumatikon*, 1 Cor. 15:44) after his death.[47] As the first-person plurals in 2 Corinthians 2:14–7:4 indicate, Paul is continuing to defend his own ministry and destiny, even if his claim also applies to all believers (cf. 2 Cor. 4:14). Similarly, his conclusion that "we will all stand before the judgment seat of Christ" (5:10 AT) is a truth for all believers that Paul applies to himself. That is, Paul still lives within Israel's narrative, expecting "the day of Christ" (1:14), his own resurrection with believers (4:14), and a day of judgment (5:10). The eschatological statement does not represent a change in Paul's eschatology but an answer to the challenge of defending his ministry. The legitimacy of his ministry rests on its ultimate significance at the day of Christ. Opponents should not judge the effectiveness of his ministry by his weak appearance, for the ultimate outcome is the transformed body. As the larger context of 2 Corinthians indicates, Paul's eschatological expectation remains, and he speaks in a variety of images to defend his ministry.

Paul's statement that he desires to "depart and be with Christ" (Phil. 1:23) also raises questions about the development of his view of the end. This echo of Socrates[48] presents Paul as a model to the Philippians of life under hostile conditions. As in 1 Thessalonians (4:14, 17), the focus is on a future "with Christ." This passage must be seen within the larger context of the eschatology of the same letter. Paul still anticipates both that he will be raised from the dead (Phil. 3:11) and that a "day of Christ" (Phil. 1:6, 10) is coming. He declares that "we wait for a Savior, Jesus Christ, who will transform our humble bodies to be conformed to the body of his glory" (Phil. 3:20–21 AT). One may compare human destiny in Romans. Paul says that "if the Spirit of the one who raised Christ from the dead dwells among you, the one who raised

---

47. Schnelle, *Apostle Paul*, 249.
48. Facing death, Socrates says, "I will choose [*airēsomai*] to die rather than to live begging meanly and thus gaining a life far less worthy in exchange for Death." Plato, *Apol.* 9; cf. *Apol.* 38e.

Christ from the dead will give life to your mortal bodies through the Spirit" (Rom. 8:11 AT). According to 8:29, the people of God are foreordained to be conformed (*symmorphon*) to the image of his Son. Both the creation and believers groan, awaiting a transformation (Rom. 8:18–22). Believers await the adoption, the redemption of the body (Rom. 8:23).

Paul offers no consistent image of the end-time. One need not assume that one can track the changes in Paul's eschatology from the expectation of the parousia in 1 Thessalonians to a Hellenized view of the departure of the soul to be with Christ. Within the same letter, for example, Paul speaks of departing to be with Christ (Phil. 1:23) and of awaiting the Savior (Phil. 3:20–21). In Paul's last letter before his imprisonment, he declares that "the day is at hand" (Rom. 13:12 AT). Paul has an inventory of eschatological images that he employs in different ways to respond to the questions that are being asked.[49]

Conclusion: 1 Thessalonians as Early Pauline Theology?

Because of the absence of subjects that become Paul's central focus in the later Pauline correspondence, interpreters have argued that 1 Thessalonians is an early stage in Pauline theology. To track a linear development of Pauline theology is problematic, however, for the practice ignores (1) the lengthy period between Paul's conversion and his first extant letter, (2) the brief period included for the undisputed letters (approximately seven years), and (3) our uncertainty about the sequence of the letters. Furthermore, these themes cannot be isolated from their rhetorical function. Nevertheless, 1 Thessalonians deserves special attention as probably Paul's first letter. This catechesis is probably the standard instruction that he gives in all of his churches and a template of Pauline theology. He develops the categories drawn from Israel's narrative and early Christian tradition—the gospel, Christology, election, sanctification, and the end-time—in subsequent letters, theologizing in response to the issues that emerge. His treatment of these topics corresponds to his rhetorical aims in each letter.

In 1 Thessalonians, Paul's argument is based on the premises and theological categories that he has inherited from the Jewish and early Christian traditions. In his pastoral goal of presenting a blameless people to Christ, he not only articulates a theology but also offers his community the identity and ethos that will reassure them of their hope. He argues from ethos, pathos, and logos, and the arrangement of the argument corresponds, at least partially,

49. Wolter, *Paul*, 212–13.

to the arrangement recommended in the rhetorical handbooks. However, the premises for his argument are drawn from the Jewish and early Christian traditions.

The absence of major Pauline themes does not indicate that 1 Thessalonians is the early example of Paul's developing theology. The themes that dominate in Galatians and Romans—the righteousness of God and justification by faith in Christ—are not present because Paul has no need to defend the inclusion of gentiles in the community, as in later letters. While Paul does not employ the terminology of God's righteousness, his reference to salvation from God's wrath (1 Thess. 1:10; 5:9) and the reminder that God is an avenger (*ekdikos*, 4:6) presuppose the Pharisaic view of God's righteous judgment when God vindicates the righteous and punishes the disobedient.[50] References to election, saving faith, and salvation from the wrath of God are connected to justification.[51] Thus Paul's doctrine of justification is implicit in 1 Thessalonians.

The incorporation of gentiles into the people of God and the claim that Christ saves the community from the coming wrath (1:10) place the Torah in a new light. While Paul's moral instructions are consistent with the requirements of the Torah (4:1–12; cf. Lev. 18–19), salvation by the death of Jesus relativizes the significance of the law for believers. Paul's later claim that no one is justified by works of the law is anticipated in 1 Thessalonians.

One cannot determine the extent to which Paul's theology develops from 1 Thessalonians to Romans, for he elaborates on the categories introduced in 1 Thessalonians in response to the challenges that he faces. First Thessalonians, like the other letters, is a pastoral work intended to guide the church toward moral formation. Paul's focus is not a systematic treatment of theological themes but the continued persuasion of his people to conduct themselves worthily of the gospel (1 Thess. 2:12; cf. Eph. 4:1; Phil. 1:27). In 1 Corinthians, for example, he offers additional reflection on the subject of relations with outsiders (1 Cor. 5:9) and of marriage (1 Cor. 7:1) in order to clarify the earlier catechetical instruction. Paul's theologizing is largely a clarification of the basic catechesis he gives in 1 Thessalonians. Thus while we cannot trace a linear development of Paul's theology, we can observe his continuing dialogue with his churches and his persuasive means of ensuring the fulfillment of his pastoral goal.

---

50. Schließer, "Paulustheologien im Vergleich," 64.
51. Hengel, "Die Stellung des Apostels Paulus zum Gesetz," 214.

6

Christology and Persuasion

When God "revealed his son" to Paul and commissioned him "to preach [Jesus] among the nations" (Gal. 1:16 AT), the apostle ceased to know Christ "from a human point of view" (2 Cor. 5:16). Having earlier regarded Jesus as a threat to the way of life based on the Torah,[1] he then reevaluated his previous commitments and identity in light of this divine revelation. When Paul defended his ministry, he asked, "Have I not seen Jesus our Lord?" (1 Cor. 9:1). He described the revelation as the occasion when God said, "Let light shine out of darkness," as in the creation, and "[shine] in our hearts for the light of the knowledge of the glory of God in the face of Jesus Christ" (2 Cor. 4:6).

This reevaluation did not involve the abandonment of his belief in Israel's God and in a narrative that extends from Adam to the ultimate reign of God. He prays regularly to God the Father (Rom. 1:8–10; 1 Cor. 1:4; 2 Cor. 1:3–4; Phil. 1:3–5; 1 Thess. 1:2–3; Philem. 4) and requests that believers join him in prayer to God (Rom. 15:30). He maintains the belief in a community composed of Abraham's children, in Israel's election, and in the hope of the Davidic messiah.

The letters consistently refer to Jesus as Christ (*christos*), Son (*huios*), and Lord (*kyrios*). Paul's new understanding of Jesus cannot be explained on the basis of the titles alone, however. He has larger questions: How could the new understanding of Jesus be incorporated into his inherited beliefs? What

---

1. See Dunn, *Did the First Christians Worship Jesus?*, 115.

role do his christological statements have in persuading his communities to be transformed by the gospel?

Paul undoubtedly viewed Jesus as the messiah of Israel. The term "Christ" identifies Jesus as the anointed one of Israel's expectation.[2] Paul's identification of Jesus as God's Son is also rooted in Israel's understanding of the Davidic messiah. The creedal statement "his Son, born of the seed of David according to the flesh, but designated Son of God in power according to the spirit of holiness" (Rom. 1:3–4 AT) may be a pre-Pauline confession, but it is also Paul's own conviction. However, Paul inherited the earliest church convictions about the messiah that were not consistent with Jewish expectation, and he elaborated on these convictions in his letters. Not only was the violent death of the messiah unknown in Jewish tradition, but the divine status of the messiah was also not consistent with messianic expectation.

Because Christology is never a point of contention between Paul and his converts, he never offers a comprehensive christological reflection but assumes that the readers share his Christology as he consistently indicates the place of Jesus alongside God. The regular greeting "Grace to you and peace from God the Father and the Lord Jesus Christ" (cf. Rom. 1:7; 1 Cor. 1:3) indicates the place of the exalted Jesus alongside God. Paul remains a monotheist, and he regularly distinguishes Jesus from God; the earthly Jesus is now the Lord who, along with God the Father, extends grace and peace in the salutation of the letters. This relationship is consistent throughout Paul's correspondence. The Thessalonians "turned to God from idols to serve the living and true God and to wait for his Son from heaven, whom he raised from the dead" (1 Thess. 1:9–10) and who saves from the coming wrath of God. Paul speaks of the Thessalonians' faith in God (1 Thess. 1:7) and prays that "God the Father and the Lord Jesus will guide [his] way to them" (1 Thess. 3:11 AT), that the Lord (*kyrios*) will increase their love (3:12), and that they will be blameless before God at the parousia of Christ (1 Thess. 3:13). It is the Lord Jesus who will come with a shout at the end (1 Thess. 4:13–18).

Paul distinguishes God from the risen Christ, but he maintains a close identification between them. He speaks of the judgment seat of God (Rom. 14:10) and the judgment seat of Christ (2 Cor. 5:10). Believers have "peace with God through our Lord Jesus Christ" (Rom. 5:1), receive the love of God through Jesus Christ (Rom. 5:6–8; 8:39), "boast in God through our Lord" (Rom.

---

2. See Hengel, *Studies in Early Christology*, 1, who observes that "the name *christos* appears 270 times in the undisputed Pauline letters. The compound name *Iēsous christos* or its variation *christos Iēsous* occurs 109 times."

5:1–11), and give thanks to God through Jesus Christ (Rom. 7:25), knowing that it was God who raised Jesus from the dead (1 Cor. 6:14; 2 Cor. 4:14).

In some instances, Paul employs *kyrios*, the common Septuagint rendering of Yahweh, in reference to God, while in other instances, the term is used for the exalted Christ. In numerous other cases, the identity of the *kyrios* is a matter of scholarly debate. While in some instances Paul maintains the traditional use of *kyrios* for Yahweh (cf. Rom. 4:8; 9:28–29; 11:3, 34; 1 Cor. 3:20; 14:21; 2 Cor. 6:17–18), he most frequently employs the term for the exalted Christ, at times citing Scriptures that originally referred to Yahweh (Rom. 10:13; cf. Phil. 2:11). In some instances, the referent is unclear (2 Cor. 3:16; 10:17; 1 Thess. 4:6).

The absence of detailed christological reflection in Paul's writings indicates that the exalted status of Jesus was not in question. Indeed, Paul's original preaching and catechesis proclaimed that "Jesus is Lord" (2 Cor. 4:5), and the church consistently expressed this conviction in worship, as the cry "Maranatha" (1 Cor. 16:22 KJV) indicates. Paul inherited the conviction from the Jerusalem church that Jesus was now at the right hand of God (Rom. 8:34; cf. Acts 2:34; 1 Cor. 15:25) and would return from heaven (1 Thess. 1:10; 4:16). In several instances, this christological confession becomes the premise for Paul's persuasive task. The rhetorical function of Paul's Christology plays a vital role in his task of ensuring the ultimate transformation of his communities.

Christology and Persuasion in Philippians

The poetic narrative in Philippians 2:6–11 offers a window into the intersection of Paul's Christology and rhetoric. This passage is the centerpiece of a letter in which Paul's goal is to lead his community to be his boast at the day of Christ and "shine like stars in the world" (2:15–16). As in all of the undisputed letters, this goal determines the nature of his persuasion. Although this letter does not precisely correspond either to ancient letters or to epistles, its focus on dissuading from one kind of behavior (cf. 2:3) and commending a future course of action (cf. 2:12–18; 4:2–9) has points of contact with deliberative rhetoric. Contrary to the numerous attempts to demonstrate that Philippians is a composite of two or more letters written on different occasions, the letter exhibits a coherent persuasive strategy that is often ignored.

The Rhetorical Situation

Having recently been imprisoned (Phil. 1:12–13), Paul writes to assure an anxious community of the advance of the gospel (1:12, 25) and to commend a course of action for the readers, who also live under precarious circumstances. The exhortation not to be intimidated by adversaries (1:28) suggests also that the Philippians are confronted by charges of sedition. Paul indicates that the Philippians suffer (1:29), are partners in tribulation (4:14), and are engaged in the same struggle with Paul (1:30). The consistent theme of suffering (e.g., 1:28–30; 2:8; 3:10; 4:14–15) suggests that the church is confronted by adversaries among the populace of this Roman colony.[3] The theme of unity (1:27–30; 2:1–4, 12–18; 4:2–3) suggests that, for Paul, a unified church is indispensable for the community's continued existence.

The Arrangement and Argument

In the opening thanksgiving, Paul reassures the community that, despite its precarious situation, "the one who began a good work among [them] will bring it to completion at the day of Christ" (Phil. 1:6 AT), and he prays that the community will be "pure and blameless" at the day of Christ (1:10). This transformation will take place as their love abounds "more and more" (1:9), and it will be complete when their lowly bodies are conformed to the image of the Son (3:21). The community faces major obstacles, however, in reaching that goal. Coming from a highly competitive society and faced with the hostility of the populace (1:28), they face major challenges in becoming the transformed community. The opening thanksgiving is not only a prayer but also a performative speech, an encouragement to the community to recognize its narrative existence and to continue toward its goal. It functions as the exordium of the letter, introducing the topic and making the audience favorably disposed.

In the narratio (1:12–26), Paul demonstrates that he, with his selfless attitude and courageous outlook in anticipation of death, is the model for others to follow.[4] Paul's example is the basis for the propositio (1:27–30), the instruction for the whole community to face the hostility of the populace, "standing in one spirit, struggling together in one soul" (1:27 AT). The remainder of the body of the letter (probatio, 2:1–3:21) is a series of three exempla (2:1–11, 19–30; 3:1–21) that lay the foundation for the community's capacity to have "one mind" (2:2; 4:2).

The primary exemplum is the poetic narrative in 2:6–11, Paul's most extended christological statement. This exemplum may already be known to the community; thus it probably has special persuasive force. Indeed, the theme of the descent and exaltation of Christ—preexistence, incarnation,

---

3. Thompson and Longenecker, *Philippians and Philemon*, 15.
4. See Ramsaran, "Living and Dying, Living Is Dying," 333–34.

and exaltation—is deeply rooted in the Christian tradition (cf. John 1:1–18; 2 Cor. 8:9; Col. 1:15–20; Heb. 1:1–4), having been developed prior to Paul.[5] One may compare Paul's declaration that "God sent his own son" (Gal. 4:4; cf. Rom. 8:3) and his appeal to the one who exchanged riches for poverty (2 Cor. 8:9) as an indication of his understanding of Christ's preexistence and incarnation.

As Paul indicates in the introduction to the poetic narrative, a shared *phronēsis* (Phil. 2:2) is necessary for unity and becomes a reality when the community holds the mind-set (2:5, *touto phroneite*) that it has "in Christ."[6] This imperative is the transition to the narrative in 2:6–11. The poetic nature of the narrative is indicated with the alternation of participles and main verbs, which describes a drama in three acts.

> Being in the Form of God
> he did not count equality with God
>   a thing to be exploited,
> but emptied himself,
>   taking the form of a slave,
>   becoming in the likeness of a human.
> Being found in human form,
>   he humbled himself to death,
>   even death on a cross.
>
> Therefore God highly exalted him
>   and gave him a name
>   that is above every other name,
> in order that in the name of Jesus
>   every knee will bow,
>   in heaven and on earth and under the earth,
> and every tongue will confess
>   that Jesus Christ is Lord,
>   to the glory of God the Father. (AT)

While scholars almost unanimously regard the passage as a hymn or poetic narrative, they disagree over the delineation of the strophes. Because 2:6–8 and 2:9–11 are of roughly equal length, Ernst Lohmeyer identified the passage as a hymn and maintained that *dio* (therefore) in 2:9 marks the beginning of its second half.[7] More persuasive is the recognition that the alternation of

---

5. Cf. Hengel and Schwemer, *Paul between Damascus and Antioch*, 373.
6. See Gorman, *Cruciformity*, 43, who maintains that the best translation of Phil. 2:5 is "Have this mindset in your community, which is indeed a community in Christ."
7. Lohmeyer, *Kyrios Jesus*, 64.

participles and main verbs marks a drama in three stages: (1) incarnation of the preexistent one (2:6–7a), (2) death on the cross (2:7b–8), and (3) exaltation (2:9–11). Although the presence of numerous words in this poetic narrative that do not appear elsewhere in the Pauline letters may suggest that Paul is citing an earlier tradition, he gives abundant evidence elsewhere that this drama corresponds to his basic conviction (cf. 2 Cor. 8:9).

Paul first refers to Jesus Christ, "who was in the form [*morphē*] of God" and "equal to God" (Phil. 2:6 AT) in his preexistent status. Although *morphē* in most instances refers to shape or outward appearance, here it refers to the nature of one's existence, as the parallel with "form of a slave" (2:7 AT) indicates. The term is the equivalent of "image" (*eikōn*) of God, a phrase that Paul uses elsewhere (2 Cor. 4:4; cf. Col. 1:15). Following early church tradition, Paul probably derives the images from the wisdom tradition. Personified Wisdom is the image of God (cf. Col. 1:15) and "reflection of God" (Wis. 7:25–26 AT). Philo identifies Wisdom with the Logos, the image of God (*Confusion* 97, 147; *Flight* 101). The "image of God" and "reflection of God" are the equivalent of the "form" (*morphē*) of God that is introduced in the poetic narrative. For Paul, it is the equivalent to "equality with God" (Phil. 2:6 AT). Paul's use of the wisdom tradition is also evident in the confessional statement in 1 Corinthians 8:6, which is the premise for the extended argument in 1 Corinthians 8:1–11:1 (see below).

Paul depicts the narrative of descent in a sequence of verbs that describe a downward spiral in which Christ is the subject of the action, followed by the climactic verbs, in which God is the subject ("he highly exalted him"). The preexistent one did not count his status as "something to be exploited."[8] As N. T. Wright has commented, "Over against the standard picture of oriental despots, who understand their position as something to be used for their advantage, Jesus understood his position to mean self-negation, the vocation described in verses 7–8."[9] Other verbs describe the downward spiral of descent: he "emptied himself" and he "humbled himself" at the cross (Phil. 2:7–8) before God "highly exalted him" (2:9).

In the first act of the narrative, he "emptied himself, taking the form of a slave" and "becoming in the likeness of a human" (Phil. 2:7 AT). This descent recalls Paul's claim that God "sent his Son, born of woman" (Gal. 4:4; cf. Rom. 8:3) and the statement that the one who was rich became poor (2 Cor.

---

8. R. W. Hoover demonstrates that *harpagmon hēgēsato* is used in antiquity for something that is at one's disposal. Hoover, "*Harpagmos* Enigma," 118. Dio Chrysostom employs *harpazō* to describe improper ways of using authority in contrast to the behavior of the ideal ruler (*4 Regn.* 4.95).

9. Wright, "Jesus Christ Is Lord: Phil. 2:5–11," 83.

8:9). With the phrase "form of a slave," he indicates the depth of the descent and the total humanity of Jesus.

The second strophe has the same alternation of participles and verbs, indicating the movement from one status to another:

> Being found in human form,
>> he humbled himself to death,
>> even death on a cross. (Phil. 2:7b–8 AT)

In the first line of the second strophe, "being found in human form," Paul builds on the last line of the first strophe, "becoming in the likeness of a human." The main verb, "humbled himself to death," indicates the further stage of the descent, and the added phrase "even death on a cross" indicates that absolute nadir of the descent.

According to the final verbs introducing the third strophe, "highly exalted him" and "gave him a name that is above every other name," what the believers now confess—"Jesus is Lord"—will be confessed by the whole creation in the future. In the culmination of the narrative, the words that are attributed to God in Isaiah 45:23 ("To me every knee shall bow, every tongue shall swear") are now attributed to the exalted Christ. The *kyrios* of the Septuagint is Jesus Christ. As in other Pauline texts, the exaltation of Christ, with the prerogatives given by God, now places him above the cosmic powers (cf. Rom. 8:38–39; 1 Cor. 15:25). Nevertheless, Paul maintains the distinction between God and Jesus, for it is God who "highly exalted" the one who emptied and humbled himself.

Otfried Hofius and Richard Bauckham have observed that this poetic narrative echoes the description of the suffering servant of Isaiah 52–53.[10] He went to his death voluntarily (Isa. 53:4, 10, 12) and in humble obedience (53:7), a death that was shameful (53:3, 9, 12). He was taken away "by oppression [*en tē tapeinōsei*] and judgment" (53:8 LXX), and he "poured himself out to death" (53:12). Nevertheless, he will be "lifted up [*hypsōthēsetai*] and shall be very high" (52:13 LXX). As a result, all nations will recognize God's sovereignty (52:15) and see the salvation of God (52:10; cf. 40:5; 45:22; 49:6).

The poetic narrative is characterized by an economy of words. Interpreters continue to analyze the terms, the form of the entire composition, and the conceptual background, seeking clarification. Paul does not elaborate on the meaning of "form of God," "equality with God" (Phil. 2:6 AT), *harpagmos* ("grasped" or "exploited"), "emptied himself" (2:7 AT), or other terms, for

10. Hofius, *Der Christushymnus Philipper 2,6–11*, 70–71; Bauckham, "Worship of Jesus in Philippians 2:9–11."

his task is to cast a rhetorical vision that will shape the mind-set of a countercultural community. The brevity gives the narrative its poetic power, for the whole is more powerful than the sum of its parts. With the poetic expression, Paul's purpose is to create an atmosphere among his readers "in order to bring his audience into a mimetic experience of Christ's self-renunciation . . . as a representation of the kind of self-renunciation" that he wishes to inculcate among them.[11]

Paul initiates the series of exempla with the memory of the one who was in the form of God (*morphē theou*, 2:6) and emptied himself into the form (*morphē*) of a slave. He concludes the probatio with the declaration that the exalted Lord (2:9–11) will return and "transform the body of our humiliation that it may be conformed [*symmorphon*] to the body of his glory" (3:21 AT). Those who are conformed (*symmorphizomenos*) to his death (3:10), will be conformed (*symmorphon*) to the body of his glory.

The remainder of the argument rests on exempla of those who took up the spirit of self-renunciation. Timothy does not think of himself (2:20), and Epaphroditus risked his life for others (2:30). According to chapter 3, Paul has applied the downward spiral to his own life, counting all of his achievements as loss for the sake of Christ (3:1–11) while he awaits the ultimate vindication (3:12–16). He invites the readers to imitate him in this self-renunciation (3:17). In the peroratio (4:1–20), Paul reiterates basic ethical instructions that unite the community (4:1–9) and concludes with an additional argument from his ethos (4:10–20). Paul thanks the Philippians for their gift, but he also depicts his own response as one who can be content under the most distressing circumstances.

While the poetic narrative of Philippians 2:6–11 may be Paul's most extended christological statement, its primary purpose is not to articulate his Christology but to persuade the community to enter into this narrative of self-renunciation, for only by this means can the community become "blameless" at the day of Christ (2:15–16). In a competitive society, believers can be a counterculture as they are shaped by the narrative of self-renunciation.

Christology and Rhetoric in the Corinthian Correspondence

In 1 Corinthians, as in Philippians, Paul expresses the hope that his converts will ultimately be "blameless at the day of Christ" (1 Cor. 1:8 AT; cf. Phil. 2:15–16). However, partisan rivalry, anticommunal behavior, and self-serving

---

11. Selby, *Not with Wisdom of Words*, 138.

conduct, expressed in a variety of ways in the multiple problems at Corinth, indicate the immense distance between the Corinthian church and that goal.[12] Paul's task is to ensure that the members "speak the same thing" (1 Cor. 1:10 AT) and practice self-denying love (cf. 1 Cor. 8:1; 13; 16:14), building up a community that will last until the end (1 Cor. 3:5–17; 8:1; 14:1–5). This challenge requires that the Corinthians acquire an alternative view of community, and Christology plays a central role.

Reinterpreting the Shema (1 Cor. 8:6)

First Corinthians, written in response to the anticommunal conduct of some of the members of the church (see chap. 7), is composed of a sequence of self-contained rhetorical units on a variety of issues. In 8:1–11:1, Paul responds to those who claim the right to eat meat offered to idols, an issue that is inseparable from the larger problem of idolatry, which Paul also discusses (10:1–22). Paul first addresses the question indirectly, finding common ground with his interlocutors in 8:1–6 and appealing to what he originally taught them. Indeed, both those who ate food offered to idols ("the wise") and those who objected to this practice ("the weak," 8:7, 9) could appeal to the same tradition.[13]

> For us, there is one God, the Father,
>   from whom [ex hou] are all things and we are unto him,
> and one Lord, Jesus Christ,
>   through whom [di' hou] are all things, and we are through him.
>   (1 Cor. 8:6 AT)

Paul adapts the words of the Shema, adding the word "Father" and distinguishing between God the Father and Jesus Christ, but includes Jesus Christ, calling him Lord. The one God is the creator, "from whom [ex hou] are all things" (cf. Rom. 4:17; 11:36; 1 Tim. 2:5). That we are "unto him" anticipates the time when God is "all and in all" (1 Cor. 15:28). God is both the origin and the goal of all things.[14] The distinction between God the Father and the Lord Jesus Christ is evident in the prepositions used in the formula. While God is the Father "from whom [ex hou] are all things," the Lord Jesus Christ is the one "through whom [di' hou] are all things, and we are through him" (1 Cor. 8:6 AT). Paul joins other New Testament writers in attributing to Christ

---

12. On the rhetorical situation in 1 Corinthians, see chap. 7 below.
13. Eriksson, *Traditions as Rhetorical Proof*, 156.
14. Schrage, *Der erste Brief an die Korinther*, 2:243.

the role that was associated with preexistent Wisdom and the Logos in the literature of Hellenistic Judaism (cf. John 1:3; Heb. 1:2).[15] This *kyrios*—not Wisdom, the Logos, or the Torah—is the mediator of creation,[16] standing "at the beginning of the creation as well as the new creation."[17] Our existence is "through him."

The confession is probably drawn from early catechesis. Paul does not offer an ontological statement about the existence of the gods but introduces the confession with "for us." That is, the believing community confesses one God and one Lord. As with the Shema, this is a confession of the absolute loyalty of believers to God, a loyalty that precludes any connection to idols. It prepares the way for the concluding argument in 1 Corinthians 10:14–22, in which Paul demands that the Corinthians "flee idolatry" (1 Cor. 10:14 AT) because one cannot drink from the cup of the Lord and the cup of demons (10:21).

By introducing a controversial topic in an indirect way, Paul makes the audience favorably disposed. Thus 8:1–6 is the exordium of Paul's argument in 8:1–11:1, and the christological confession in 8:6 is part of the exordium. He builds on the argument with a refutatio in 8:7–13 and exempla in 9:1–10:22 before concluding with the resolution in 10:23–11:1.

The implications of the christological confession become evident in the developing argument. Paul argues that anyone who destroys the weaker believer through the exercise of one's knowledge not only sins against that believer but also sins against Christ (8:12). This recalls the claim that individuals are members of Christ (6:15). In the example of Israel's journey in the wilderness, Paul recalls the Jewish haggadic tradition of the rock that followed Israel and from which Israel drank, concluding that "the rock was Christ" (10:4). Once more, Paul draws on traditions of Hellenistic Judaism. Philo speaks of the rock as Wisdom (*Alleg. Interp.* 2.86) and as the divine Logos (*Worse* 115–18).

Paul challenges the listeners not to "test Christ" (1 Cor. 10:9 AT), as some of the Israelites in the wilderness tested God (Ps. 78:18). When he compares the Lord's Supper to pagan sacrificial meals, he reminds the readers that they cannot drink from the cup of the Lord and the cup of demons (1 Cor. 10:21) and exhorts them not to "provoke the Lord to jealousy" (1 Cor. 10:22 AT), echoing the statement that Israel provoked God to jealousy (Deut. 32:21). Paul begins the discussion of idolatry by placing Jesus Christ within the Shema, and he concludes by identifying Jesus as the *kyrios* who demands total loyalty. Just as he argued earlier that individual bodies are "members of

---

15. Dunn, *Theology of Paul*, 81. For the denial of the influence of wisdom traditions, see Fee, *Pauline Christology*, 595–619.

16. Schrage, *Der erste Brief an die Korinther*, 2:244.

17. Schrage, *Der erste Brief an die Korinther*, 2:244.

Christ" (1 Cor. 6:15), he now argues that the community that participates in the table of the Lord is "one body."

Although Paul offers no developed Christology, his exhortation to the Corinthians assumes a Christology that serves a rhetorical purpose. The confessional statement in 8:4–6 is an appeal to the community's tradition; thus it is an argument from logos. It is the basis for the argument demanding absolute loyalty to Christ and the foundation for the demand to "flee idolatry" (1 Cor. 10:14 AT).

Christ as Subordinate to God

First Corinthians 3:23. In response to the partisan cries "I am of Paul," "I am of Apollos," "I am of Cephas," and "I am of Christ" (1 Cor. 1:12 AT), Paul offers an extended theology of the cross (1:18–2:17), demonstrating that the cross destroys all boasting about human leaders (3:21) and that Paul and Apollos are only servants (see chap. 7 below). At the conclusion of the argument, Paul offers a final reason for not boasting about human leaders: "All things are yours, whether Paul or Apollos or Cephas, . . . all things are yours, and you are of Christ, and Christ is of God" (3:21–23 AT). The genitive plural "yours" (*hymōn*) stands in sharp contrast to the genitive with the first-person singular of "I am of ___" (1:12), as Paul appeals to corporate rather than individual identity. He concludes, "You—the community—are of Christ, and Christ is of God" (3:23 AT). The genitive with the person's name was commonly used for the relationship of children to parents and slaves to masters. Thus the NRSV appropriately translates, "You belong to Christ"; that is, the corporate community belongs to Christ, not to human leaders. To be "of Christ" is to demonstrate that Christ is not divided (cf. 1:13), to be "members of Christ" (6:15) and parts of the body of Christ (12:13–31).

Paul concludes the argument, "And Christ is of God" (1 Cor. 3:23 AT). Although Paul has frequently described Christ as "equal to God" (Phil. 2:6 AT) and the "image of God" (2 Cor. 4:4) and even applies *kyrios*, the term for God in the Septuagint, to Jesus Christ, here he declares that Jesus Christ is subordinate to God. As Paul has already declared, believers are "in Christ," who is "wisdom from God" (1 Cor. 1:30). To place Christ in a subordinate position to God is to place the subordination of believers into the larger context and reinforce the insistence that one cannot boast about people.

First Corinthians 11:2–16. Whereas the christological claim of subordination is the conclusion to Paul's treatment of factionalism in chapters 1–4, in 11:2–16 it is the premise of the argument over head coverings. This self-contained unit is the introduction to the larger discussion of public worship.

Before Paul addresses practices in worship, he addresses issues of attire. He does not indicate what evoked the discussion but argues that the church must have common expectations on head coverings in conformity with all of the churches (11:16). Indeed, the *captatio benevolentiae* in 11:2 ("I praise you . . . that you keep the traditions," AT) forms an inclusio with the reference to the practice of all the churches in 11:16.

Paul begins with the exordium (11:2) that makes the audience favorably disposed. The propositio of the argument is the christological statement of 11:3. The probatio, based on arguments from scriptural interpretation, comes next in 11:4–12 and is followed by a peroratio in 11:13–16. Paul appeals to arguments derived both from Scripture (11:4–12) and from the customary rhetorical proofs.[18]

Because the issue is the head covering, Paul formulates the christological statement in 11:3. "I want you to know" may introduce a tradition that is unknown to the Corinthians (cf. 10:1) that Paul delivers on his own authority.[19] Before giving rules for covering the head (11:4–12), he describes an order of creation, using the word "head" in the metaphorical sense to describe the hierarchy of being. Whereas Paul speaks directly to the whole church in the similar passage in 3:23 ("You are of Christ, and Christ is of God," AT), his focus is on an order of creation involving men and women here, as the unusual sequence suggests.[20] In other words, the conclusion "the head of Christ is God" (AT; cf. 11:23) is reminiscent of the christological statement in 3:23 ("You are of Christ, and Christ is of God," AT). Paul elaborates on this sequence, maintaining that "the man is the image and glory of God" and "the woman the glory of the man" (11:7 AT). The primary function of this statement in the argument is the focus on hierarchy.[21] This premise is based on Paul's understanding of Scripture, as the elaboration in 11:4–12 indicates. Paul does not focus on the subordination of Christ but introduces the principle of subordination that he will apply to the issue of head coverings. He does not lay out a developed Christology but appeals to the place of Christ in the order of creation to encourage the readers to subordinate themselves to the divine order.

First Corinthians 15:20–28. These verses are the core of Paul's argument in response to one aspect of the rhetorical situation in Corinth: some say that

18. Paul argues on the basis of what is "fitting" (*prepon*) in 11:13. For *prepon* in argumentation, see Lausberg, *Handbook of Literary Rhetoric*, §1055.

19. On Paul's use of "I want you to know" or "I do not want you to be ignorant" to introduce his prophetic voice, see Rom. 11:25; 1 Thess. 4:13.

20. In 3:23, the ascending sequence is you (plural), Christ, God. Cf. the sequence in 11:3: the head of every man is Christ; the head of the woman is the man; the head of Christ is God.

21. Fenske, *Die Argumentation des Paulus*, 155.

there is no resurrection of the dead (15:12). What the Corinthians meant by this claim is debatable. However, Paul's response to the Corinthians indicates that the resurrection of Christ was not disputed. The response to the question "By what body?" suggests that the Corinthians have ridiculed the concept of the bodily resurrection (15:35–39). This issue is particularly pertinent because some in the community have died (11:30). Having earlier alluded to the resurrection of the body (6:14), Paul faces the challenge of persuading his readers that the bodies of believers will be transformed and raised. As an argument attempting to dissuade his readers from one belief and encourage future conduct (cf. 15:58), the discussion has the marks of deliberative rhetoric.[22] The christological claim in 15:20–28 is the core of the argument, expanding on earlier confessional statements (3:23; 11:2–3), both of which declare the subordination of Christ to God.

As the inclusio marking the beginning and end of this discussion indicates, belief in the bodily resurrection determines whether the Corinthians have believed in vain (15:2, 58), a theme that recurs in the argument (cf. 15:10, 14). Paul's desire for a transformed community requires that they believe the gospel that he has preached (15:1–2). The introduction reminding them of the gospel that he preached and what they believed (15:1–3a, 11) begins the argument by finding common ground with the Corinthians; thus it is the exordium of this self-contained unit.[23] The list of witnesses to the resurrection (15:3b–11) is the narratio summarizing the history of the case.[24] In 15:12–19, Paul refutes the claim that "there is no resurrection" with a series of syllogistic arguments, indicating that the Corinthians' claim would be a denial of what they have already believed, for one cannot separate the resurrection of Christ from that of other believers.[25] This argument from the contrary is the refutatio pointing out the absurd contradictions to which a denial of the resurrection leads and the consequences for the Corinthians themselves.[26]

Having refuted the opponents' view in 15:12–19, Paul states in positive terms the inseparability of the resurrection of Christ and the believers' resurrection. The propositio of this chapter is the affirmation "now Christ has been

22. Eriksson, *Traditions as Rhetorical Proof*, 245.

23. Schrage, *Der erste Brief an die Korinther*, 4:17. Eriksson, *Traditions as Rhetorical Proof*, 246, describes the opening words of 1 Cor. 15 as *insinuatio*, in which the speaker gains the goodwill of the listeners by indirectly approaching the topic, especially in instances in which they have been won over by the opposing side. See Lausberg, *Handbook of Literary Rhetoric*, §280.

24. Eriksson, *Traditions as Rhetorical Proof*, 246.

25. See Eriksson, *Traditions as Rhetorical Proof*, 255–56.

26. Eriksson, *Traditions as Rhetorical Proof*, 261; Schrage, *Der erste Brief an die Korinther*, 4:110.

raised, the firstfruits of those who sleep" (15:20 AT),[27] which Paul develops in the probatio in 15:21–49; he then concludes with the stirring peroratio in 15:50–58.

Paul elaborates on the propositio in 15:21–28, beginning with a premise that is apparently known to the readers (death came by one man; in Adam, all die) as a basis for the comparison (through a man is the resurrection of the dead; in Christ, all will be made alive).[28] Paul focuses his comparison of Christ to Adam not, as in Romans (5:12–21), on the entrance of and spread of sin but on death and resurrection as he shapes the interpretation of the creation story to fit the rhetorical situation. As in Romans, Christ is the second Adam.[29]

Paul develops the christological claim further in 1 Corinthians 15:23–28 with his focus on "each in his own order," describing a sequence of events that leads to the end, which is unparalleled elsewhere in Pauline literature. As the firstfruits (aparchē; cf. 1 Cor. 15:20; Rom. 8:23), Christ is at the beginning of the sequence (1 Cor. 15:23b), followed by those who are "of Christ" (cf. 1 Cor. 3:23) at the parousia, and then the end (telos) (1 Cor. 15:24). Two parallel clauses introduced by "when" (hotan) describe the events associated with the end:

when he delivers the kingdom to God the Father,
when he destroys every rule and authority and power. (15:24 AT)

Paul clearly distinguishes between the exalted Christ and God. He also distinguishes between the parousia and the end (telos), but he does not indicate the amount of time between the two events. The parousia is the return of Christ (cf. Matt. 24:3, 27, 37, 39; 1 Thess. 2:19; 3:13; 4:15; 5:23); telos is the term for the end of time (Matt. 10:22; 24:6 par.; 1 Cor. 1:8; 2 Cor. 1:13) frequently used in Jewish literature. The exalted Christ now rules over the kingdom in the interim before turning it over to the Father. Whereas elsewhere his exaltation is the victory over the powers (cf. Rom. 8:35–39; Eph. 1:19–22; Phil. 2:11; 3:21; Col. 1:15–20; Heb. 1:4; 1 Pet. 3:22), here the conquest of the powers remains unfinished until the end. That is, the church lives between the beginning of the new creation and the end. Paul does not refer to the details that he gives in 1 Thessalonians 4:13–18 or to other events related to the end, including the final judgment (cf. Rom. 2:6–11; 14:10–12; 2 Cor. 5:10), but he gives scriptural

27. Eriksson, Traditions as Rhetorical Proof, 261.
28. Comparison (Greek synkrisis) is the presentation of a parallel case or item that may be compared in some detail in order to show that one is worse or better than the other. See Lausberg, Handbook of Literary Rhetoric, §395.
29. See Dunn, Theology of Paul, 281–93.

support for this sequence in 1 Corinthians 15:25–28. *Dei gar* in 15:25 indicates the apocalyptic necessity of the course of events,[30] which he derives from his christological reading of Psalm 110:1. His focus is not on the place of Jesus at God's right hand, as in the allusions to this psalm elsewhere in the New Testament (cf. Matt. 22:44; 26:64 parr.; Acts 2:34; Rom. 8:34; Heb. 1:3, 13; 8:1; 10:12), but on the present as the time when "he must rule" (*basileuein*, 1 Cor. 15:25; cf. *katakyrieue*, Ps. 110:2 [109:2 LXX]) before the enemies are defeated. "Until" (*heōs an*) in Psalm 110:1 (109:1 LXX) becomes *achri hou* in 1 Corinthians 15:25. While Jesus is subordinate to God, he is granted a role that in the Old Testament belongs to God. The theme of God's victory over all enemies goes back to Exodus 15 and becomes pervasive in the Psalms.[31] That is, Psalm 110, which is commonly a reference to the triumph of Christ over cosmic powers, describes a victory that is still incomplete.

According to Psalm 110:1, God speaks in the first person, saying, "Until I put all your enemies under your feet," while in 1 Corinthians, Paul says, "Until he places all [his] enemies under his feet" (1 Cor. 15:25). The antecedent of "he" is apparently the Son, who will ultimately turn the kingdom over to the Father. Turning from the reference to the principalities and powers, Paul concludes that "the last enemy that is being destroyed is death" (15:26 AT), alluding to the situation at Corinth, in which some have died (11:30). Indeed, the outcry in the peroratio (15:54–55) indicates that death is the problem that demands a resolution for the Corinthians. He confirms this with the citation of Psalm 8:6, "He has put all things under his feet" (1 Cor. 15:27 AT). Paul may be the first to combine Psalm 110:1 and Psalm 8:6 (8:7 LXX)—both of which have the phrase "under his feet"—in a christological interpretation (cf. Eph. 1:22; Heb. 2:5–8). His argument is based on the appeal to Scripture—the authority of an ancient witness—and the assumptions that were persuasive only within the Christian subculture.[32]

While Christ is the subject of the action in 1 Corinthians 15:20–26, Paul returns to the role of God in 15:27–28. God is, in fact, the one who subjected all things to the Son (15:27), and the Son will ultimately be in subjection to God, who will be "all and in all" (15:28).

This is the primary proof in a deliberative argument intended to demonstrate that our labor is not in vain. It is probably addressed to those who do not see the victory as a present reality and thus recognize that death, the last enemy, has not been conquered. Paul's extended christological statement

---

30. Cf. *dei* for apocalyptic necessity in Mark 8:31; Luke 24:26; Rev. 1:1; 13:10.
31. Wright, *Paul and the Faithfulness of God*, 736.
32. See Eriksson, *Traditions as Rhetorical Proof*, 263.

differs from others because of the rhetorical situation. His portrayal of eschatology and Christology is framed to assure people who struggle with death that the victory is still to come. The battle with overwhelming powers that is in progress is a prelude to the ultimate victory.

While 1 Corinthians 15 indicates Paul's reshaping of the Pharisaic theology of the resurrection, this self-contained unit is the assurance that believers will ultimately be transformed, without which the conviction in 1:8 would not become a reality. Only those who believe in the resurrection will conform their lives to the crucified one; and only they will follow Jesus to resurrection and transformation. An understanding of Christology is necessary for the ultimate transformation.

Conclusion: Christology and Persuasion

Paul never engages in an extended discussion about the nature of Christ in the letters because Christology was not a matter for debate. Nor does he offer a consistent delineation of the relationship of the exalted Christ to God. Indeed, he employs christological statements as premises and proofs in deliberative arguments in which he attempts to shape the behavior of the readers. While he consistently argues on the basis of the work of Christ (see chaps. 7 and 8 below), he only occasionally argues from the person of Christ. The most prominent examples are in Philippians and 1 Corinthians, as I have argued in this chapter.

In all of his letters, Paul assumes the narrative of the preexistence, incarnation, and exaltation of Jesus Christ, and he employs this narrative for different purposes. In Philippians, Paul addresses a church living in a competitive society to encourage a *phronēsis* (cf. 2:2–4) that rejects self-seeking and looks to the good of others, appealing to the poetic narrative in Philippians 2:6–11. Similarly, in 1 Corinthians 3:23 and 11:3, he describes the subordination of Christ in order to encourage subordination among the believers; in the proof in the argument for the resurrection (1 Cor. 15), he describes the role of Christ in defeating the enemies (1 Cor. 15:23–28) for those who still live where death, the last enemy, has not yet been defeated. In this instance, Christ acts on behalf of God, who, in Jewish expectation, defeats the enemies (Ps. 110:1). The adaptation of the Shema (1 Cor. 8:6) is the common ground between Paul and his interlocutors, the premise for his argument to reject idolatry. The debates among scholars about Pauline Christology probably reflect the absence of precise delineation in Paul, who employs the community's common confession to address a variety of rhetorical situations.

7

Greco-Roman Values
and the Theology of the Cross

The Corinthian Correspondence

The evidence of 1 Corinthians suggests that the postbaptismal catechesis in Corinth includes the same topics that Paul gave to the Thessalonians. Paul initiates the gentile community into Israel's narrative world, gives moral instructions that are consistent with the Jewish tradition (cf. 1 Cor. 5:9), and teaches them the traditions that define their existence (cf. 1 Cor. 11:2, 23–26; 15:3; 1 Thess. 4:1–2). Paul's frequent appeals to what the Corinthians already know (cf. 1 Cor. 3:16; 5:6; 6:2–3, 9, 15–16; 8:1, 4; 15:1–3, 11) suggest the extent of the catechesis and serve as the premise for his theological arguments.[1] He assumes that both communities recall his earlier catechesis, the basic convictions that called the church into being.

The Cross and Pauline Catechesis

Paul taught both communities that Christ "died for us" (1 Thess. 5:10). In 1 Thessalonians, he assumes that the readers "believe that Jesus died and arose" (1 Thess. 4:14 AT), while in 1 Corinthians, he recalls that "Christ died

---

1. Cf. Eriksson, *Traditions as Rhetorical Proof*. On the argument from what the readers know, see Long, *Ancient Rhetoric and Paul's Apology*, 49.

for our sins in accordance with the Scriptures, that he was buried, and that he was raised on the third day according to the Scriptures" (1 Cor. 15:3–4 AT; cf. 8:11). Paul inherited this tradition from the Jerusalem church, and it is the gospel that he preached (1 Cor. 15:1) and that the Corinthians believed (1 Cor. 15:11).

While Paul summarizes his gospel in a variety of ways, a consistent feature in his summaries is the formulation with *hyper* (on behalf of) followed by the genitive object.[2]

Christ died for [*hyper*] the ungodly. (Rom. 5:6)

Christ died for [*hyper*] us. (Rom. 5:8)

He gave himself up for [*hyper*] all of us. (Rom. 8:32)

One for whom [*hyper*] Christ died. (Rom. 14:15; cf. 1 Cor. 8:11).

One died for [*hyper*] all. (2 Cor. 5:14 AT)

The one who knew no sin he made to be sin for [*hyper*] us. (2 Cor. 5:21 AT)

[The one] who loved me and gave himself for [*hyper*] me. (Gal. 2:20)

Christ . . . becoming a curse for [*hyper*] us. (Gal. 3:13)

The *hyper* formula to designate the saving significance of the death of Christ continues in the disputed Pauline letters (Eph. 5:2, 25; 1 Tim. 2:6; Titus 2:14) and appears among other New Testament witnesses (Mark 14:24 parr.; John 10:11, 15; 11:50–51; cf. Heb. 2:9; 6:20; 7:25, 27; 9:24; 10:12; 1 Pet. 2:21; 3:18).

In numerous instances, Paul employs different prepositions interchangeably to associate Jesus's death with the removal of sin. According to 1 Corinthians 15:3, "Christ died for [*hyper*] our sins" (cf. Gal. 1:4), while according to Romans 8:3, he died "because of [*peri*] our sins" (AT). According to Romans 4:25, he died "because of [*dia*] our trespasses [*paraptōmata*]" (AT).

The idea of one dying for another is commonplace in the literature of antiquity.[3] However, Pauline usage is probably indebted to the Septuagint. The suffering servant of Deutero-Isaiah provides the vocabulary for interpreting the death of Jesus. The servant was "wounded for [*dia*] our transgressions, crushed for [*dia*] our iniquities" (Isa. 53:5), and he "bore the sins of many and was handed over for [*dia*] their sins" (Isa. 53:12 AT). These prepositions indicate the saving significance of the servant's death.

The sacrificial system also provides the context for the interpretation of the death of Jesus. The sin offering prescribed in the Torah was "for sin," *peri*

2. Wolter, *Paul*, 101–2.
3. Wolter, *Paul*, 101–2; Hengel, *The Atonement*, 4–13.

tēs hamartias (LXX: Lev. 5:8, 9; 6:18, 23; 7:7; 8:14; 9:7–8, 10) and *to hyper [tēs] hamartias* (LXX: Ezek. 40:39; 43:22, 25; 44:29; 45:17, 22–23, 25; 46:20). Paul also used the terminology of the sacrificial animal to interpret the death of Jesus (1 Cor. 5:7).

The Cross and the Rhetorical Situation in the Corinthian Letters

While Paul frequently cites variant forms of the *hyper* formula without further elaboration, the situation in the Corinthian church compels him to elaborate extensively on the meaning of the death of Jesus. Despite Paul's eighteen-month stay in the city, many in the community have either misunderstood Paul's catechesis (cf. 1 Cor. 5:9–10) or asked for clarification (cf. 7:1, 25; 8:1; 12:1). Paul not only restates his basic convictions but also clarifies earlier traditions, using them as the basis for further elaboration, assuming that opponents will acknowledge the traditions as the premise for his argument (cf. 8:6; 11:23–26; 12:3, 13).[4]

The extent to which the numerous issues at Corinth reflect a coherent Corinthian theology is an unresolved issue. However, one can ascertain certain elements of the Corinthian point of view. The partisan rivalry (1:10–17; 3:1–5), expressed in the slogans "I am of Paul" and "I am of Apollos" (cf. 3:4), reflects the allegiance to a leader in partisan politics in Greco-Roman cities.[5] This rivalry was apparently associated with a claim to wisdom (3:18), the boasting about human leaders (3:21), and the questioning of Paul's authority (cf. 4:1–5). "The wisdom of this age" (2:6; cf. 3:18), expressed in the gift of rhetoric, was apparently the criterion of assessing leadership within the community. The contrast between Paul's preaching and "persuasive words of wisdom" (2:4 AT) suggests that the Corinthians equated wisdom with rhetoric. The insistence on "the wisdom of word" (1:17 AT) reflects the ancient emphasis on wisdom and rhetoric, leading the Corinthians to doubt the efficacy of their founder (4:1–5). As Cicero said, "The best rhetorician but also the wisest man . . ." (*De or.* 3.22.82).[6] The Corinthians were apparently judging their leaders according to these standards.

The repeated phrase "All things are lawful" (1 Cor. 6:12; 10:23) echoes Greek formulations,[7] and the slogan "Food is for the belly and the belly for food" (6:13 AT) is probably a reference to a common Greek understanding

4. See Eriksson, *Traditions as Rhetorical Proof*, passim.
5. Mitchell, *Paul and the Rhetoric of Reconciliation*, 82–84.
6. Cf. Betz, "Problem of Rhetoric and Theology," 32.
7. See Winter, *After Paul Left Corinth*.

of the body and sexuality. The Corinthian conduct at the Lord's Supper was influenced by the ancient meal practices,[8] and the denial of the resurrection likely represented the basic Greek point of view of the body (cf. 6:12–20), according to which only incorporeal souls survived death.

Thus numerous scholars have observed that the issues in Corinth are intertwined with the socioeconomic divisions within the church. Those who acquired wealth expected leaders to conform to the Greco-Roman standards of rhetoric, to take others to court (cf. 6:1–11), to have the opportunity to eat meat (cf. 8:1–11:1), and to demonstrate class distinctions at meals (cf. 11:17–34).[9] Paul's work with his hands and his refusal to accept their financial support alienated those who wished to be his patrons. Thus the Corinthians maintained many of the Greco-Roman values, despite Paul's eighteen-month stay among them. Jürgen Becker has argued persuasively, "This Corinthian development took place under the conditions of a newly arisen Gentile-Christian church, which did not simply lay aside its former culture, understanding of religion, and interpretation of the world, nor did it adapt itself fully to the apostle's understanding during Paul's stay in Corinth. Thus the problem of the Corinthian church was, first, how the Paulinism known to it stood in contrast to the old ways or to what extent the old ways could also be a help in giving life to the new."[10]

Although a disturbing sequence of events occurs between 1 and 2 Corinthians (cf. 2 Cor. 2:1–11), many of the issues remain the same. Paul continues to play the role of fool among those who claim to be wise (2 Cor. 11:16–19; cf. 1 Cor. 1:18, 23; 4:10). While comparisons with Apollos and others is no longer the issue, the coming of rival apostles and "ministers of Christ" (2 Cor. 11:23) has resulted in the Corinthians' renewed questions about Paul's leadership. Paul's physical presence and rhetorical ability also remain an issue (2 Cor. 10:11; 11:6), and his refusal to accept financial support is still the source of suspicion among them (2 Cor. 11:7–11; 12:13–18). This issue has been exacerbated by the demands of the rival apostles, who, according to Paul, "enslave" and "prey upon" the community (2 Cor. 11:20). Paul defends himself, distinguishing himself from "the many" who, like the Sophists,[11] peddle their teachings (2 Cor. 2:17).

8. Pogoloff, *Logos and Sophia*, 237–71.
9. Theissen, *Social Setting of Pauline Christianity*, 69–174.
10. Becker, *Paul*, 199.
11. Cf. Plato, *Prot.* 313c–d: "Is a Sophist not a merchant or shopkeeper [*emporos kai kapēlos*], selling the commodities that nourish the soul, . . . those who peddle their knowledge from city to city, selling it wholesale and retail [*polountes kai kapeleuontes*], praising to their buyers all that they offer for sale?"

In both letters, Paul's challenge is to confront the common values of Greco-Roman culture, which he describes in a variety of ways. According to 1 Corinthians, he confronts those who are "of the flesh" (1 Cor. 3:3) and behave at "a purely human level" (*kata anthrōpon*). They are people whose knowledge is "of this age" (1 Cor. 3:18 AT; cf. 2:6); thus they do not grasp the wisdom that God has revealed. According to 2 Corinthians, Paul confronts those who charge that he conducts himself "according to the flesh" (*kata sarka*, 2 Cor. 10:2), insisting that he conducts a warfare that is not *kata sarka* (2 Cor. 10:3) but that others boast *kata sarka* (2 Cor. 11:18). Indeed, he describes his conversion from an epistemology that was *kata sarka* (2 Cor. 5:16) to one of the new creation (2 Cor. 5:17).

Rhetoric and the Theology of the Cross in 1 Corinthians

The Rhetorical Situation

As a letter intended to persuade the Corinthians toward a specific course of action in the future and dissuade them from specific behavior, 1 Corinthians "is largely deliberative rhetoric,"[12] consisting of Paul's attempts to correct practices that undermine communal solidarity within the Corinthian church. Paul proceeds from one behavioral issue to another, in each instance offering theological arguments for the course of action that he commends. His goal for a blameless community at the day of Christ (1 Cor. 1:8) can become a reality only if he is able to persuade his readers to follow the practices that he commends. In the invention and arrangement of the letter, the theology of the cross plays a decisive role.

Invention and Arrangement

First Corinthians 1–4. Before Paul addresses the conflicts at Corinth, he introduces the topics in the opening thanksgiving, expressing gratitude that the believers "have become rich in [Christ], in all word and knowledge" (1:5 AT) and that they "do not lack any spiritual gift [*charisma*]" (1:7 AT). These issues, however, are the sources of conflict, as Paul's later complaint "Already you are rich!" (4:8 AT) and his discussion of speech and knowledge indicate (cf. 1:17–18; 2:1; 8:1, 7, 10; 12:8; 13:2; 14:6). Indeed, as Hans Dieter Betz has indicated, "Paul's correspondence with the Corinthians is basically nothing but an extended wrestling with this claim, concisely stated in the words 'rich . . . in every kind of speech and every kind of knowledge.'"[13]

---

12. Kennedy, *Interpretation through Rhetorical Criticism*, 87. See also Schrage, *Der erste Brief an die Korinther*, 1:80; Mitchell, *Paul and the Rhetoric of Reconciliation*, 20–22.
13. Betz, "Problem of Rhetoric and Theology," 26–27.

By introducing the controversial topics in a positive way, Paul undoubtedly hopes to make the audience favorably disposed. The assurance that God will "confirm [them] blameless to the end at the day of our Lord Jesus Christ" (1:8 AT), despite the many problems in the community, is also intended to gain a favorable hearing among the Corinthians. This affirmation corresponds to the pastoral goal that he states frequently (cf. 2 Cor. 1:14; Phil. 2:16; 1 Thess. 2:19). The telos of Paul's work is the ultimate formation of a community. Thus the thanksgiving in 1 Corinthians 1:4–9 serves as the exordium of the letter as it introduces the topics of the letter and places the issues at Corinth in the wider context of Paul's pastoral purpose.

The assurance expressed in the exordium that God "will confirm [the Corinthians] blameless to the end" (1:8 AT) is in sharp contrast to the existing reality indicated in the opening words in 1:10–17 and the indictment in 3:1–5, which describe the partisan politics at Corinth. The Corinthians have not made progress consistent with Paul's hope for their moral formation (1:8–9). The appeal to the Corinthians to "say the same thing" and "have the same mind" (1:10 AT) is the propositio of the letter, not only addressing the partisanship of the Corinthians but also confronting the numerous anticommunal activities in the community that Paul addresses throughout the letter.[14] The brief statement of the facts in 1:11–17 is the narratio of the letter, which explains Paul's reason for writing (1:11–12) and gives a brief defense of Paul's ministry among the Corinthians.[15] The Corinthians' competitiveness over their respective leaders, including their pride over the one who baptized them, forces Paul to reaffirm his basic mission. The claim in 1:17 that Christ sent him not to baptize but to preach (*euangelizesthai*) recalls his basic mission as the herald of Deutero-Isaiah who announces the good news (Isa. 52:7; 61:1; cf. 1 Cor. 9:16; 15:1; Gal. 1:16). In his statement that his preaching was "not in the wisdom of word, lest the cross be emptied of its power" (1 Cor. 1:17 AT), he echoes the claim in 1 Thessalonians that his gospel did not come "in word alone, but in the power of the Holy Spirit" (1 Thess. 1:5 AT) and his detailed contrast between his preaching and the speech that "pleases humans" (1 Cor. 2:4) and seeks glory from others (1 Cor. 2:6). Paul thus draws a sharp contrast between his preaching and the rhetoric of his time in response to those who measure preaching by the standards of Greco-Roman rhetoric. As the argument indicates, the good news of the herald is the death of Jesus on the cross. Paul develops the argument in the probatio in 1:18–15:58, which consists of a series of arguments on the issues that have emerged.

14. Mitchell, *Paul and the Rhetoric of Reconciliation*, 198–200.
15. Kennedy, *Interpretation through Rhetorical Criticism*, 24–25.

In the first argument, 1:18–4:21, Paul lays the foundation by elaborating on the theology of the cross. The sharp distinction between "the wisdom of word" and the cross of Christ (1:17 AT) provides the transition to the extended contrast in 1:18–2:16. The place of this section within the discussion of factionalism suggests that the theology of the cross is the answer to the partisan rivalry at Corinth. Paul elaborates on his preaching in 1:18–2:16 before he returns to the dispute at Corinth in chapter 3. The content of his preaching is "the word of the cross" (1:18 AT), an interpretation of his original preaching that "Christ died for our sins" (15:3) and the opposite of "the wisdom of word" (1:17 AT).

This contrast is the first of several antitheses that Paul presents in 1:18–2:16. Paul contrasts "those who are being saved" with "those who are perishing" (1:18), foolishness with power (1:18), foolishness with wisdom (1:23–24), the foolishness of God with human wisdom (1:25), God's weakness with human strength (1:27), persuasive words of wisdom with Christ crucified (2:1–2), and the wisdom of this age with the wisdom of God (2:6). Paul speaks in these sharp antitheses because the Corinthians' claim to be "wise in this age" (3:18) is contrary to the word of the cross.[16]

Paul's question "Was Paul crucified for [*hyper*] you?" (1:13) indicates that the Corinthians acknowledge the original message that "Christ died for our sins" (cf. 15:3) without recognizing the dichotomy between the word of wisdom and the gospel. Indeed, while Paul summarizes his preaching in a variety of ways in his letters, the expression "the word of the cross" (1:18 AT) is more than to say that "Christ died." This designation is a sharp reminder of the means of Jesus's execution and the horrors of the cross. Paul reiterates, "We preach Christ crucified" (1:23; 2:2 AT). The emphasis on "Christ crucified" suggests that, while the Corinthians did not question that "Christ died for [their] sins," they also had not grasped the significance of the message. Jürgen Becker has suggested that the Corinthians' views might have corresponded to a basic trait of Hellenistic hero worship, according to which the victorious hero is acclaimed after overcoming various trials. For example, Heracles was worshiped as a hero and god after he endured trials and sufferings before becoming victorious.[17]

Paul does not give a comprehensive theology of the cross but describes it in terms that address the Corinthian situation. Over against those who

16. The place of antithesis (Greek *antitheton*) in argumentation is a topic in the rhetorical handbooks. See Lausberg, *Handbook of Literary Rhetoric*, §787. According to Aristotle, *Rhet.* 3.9.8, antithesis (of opposite terms) is pleasing because matters that are well known become better known when placed alongside their opposites. See Anderson, *Glossary of Greek Rhetorical Terms*, 21.
17. Becker, *Paul*, 201.

celebrate human wisdom, Paul declares that the cross is the ultimate example of God's sovereign choice and the infinite distance between divine and human wisdom, appealing to Old Testament traditions of the God who destroys the pretensions of the wise (1 Cor. 1:19; cf. Isa. 29:14; Jer. 9:23–24).[18] Indeed, the Corinthians' existence as a people composed of "not many . . . wise according to human standards" (1 Cor. 1:26) is an additional example of God's sovereign call (1:26–31) and the refutation of all human boasting (1:30–31). Even Paul's demeanor as a speaker is contrary to the human wisdom that the Corinthians admire, for he appeals to his own ethos, claiming that he did not come with "excellence of speech or wisdom" (2:1 AT) or "persuasive words of wisdom" (2:4 AT). He came "in weakness and in fear and trembling" (2:3 AT), preaching only "Christ crucified" (2:2), not the human wisdom of the orator.

In 2:6–16, Paul elaborates on the word of the cross, declaring that it is not human wisdom but the divine wisdom that is "not of this age" (2:6 AT) and thus not intelligible to the world—even to the rulers of this age—because it is a mystery that has been hidden away but has now been revealed through the Spirit (2:10). Thus Paul speaks as a prophetic seer who argues on the basis of divine revelation[19] rather than common rhetorical proofs. While the worldly (*psychikos*) person does not receive this divine wisdom (2:14), those who have the Spirit discern all things and have the mind of Christ (2:15–16). That is, only those who have an epistemology of the new age can understand the message of the cross. According to Charles Cousar, "What must be taken seriously is the epistemological thrust of 1:18–2:16. The section confronts the readers with a way of knowing God radically different from the way of knowing that has resulted in factionalism."[20] In contrast to the appeal to rationality in Greek rhetoric, Paul speaks with prophetic rhetoric, appealing to knowledge that is not publicly accessible. The community must radically readjust its way of knowing God and living together in community.

As the inclusio of 1:10–17 and 3:1–5 indicates, Paul's challenge is to reorient the Corinthians' understanding of leadership with a theology of the cross. In 3:1–5, Paul indicates that the dichotomies of 1:17–2:16 extend to the readers, who have demonstrated that they belong to this age, unable to grasp spiritual matters. Their partisan politics indicate that they are still "people of the flesh" (*sarkinoi*, 3:1; *sarkikoi*, 3:3 bis) who conduct themselves by worldly standards (*kata anthrōpon*, 3:3; *anthrōpoi*, 3:1, 3, 4; "worldly," NIV) and whom Paul must address as infants (*nēpioi*, 3:1).

18. Brown, *Cross and Human Transformation*, 81.
19. See chap. 1 above for Paul's prophetic rhetoric.
20. Cousar, "Theological Task of 1 Corinthians," 94.

The argument of the letter builds on the theology of the cross articulated in 1:18–2:16 as Paul presents the implications of this new epistemology. Those who understand the theology of the cross will abandon a this-worldly understanding of leadership. Recognizing that their leaders are only *diakonoi* (3:1–5)—gardeners in God's vineyard (3:6–9) and construction workers in God's building—transforms the believers' understanding of leadership and confronts those who are "wise in this age" (3:18) and boast about people (3:21).

This dichotomy of values is nowhere more evident than in the conclusion to the argument over leadership in 4:6–13 in Paul's contrast between his own demeanor and the Corinthians' Greco-Roman understandings of leadership. In keeping with the message as foolishness, Paul is a fool for Christ, while the Corinthians are wise, weak while they are strong, inglorious while they are glorious (4:10). While they are "puffed up" against each other (4:6) and boast (4:7) without a basis for boasting, Paul describes himself as "condemned to death" (*epithanatios*) and a spectacle (*theatron*) to the world (4:9). Consistent with the foolishness of his preaching of the cross, he has become a fool (4:10). The catalog of sufferings in 4:9–13 endured by Paul is an indication of his participation in the cross. Thus while the Corinthians agree with the creedal statement "Christ died for our sins," they do not recognize the implications for their common life. Paul argues on the basis of an ethos that is determined by the message he preaches, the Christian tradition, and Scripture, offering arguments that would be persuasive only within the subculture of the believing community.

First Corinthians 5:1–11:1. The theology of the cross is the answer not only to the problem of factionalism in Corinth (1:18–4:21) but also to other issues. While Paul addresses a variety of issues in 5:1–11:1, the consistent thread is relationship between insiders and outsiders as Paul confronts believers who fail to draw sharp boundaries between their practices and those of the surrounding culture. The slogan "All things are lawful," which Paul cites in two verses (6:12; 10:23), only to correct it in each case, is apparently the slogan of some who insist on their individual rights at the expense of community cohesion.

Paul confronts this issue first in the case of the man who is living with his father's wife, a practice that is forbidden in the Torah (Lev. 18:8) and among Paul's churches. Corinthians who boast about human leaders (cf. 1 Cor. 1:29, 31; 3:21; 4:7) also boast about this practice (1 Cor. 5:2). After Paul has instructed the community to "deliver this one to Satan" (5:5 AT), he employs the images from the exodus to reiterate his demand, adding, "Cleanse out the old yeast, in order that you may be a new batch of dough" (5:7 AT).

The demand is followed by the theological warrant "For our paschal lamb, Christ, has been sacrificed" (5:7). This image is an example of Paul's use of synecdoche, recalling the entire gospel narrative.[21] As in 1:18–2:16, the death of Jesus is the warrant for the new behavior. In this instance, Paul interprets the basic creed "Christ died for our sins" (cf. 15:3), using images from Israel's narrative, speaking with a prophetic voice. The church is the heir of Israel, and Christ is the sacrificial lamb that redeems the people (cf. Exod. 12:21). Just as ancient Israel perpetually celebrated a feast of remembrance (Exod. 12:14), the church regularly celebrates a feast (1 Cor. 10:14–21; 11:17–34).

The sacrifice of Christ has shaped Christian identity, the decisive break between old and new ways of thinking—between the old leaven and the new.[22] A community defined by the cross will recognize sharp boundaries between the church and the world (cf. 5:9) and its understanding of freedom. As Paul says elsewhere, "No one lives to himself and no one dies to himself" (Rom. 14:7; cf. 2 Cor. 5:15).

When Paul addresses the problem of lawsuits (1 Cor. 6:1–11), he also confronts the problem of the church and the world. His argument is based on what believers already know as a result of prior catechesis (cf. "Do you not know?" in 6:2, 3, 9). He is probably confronting wealthier people who are insisting on their own rights; his counsel to "be wronged" (6:7) is consistent with the theology of the cross.

Paul corrects the Corinthian claim in 6:12 that "all things are lawful," adding, "But not all things are beneficial [*sympherei*]," as he addresses the Corinthians on sexuality and the body and the right of men to go to prostitutes (6:12–20).[23] However, he redefines *sympherein*, appealing to the assumptions of his Christianized Jewish apocalyptic literature (6:14).[24] Paul responds with a theology of the body, declaring that the body is destined for resurrection (6:14) before appealing to what the Corinthians already know: that the body is a member of Christ (6:15) and that the body is the temple of the Holy Spirit (6:19). In his concluding argument, he declares, "You are not your own; you were bought with a price" (6:19–20 AT), once more indicating that the

21. See Mitchell, "Rhetorical Shorthand in Pauline Argumentation," 70–72. See also Peterson, "Christ Our Pasch," 134–35.

22. Wolter, *Paul*, 105.

23. The appeal to the beneficial or advantageous (*sympheron*) was commonplace in Greco-Roman popular philosophy and rhetoric. The handbooks recommend that the orator demonstrate that a course of action is advantageous (*sympheron*), just (*dikaion*), possible (*dynaton*), and fitting (*prepon*). While the lists vary among the handbooks, *sympheron* is consistently present. See Lausberg, *Handbook of Literary Rhetoric*, §375. Paul also argues on the basis of *sympheron* in 1 Cor. 12:7; 2 Cor. 8:10; 12:1; cf. the related *symphoron* in 1 Cor. 7:35.

24. "God raised the Lord and will raise us with him" (AT).

community is defined by the death of Christ and arguing from the premises that were common knowledge within the community.

The image of the purchase is derived from the practice of buying slaves.[25] The image may also be drawn from the exodus story, signifying that the death of Jesus was the liberation from the power of the old age. Paul uses the image also in Galatians, describing believers as "liberated from the curse of the law" when Christ took the curse upon himself at the cross (Gal. 3:13 AT; cf. 4:5). A similar image appears at the beginning of Galatians, as Paul declares that Christ gave himself for our sins "in order that he might deliver us from the present evil age" (Gal. 1:4 AT). Paul employs the image of slavery also in Romans, using language associated with the liberation of slaves from Egypt to depict the redemption (*apolytrōsis*) in Christ (Rom. 3:24; cf. 1 Cor. 1:30; Eph. 1:7; Col. 1:14).[26] The Corinthians' freedom is not, however, that which they claim, for it is defined by the cross. Those who are liberated by the cross are no longer enslaved to the power of sin over the body (Rom. 6:16–19), and they no longer live for themselves.[27]

In 1 Corinthians 8:1–11:1, Paul continues to address those who insist that their own knowledge (8:1–4, 7) and freedom (8:7; 10:23) give them the right (*exousia*, 8:9) in the market to purchase meat offered to idols (10:25) or to accept invitations to dine at pagan meals (8:10; 10:27–28). This freedom is an additional source of division, for not all share this knowledge (8:7). Paul faces a similar situation in Romans over meal practices (14:1–15:13) and offers the same answer in both letters. While he agrees with those who eat the meat (1 Cor. 8:1–7; cf. Rom. 15:1), he instructs them to beware that their freedom not destroy those who do not share their knowledge and whose consciences are weak, for the weaker believers are those "for whom Christ died" (1 Cor. 8:11; cf. Rom. 14:15). As in the preceding argument (1 Cor. 1:17–2:16; 5:7; 6:20), Paul applies the creedal statement "Christ died for our sins" to the divisions in Corinth. The death of Christ "for our sins" has profound ecclesiological consequences. A diverse community is united by the fact that all are those "for whom Christ died." To sin against the fellow believer is to sin against Christ (8:12). What is at stake is not just the conscience of "the weaker fellow believer" but the saving death of Christ.[28] The community is defined by

---

25. Spicq, "ἀγοράζω," *TLNT* 1:28.

26. *Apolytrōsis* is not used in the Old Testament in a theologically significant way; λυτρόω is employed for God's act of redemption. God "redeemed" Israel from slavery in Egypt (cf. LXX: Deut. 7:8; 9:26; 13:6 [13:5 Eng.]; 15:15; Pss. 73:2 [74:2 Eng.]; 76:16 [77:15 Eng.]). See Kertelge, "ἀπολύτρωσις," *EDNT* 1:139.

27. Schrage, *Der erste Brief an die Korinther*, 2:36.

28. Eriksson, *Traditions as Rhetorical Proof*, 159.

the cross, and believers participate in the cross by living on behalf of (*hyper*) others. According to 1 Corinthians 9, Paul offers his practice as an exemplum of one who abandons his rights in order to be a slave of all. Thus he embodies the renunciation of rights that grows out of the theology of the cross.

The focus on the cross is also apparent in Paul's continuing comments about idolatry in 1 Corinthians 10. Responding to the Corinthian claim for the right to eat meat offered to idols (10:23), Paul recalls the disastrous consequences that befell the Israelites after the exodus. Although the ancestors, like the Corinthians, "ate spiritual food" and "drank spiritual drink" (10:3–4), they died. This story is an exemplum—*typikōs* (10:11)—for the believers. Participation in a sacred meal does not guarantee their salvation. Paul warns his readers about the consequences of crossing the boundaries between their confession and the world of idolatry, concluding, "Therefore, flee from idolatry" (10:14 AT).

Paul supports the imperative with a series of rhetorical questions (10:16, 18–19, 22) interspersed with his conclusions (10:17, 20–21), assuming that the Corinthians will agree on the answers to the rhetorical questions but not to Paul's conclusions. In the rhetorical questions in 10:16, the premise for the argument is what the Corinthians already acknowledge (cf. 6:2–3, 9, 15–16), which is recognized only within the community. The questions "The cup of blessing, is it not a participation [*koinōnia*] in the blood of Christ?" and "The bread which we break, is it not a participation [*koinōnia*] in the body of Christ?" paraphrase the words of institution, which Paul recites in 11:23–26. Paul assumes that the Corinthians will agree that the Lord's Supper is a *koinōnia* in the body and blood of Christ. The parallel with the words of institution (cf. 11:23–26) suggests that *koinōnia* is an interpretation of "is" (*estin*) in the words of institution (i.e., "This is my body; . . . this cup is . . .").[29]

Paul's additional rhetorical questions indicate that all agree that sacrificial meals both in Israelite and Greco-Roman religion establish *koinōnia* (1 Cor. 10:18, 20–21) with the deity and among the participants. They do not understand, however, that the table of the Lord is *koinōnia* in the body and blood of Christ, which is metonymy for Jesus's death on the cross. Paul's use elsewhere of *koinōn-* with the genitive indicates the nature of this participation. He indicates in the exordium (1:9) that believers were called into the fellowship (*koinōnia*) of God's Son. Thus, Paul presents himself as a model to others, describing the "fellowship [*koinōnia*] of his sufferings" (Phil. 3:10 AT) and stating that believers are "partners" (*koinōnoi*) in the sufferings of Christ (2 Cor. 1:7 AT).

29. Thompson, *Church according to Paul*, 84.

Paul makes analogous statements using the preposition *syn* and compound words that use *syn* as a prefix. Addressing the Christian community, Paul regularly speaks of sharing the destiny of Christ. "If we suffer [*sympaschomen*] with him, we shall also be glorified with him [*syndoxasthōmen*]" (Rom. 8:17 AT). Paul declares, "I have been crucified with Christ" (Gal. 2:19). In baptism, believers have been "baptized into his death" (Rom. 6:3), have "died with Christ" (Rom. 6:8), have been "buried with him" (Rom. 6:4), and have been "planted with him in the likeness of his death" (Rom. 6:5 AT). The old human "has been crucified with him" (Rom. 6:6 AT). Thus the community shares the destiny of Christ in baptism—a once-for-all event—participates in the destiny of Christ in the regular observance of the Lord's Supper in daily lives, and hopes to be with him in the future.

While Paul draws analogies between the Lord's Supper and other sacred meals, he points to the fundamental difference. Believers share in the death of the crucified Lord. As Paul's comment in 1 Corinthians 10:17 indicates, their *koinōnia* is not that of friends in a social hour. They become one body by participating in the body of Christ.

Paul's discussion of the Lord's Supper is only an illustration of the larger point that he makes. Within the context of participation in pagan sacred meals, Paul's point is the incompatibility between the table of the Lord and the table of demons (1 Cor. 10:21). Participation in Christ is exclusive. Unity is preserved when the whole community becomes participants in the crucified Lord, recognizing the exclusivity of the community in the Lord's Supper.

First Corinthians 11:17–34. While the interpretation of the Lord's Supper in 10:16 is only an illustration in Paul's instructions on the avoidance of pagan meals, the Lord's Supper becomes the major focus of his attention in 11:17–34, which addresses chaos in public meetings (11:2–14:40). Paul has heard of divisions (*schismata*) not only in the Corinthians' partisan politics (1:10) but also in the Lord's Supper (11:18). The Corinthians have not become "one body" (cf. 10:17) in the participation of the Lord's Supper; thus "it is not the Lord's Supper" (11:20 AT) that they eat. The divisions (*haireseis*, 11:19) reflect socioeconomic realities that were common at Greco-Roman meals, in which rich and poor ate unequal portions.[30] Just as the Corinthians interpreted earlier issues through the lenses of Greco-Roman values, they interpreted the meal according to ancient analogies.

Paul responds with an appeal to the Christian tradition, once more recalling what the Corinthians already know (11:23–26) as a basis for the conclusions

30. See Winter, *After Paul Left Corinth*, 154–58; Pogoloff, *Logos and Sophia*, 239.

that he will draw (11:27–34).[31] Consistent with the Lukan account, he repeats, "This is my body which is for [*hyper*] you" (1 Cor. 11:24 AT), using a preposition that appears in other accounts of the Last Supper (cf. Matt. 26:28, *peri pollōn*; Mark 14:24, *hyper pollōn*; Luke 22:19–20, *hyper hymōn*). This new covenant inaugurated by blood recalls Exodus 24. Christ inaugurated the new covenant by his blood, and Paul is its minister (cf. 2 Cor. 3:3–6). Together the body and the blood are a metonymy for the death on the cross. The citation of the tradition indicates that the cross is the norm for Christian behavior, as in 1 Corinthians 8:11. When Paul declares that participation in the Lord's Supper is a proclamation of the death of Jesus (1 Cor. 11:26), he refers to the body and the blood of the cross. Just as Paul proclaims Christ crucified, the church proclaims the death of Jesus.

Paul then offers theological conclusions, introduced by *hōste*, in 1 Corinthians 11:27–34. Participation in the Lord's Supper is an ecclesial act. Those who participate unworthily (11:27), not discerning the body, receive judgment, just as the Israelites did. Indeed, some have already received the judgment. To "discern the body" is shorthand for discerning the body and the blood of Jesus. The end result is the imperative "Wait for one another" (11:33). The Corinthians have failed to see the ecclesial nature of the Lord's Supper. While the Lord's Supper, according to 10:14–21, is an exclusive act, in 11:17–34, it is also an inclusive act. In each instance, the cross defines ecclesial identity as believers participate in it. Paul's theology of the cross in 1 Corinthians is not a comprehensive analysis of the meaning of Jesus's death but the response to the rhetorical situation in Corinth.

Rhetoric and the Theology of the Cross in 2 Corinthians

The Rhetorical Situation

Although a year passes between 1 and 2 Corinthians (2 Cor. 8:10), many of the same issues remain. Paul offers frequent statements of his credentials in the form of catalogs of sufferings (2 Cor. 4:7–10; 6:4–10; 11:23–33; 12:10) because the opponents have forced him into competitive boasting (2 Cor. 10:12; 11:18, 22–23; 12:11).[32] Rival apostles probably joined with those who questioned Paul's authority in 1 Corinthians, bringing letters of recommendation (2 Cor. 3:1), boasting of their credentials (cf. 2 Cor. 5:12; 11:18), and comparing themselves with Paul (2 Cor. 10:12–18). The criticisms that "his bodily presence

31. See Eriksson, *Traditions as Rhetorical Proof*, 100–106.
32. Judge, "Paul's Boasting," 46–47.

is weak and his speech is of no account" (2 Cor. 10:10 AT) and that he is un-skilled in speaking (2 Cor. 11:6) indicate that the issues of 1 Corinthians 1–4 are still present. Paul's refusal of patronage and his manual labor (cf. 4:9–11; 9:1–3) also continue to be an issue (2 Cor. 11:7–11, 20; 12:14–18; cf. 2:17). He defends himself against the opponents' charges, that he conducted himself "with worldly wisdom" (*en sophia sarkikē*, 2 Cor. 1:12) and that he made his decisions "in a worldly way" (*kata sarka*, 2 Cor. 1:17; cf. 10:2), turning those charges against them. He insists that, since his conversion, he no longer regards anyone "in a worldly way" (*kata sarka*), although he once regarded Christ in this way (2 Cor. 5:16). Now, however, living in the new creation, he has a new way of knowing (2 Cor. 5:17). It is the opposition that boasts "in a worldly way" (2 Cor. 11:18)—that is, according to the standards of the old aeon.

The standards of the old aeon are those that conformed to the values of Greco-Roman culture. The charge that Paul is humble (*tapeinos*, 2 Cor. 10:1) and that he has humiliated (cf. *tapeinōn*) himself by working with his hands (2 Cor. 11:7) reflects the negative Greco-Roman attitudes toward humility and manual labor.[33] The accusation that "his bodily presence is weak" also reflects Greco-Roman values regarding physical beauty and strength.[34] Thus Paul's challenge in both Corinthian letters is to inculcate values that correspond to the *new* aeon.

Invention and Arrangement

Second Corinthians, unlike the other Pauline letters, contains little ethical advice regarding future conduct, for it is a defense speech in which Paul's argument consistently appeals to ethos and pathos. As a defense speech about Paul's past conduct, it approximates judicial rhetoric.[35] Although the letter is frequently regarded as a compilation of separate letters, a singular thread indicates that the same rhetorical situation and theme lie behind all parts of the letter. Consequently, one may observe the invention and arrangement of a unified letter.

In the exordium (1:3–7), Paul introduces the topic that is under dispute without indicating that it is the subject of controversy. Having been criticized for his weakness (10:10; cf. 11:21, 29–30; 12:10; 13:3–4), he echoes the psalmist (cf. Pss. 116:1–11; 118:5; 119:50) in praising the God who "comforts us in all our afflictions" (*thlipseis*, 2 Cor. 1:4), the pervasive theme in 2 Corinthians

---

33. Spicq, "ταπεινός," *TLNT* 3:369; see Hock, *Social Context of Paul's Ministry*, 64–65.

34. See Marshall, *Enmity at Corinth*, 61–62.

35. Kennedy, *Interpretation through Rhetorical Criticism*, 86–96; Long, *Ancient Rhetoric and Paul's Apology*, 17–70.

(2:4; 4:17; 6:4; 7:4). With this imitation of the elevated language of the Psalms, he invites the readers into the liturgy in order to shape values that meet with resistance among the readers before he argues the case.[36] The first-person plural refers primarily to Paul, as the distinction between the first- and second-person plural indicates in 1:6–7. The claim that his own afflictions are nothing less than "the sufferings [*pathēmata*] of Christ," which overflow to him (1:5), anticipates the argument of the letter (cf. 4:7–11; 5:14–15; 13:3–4). It is not only Paul who participates in suffering, however. Despite the conflict in Corinth over Paul's suffering, he indicates that the Corinthians are partners (*koinōnoi*) in the same sufferings (1:6–7). The absence of this claim elsewhere in the letter suggests that Paul is describing a desire rather than the reality at Corinth. His words are more performative speech—an implied appeal for solidarity—than existing reality. The repeated claim that his sufferings are for their comfort (*hyper tēs hymōn paraklēseōs*, 1:6) is an appeal to ethos and pathos and the anticipation of his frequent reminder that his sufferings are on their behalf (1:23; 2:4; 4:15; 5:13–15). In the narratio (1:8–11), Paul offers a specific example of the sufferings (*thlipseis*) that he has endured, a theme that is central to Paul's defense.

In the propositio (1:12–14), Paul initiates his defense, claiming that he has behaved "not in worldly wisdom [*en sophia sarkikē*] but by the grace of God" (1:12 AT). He introduces the theme of boasting in 1:14, affirming that "we are your boast and you are ours at the day of Christ" (AT). Throughout the letter, he calls for reciprocal boasting (cf. 5:12). In 1:15–9:15, Paul offers proofs of his boast for them (7:4, 14; 8:24; 9:2–3), while in chapters 10–13, he boasts of his own deeds because the Corinthians have not reciprocated his boasting (12:11; cf. 5:11–13), leaving his desire for a reciprocity of boasting (1:14) unfulfilled. Paul's desire to boast of his converts at the day of the Lord corresponds to the goal that he consistently states in his letters (cf. Phil. 2:15–16; 1 Thess. 2:19). Chapters 10–13 of 2 Corinthians summarize the issues in chapters 1–9 and thus function as the peroratio of the letter.

In the first proof (2 Cor. 1:15–2:13), Paul defends himself against the charge that he makes his decisions in a worldly way (*kata sarka*, 1:17; cf. 10:2–3); even though he fails to keep his promise to visit them, he indicates that his actions were always for their benefit. His change of travel plans was "to spare" them (1:23) and was based on his love for them (2:4) because his "joy is [their] joy" (2:3 AT). Indeed, everything was "on [their] behalf" (*di' hymas*, 2:10). The repeated claims that his decisions were for their sake are consistent with the affirmation in the propositio that they are "his boast" (1:14). This language

36. See Selby, *Not with Wisdom of Words*, 106. For the form "Blessed be the Lord, who . . . ," see Luke 1:68; Eph. 1:3–14; 1 Pet. 1:3–11.

of pathos prepares the way for his appeal for reconciliation at the end of his defense (5:20; 6:1–2; 6:11–7:4).[37]

In 2:14–7:4, Paul's defense moves from a sequence of events in the past (1:8–11; 1:13–2:13) to the present tense, and from the first-person singular (1:15–2:13) to the first-person plural, which refers primarily, if not exclusively, to Paul himself. Thus he turns from a specific instance to what is "always" (*pantote*) the case in his ministry (cf. 2:14; 4:10; 5:6). The defense begins with a second exordium celebrating the victory in Paul's ministry (2:14–17) and concludes with an appeal for the reciprocity of boasting that he mentions in the propositio (1:14). In 2:14–5:10, Paul describes the paradoxical nature of this victory, while 5:11–7:4 offers the theological foundations for the appeals to the community (5:20; 6:1–2; 6:11–7:4).[38]

In the second proof of the letter (2:14–4:6), Paul distinguishes his preaching ministry from that of those who merely peddle the word (2:17; cf. 4:2). Evoking the image of the triumphal procession, he describes himself as a participant through his preaching ministry as he "spreads the fragrance of the knowledge [of God] in every place" (2:14 AT). While he is not the victorious general in the victory processional but apparently the captive who is being led to his death, his focus is a ministry that determines the salvation or the destruction of his listeners (2 Cor. 2:16; cf. 1 Cor. 1:18). Despite the appearances, this ministry is of such magnitude that he echoes Moses, asking, "Who is sufficient for these things?" (2 Cor. 2:16; cf. Exod. 4:10).

Paul recalls the story of Moses as an exemplum in chapter 3, employing *synkrisis* (comparison) to demonstrate, against his detractors, the glory of his own ministry (2 Cor. 3:7–11).[39] Paul is the minister of the new covenant promised by Jeremiah (2 Cor. 3:1–6; cf. Jer. 31:31–34; Ezek. 11:19; 36:26), which is written not on stone but on human hearts (2 Cor. 3:2–5). The result is a community that, unlike the Israelites, can behold the glory of the Lord and be transformed into the image of Christ "from glory to glory" (2 Cor. 3:18 AT). As Paul will demonstrate in the argument that follows, transformation occurs as he and the entire community ("we all") participate in the cross of Christ (4:10–11; cf. 1:6). The existence of the Corinthian church empowered by the Spirit is the demonstration that they are his letter of recommendation—his

---

37. Gorman, *Cruciformity*, 204.

38. See Bieringer, "2 Korinther 5,14a und die Versöhnung der Welt," 431.

39. Comparison (Greek *synkrisis*) was a common rhetorical device designed to demonstrate the greatness of the speaker's subject. Thus Aristotle, *Rhet.* 1.9.39: "And you must compare him with illustrious personages, for it affords ground for amplification and is noble, if he can be proved better than men of worth. Amplification is with good reason ranked as one of the forms of praise, since it consists in superiority, and superiority is one of the things that are noble."

"boast" (cf. 1:14)—and the evidence that the outpouring of the Spirit in the new age has become a reality.

Paul describes the paradoxical nature of this glory in the third proof (4:7–5:10). In response to the opponents' criticism of his weakness, Paul declares, "We hold this treasure in earthen vessels, in order that the extraordinary power may be God's and not ours" (4:7 AT), reiterating with striking images the theme of power in weakness that he recalled in 1 Corinthians (1 Cor. 1:18–2:5). The treasure is the glorious gospel that he preaches (2 Cor. 2:14–17; 4:5–6), and the earthen vessel, a common metaphor for the fragile human body,[40] is frail existence. That is, God has placed the ministry that surpasses that of Moses (2 Cor. 3:1–18) in an unlikely place. Thus Paul responds to the opponents' complaints about his weakness (2 Cor. 10:10–11) with the claim that this weakness is the arena in which God's power is present. This claim appears both in the exordium (2 Cor. 1:3–7) and in the peroratio (13:3–4) of the letter.

The carefully crafted antitheses in 4:8–9 illustrate the theme of power in weakness. Both the list of sufferings and the rhetorically crafted antitheses echo the contrast between Paul's ministry and the values of the Corinthians, as in 1 Corinthians 4:9–13. They are a distinctive feature in 2 Corinthians because opponents have boasted of their own credentials and the adversities they have overcome (cf. 11:18, 21–23). For Paul, however, these adversities are not evidence for his achievements but of his weakness (11:29–30; 12:9–10) as he demonstrates that God's power is present in his weakness (12:9; cf. 1:3–7).

The sufferings and the empowerment described in 4:8–9 are nothing less than the participation in the death and resurrection of Jesus, as Paul indicates in 4:10–15. In the two parallel statements in 4:10–11, he indicates why he is not destroyed. Just as he is "always" (*pantote*) being led in the triumphal processional (2:14), he is "always [*pantote*] carrying around the dying [*nekrōsis*] of Jesus" in his body and "always [*aei*] being handed over [*paradidometha*] to death" (4:10–11 AT). This description corresponds to the first part in each of the antitheses. Being hard pressed (*thlibomenoi*), distressed (*stenochōroumenoi*), bewildered (*aporoumenoi*), persecuted (*diōkomenoi*), and knocked down (*kataballomenoi*) is the equivalent of "carrying around the dying of Jesus" (4:10 AT).

Nekrōsis, used elsewhere in the New Testament only once (cf. Rom. 4:19), denotes the process of dying.[41] It is a graphic way of describing a common theme in 2 Corinthians as well as the other letters. In the exordium, Paul already declares that "the sufferings of Christ overflow to us" (2 Cor. 1:5 AT),

40. See texts in Schmeller, *Der zweite Brief an die Korinther*, 255.
41. BDAG 668.

and at the end of the letter, he declares that "Christ was crucified in weakness, but lives by the power of God, and we are weak in him, but we will live with him in the power of God" (2 Cor. 13:4 AT). Likewise, in Philippians, he desires to know "the fellowship of [Christ's] sufferings" (Phil. 3:10 AT).

Paul's description of himself as "handed over to death" recalls the fate of the suffering servant of Isaiah 53, who was "handed over to death" (Isa. 53:12 LXX). Thus he not only identifies the suffering of Jesus with the suffering servant but also identifies himself with the suffering of Jesus.

Paul reiterates in 2 Corinthians 4:10–11 that power is present in human weakness, indicating that "the life of Jesus is manifested" as he participates in the dying of Jesus (2 Cor. 4:10 AT). Paul's dying means life for the Corinthians in the present because he knows of the future resurrection (4:14–15).

Mention of the future resurrection provides the transition to 4:16–5:10, in which Paul elaborates that empowerment takes place in the present (4:16–18) and will culminate in the future (5:1–10). The expectation of the final judgment (5:10), which Paul inherited from his Pharisaic background, provides the telos of Paul's ministry, as he indicates in 5:11–6:2. In order to reach the goal of a people who are his "boast at the day of Christ" (1:14 AT), he engages in persuasion (5:11).

While he denies elsewhere that he speaks with "persuasive words of wisdom" (1 Cor. 2:4 AT), associated with the Sophists (cf. Gal. 1:10; 1 Thess. 2:4), he insists that he "persuades others" (2 Cor. 5:11 AT). He does not, however, employ the sophistic persuasion that merely pleases others (Gal. 1:10; 1 Thess. 2:4) but the proclamation that urges them to "be reconciled to God" (2 Cor. 5:20). The chiasm below indicates the relationship between Paul's persuasion and his theology.[42]

A 5:11–13 Paul persuades others in a ministerial existence for their sake (*hymin*).

   B 5:14–15 (*gar*) Because of the death of Christ "for us," we die with him.

      C 5:16 (*hōste*) Paul has a new epistemology as a result of Christ's sacrifice.

      C′ 5:17 (*hōste*) All who are in Christ participate in a new world.

   B′ 5:18–19 The death of Christ is both reconciliation of the world and the source of Paul's ministry.

A′ 5:20–6:2 Paul persuades the Corinthians to be reconciled to God. (AT)

42. The chiasm appears also in my chapter "Reading the Letters as Narrative," 94–95.

The outer frame (A, A') indicates the nature of Paul's persuasion. Paul's task is to enable the community to answer those who boast "according to appearances" (*en prosōpō*; i.e., according to Greco-Roman standards; cf. 10:10–11; 11:18). In keeping with his desire to be their boast, which he stated in the propositio (1:14), he wants them to be able to boast about him—that is, to articulate a theological position. At the end of the unit, Paul engages in persuasion, taking on the role of the servant, urging the readers not to receive the grace of God in vain (6:1), citing the servant's words (6:2; cf. Isa. 49:8), and declaring that "now is the day of salvation."

In the most densely argued theological statement in the letter, Paul demonstrates the inseparability of persuasion and theology. He summarizes his gospel three times with different formulations (2 Cor. 5:14–15, 18–19, 21), in each instance indicating its significance for his ministry and for the community. In some instances, the first-person plural refers to Paul himself (5:14, 16, 18–19), while in other instances, it refers to the entire believing community (5:21b). The second-person plural refers to the readers (5:11–13, 20; 6:1–2), and it is in the third person that Paul enunciates a theological principle (5:14–15, 17, 18a, 19a, 21a).

In keeping with the telos of his ministry (1:14), he declares that his ministry is "for you" (*hymin*, 5:13; cf. 1:23–24; 2:3; 4:15).[43] In the theological argument, he demonstrates that his ministry is the embodiment of his theology. As *gar* indicates in 5:14, Paul defends his ministerial conduct with the theological foundation. In saying "the love of Christ controls us," he reiterates that he is not his own man (AT; cf. 1 Cor. 9:15–18; 2 Cor. 2:14). As Paul says elsewhere, the love of God was evident in the giving of God's Son (cf. Rom. 5:7–8; Gal. 2:20). Paul offers the reason for his conduct in the creedal statement, assuming that his readers will agree. "One died for [*hyper*] all" (2 Cor. 5:14 AT) is an alternative form of the foundational story "Christ died for [*hyper*] our sins" (2 Cor. 15:3 AT; cf. Rom. 4:25; 5:7–8). The phrase "die for" (*apothnēskō hyper*) appears three times in 2 Corinthians 5:14–15. Paul probably replaced "for our sins" with "for all" to prepare the way for "all" in 5:14c: "therefore all died" (AT).[44] He thus argues on the basis of received traditions, as in 1 Corinthians.

Paul offers an initial interpretation of the creedal statement in 2 Corinthians 5:14c: "Therefore all died" (AT). The surprising conclusion is not that,

---

43. *Hymin* is a dative of advantage, "in your interest." BDF 188.

44. In Paul's use of the formula "die for," the subject is Christ (cf. Rom. 5:8; 14:15; 1 Thess. 5:10), while here in 2 Cor. 5:14 it is "one" (*heis*). Elsewhere the object of the *hyper* formula is the first-person plural (Rom. 5:8; 1 Thess. 5:10) or "for our sins" (1 Cor. 15:3); here the object is "all" (*pantōn*).

because one died, others may live, but that "all died." In contrast to earlier passages in which Paul has described his own experience as involving the sharing in the sufferings of Christ (1:3–7; 4:10–11), here he extends his own experience to indicate the general principle that "all"—the entire believing community—died. As he indicates in the exordium (1:5–7), all believers are "partners" (*koinōnoi*) in the sufferings of Christ that overflow to Paul (cf. Phil. 1:30). Paul also indicates elsewhere that the destiny of one affects the many (Rom. 5:12–21; 1 Cor. 15:45–49) and that in baptism believers are "buried with" Christ (Rom. 6:4) and crucified with him (Rom. 6:6). He makes a similar claim when he says, "I have been crucified with Christ" (Gal. 2:19) and when he speaks of "the fellowship of his sufferings" (Phil. 3:10 AT), presenting himself as a paradigm for others.

"All died" is an elaboration on the earlier affirmation that "we all" are being transformed into Christ's image (2 Cor. 3:18). Paul elaborates on this claim, repeating the basic creed in 5:15 and adding an interpretation: "In order that those who live may no longer live for themselves, but for the one who died and was raised" (AT). This principle applies to Paul, whose ministry is for the sake of others ("for you," 5:13; cf. 1:23; 4:15), but the general principle applies to all believers. As Paul says to the Romans, "No one lives to himself, and no one dies to himself" (14:7 AT).

While the readers agree with the basic premise that "one died for all," their opposition to Paul indicates that they do not draw the same theological conclusions. In the parallel statements in 2 Corinthians 5:16–17, Paul recalls his own journey, indicating that he once regarded Christ from a worldly point of view (*kata sarka*, 5:16) but that he no longer regards him in this way. That is, before his conversion, he had shared the opponents' epistemology, but now he has a new way of knowing insofar as the cross is the defining aspect of his ministry. When opponents criticize his weakness and suffering, they are thinking in a worldly way.

The parallel statement in 5:17 clarifies Paul's new epistemology. Paul speaks not only of his own ministry but also of "anyone who is in Christ." They belong to the new creation, while those who live "in a worldly way" (*kata sarka*) do not recognize that the death on the cross is not only a past event but also the reality that marks the turn of the ages. Having indicated earlier that he is the minister of the new covenant (3:6) promised by Jeremiah (Jer. 31:33–34), he now speaks of "the new creation," an allusion to Israel's hope for "new heavens and a new earth," when "the former things shall not be remembered" (Isa. 65:17; cf. 66:22). Christ has assumed the role of the suffering servant of Isaiah, who "died for all" (2 Cor. 5:14), an event that inaugurated the new covenant and the new creation.

Paul reformulates in 5:18–19 the soteriological affirmation that "one died for all," employing the image of reconciliation in two parallel statements:

A   God, who reconciled us to himself through Christ,

  B   and has given us the ministry of reconciliation.

A′ That is, God was in Christ reconciling the world to himself, not counting their trespasses against them,

  B′ and entrusting to us the word of reconciliation. (alt.)

As in 5:14–15, Paul repeats the soteriological statement while making slight alterations. In 5:18, he uses the aorist tense to describe the event ("the one who reconciled," AT), while in 5:19, he uses the imperfect tense ("God . . . was reconciling," AT). According to 5:18, God reconciled "us," while in 5:19, God was reconciling the world. The parallel statements declaring that God reconciled both us and the world recall the statement that "one died for all." The *kosmos* is the world of humanity that is enslaved to sin.

The term "reconciliation" is a rare soteriological word in Paul (cf. Rom. 5:11). It is used elsewhere in the Septuagint only in 2 Maccabees (2 Macc. 1:4–5; 5:20; 7:33; 8:29), where the author prays that God, in his mercy, will be reconciled to the people (2 Macc. 1:4–5; 7:33) after a time of divine wrath. In 2 Corinthians 5:18–19, however, God is the initiator. We do not plead for him to be reconciled to us.

While this specific image is not used in the Septuagint, the consistent theme in Deutero-Isaiah is the hope for peace with God. Israel's exile, according to Isaiah 40–66, is the result of the people's sin. Israel suffers under God's wrath (Isa. 51:20; 60:10), God's anger (47:6; 51:17, 22; 54:8; 57:16–17), and separation from God (59:2). God's restoration of Israel is described not only as a redemptive and new creation but also as a time when the nation will "not be forsaken" (62:12 AT). Peace is reestablished between the nation and its God (cf. 48:18; 52:7; 57:19), a peace that results from, and is characteristic of, the new creation. According to Isaiah 43, this is considered a ransom (43:3) and the forgiveness of sins (43:22–25).[45]

Paul has employed the soteriological statement as a defense of his ministry, as the parallel statements "giving us the ministry of reconciliation" (2 Cor. 5:18 AT) and "entrusting to us the word of reconciliation" (5:19 AT) indicate. His ministry is defined by the cross and appointed by God. Paul indicates the significance of the soteriological statement, declaring that he is the ambassador of God, "making his appeal through us" to "be reconciled to God" (5:20).

45. Beale, "Old Testament Background of Reconciliation."

The next soteriological statement appears without a transition, appearing between "God making his appeal through us" (5:20 AT) and "We appeal to you" (6:1 AT). Verse 21 is a reformulation of Paul's preaching and a transition to the appeal in 6:1–2. The antithetic style suggests that it is a formula worked out by Paul in which he declares his gospel, followed by the purpose clause.

> God, sending his own Son in the likeness of sinful flesh and for sin, condemned sin in the flesh, in order that the just requirement of the law may be fulfilled in us. (Rom. 8:3–4 AT)

> You know the grace of our Lord Jesus Christ, that for your sake [di' hymas] he became poor, although he was rich, in order that you may become rich through his poverty. (2 Cor. 8:9 AT)

> Christ redeemed us from the curse of the law, becoming a curse for us, . . . in order that in Christ Jesus the blessing of Abraham might come to the gentiles. (Gal. 3:13–14 AT)

> The one who died for us (hyper hēmōn), in order that whether we wake or sleep we will be with him. (1 Thess. 5:10 AT)

Scholars have offered alternative attempts to recognize a chiasm in the antithetical statement in 2 Corinthians 5:21.

The one who knew no sin	he made to be sin.
(We who know sin)	become the righteousness of God in him.

The formulation is what Morna Hooker calls "interchange." Christ became sin, while we become the righteousness of God.[46] "For us" (hyper hēmōn; "for our sake," NRSV) reformulates "for all" (hyper pantōn) in 5:14, and "so that" (hina) recalls 5:15. The "one" who "died for all" (5:14) is the one "who knew no sin" (5:21).

Nowhere else does Paul refer to Christ as "the one who knew no sin." Paul may have in mind the unblemished sacrificial animal of Leviticus 4 and 16 or the suffering servant of Isaiah 53:9, who had "done no violence" and had "no deceit in his mouth." That he "became sin" is reminiscent of Paul's claim that he came "in the likeness of sinful flesh" (Rom. 8:3). The expression probably echoes Isaiah 53:12, according to which the servant was "numbered with the transgressors, yet bore the sin of many" (AT).[47]

---

46. Hooker, "Interchange in Christ and Ethics," 5.
47. See Bieringer, "Sünde und Gerechtigkeit," 469.

The purpose clause, "in order that we might become the righteousness of God," is the transition to the appeal in 2 Corinthians 6:1–2 (AT). To become God's righteousness is the equivalent of living no longer for ourselves (2 Cor. 5:15) and being reconciled to God (5:20). The effect of the cross, therefore, is transformation (cf. 3:18). "We" here is the whole community, the equivalent of "us" in the first half of the statement. Paul is probably still echoing the words about the servant, the righteous one, who makes many righteous (Isa. 53:11).

Paul continues to echo Deutero-Isaiah as he concludes, "We appeal to you not to receive the grace of God in vain" (2 Cor. 6:1 AT; cf. Isa. 49:4), citing the words of the servant, "Now is the time of salvation" (2 Cor. 6:2 AT; cf. Isa. 49:8). Paul's defense resumes in 2 Corinthians 6:3–10 (cf. 2 Cor. 4:7–11) as the basis for further appeals in 6:11–7:2a. In chapters 7–9, he describes the Corinthians as his "boast," but the sequence of appeals in 6:13–7:4 is based on Paul's theological explanation.

The central focus of the peroratio (chaps. 10–13) is the "fool's speech" in 11:16–12:10, which expands on the earlier catalogs of sufferings (4:7–10; 6:4–10) and is the basis for Paul's appeal to the Corinthians to reciprocate his boasting on their behalf (12:11; cf. 1:14). As Paul has indicated in 4:7–11, the list of sufferings is an indication of his participation in the sufferings of Christ and evidence of God's power in human weakness (cf. 13:4). Paul thus confronts Greco-Roman values with a defense of his ministry based on participation in the sufferings of Christ. However, this argument is plausible only for those who accept the original premise that "Christ died for our sins" (1 Cor. 15:3).

Conclusion: The Theology of the Cross in the Corinthian Correspondence

Paul's "theology is not a dead exercise of repeating formulae, but filling a faith statement with new life under specific historical conditions in the Corinthian community."[48] Because of the situation in Corinth, Paul theologizes about the meaning of the cross in the life of the church. While he assumes that his readers acknowledge that "Christ died for our sins," the telos of his ministry is threatened by the Corinthians' failure to grasp the meaning of the creed that Paul once preached and that they had believed (1 Cor. 15:3, 11). In both Corinthian letters, Paul confronts believers who live by the values of their culture, failing to recognize that the message of the cross is the revelation of a new era that transforms the values of believers.

48. Bieringer, "Dying and Being Raised For," 175.

The cross, the epitome of shame in the Greco-Roman world, now defines Christian existence and Paul's ministry. The tradition that "one died for all" (2 Cor. 5:14), which Paul restates with a variety of images (cf. 2 Cor. 5:18–19, 21), is the central premise in 2 Corinthians. Paul appeals to logos (the Old Testament and inherited creedal statements), ethos, and pathos to persuade the community to be reconciled to God and ultimately to be his boast at the day of Christ (2 Cor. 1:14; cf. 11:2–3). Participation in the cross is the focal point of Paul's theology, for by participating in that event, the community is being transformed into the image of Christ. In the cross, Paul sees the culmination of the promises of the exilic prophets. The gospel promised by Deutero-Isaiah has become a reality in the death of Jesus.

8

The Theology of the Cross and Justification by Faith

From the time of his call, Paul understood his mission as the apostle to the gentiles. In a radical break from the Jewish tradition, he welcomed them without requiring circumcision. Gentiles thus became incorporated into the people of God as heirs of ancient Israel with an identity and ethos as the elect people. Their task, like Israel's, was to lead holy lives that separated them from family and neighbors. While Paul introduces the topics of justification (*dikaioō*, 1 Cor. 6:11; *dikaiosynē*, 1 Cor. 1:30; 2 Cor. 3:19; 5:21; 9:9) and faith in the earlier correspondence—and presumably in his catechesis—he neither develops these themes nor combines the topics of *dikaiosynē* (righteousness, justification; *dikaioō*, justify) and *pistis* (faith, faithfulness).[1] In Galatians and Romans, he brings these categories together as primary themes in his interpretation of the death of Jesus. The predominant place of these themes in Galatians is probably determined by the rhetorical situation. Although Paul insists that he does not "persuade people" (Gal. 1:10 AT), his task in Galatians, as in the other letters, is to ensure that Christ will be "formed" among them (Gal. 4:19). He attempts to persuade the readers to take the right course of action (Gal. 4:12; 5:13–6:10); thus Galatians has a functional similarity to deliberative rhetoric.[2] In this

1. Philippians, which has this language (3:9–11), was probably written during Paul's Roman imprisonment.
2. See Kennedy, *Interpretation through Rhetorical Criticism*, 144–45.

chapter, I will explore the rhetorical function of these themes in Paul's persuasive task.

Faith and Righteousness outside of Galatians and Romans

Paul, like other New Testament writers, gives a prominence to the noun "faith" (*pistis*) and the verb "believe" (*pisteuō*), which distinguishes him from both Old Testament and Greco-Roman writers.[3] *Pistis*, which can be rendered as "trust," "faith," "proof," or "faithfulness,"[4] is the attribute that Paul inculcates in his converts. For example, he expresses gratitude for the Thessalonians' "work of faith" (1 Thess. 1:3) after he has sent Timothy to encourage their faith (*pistis*) in the context of persecution (1 Thess. 3:2–3) and has received a positive report of their faith (*pistis*) and love (1 Thess. 3:6). Their faith is, however, incomplete, for Paul hopes to strengthen what is lacking in their faith (1 Thess. 3:10) and encourages them to put on "the breastplate of faith and love" (1 Thess. 5:8). Similarly, Paul expresses gratitude for Philemon's faith and love (Philem. 5). He also declares to the Corinthians that "we walk by faith and not by sight" (2 Cor. 5:7 AT) and commends their faith (2 Cor. 8:7). Additionally, Paul declares to the Philippians that "it has been granted to [them] not only to believe, but also to suffer for Christ" (Phil. 1:29 AT). He also employs the participle *hoi pisteuontes* to describe communities as "those who believe" (1 Cor. 1:21; 14:22; 1 Thess. 1:7; 2:10; cf. 1 Cor. 3:5). This description assumes the boundaries between believers and unbelievers (*apistoi*, 1 Cor. 6:6; 7:12; 10:27; 14:22–23; 2 Cor. 4:4; 6:14) and reflects the conviction that *pistis* is the distinguishing feature of Christian existence.[5]

"The faith," mentioned in Galatians (1:23), becomes especially prominent in the disputed letters of Paul. *Pistis* and *pisteuō* appear in these disputed letters without an object and as a primary Christian attribute. Paul has heard of the faith of the Colossians (Col. 1:4; cf. Rom. 1:8) and writes to ensure that they remain strengthened and established in the faith (Col. 1:23; 2:7). He reminds the Ephesians that "by grace [they] are saved through faith" (Eph. 2:8 AT) and prays that Christ will take up residence in their hearts through faith (Eph. 3:17). *Pistis* also has an especially important place in the Pastoral Epistles (1 Tim. 1:2, 4–5, 19; 2:7, 15; 4:1, 6, 12; 5:8, 12; 6:10–12, 21; 2 Tim. 1:5, 13; 3:8).

3. On the subject of faith in antiquity, see Morgan, *Roman Faith and Christian Faith*.
4. BDAG 819.
5. Wolter, *Paul*, 81.

While Paul frequently employs *pistis* and *pisteuō* without an object to describe a life orientation, he also employs both the noun and the verb to describe the content of faith. He describes the Thessalonians' faith in God (1 Thess. 1:7) and reminds them that "we believe [*pisteuomen*] that Jesus died and arose" (1 Thess. 4:14 AT). Similarly, he reminds the Corinthians that the gospel of the death and resurrection of Christ was preached, adding "and so we believed" (1 Cor. 15:1, 11 AT). He wants to ensure that their faith is not in human wisdom but in the power of God (1 Cor. 2:5).

However, Paul speaks of the righteousness of God (*dikaiosynē tou theou*) prior to Galatians and Romans rarely (2 Cor. 5:21; cf. 9:9). The verb *dikaioō* (justify, vindicate, declare righteous) appears only in Paul's reminder to the Corinthians: "You have been washed, you have been justified [*edikaiōthēte*], you have been sanctified" (1 Cor. 6:11 AT). While the concepts may be present implicitly in the earlier letters, the combination of *dikaiosynē/dikaioō* with *pistis/pisteuō* appears outside of Galatians and Romans only in Philippians 3:9–10.

Justification by Faith and Transformation in Galatians

The Rhetorical Situation

New issues undoubtedly evoked the dominance of these themes in Galatians and Romans. While they may be implicit in Paul's earliest letter, as I argued in chapter 5, Paul develops them as weapons in the defense of his gospel in Galatians. He has shaped gentile converts into communities on the basis of faith and without requiring circumcision, but only in Galatians and Romans (see chap. 9 below) does he offer a theological defense of this practice. From the evidence offered in Galatians itself, we can determine the rhetorical situation. Paul faces opponents who proclaim what Paul calls "another gospel" (Gal. 1:8–9 AT). Since Paul's task is not to give an objective description of the proponents of the "other gospel," we can discern their point of view only through the filter of Paul's highly polemic rhetoric. He describes them as those "who trouble you" (1:7; 5:10 AT), "who unsettle you" (5:12), and "who want to make a good showing in the flesh" (6:12)[6] by compelling the converts to be circumcised (6:12). Indeed, at least some of the gentile converts in Galatia have been circumcised (1:6–9; 5:2; 6:13). Paul's insistence that neither circumcision nor uncircumcision benefits the believer (5:6; 6:15) is undoubtedly addressing that issue.

6. Cf. chap. 4 above.

John Barclay has rightly cautioned against mirror reading the letter to gain additional information about the historical situation.[7] Nevertheless, one can make reasonable judgments about the events that lie behind Galatians on the basis of historical plausibility and the argument of the letter. The attention to Abraham in Galatians 3:6–29 suggests that Paul is responding to opponents who insist that, because Abraham himself sealed his covenant with God by being circumcised, all of his children must submit to the same rite. Indeed, they probably agreed with Philo that Abraham was the first proselyte (*Virtues* 212–19) and thus a model for others. Paul's opponents probably believed that Jesus was the messiah of Israel but insisted that gentile converts keep the law. The evidence of Galatians suggests that the demand for obedience to the law was attractive to the Galatians, probably because the law provided a means of self-control and a moral structure. Paul, however, declares that they deserted the one who called them (Gal. 1:6), became estranged from Christ, and fell from grace (Gal. 5:4). Thus he fears that his work as the herald of the good news announced in Deutero-Isaiah is "in vain" (Gal. 4:11 AT; cf. Isa. 49:4) but writes to reclaim his converts for the gospel. Like a woman in birth pangs, he agonizes over the community, for his labor will not be in vain only if Christ is "formed" (*morphōthē*) among the Galatian churches (Gal. 4:19).

Argumentation and Theology

Hans Dieter Betz argued that Galatians is an apologetic letter that "presupposes a real or fictitious situation of the court of law, with jury, accuser, and defendant."[8] In the case of Galatians, the addressees are the jury, Paul is the defendant, and the opponents are the accusers. Thus, according to Betz, Galatians is a letter of self-defense, a speech in letter form that conforms to ancient judicial rhetoric and can be analyzed accordingly. Betz identifies the parts of the ancient speech in Galatians: the exordium (Gal. 1:6–9), the narratio (1:10–2:14), the propositio (2:15–21), the probatio (3:1–4:31), and the exhortatio (5:1–6:10). He identifies 1:1–5 as the epistolary prescript and 6:11–18 as the epistolary postscript. As numerous interpreters have argued, this approach fails to account for the full argument of Galatians. "Exhortatio" is a category invented by Betz that is never mentioned in ancient descriptions of the parts of the oration. Indeed, the extended exhortation—especially the proportion that is devoted to it in Galatians—is absent from ancient speeches. Furthermore, the designation of 1:1–5 as prescript and 6:11–18 as postscript does not account for the place of these passages in the rhetoric of Galatians.

---

7. Barclay, "Mirror Reading a Polemical Letter."
8. Betz, *Galatians*, 24.

Thus any analysis of the rhetoric and theology of Galatians must observe the place of the extended ethical exhortation (esp. 5:13–6:10) as well as the introduction (1:1–5) and the conclusion (6:11–18) in the argument.[9] The exhortation is not an appendix to the argument but an integral part of it. Galatians is not, like judicial rhetoric, a call for a judgment about the past but an attempt to dissuade the readers from the direction that they have taken and to persuade them toward appropriate behavior in the future. Paul's ultimate hope is that Christ "be formed" among the Galatians (4:19 AT). If he fails, he will have "labored in vain" (4:11 AT).

The exordium. Despite the limitations in Betz's analysis, his use of ancient categories for the parts of the speech is beneficial for demonstrating the coherence of the argument. The salutation in Galatians (1:1–5) is not merely an epistolary prescript but an introduction to the issues that are at stake. Paul begins his response to the Galatians not with the traditional thanksgiving announcing the topics for discussion but with the extended salutation (1:1–5) and expression of dismay at the Galatians' reception of another gospel (1:6–9). While he does not make the audience favorably disposed, as he does in the exordium of other letters, his opening words express one aspect of the exordium;[10] he introduces the topic for discussion: the validity of the gospel and his role in proclaiming it. Paul's statement of his apostolic credentials (1:1) anticipates the autobiographical section (1:10–2:14), answering the issue that is under dispute. The extended statement of his credentials ("not from humans nor through humans," 1:1 AT) introduces the claim that his calling and gospel came by revelation (1:15–16) and indicates that his message is not based on common rhetorical proofs but on his prophetic rhetoric.[11] The premise of the entire argument is the revelation from God. If Paul has challenged the traditional norms for gentile membership in the people of God, it is because he, like the prophet of Deutero-Isaiah and Jeremiah (Isa. 49:1; Jer. 1:5), was set apart from his mother's womb.

Anticipating the argument that follows, Paul summarizes the gospel, describing Christ as the one "who gave himself for our sins" (Gal. 1:4), a variant form of the early Christian creed, "Christ died for our sins according to the Scriptures" (1 Cor. 15:3). As a summary of the gospel that was probably

9. See Hübner, "Der Galaterbrief," 243.

10. For a speech that opens with a blistering accusation, see Cicero's *First Oration against Cataline.*

11. On Paul's prophetic rhetoric, see chap. 1 above. See also chap. 1 on Paul's consistent contrast between himself and the rhetoricians. Unlike the rhetoricians, he does not "please men" (Gal. 1:10 AT). See also Tolmie, *Persuading the Galatians,* 33. Although a major part of the argument of Galatians is an appeal to Paul's ethos, he recalls values that are in sharp contrast to those of the rhetoricians.

delivered to all of the churches (cf. Rom. 4:25; 5:6–8; 1 Cor. 15:3; 2 Cor. 5:14, 21; 1 Thess. 5:10), the statement in 1:4 presents common ground with the readers by mentioning a matter that was not in dispute.[12] This formula echoes the description of the suffering servant of Deutero-Isaiah, whom the Lord delivered over "for our sins" (Isa. 53:5 AT) and gave up "because of our sins" (Isa. 53:12 AT)—the one who "bore the sins of many and was delivered over because of our sins" (Isa. 53:12 AT). This was the creed that Paul had received from the earliest disciples. The description of Christ as the one who "gave himself [*dontos heauton*]" (Gal. 1:4) anticipates the later reference to "the one who loved me and gave himself [*paradontos heauton*] for [*hyper*] me" (Gal. 2:20) and is reminiscent of other summaries in which Christ is the one who "gave himself" for others (cf. Rom. 8:32; Eph. 5:2, 25). While "our sins" originally referred to the trespasses of Israel that are borne by the servant in Deutero-Isaiah (Isa. 53:4–5, 12), for Paul, they include the sins of Jews and gentiles.

Paul frequently interprets the death of Jesus with a purpose clause (cf. Rom. 8:3–4; 2 Cor. 5:21; Gal. 3:14; 4:4–5). Here Christ died "in order to rescue us from the present evil age" (Gal. 1:4 AT). The verb *exaireō*, suggesting rescue from perilous circumstances,[13] was used for the Hebrews' rescue from Egyptian slavery (Acts 7:34). Its use here anticipates the later claim that Christ "delivered [*exēgorasen*] us from the curse of the law" (Gal. 3:13 AT; cf. 4:5). The image suggests deliverance from slavery, a theme that Paul introduced in 1 Corinthians (1 Cor. 6:20; 7:23) and develops in Galatians (cf. Gal. 4:21–31; 5:1, 13): the readers were once enslaved to the law (Gal. 4:5), to world powers (*stoicheia*), and to beings that were not gods (Gal. 4:8–9). He also develops this theme in Romans, indicating that believers, who were once enslaved to sin (Rom. 6:17, 20), are now liberated (Rom. 6:18). The reminder in Galatians that the readers have been "rescued from the present evil aeon" (Gal. 1:4 AT) anticipates the later theme that the readers have relapsed into the old aeon. That is, in keeping with the Pharisaic tradition, Paul envisions two successive aeons, maintaining that believers, with the death of Christ, have entered the new aeon.

The rescue from the present evil age at the beginning of Galatians (1:4) forms an inclusio with the announcement of the new creation in 6:15. Paul's gospel is the message of the new aeon, but circumcision belongs to the old aeon. The numerous antimonies are actually about the breaking in of the new

---

12. See Hübner, *Theologie des Neuen Testaments*, 2:58: "The soteriological accent given here has programmatic significance for the whole letter."

13. BDAG 344.

aeon, which occurred at the cross. On one side of the dualities in Galatians is the reality of the present evil age, while on the other side is the reality of the new creation.

1:4	The present evil age	6:15	The new creation
2:16	Works of the law	2:16	Faith(fulness) of Christ
2:19	Law	2:19–20	Christ
3:2, 5	Works of the law	3:2, 5	Hearing of faith
3:3; 5:16	Flesh	3:3; 5:22	Spirit
3:9–10	Curse	3:6–9	Blessing
3:11–12	To do	3:11	To believe
3:18, 21	Law	3:16–18	Promise
4:4–7, 21–31	Slave	4:26, 31; 5:1, 13	Free person

The death of Christ is the inauguration of the new age; Paul interprets the Galatians' turn to the law as a relapse into the old age. The argument of Galatians elaborates on the claim that Christ "rescued us from the present evil age" (AT) by his death on the cross.

The narratio. In the autobiographical section, Paul elaborates on his role as herald of the gospel of the new aeon, his ministry to the gentiles, and the full agreement of the Jerusalem pillars (Gal. 1:10–2:10). As one who, like Jeremiah (Jer. 1:5) and the prophet of Isaiah 49:1–6, was set apart from his mother's womb, Paul is the herald who is the light to the nations (Isa. 49:6). The establishment of the divine origin of his gospel gives authority to his message.[14] Then, in recalling the insistence that Titus remain uncircumcised during his visit to Jerusalem (Gal. 2:1–10), Paul describes a situation that is parallel to the problem faced by the Galatians. With the resolution that Titus could remain uncircumcised, the truth of the gospel remained (Gal. 2:5). By laying his gospel before the pillars, the leaders of the church, who accepted his mission to the gentiles, Paul demonstrates his authority (Gal. 2:7–10). The Antioch incident, in other words, offers an exemplum from recent experience, indicating that all sides accepted his gospel to the uncircumcised.[15]

The truth of the gospel (cf. Gal. 2:14) was also at stake over another issue parallel to the problems among the Galatian churches. Those Jewish Christians at Antioch who refused table fellowship with gentiles were guilty, according to Paul, of not acting consistently with "the truth of the gospel"

14. See Anderson, *Ancient Rhetorical Theory and Paul*, 147. Anderson cites parallels to Paul's defense in Demosthenes, *Or. 5*, and in Dio Chrysostom, *Conc. Apam.* Both met hostility from the audience with lengthy apologetic narratives.

15. On the importance of the term *exemplum* (example) in ancient rhetoric, see n. 26 below.

(Gal. 2:14), for they denied the full membership of gentiles among the people of God. These past examples of the victory of the truth of the gospel were examples of the issues before the Galatians (cf. Gal. 1:6–9). Paul's point is that "the truth of the gospel" stands in contrast to the boundaries created by the observance of the law.

These events are examples not only of the truth of the gospel but also of Paul's authoritative voice. He does not employ common rhetorical proofs but speaks on the basis of divine revelation. Like ancient orators, Paul appeals to his ethos, knowing that the character of the speaker is necessary for persuasion. In order to overcome reservations about himself, he removes any prejudices against himself (cf. Cicero, *Inv.* 1.22–23).

The propositio. Paul's address to Peter in Galatians 2:15–21 is not only a challenge to Peter but also the answer to the Galatian situation, the propositio of the argument.[16] In the chiasm, Paul again speaks in sharp dichotomies, introducing new topics into the discussion.

A Knowing that a person is not justified by works of the law, but by the faith in/of Christ,[17]

B And we have believed in Christ,

B′ in order that we may be justified by the faith in/of Christ,

A′ For by works of the law no one will be justified. (Gal. 2:16 AT)

With this statement, Paul introduces new categories into the discussion that play a major role in both Galatians and Romans. The passive voice in A and A′ indicates that God is the one who justifies. The reference to what Peter should know indicates that Paul is appealing to a premise that he shares with Peter, and perhaps with the Galatian readers. The verb is a forensic image, suggesting that God is the righteous judge who punishes the wicked and declares others in the right. In other words, Paul enters into a conversation in Judaism over whom God will ultimately justify, introducing the verb *dikaioō* in both the present and the future tenses to argue who will and who

---

16. Hübner, *Theologie des Neuen Testaments*, 2:64.

17. The KJV renders *pistis christou* as "faith of Christ," but subsequent translations have rendered it "faith in Christ." See below for the discussion. In Gal. 2:16, Paul adapts the citation from Ps. 142:2 LXX (cf. 143:2 Eng.), "All flesh will not be justified [*ou dikaiōthēsetai*] before you," to which Paul adds "by works of the law" (*ex erga nomou*). In the original passage, the psalmist stands before God's judgment, knowing that his only hope is in God's righteousness (*dikaiosynē*, 142:1 LXX [143:1 Eng.]). Paul agrees with the psalmist that the sinful person relies on the righteousness of God. While the psalmist concludes that no one is justified before God, Paul adds a phrase to the citation, "by works of the law," and declares that it is by faith in Christ that one is justified. See Hübner, *Theologie des Neuen Testaments*, 2:66.

will not be justified. This imagery, which is central to Paul's argument, has a rich history in the Old Testament and Judaism. Both the noun (*dikaiosynē*, righteousness) and the verb (*dikaioō*) suggest a courtroom in which God is the righteous judge who may declare in favor of the accused. The terminology is especially noteworthy in Deutero-Isaiah. The prophet tells the exiles that God's righteousness (*dikaiosynē*) is forever (Isa. 51:8 LXX). "For the sake of his righteousness, [God] . . . will magnify his teaching and make it glorious" (Isa. 42:21). He has aroused Cyrus in righteousness to end the exile (Isa. 45:13) and bring salvation. Thus God's righteousness is the equivalent of the salvation that comes from God (Isa. 51:6), and God will now come near Israel in righteousness (Isa. 46:13). The prophet declares that "the one who justifies [*dikaiōsas*] me is near" (Isa. 50:8 LXX), and "all the sons of Israel will be justified [*dikaiōthēsontai*]" (Isa. 45:25 LXX). The "righteous one . . . shall make many righteous" (Isa. 53:11), for he will bear the sins of Israel. Thus, according to Deutero-Isaiah, God's righteousness is the basis for Israel's salvation, the equivalent of salvation and the bearing of the sin of the people.

Paul uses two genitive phrases that have been the center of controversy— *erga nomou* (works of the law) and *pistis christou* (faith in/of Christ)— which correspond to the numerous antinomies described above and are apparently shorthand for the alternatives that Paul develops in the midrash in Galatians 3. Paul lays out these alternatives as general principles in A and A' (above). In B and B', he employs the first-person plural, "We have believed in Christ, in order that we may be justified by the faith in/of Christ and not by works of the law." While the opponents have proposed both faith in Christ and obedience to the Torah, Paul speaks in sharp antitheses—faith in/of Christ or works of the law. This claim recalls the summary of the gospel in 1:4. To be rescued from the present evil world is to be justified. As Paul argues in Galatians 3, the works of the law belong to the old aeon, while faith belongs to the new aeon.

Erga nomou and *pistis christou* are shorthand for major themes, and the development of these themes in Galatians 3, where Paul continues to speak in sharp antinomies, provides some clarification. In A and A', no one will be justified "by works of the law" (*erga nomou*). Paul then repeats variant forms of this statement, indicating in 3:11 that no one is justified by the law. While he speaks positively elsewhere about work (1 Cor. 3:13; 15:58; 16:10; Phil. 1:22; 1 Thess. 1:3; cf. Phil. 2:12; Gal. 6:10)—even the "work of faith" (1 Thess. 1:3)—and the final judgment on the basis of the deeds done in the body (Rom. 2:6; 2 Cor. 5:10), he always speaks negatively about "works of the law," which he abbreviates at times to "law" (Gal. 2:21; 3:11, 19, 21). In Galatians and Romans, "works of the law" are always the opposite of faith(fulness). The context suggests that, while "works of the law" in Jewish sources are all of the deeds required by the Torah,[18] the issue in Galatians involves circumcision and food laws, two of the identifying marks of Jewish identity. As the dichotomy indicates, "works of the law" refers to the practice of the law as the source of one's righteousness.[19] Paul clarifies the matter in 2:21, concluding that "if righteousness [*dikaiosynē*] is by the law, Christ died in vain" (AT). Thus those who insist on circumcision have negated the meaning of the cross.

The alternative to "works of the law," according to 2:16, is *pistis christou*, on the basis of which one is justified. Although the KJV renders *pistis christou* as "faith of Christ," subsequent translations have rendered it as "faith in Christ" and thus parallel to "We have believed in Christ, in order that we may be justified by *pistis christou* and not by the works of the law" (AT). Recent studies have maintained that *pistis christou* should be rendered "faithfulness of Christ." That is, *pistis christou* is regarded as the divine initiative, the equivalent of the obedience of Christ in his death on the cross (cf. Rom. 5:19; Phil. 2:8).[20] Since these antithetical genitive phrases are shorthand for the alternatives for salvation, their significance becomes clarified when we observe Paul's frequent antitheses of works and faith.[21]

Works of the law (*erga nomou*)	Faith in/of Christ (*pistis christou*) (Gal. 2:16 bis)
Works of the law	*Pistis christou* (Rom. 3:21–22)
Works of the law	Hearing of faith (Gal. 3:2)
Works of the law	Faith (Gal. 3:10–11)
Works of the law	Faith (Rom. 3:28)
Law of works	Law of faith (Rom. 3:27)
Working	Believing on (*epi*) the one who justifies the ungodly (Rom. 4:5)
Works (Rom. 4:6)	Faith (Rom. 4:9)
Works	God's call (Rom. 9:12)
Works	Faith (Rom. 3:31)
Righteousness from the law	Death of Christ (Gal. 2:21)
One's own righteousness	*Pistis christou* (Phil. 3:9)

These variant forms of the antithesis between *erga nomou* and *pistis christou* in Galatians 2:16 indicate that Paul's primary concern with this antithesis is the human response to the gospel, which Peter and the others have ignored

18. See Wright, "4QMMT and Paul."
19. See Barclay, *Paul and the Gift*, 374.
20. Hays, *Faith of Jesus Christ*, 188; Wright, *Paul and the Faithfulness of God*, 857.
21. For Paul's use of antithesis and its significance in rhetorical argument, see chap. 7, n. 16 above.

in compelling gentiles to "live like Jews" (cf. 2:14). The elaboration in Galatians 3 leaves little doubt that the human response plays an important role in justification. When Paul uses *pistis* without an object, he is referring to the human response (cf. 3:10–14, 24). However, *pistis christou* is more than the human response, as Paul's own example indicates (2:19–21), for he is himself the example of the contrast between law (*nomos*) and faith (*pistis*). When he says, "I died to the law in order that I might live for Christ" (2:19 AT), he presents himself as an example to the Galatians. In the claim "The life that I live by faith in the Son of God, who loved me and gave himself for me" (2:20 AT), he offers a paradigm for life in the new aeon, an anticipation of the exhortation in 5:13–6:10. The focus is not only on the human response but also on the total reliance on Christ. The parallels in 2:19–21 indicate that the response of faith is the equivalent to "living for Christ" and being "crucified with Christ" (2:19). Michael Wolter has suggested that the choice between the subjective genitive ("faithfulness of Christ") and the objective genitive ("faith in Christ") is a false alternative, for the focus is on both the orientation toward Christ and Christ himself. Indeed, as the antinomies above suggest, the alternative to the law is not only the human response but also "the death of Christ" (2:21 AT). For example, when Paul says in 3:23 "When faith came" (AT), he speaks of the coming of Christ himself. Thus the *pistis christou* that justifies is both the human response and the saving act of Christ.[22] As John M. G. Barclay maintains,

> This recognition is accorded on the basis of "faith in Christ," not because this faith in itself establishes a kind of "worth," but because it is directed to the event in which was created, without regard to worth, a new source and mode of life in relation to God (2:19). Just as the emphasis in the first of the two antithetical phrases, "works of the law" (*erga nomou*), falls on the second term (the practice of the Torah) . . . , so in the second, "faith in Christ" (*pistis christou*), the emphasis falls not on "faith" but on the *Christ* on whom this faith is founded.[23]

The *propositio* in 2:15–21 is both a word to Peter regarding the conflict in Antioch and a word to the Galatian church. Paul did not invent the doctrine of justification by faith merely as a rhetorical strategy to confront a sociological problem,[24] for these categories are implicit in the earlier writings. However,

22. Wolter, *Paul*, 75–76.
23. Barclay, *Paul and the Gift*, 379.
24. See F. Watson, *Paul, Judaism, and the Gentiles*, 36: "Paul insists that his reasons for dispensing with the law are strictly theological (2:15–5:11), but his own words in 1 Cor. 9:21 and 10:32–33 prove that the setting aside of parts of the law was originally not a matter of theological principle but of practical expediency."

Paul's statement to Peter serves a rhetorical purpose. He develops this doctrine when the gentile mission is at stake. His appeal to what he and Peter know (2:16) indicates that "one is justified by faith and not by works of the law" (AT) and is intended as a shared premise for the argument that follows. Thus he employs a premise that is intelligible only to those who share the community of faith. His description of himself as "crucified with Christ" (2:19) also indicates that the life of faith involves participation in the sufferings of Christ.

The probatio. Paul offers a series of arguments to support the claim of the propositio in Galatians 2:15–21. In 3:1–5, he argues on the basis of the experience of the Galatians, introducing the dichotomy between the Spirit and the flesh that he will develop in 5:16–25. The series of rhetorical questions indicates that the Galatians had earlier received the Spirit on the basis of "the hearing of faith" (3:2 AT) and that God had supplied them with powers apart from the works of the law (3:5).[25] That is, the Galatians' rescue from "the present evil age" was evident in the power of the new age that they had experienced (3:5). To accept the "works of the law" was to relapse into the old age from which they had been rescued. The dichotomy between works of the law and hearing of faith (3:2, 5 AT) is the equivalent of the dichotomy between flesh and Spirit that becomes the focus of 5:14–26. If the Spirit is the power of the new age, the flesh is the reality of the old age.

To make his case, Paul turns from the argument from experience to the argument from Scripture, citing Genesis 15:16, "Abraham believed [*episteusen*] God, and it was reckoned as righteousness [*dikaiosynē*]" (Gal. 3:6), concluding that those who are "of faith" (*ek pisteōs*) are the children of Abraham (Gal. 3:7, 9). While Abraham in the Jewish tradition is an example of one who was faithful in keeping the law (cf. Sir. 44:19–21; 1 Macc. 2:52), for Paul, he is the exemplum for the argument that Paul made in Galatians 2:15–21: righteousness by faith apart from works of the law. The fact that Paul employs the identical text from Scripture and the example of Abraham to make a different argument elsewhere (cf. Rom. 4) indicates that he frames the exemplum to fit the circumstances and to serve as a proof for the argument that is at stake.[26]

As the contrast in Galatians 3:10–14 indicates, *ek pisteōs* (by faith) is the opposite response of *ex erga nomou* (by works of the law). When Paul says

25. On the place of rhetorical questions in persuasion, see Tolmie, *Persuading the Galatians*, 101–2.

26. Anaximenes of Lampsacus (*Rhet. Alex.* 8) says that examples (*paradeigmata*) may be used to bolster arguments considered by the audience to be implausible. Examples can also be used to make the opponents' argument less probable. Aristotle (*Rhet.* 2.20) divides the *paradeigmata* into two types: historical examples and invented examples. See Anderson, *Glossary of Greek Rhetorical Terms*, 87. Cf. the Latin *exemplum*.

that the gentiles receive the blessing "through faith" (3:14), that "the just shall live by faith" (3:11 AT), and that "we may be justified by faith" (3:24 AT), he describes faith in the human response as a condition of justification, elaborating on 2:16, "We have believed in Christ" (AT). In 3:22, he says that the promise is "from *pistis . . . christou* to those who believe" (AT). He concludes the argument, declaring that they "are all children of God through faith [in Christ]" (3:26). Thus works of the law are the antithesis of faith in 3:10 (cf. Rom. 3:28). When Paul abbreviates the antithesis to "works" and "faith," he is speaking of alternative responses to the gospel. This focus is consistent with Paul's usage in Romans, where *pistis* and *pisteuō* are employed for the human response to the gospel and are antithetical to works. Undoubtedly, the opposite of works of the law is faith as the human trust in Christ as the basis for justification.

The numerous antitheses involving faith and works indicate that *pistis christou*, often abbreviated to *pistis*, does not refer exclusively to "the faithfulness of Christ." Paul never makes Christ the subject of *pisteuei*. When he speaks of faithfulness, he describes God as faithful.[27] When he says, "We believed in Christ," he is declaring that he and others have met the conditions in which one is justified by faith in Christ (*pistis christou*).

Paul is the model of this principle, as he indicates in the brief autobiographical comment in Galatians 2:19–20. He lives by faith in the Son. Both "faith" and "faith in Christ" are abbreviations for the actual content of faith, which Paul describes in 2:20. It is faith in "the one who loved me and gave himself for me" (2:20 AT). That is, it is faith in the crucified Savior as the basis of one's salvation. This faith is not a singular event. It is inseparable from the comment "I have been crucified with Christ. It is no longer I who live, but Christ who lives in me" (2:19–20 AT).

Faith is not only a human response, however. Twice Paul employs the enigmatic phrases "before faith came" (3:23) and "when faith came" (3:25 AT) as ways of describing the two aeons (cf. 1:4) "in the fullness of time" (4:4 AT). As the verb indicates, "faith" is metonymy for Christ, whose coming marks the change of aeons. One is justified by the coming of Christ, who inaugurated the new aeon of faith.

Paul repeatedly employs purpose clauses to describe these dynamics of faith:

> Christ rescued us from the curse, becoming a curse for us, . . . in order that we may receive the promise through faith. (3:13–14 AT)

27. Silva, "Faith versus Works of the Law," 232.

Scripture imprisoned all things under sin, in order that the promise may be given from the faithfulness of Christ to those who believe. (3:22 AT)

The law is our pedagogue until Christ came, in order that we may be justified by faith. (3:24 AT)

When the fullness of time came, God sent his Son, . . . in order to rescue those who are under the law, in order that we may receive adoption. (4:4–5 AT)

As Paul indicates in 3:13–14, the death on the cross created the possibility for the response of faith. The purpose clauses indicate that the divine act at the turn of the ages brought the new era of justification by faith. As Paul says in 2:21, "If righteousness were by the law, Christ died in vain" (AT).

Paul further illustrates the coming of the new aeon with an exemplum from family life (4:1–7), comparing young children to slaves (4:1) until they reach adulthood and freedom. He concludes that the gentile believers in Galatia, now living "in the fullness of time" (4:4 AT), have the freedom of adult children who now, because they have the Spirit, can cry "Abba! Father!" (4:6). They have nevertheless abandoned their freedom, returning to the slavery of the old age (4:8–11).

The imperative in 4:12 introduces one of the major challenges of delineating the rhetorical structure of Galatians. The call for imitation in 4:12 is the first of the imperatives in the letter. However, the imperatives here and in 5:1 introduce further arguments before the extended exhortation in 5:13–6:10. In 4:12–20, the call for imitation introduces an argument from pathos, a recollection of the deep ties of affection that accompanied Paul's first visit. He concludes with a climactic appeal to pathos in 4:19, indicating that he is a mother in the pangs of childbirth "until Christ is formed among [them]" (4:19 AT). The rhetoric of pathos is combined with Paul's theological vision. Justification by faith is not only an initial experience but also a continuing process of formation, the maintenance of the freedom that the converts have experienced (cf. 4:1–6).

The allegory of Hagar and Sarah in 4:21–31[28] expands on the dichotomy of freedom and slavery introduced earlier in the letter (2:4–5; 4:1–6) and prepares the way for the imperatives "Stand fast, therefore, and do not submit again to a yoke of slavery" (5:1 AT) and "Do not let your freedom become an opportunity for the flesh" (5:13 AT). The ethical exhortations are the climax of the argument of the letter, for now Paul challenges the readers to implement the theological principle that has been argued in 1:10–5:12. Their imitation of

---

28. On allegory as a rhetorical proof, see Quintilian, *Inst.* 8.6.44–47.

Paul (cf. 4:12) and the formation for which he suffers (4:19) become a reality in the exercise of freedom described in the exhortation. Paul indicates that the adherence to the law that has attracted the Galatians does not require circumcision, for the whole law has been fulfilled in one word, "Love your neighbor as yourself" (Gal. 5:14; cf. Lev. 19:18). The conflict between flesh and Spirit (cf. Gal. 5:17) is between the old aeon, from which they have been rescued (Gal. 1:4), and the new aeon; they may choose between the two (Gal. 5:16).

While Paul does not mention in Galatians Jeremiah's promise of a new covenant, he probably assumes the reality anticipated by Jeremiah and the other exilic prophets. Jeremiah anticipated the return from exile and the restoration of Israel, a time when God would provide a new covenant unlike the one that Israel did not keep (Jer. 31:32). In the new era, the restored Israel would keep the law written on their hearts. According to Ezekiel, God would gather the scattered people, give them a new heart, and place a new spirit within them (Ezek. 11:19) so that Israel would again keep God's commandments (Ezek. 11:20; 36:26–27). What the prophets promised for a dispersed Israel, Paul extends to gentile converts. Believers are not, as the opponents probably argued, antinomians but people who keep "the law of Christ" (Gal. 6:2). In the works of the flesh and the fruit of the Spirit (Gal. 5:22–25), Paul gives examples of the conduct that corresponds to the love command (Gal. 5:14). As people empowered by the Spirit, they live under a new covenant in the new aeon. Following Paul's example (Gal. 2:20–21; 4:12), they live for Christ.

The peroratio. The peroratio of a speech should summarize the argument with intensity. In Galatians 6:11–18, Paul summarizes his argument (6:12–13), concluding that "circumcision is nothing and uncircumcision is nothing, but a new creation is everything" (6:15 AT; cf. 5:6). This claim appropriately summarizes the entire letter. "The new creation," which recalls the promise of Isaiah 65:17 and 66:22 (cf. 2 Cor. 5:17), is the era of the restoration of Israel in which gentiles may now participate. This concluding claim forms an inclusio with the declaration at the beginning of the letter that believers have been rescued from the present evil age (Gal. 1:4). Only if believers live in the new aeon will Christ be formed among them (Gal. 4:19).

Conclusion: Rhetoric and Theology in Galatians

Galatians is a carefully structured rhetorical argument in which the arrangement is at least partially analogous to the parts of an ancient oration as Paul appeals to ethos, pathos, and logos to persuade his gentile converts to take the right course of action. While the doctrine of justification by faith is implicit in Paul's other letters, it becomes the central focus when Paul defends the admission of gentiles to the people of God. This argument fits Paul's rhetorical needs, but it cannot be reduced to mere rhetorical strategy, for the argument is implicit in other letters and consistent with Paul's basic conviction that the admission of gentiles into Israel's narrative requires a response other than circumcision. Justification by faith is thus the foundation for a united church.

As the structure of Galatians demonstrates, justification by faith is not merely an image for the admission of gentiles but also a life orientation that reaches its culmination when Christ is "formed" in the community. Thus the culmination of the argument is the exhortation that depicts the moral formation of the community of the new aeon. The church is empowered by the Spirit to do the will of God.

Although the arrangement of Paul's argument is analogous to that of Greco-Roman rhetoric in some respects, it would have been unintelligible outside the subculture of the Christian community. Paul's argument is based not on traditional rhetorical proofs but on revelation. His speech is prophetic, and his proofs rely on premises of the Christian revelation. The major theme of justification by faith is implicit in 1 Thessalonians (see chap. 5 above); it is developed in Galatians because of the demands of the rhetorical situation. Paul's theologizing cannot be reduced to a mere rhetorical strategy, but the argument serves the rhetorical purpose of answering the opponents in the hope that Christ "will be formed" among the Galatian churches (Gal. 4:19 AT) and demonstrated in their ethical practices (5:1–6:10).

9

Romans, the Righteousness of God, and the Defense of Paul's Ministry

At the beginning of Galatians, Paul defends his gospel of inclusion of the gentiles, recalling that God called him to preach to the nations (Gal. 1:16). Against those who challenge Paul's ministry, the apostle responds in Galatians with a new vocabulary, a nexus of words that are scarcely used in the other letters. He speaks for the first time of "works of the law" (*erga nomou*), often abbreviated to "the law" (*nomos*), with a frequency that is unprecedented in his other letters.[1] The verb *justify* (*dikaioō*) also appears with a frequency that is unparalleled in the earlier letters. The dichotomy of works of the law/works and faith in/of Christ (*pistis christou*) appears first in Galatians, and these words compose a semantic field that is central to Paul's defense of the gentile mission.[2]

The same semantic field appears elsewhere only in Romans, which was apparently written after Galatians. Indeed, Romans shares with Galatians the declaration that "no one will be justified by works of the law, but by faith in Christ" (Gal. 2:16 AT; cf. Rom. 3:20, 28). It also shares with Galatians the dichotomies of works/faith and flesh/Spirit as well as the reference to

---

1. The phrase "works of the law" (*erga nomou*) appears eight times in the undisputed letters, of which six are in Galatians (2:16 [three times]; 3:2, 5, 10) and two are in Romans (3:20, 28); it does not appear in the disputed letters. The negative use of "works" (*erga*) appears six times in Romans (3:27; 4:2, 6; 9:11–12, 32; 11:6) and twice in the disputed letters (Eph. 2:8–9; Titus 3:5). Paul speaks of the law (*nomos*) 118 times, of which 74 are in Romans and 32 are in Galatians.

2. Cf. Schnelle, "Gibt es eine Entwicklung?," 290.

the time when "we cry 'Abba! Father!'" (Gal. 4:6; cf. Rom. 8:15). However, scholars have noted that arguments in Romans stand in tension, if not contradiction, to the argument in Galatians. In Romans, Paul speaks more positively of the law than in Galatians. Paul's claim that "the law is just and good and holy" (Rom. 7:12 AT) is inconsistent with the reference to "the curse of the law" in Galatians 3:13. The argument that the law is spiritual (Rom. 7:14) but powerless because of the reality of sin (Rom. 7:14–25) has no parallel in Galatians. Indeed, Paul mentions the singular "sin" (*hamartia*) forty-eight times in Romans but only three times in Galatians and eight times in the other undisputed letters.[3] While in Galatians Paul identifies the gentile community as "the Israel of God" (Gal. 6:16) and presents Israel as the slave girl Hagar (Gal. 4:21–31), in Romans, he agonizes over the future of Israel (Rom. 9:1–5) and finally concludes that "all Israel will be saved" (Rom. 11:26).[4]

These theological differences have been explained in a variety of ways. For some, they are evidence of the basic inconsistency in Paul's theology,[5] while for others, these changes reflect a process of development in his thought.[6] Thomas Tobin argues that Paul is responding to readers who have reacted negatively to the argument of Galatians.[7] Another possibility is that Paul is answering questions that have emerged from his teaching. Paul is thus clarifying the argument of Galatians, giving a more positive view of the law and the future of Israel. However, the pervasive use of the diatribe in Romans suggests that Paul's earlier teaching demands clarification. While the interlocutor may be a literary fiction, the questions are nevertheless real. Hans Hübner asks an important question: "What is theologically new in Romans in comparison with what Paul has written in the earlier letters, especially Galatians?" He adds, "Is the new that is expressed in Romans so clearly perhaps conditioned by the rhetoric of Paul?"[8] An analysis of the rhetorical situation provides further insight into the new dimension in Pauline theology that the apostle had not yet offered.

---

3. Cf. Schnelle, "Gibt es eine Entwicklung?," 290.

4. See Hübner, *Theologie des Neuen Testaments*, 2:235.

5. Cf. Räisänen, *Paul and the Law*, 266: "It is a fundamental mistake of much Pauline exegesis in this century to have portrayed Paul as the 'prince of thinkers' and 'the Christian thinker par excellence.' Paul was indeed an original and imaginative thinker, and his letters are full of seminal insights and thought-provoking suggestions. He is, however, first and foremost, a missionary, a man of practical religion who develops a line of thought to make a practical point, to influence the conduct of his readers."

6. See the discussion in Schnelle, "Gibt es eine Entwicklung?," 289–307.

7. Tobin, *Paul's Rhetoric in Its Contexts*, 6–15.

8. Hübner, *Theologie des Neuen Testaments*, 2:232–33.

The Rhetorical Situation

Unlike Galatians, Romans offers no concrete evidence of Paul's knowledge of the situation of the readers. Although scholars have made a plausible reconstruction of the demographics of the Roman church and the historical background of the letter based on the conflict that he addresses in 14:1–15:13[9] and the list of names in chapter 16,[10] Paul speaks only of his own situation as he writes the letter. He has completed his work in the eastern Mediterranean (Rom. 15:23)—"from Jerusalem to Illyricum" (15:19 AT)—and plans to come to Rome before he goes on to Spain (15:24). He must first go to Jerusalem with the collection from the gentile churches for the Jerusalem church, a project that has occupied him for several years (15:25–29). Because of the tensions involved in his ministry to the nations, he is fearful that the Jewish church will not accept the collection, which, for Paul, is a sign of the unity of Jewish and gentile churches. He also recognizes danger from the wider Jewish community (15:30–32).

As Paul indicates in 15:14–15, he writes to remind the Romans of what they already know,[11] the catechesis that is common in the churches. He writes "quite boldly" by virtue of the grace given to him "to be a minister [*leitourgos*] of Christ Jesus to the nations, doing priestly service in the gospel of God, in order that the sacrifice of the gentiles may be acceptable, sanctified in the Holy Spirit" (15:15–16 AT). With the priestly language, Paul is describing himself with the terminology of the priest in the Jerusalem temple.[12] The offering of the gentiles is "the sacrifice" that Paul presents to God.[13] As Paul indicates elsewhere, he hopes that they will be "sanctified in the Holy Spirit" (cf. 1 Thess. 4:3–7; 2 Thess. 2:13). A sanctified people is thus the ultimate outcome of Paul's work. He prays elsewhere that God will "establish the hearts of the people blameless in sanctification before our God and Father at the parousia of our Lord Jesus Christ" (1 Thess. 3:13 AT), that "the God of peace may sanctify you wholly, and that your spirit and soul and body be kept blameless at the parousia of the Lord Jesus Christ" (1 Thess. 5:23 AT). Paul's calling, in other words, is to present a transformed people to God.

Romans is, therefore, an account of Paul's calling and mission to the gentiles.[14] The reference to what some maliciously report about him (Rom. 3:8)

---

9. See Minear, *Obedience of Faith*; Karris, "Romans 14:1–15:13," 65–84.
10. Cf. Lampe, "Roman Christians."
11. Fitzmyer, *Romans*, 711.
12. Fitzmyer, *Romans*, 711.
13. *Hē prosphora tōn ethnōn* is an objective genitive, referring not to the sacrifice that the gentiles make but to the gentiles *as* the sacrifice.
14. See Stendahl, *Final Account*, ix.

suggests that an important dimension of Paul's argument is a defense of his ministry. As the list of names in Romans 16 indicates, believers from the eastern Mediterranean have, along with Prisca and Aquila (16:3–5), come to Rome with reports about Paul. The address to the strong and the weak in Romans 14:1–15:13, with its apparent description of conflict, may reflect Paul's knowledge of the Roman situation but would also apply to other churches facing the issues of bringing Jews and gentiles into one body. Paul specifically addresses gentiles (1:13; 11:13), but his argument suggests that he is addressing Jewish Christians as well. Issues dividing Jews and gentiles (cf. 15:1–13) reflect problems that have arisen in the Roman church. Since Paul is opaque in describing the local situation, more precise reconstructions based on external evidence remain speculative.[15]

While Paul writes Romans against the background of a rhetorical situation that is different from that in Galatians, he probably faces an issue that he is confronting in many churches, including the Jerusalem church and the churches in Galatia: the conditions for the admission of gentiles into the people of God. Although Paul makes no explicit reference to this issue in Romans, the evidence suggests he is facing it here also. As a defense of his ministry to the gentiles, his persuasive task is to justify his ministry to the nations, answer objections, and lay the foundation for Jews and gentiles to praise God with one voice (Rom. 15:6) in a united community.

Argument and Theology

Interpreters have observed the clear distinction between the outer frame of Romans (1:1–15; 15:14–32) and the argument of the letter (1:16–15:13). Only in the outer frame does Paul indicate his circumstances. Indeed, the opening and the closing sections are parallel: Paul claims that his mission is based on the grace of God (1:5; 15:15) for "the obedience of faith among the gentiles" (1:5; 15:18 AT). He has wanted to visit Rome for a long time, but he has been unable to do so (1:9–10, 13; 15:22–23). While the argument in 1:16–15:13 refers neither to the situation of Paul nor to the readers, its themes make the case for Paul's mission regarding "the obedience of faith among the gentiles." This outer frame indicates that the ethical section in 12:1–15:13 is a vital part of the argument, if not its climax.[16]

---

15. Barclay, *Paul and the Gift*, 456: "Many recent reconstructions of the Roman churches' historical context place inordinate weight on the opaque notice of Suetonius that Claudius expelled Jews from Rome (in 49 CE?) *impulsore Chresto* (*Claud.* 25.4)."

16. Contra Hübner, "Die Römerbrief und die rhetorische Kompetenz des Paulus," 170, whose analysis of the argument ends in 11:36.

The Exordium and the Narratio

In the opening section (1:1–15), Paul introduces himself and his gospel (1:1–7), indicating the credentials that give him the right to speak. As an apostle, he speaks for God, and his rhetoric is determined by his prophetic call.[17] He makes the audience favorably disposed through his thanksgiving that the Romans' faith is known throughout the world (1:8). His expression of longing to see them (1:9–11) introduces both ethos and pathos, and his desire to be mutually encouraged (1:12) adds to the goodwill that Paul hopes to elicit from his readers. The identification of his mission as "the obedience of faith among the gentiles" (1:5 AT) and his claim that the gospel is "promised beforehand" (1:2) in the Scriptures anticipate the topics that he will develop in the letter. Thus 1:1–12 functions as the exordium of a carefully structured letter, and 1:13–15 functions as the narratio. The repetition of these themes in 15:14–16:23 indicates that the latter passage is the peroratio of a well-crafted argument in which Paul once more appeals to ethos and pathos in his persuasion. Even the final greetings (16:1–23), with inclusion of Jewish and gentile Christians, advances the argument and is a part of the peroratio.[18]

The Propositio

Having expressed his desire to preach (*euangelisasthai*) in Rome (1:15) in the narratio, Paul introduces his gospel (*euangelion*) in the propositio in 1:16–17, offering a personal apologia: "I am not ashamed of the gospel." As an apostle chosen by God (1:1, 5) for a specific task, Paul does not begin with conventional rhetorical arguments but with the prophetic insight to interpret God's plan. While he summarizes the gospel elsewhere in a variety of ways (cf. 1 Cor. 1:18; 15:1–3; 2 Cor. 4:5), here it is "the power [*dynamis*] of God to salvation for everyone who believes, to the Jew first and then to the Greek" (Rom. 1:16 AT). He thus adapts his definition of the gospel to fit the rhetorical situation. That his gospel is power is a familiar theme (cf. 1 Cor. 1:18; 2:4–5; 4:20; 1 Thess. 1:5). The claim anticipates the argument of the letter, which consistently describes the powerlessness of all humankind, for both Jews and Greeks are "under sin" (Rom. 3:9 AT), enslaved to the passions (6:6, 16; cf. 7:5, 7–25) that rule (6:12) over the body, and are unable to do the good (8:8–9). God's *dynamis* thus stands in sharp contrast to what "the law was unable to do" (*to adynaton*, 8:3 AT) and to the good that unredeemed humans "cannot

---

17. See chap. 1 above.
18. Wuellner, "Paul's Rhetoric of Argumentation in Romans," 339–40.

do" (*ou dynantai*, 8:7–8). In the argument, Paul will demonstrate that this power will overcome the opposing power of sin (cf. 5:12–8:17).

Salvation (*sōtēria*) includes the moral transformation that is a prelude to God's ultimate triumph (cf. 8:18–39). Believers have been saved already (cf. 8:24), but they await the ultimate salvation (5:9; 9:27; 10:9; 11:14, 26) when they will be conformed to the image of the Son (8:29).

Anticipating the argument that follows, Paul indicates that God's power for salvation extends not just to the physical descendants of Abraham but to "everyone who believes, to the Jew first and then to the Greek" (1:16 AT). One may observe the remarkable frequency of the word *pas* ("all," "every") throughout Romans to declare that "all" are under the power of sin (3:9; cf. 3:12, 23; 5:12, 18) and that all who believe will be saved (cf. 3:22; 10:4, 11–13). The insistence on the salvation of all is undoubtedly a response to those who limit membership in the people of God to the physical descendants of Abraham.

The reference to Jew and Greek is also a theme throughout Romans. Inasmuch as God is no respecter of persons (2:11), both Jew and Greek will receive reward and punishment, depending on whether they have done good or evil (2:9–10). Both Jew and Greek are under the power of sin (3:9). There is no distinction between them (10:12), for all who call on the name of the Lord will be saved. Indeed, Paul anticipates a time when both gentiles and Jews "will be saved" (cf. 11:26).[19] As the ensuing argument indicates, both Jews and Greeks may be excluding each other from the people of God (cf. 11:13–26).

The supporting claim, that in the gospel "the righteousness of God [*dikaiosynē theou*] is being revealed from faith to faith" (1:17 AT), indicates the relationship between God's righteousness and God's power to salvation. While Paul has used the verb *dikaioō* (justify, vindicate, declare righteous) previously (1 Cor. 6:11), especially in Galatians (cf. Gal. 2:16–17; 3:8, 11, 24), the phrase *dikaiosynē tou theou* is a major theme only in Romans.[20] The language is drawn from Israel's hope in a time of distress for the manifestation of God's righteousness. The psalmist, for example, cries out, "In your righteousness deliver me" (Ps. 31:1). The prophet of the exile promised the righteousness of God to the despairing exiles, indicating the relationship between righteousness and salvation: "I will bring near my deliverance [*dikaiosynē*] swiftly, my salvation has gone out and my arms will rule the peoples" (Isa. 51:5). According to the *Psalms of Solomon*, "God is a righteous judge who

---

19. See Hübner, *Theologie des Neuen Testaments*, 2:237: "The '*heilsgeschichtliche*' chiasm is evident: Rom. 1:16 has the sequence 'Jew-Greek'; Rom. 9–11, however, has 'gentiles-Israel.'"

20. The only other Pauline reference to the phrase is 2 Cor. 5:21, "That we might become the righteousness of God in him."

will not be impressed by appearances" (*Pss. Sol.* 2:18) but will judge the world in righteousness (*Pss. Sol.* 8:24; 9:2; 10:5).[21] In the Dead Sea Scrolls, an unknown writer cries out, "If I stumble by reason of the wickedness of my flesh, my justification lies in the righteousness of God" (1QS 10.11; cf. 1QH[a] 12.36–37; 19.8–10). Thus *dikaiosynē tou theou* describes an attribute of God as the one who comes to save Israel in keeping with God's promise. Paul develops the theme of the righteousness of God throughout Romans (cf. Rom. 3:21, 26; 10:3), adding new aspects to the concept.

A new dimension to Paul's announcement about the righteousness of God is that the righteousness of God "is being revealed" (*apokalyptetai*, Rom. 1:17). Paul is the prophetic figure who announces the divine revelation that the promises that the Jews expected to be fulfilled at the end of history have become a reality in Jesus Christ (cf. 1 Cor. 2:10). The present tense indicates that the revelation of God's righteousness is not a singular event but a continuing reality. In a restatement of the thesis of Romans, Paul declares, "But now, the righteousness of God has been manifested [*pephanerōtai*] . . . to all who believe" (Rom. 3:21–22 AT). The perfect tense *pephanerōtai* points to an event of the past that has a continuing significance.[22]

Unlike his contemporaries who claim that God's righteousness is the vindication of those who are faithful in keeping the law, Paul argues that the righteousness is "from faith to faith" (Rom. 1:17 AT), reiterating the statement that salvation is for "everyone who believes" (1:16 AT). He cites Habakkuk 2:4: "The righteous [*ho dikaios*] will live by faith [*ek pisteōs*]" (AT). However, while Jewish tradition understood the passage to refer to those who were faithful in keeping the law (cf. 1QpHab 7.15–8.3, on Hab. 2:4), Paul consistently argues throughout the letter that the human response is not the works of the law but faith in Christ (cf. Rom. 3:22, 26; 10:9–11; cf. 4:3, 5, 9, 11, 16; 5:1; 9:30, 32). Both the phrase "from faith to faith" (*ek pisteōs eis pistin*) and the Habakkuk citation (in Rom. 1:17) indicate that faith is the continuing response to the gospel that is expressed in "the obedience of faith" (Rom. 1:5 AT; cf. 6:16–17; 10:16; 15:18).

As in Galatians, believing is the antithesis of working. Paul's elaboration on the *propositio* in Romans 3:21–26 offers the alternative to his claim

---

21. See chap. 3 above.

22. See Hübner, *Theologie des Neuen Testaments*, 2:241. Note the significance of *now* (*nyn*) in Paul's thought (cf. Rom. 3:21). We live in the "now age" (Rom. 3:26 AT) of the fulfillment of God's promises. We "have *now* been justified by his blood" (5:9 AT) and have *now* received reconciliation (5:11). At a critical point in the discussion, he says, "There is therefore *now* no condemnation to those who are in Christ" (8:1 AT). "Now" (*nyn*) reflects the apocalyptic distinction between this age and the age to come.

(Rom. 3:20) that "all flesh will not be justified by works of the law," as *nyni de* indicates (3:21 AT). The declaration that "the righteousness of God has been manifested [*pephanerōtai*]" (3:21 AT), like the earlier claim that "the righteousness of God is revealed [*apokalyptetai*]" (1:18 AT), indicates that the eschatological event anticipated by the law and the prophets has become a reality. Both the divine initiative and the human response are evident.

In declaring that God's righteousness is revealed "for all who believe," Paul is laying the foundation for his appeal for a united church. As he declares, God will justify both the circumcised and the uncircumcised by faith (3:30), taking away the advantages of those who have kept the law. While this argument is consistent with the earlier message in Galatians, the new dimension is the association of God's righteousness with God's power. Indeed, as Paul indicates at the end of the argument, Jewish and gentile house churches should "welcome one another" (15:7) because Christ has become a servant of the circumcised (15:8) in order that the gentiles may glorify God (15:9).

The *propositio* is the premise for the argument that follows. Paul will make his case with an arrangement that is consistent with ancient rhetorical theory,[23] sometimes using established rhetorical arguments.[24] His starting point, however, is his own prophetic voice and a premise based on a revelation from God.

The Probatio

Just as a symmetry exists in the outer frame of the letter (1:1–15; 15:14–32), a symmetry is also present in the opening and concluding arguments. In 1:18–3:20, Paul describes the revelation of God's wrath on all unrighteousness (*adikia*, 1:18), while in 12:1–15:13, he depicts the transformed life of the community of the new aeon (12:2). According to 1:28, God gave humanity up "to a reprobate mind [*nous*]" (AT), while in 12:2, he encourages the readers to be "transformed by the renewing of the mind [*nous*]" (AT). Those who are under the wrath of God engage in false worship; they "worshiped [*elatreusan*] . . . the creature rather than the Creator" (1:25), but Paul encourages the transformed community to offer to God spiritual worship (*logikē latreia*, 12:1). While both Jews and gentiles are under the power of sin (3:9), Paul envisions a community that does the will of God (12:2) and offers concrete instructions for the righteous community (12:3–15:13). The exhortation in 12:1–15:13 is thus not an addendum to Paul's argument but the fourth in a series of arguments

23. Cf. Wuellner, "Paul's Rhetoric of Argumentation in Romans."
24. Exempla are in chap. 4 and 5:12–21; a fortiori argument in 5:12–21 and 11:24; apostrophe in 2:1–16.

that elaborate on the *propositio*. These arguments are linked together but are also self-contained units in which each section is complete and autonomous, having a *dispositio* that includes an introduction, several propositions, and a conclusion.[25] The final unit (12:1–15:13) is a demonstration of the effect of the righteousness and power of God in creating the community of the new age (12:1–2).

The Wrath and Righteousness of God

In the first argument, Romans 1:18–4:25, Paul speaks in the third person, describing the past event that continues into the present, the revelation of God's righteousness for all who believe. This claim requires that Paul answer the questions that have emerged from his gospel. These rhetorical questions posed by an imaginary interlocutor are central to the structure of the letter.[26]

"What is the advantage of the Jew? What is the benefit of circumcision?" (3:1 AT)

"What if some were unfaithful? Will their unfaithfulness nullify the faithfulness of God?" (3:3)

"If our injustice [*adikia*] confirms the justice [*dikaiosynē*] of God, what shall we say? That God is unjust [*adikos*] to inflict wrath on us?" (3:5 AT)

"If the truth of God abounded to his glory through my lie, why am I judged a sinner?" (3:7 AT)

"Is it so, as some blasphemously report that we say, 'Let us do evil that good may come'?" (3:8 AT)

"Do we nullify the law through faith?" (3:31 AT)

"Shall we continue in sin that grace may abound?" (6:1 AT)

"Is the law sin?" (7:7 AT)

"Is God unjust?" (9:14 AT)

"You will say to me then, 'Why does he still find fault? Who can resist his will?'" (9:19 AT)

"Has God rejected his people?" (11:1)

In the second argument, 5:1–8:39, Paul turns to the future, speaking for the first time in the first-person plural to those who believe in "the one who raised

---

25. See Aletti, "Rhetoric of Romans 5–8," 295.

26. See, Hübner, *Theologie des Neuen Testaments*, 2:239–40; Hübner, "Die Rhetorik und die Theologie," 171. On the use of rhetorical questions in the rhetorical handbooks, see Aristotle, *Rhet.* 3.19.5; Quintilian, *Inst.* 9.2.6–11.

Jesus from the dead" (4:24 AT), who are primarily gentiles. He answers objections to his gospel ("Shall we continue in sin that grace may abound?" [6:1 AT; cf. 6:15] and "Is the law sin?" [7:7 AT]) as he describes existence between the "now" (cf. 3:21, 26; 8:1) and the "not yet" of God's final triumph. The celebration of the predominantly gentile church (8:18–39) raises the question that Paul answers in the third argument, chapters 9–11 ("Is God unjust?" [3:5 AT]). The final section (12:1–15:13) appeals to the community to live out the righteousness of God by living as a body (12:3–8) in a multiethnic church (14:1–15:13).

GOD'S RIGHTEOUSNESS AND WRATH IN THE PAST AND THE PRESENT (1:18–4:25)

Paul introduces the opening argument (1:18) with the declaration that "the wrath of God is being revealed [*apokalyptetai*] on all who hold the truth in unrighteousness [*adikia*]" (AT). The parallel to the previous statement, "the righteousness of God is being revealed [*apokalyptetai*]" (1:17 AT), indicates the close relationship between God's righteousness and God's wrath, both of which are the eschatological events in Jewish expectation. Paul shares the Jewish expectation of a day of wrath (Rom. 2:5, 8; 5:9; cf. Amos 5:18–20; Zeph. 1:14–15; 1 Thess. 1:10; 5:9), which will also be the manifestation of the righteous judgment of God (cf. Isa. 60:10), who will vindicate the righteous and punish the wicked. God will separate the righteous and the sinners to "repay the latter according to their actions" (Rom. 2:6 AT). According to the Wisdom of Solomon, God is righteous and rules all things righteously (Wis. 12:15), showing mercy on Israel and punishing with wrath those who deserve to be punished (cf. Wis. 11:9). God tormented those who "lived unrighteously . . . through their own abominations" (Wis. 12:23). Thus Paul's parallel statements, "the righteousness of God is being revealed" (Rom. 1:17 AT) and "the wrath of God is being revealed" (Rom. 1:18 AT), reflect the traditional understanding of God's righteousness as mercy on the faithful and punishment for the wicked. Paul indicates that the righteous judgment that was anticipated as a future event is a present reality.

The new dimension in Paul's argument is that Paul does not distinguish between the righteous who receive mercy and the unrighteous who receive wrath. "Those who hold the truth in unrighteousness" (1:18 AT) include gentiles and Jews, all of whom are "under sin" (3:9 AT). While Paul does not specifically speak of gentiles, he lists the vices commonly associated with gentiles in Jewish literature, echoing Wisdom 13–14, concluding that they know God's decree (*dikaiōma*) that those who practice these vices deserve to die but that they both practice them and approve of others who do them (Rom. 1:32). They have a revelation in nature (1:18–24), but they do not follow the good that they know.

Similarly, the one who judges is without excuse (2:1), for the one who stands in judgment practices the same things (2:1, 3) and is thus subject to God's wrath (2:5, 8). Indeed, both Jews and gentiles will be measured by the same standard (2:9). Inasmuch as God's impartial justice is for Jews and Greeks, Paul does not follow the traditional division between the righteous and the unrighteous, for "no one is righteous" (3:10 AT). In Romans 2:12–29, Paul compares Jewish and gentile obedience, concluding that those who stand in judgment and boast in the law (2:23) do not, in fact, keep the law. Thus like the gentiles, they know God's will but do not follow it. Therefore, the description of humanity "under sin" (3:9 AT) indicates the powerlessness of humankind to do the will of God and its need for "the power of God to salvation" (1:16 AT).[27]

In view of Paul's indictment of all humankind, scholars have pointed to the apparent contradiction between Paul's description of the righteous gentile (2:14) who does "the things of the law" (AT) and the one who has the law but does not keep it (cf. 2:17–29). Those who identify the contradictions between Romans 2 and Paul's argument elsewhere do not adequately observe the rhetorical purpose of chapter 2, in which Paul employs an apostrophe, using the rare second-person singular in 2:1, 17, as if it is addressed to one individual.[28] The suggestion that gentiles may have the law written on their hearts while the interlocutor fails to keep the law is intended for rhetorical effect. Wayne Meeks has demonstrated the parallels between chapters 2 and 14 in Romans.[29] In each instance, Paul warns against exercising judgment against the other. He employs the apostrophe in Romans 2 in order to lay the foundation for a united church.[30] Thus Paul is not offering a theology of natural law or speculating about the righteous gentile. Throughout the chapter, he addresses readers who boast in the law and stand in judgment over those

---

27. For an analysis of Rom. 2, see my discussion under "God's Righteousness and Wrath in Romans" in chap. 2 above.

28. Cf. Quintilian, *Inst.* 9.2.28. An apostrophe is a diversion from the primary audience that may be used to attack an adversary or turn to make an appeal.

29. Meeks, "Judgment and the Brother," 296.

30. On the use of the apostrophe in ancient rhetoric, see Lausberg, *Handbook of Literary Rhetoric*, §§762–65, especially §762: "Apostrophe . . . is 'turning away' from the normal audience (the judges . . .) and the addressing of another, second audience, surprisingly chosen by the speaker. This practice has an emotive . . . effect on the normal audience, since it is an expression, on the part of the speaker, of a pathos . . . which cannot be kept within the normal channels between speaker and audience."

who do not keep the law. Paul undermines their self-confidence by offering the possibility of gentiles who exceed them in righteousness.

Paul reiterates the thesis in 3:21–31, expanding on the basic premise announced in 1:16–17, indicating in the inclusio that his gospel is "witnessed by the law and the prophets" (3:21 AT) and that he "establishes the law" (3:31 AT), although this new event is "apart from the law" (3:21). This reiteration of the premise of the argument (cf. 1:16–17) is again based on Scripture and Paul's eschatological interpretation of it; thus it is persuasive to insiders who accept Paul as the interpreter. The dense syntax in 3:21–26 was probably intended for rhetorical effect as Paul reiterates themes. The righteousness of God "has now been manifested" (3:21 AT) "in the now age" (3:26 AT). Twice Paul mentions "the righteousness of God" (3:21; cf. "his righteousness," 3:26 AT) but then expands, using the verb *dikaioumenoi* in the present tense, which he repeats twice in this statement (3:24, 26) and repeatedly in the letter (cf. 3:28, 30; 4:5), further indicating that the eschatological vindication is a present reality. That is, God is righteous (*dikaios*) and "makes righteous" those who fall short of the glory of God. As in Isaiah 53:11, "The righteous one will make many righteous" (AT). Thus *dikaiosynē theou* is a subjective genitive, recalling Israel's appeal to the righteousness of God for its salvation (Rom. 3:22). In Romans, it is the equivalent of the love of God (cf. Rom. 5:8; 8:35, 39). To "make righteous" is, as Deutero-Isaiah indicates, to take away sin. To be justified is no mere pretense,[31] for it involves being liberated from the power of sin (cf. Rom. 6:7). As the argument in Romans 5–8 indicates, it is the life in the new aeon under a new power.

Paul then stacks up synonyms to describe the demonstration of God's righteousness, emphasizing the enormousness of the gift. He speaks of the gift (*dōrea*) by God's grace (*charis*), using a hendiadys that he employs again in 5:15 ("the grace of God and the gift in grace," AT), the equivalent of "the gift of righteousness" (5:17). The terms indicate that the gift shows no correspondence to the worth of the recipients. The dismal condition described in 1:18–3:20 is overcome by God's gracious gift.

For the first time in the argument, Paul indicates that the manifestation of God's righteousness is in the death of Christ. By calling it the redemption (*apolytrōsis*, 3:24) in Jesus Christ, Paul echoes the language of the exodus, the liberation of Israel from slavery. The Israelites looked back to the exodus as the moment when God redeemed (*elytrōsato*) Israelite slaves from Egypt (Deut. 7:8; cf. 9:26; 15:15; Pss. 24:22 LXX; 30:6 LXX). Deutero-Isaiah employs the word to describe the redemption from Babylonian captivity (Isa.

---

31. See Barclay, *Paul and the Gift*, 476. Barclay renders *dikaioō* "consider righteous."

43:1, 14; 44:22–24). God both justifies and sets forth Christ as the *hilastērion*, which translations render as "expiation" (Rom. 3:25 RSV) or "sacrifice of atonement" (NIV, NRSV). While this word in Greco-Roman sources means "propitiation," a means of appeasing the gods,[32] in the Septuagint, it was employed for the mercy seat, the gold plate on the ark of the covenant (cf. Exod. 25:17–22; cf. Heb. 9:5). In 4 Maccabees, the death of the martyrs is the *hilastērios* ("atoning sacrifice," NRSV) that preserved Israel. The association of the image with "his blood" and the removal of sin (cf. Rom. 3:9; 4:7; 5:20) suggests that Paul is alluding to the ritual of the Day of Atonement, when the high priest purified Israel from its sins by sprinkling the blood of the goat on the mercy seat (*hilastērion*).[33] Paul employs the metaphor to clarify God's act of justifying the ungodly, using the image of the ancient sacrifice for sins. This anticipates the later comment that we are justified by his blood (Rom. 5:9).

As the repetition of "faith" (*pistis*), along with the verb "believe" (*pisteuō*), indicates (Rom. 3:22, 25–26), in the new situation, God's justice is no longer the prerogative of those who keep the law but is "for everyone who believes" (3:22 AT; cf. 3:26). Scholars debate over whether to render the translation of the twofold *dia/ek pisteōs christou* (3:22, 26) as "faith of Christ" (subjective genitive) or "faith in Christ" (objective genitive). The context indicates that the traditional reading "faith in Christ" is to be preferred, for Paul abbreviates the phrase to "everyone who believes," and he illustrates the case with the example of Abraham, "who believed God." The summary statement "A person is justified by faith and not by works of the law" (3:28 AT) and the statement that God will justify the uncircumcised as well as the circumcised on the basis of faith (3:29) indicate that Paul focuses on a response to God's righteousness that does not include circumcision. A united church comes together on the basis of faith.

The rhetorical aim of the argument, as 3:27–4:2 indicates, is to undermine all boasting. Paul writes to ensure that neither gentiles nor Jews boast of their status. Having argued from revelation, Paul now offers Abraham as an exemplum of the principle he has stated in the premise.[34] Paul had employed the example of Abraham in Galatians 3 to justify his mission to the gentiles, and in Romans 4, he develops the argument further. The focus of Romans 4 is on Abraham as the father of a multiethnic family on the basis of faith. After citing the primary text that contains both *pisteuō* and *dikaiosynē* (4:3; cf. Gen.

---

32. BDAG 474.

33. Wolter, *Paul*, 105.

34. Aristotle lists two kinds of proofs: the example and the enthymeme. One type of example consists in relating things that have happened, and the other consists of invention by the speaker. See the discussion in Aristotle, *Rhet.* 2.20.

15:6), Paul reiterates the focus on *pistis* repeatedly. In the articular infinitives in Romans 4:11, 16, 18, he focuses on Abraham as the father of gentiles who believe. Those who believe in the one who raised Jesus from the dead (Rom. 4:24) follow in the footsteps of Abraham and belong to his family.

Paul thus addresses the rhetorical situation with the theological basis for a united church. He does not use traditional rhetorical arguments but begins with the premise that would have been plausible only within the subculture of the Christian community. Paul is the prophetic figure who announces the divine revelation of God's righteousness and the response of faith as the response to God's righteousness. While he begins with the premise of divine revelation, he employs traditional rhetorical arguments (apostrophe, exemplum) to develop the case.

Living between the Times (5:1–8:39)

In Galatians, Paul's argument for justification by faith makes only a passing reference to the eschatological hope (Gal. 5:5) but focuses on the presence of salvation (cf. Gal. 1:4; 3:23; 4:4). The argument in Romans 1:18–4:25, which focuses on the event of the recent past, calls for further clarification, as the questions of the interlocutor indicate (see above). As Paul indicates in 3:8, his message is widely misunderstood or maliciously misrepresented. Thus his defense of his ministry requires that he answer these questions in the remainder of the letter. In chapters 5–8, he answers the questions "Shall we continue in sin that grace may abound?" and "Is the law sin?" (cf. 6:1; 7:7), and he gives an extended statement on eschatological hope (5:1–11; 8:18–39). We may read Romans 5–8 as a carefully crafted sermon-within-a-sermon that is answering the questions raised by the announcement of the "now" of salvation in chapters 1–4 and describing the situation of believers who live between the "now" and their ultimate salvation. Indeed, Romans 5–8 answers the perennial question that has faced believers: How do we believe in God's ultimate triumph if we do not see the evidence of the new creation? How do we live the transformed life if we are still living with the temptations of the old age? His answer requires an exploration of anthropology (5:12–21; 7:7–25) and pneumatology (8:1–17) in a new way.

Paul introduces the new topics in 5:1–11 in the exordium of this section and concludes with a peroratio in 8:18–39 that recapitulates these themes in a lyrical and triumphant composition. Here Paul guides his ancient readers through the meaning of Christian hope, reminding them that those who are surrounded by hopelessness may endure in hope because of what God has done in Christ. Indeed, while *pistis* and *pisteuein* appear only rarely in Romans

5–8 (cf. 5:1–2; 6:8), hope is the constant thread that runs through these chapters (5:2, 4; 8:20, 24–25). Paul has already indicated the close relationship between faith and hope in the story of Abraham, who "believed" and "hoped against hope" (4:18 AT). The correspondence between the beginning and the end of this minisermon suggests the coherence of Paul's message of hope. This correspondence is evident in the parallels indicated below.

"hope of the glory of God" (5:2)	"the glory to be revealed" (8:18) "We were saved in hope, but hope that is seen is not hope." (8:24)
"sufferings" (5:3)	"sufferings" (8:35)
"endurance" (5:4–5)	"We wait with endurance." (8:25)
"the love of God" (5:5)	"Who shall separate us from the love of God?" (8:35) "[Nothing] is able to separate us from the love of God." (8:39)
"The Holy Spirit has been poured out." (5:5)	"having the firstfruits of the Spirit" (8:23) "The Spirit helps us in our weaknesses." (8:26)

The premise of the argument of Romans 5:1–11 is the Christian confession in 5:1: "Having been justified by faith" (AT). This reiterates the premise of the letter and is the basis for the *synkrisis* (comparison) in 5:9–11 between salvation in the Christ event and salvation in the future. Paul makes the logical step, using the argument from the lesser to the greater.[35] The beginning and the end of the argument are shaped by comparisons (*synkrises*): between the sufferings of this age and the future glory (8:18) and between God's act in the past and what God will do in the future (cf. 8:32, 34–39).[36]

God's love, which has been demonstrated in the past (5:7; 8:35, 39), is the expression of God's righteousness and his continuing assurance in the midst of the present sufferings. Paul begins and ends Romans 5 and 8 with reflection on the hope of salvation for those who have already been saved.

Chapters 5–8 indicate that the "now" of salvation is not the end of God's narrative. Paul turns from the past tense of chapters 1:17–4:23 to the present and future and from the third person in chapters 1–4 to the first-person plural in 4:24–8:39, describing the experience of the predominantly gentile

35. On the argument from the lesser to the greater (*a minore ad maius*), see Aristotle, *Rhet.* 1.2.21.

36. On *synkrisis*, cf. Quintilian, *Inst.* 8.4.9: "Just as this form of amplification rises to a climax, so too, the form which depends on comparison seeks to rise from the less to the greater, since by raising what is below it must necessarily exalt that which is above." Quintilian discusses a variety of forms of *synkrisis*, including one that relies on reasoning: "One thing is magnified in order to effect a corresponding augmentation elsewhere, and it is by reasoning that our hearers are then led on from the first point to the second which we desire to emphasize" (8.4.15).

community that now participates in Israel's narrative. The God who has already revealed his righteousness will ultimately reveal his glory (8:18). The community has been justified (5:1), reconciled (5:11), and saved (8:24). Now it has peace with God (5:1), but it lives in hope that it "will be saved" (5:9–10 AT). In the present, the community joins the whole creation in waiting for the ultimate redemption (8:18–24).

For the believing community, redemption will be adoption (*huiothesia*; cf. 8:15), the redemption of the body (8:23). God's ultimate purpose is that the community be "conformed to the image of the Son" (8:29 AT). This hope is consistent with Paul's emphasis on the ultimate hope of believers in the earlier letters. With the first-person plural that began in 4:24, Paul includes all who believe that God raised Jesus from the dead.

The lyrical peroratio (8:18–39) is an argument from pathos and an invitation for the community to experience the good news of God's righteousness. Paul concludes this section with a change of tone and style that includes the gradation in the form of a climax in 8:29–30.[37]

> Because whom he foreknew he also foreordained.
> Those whom he foreordained he also justified.
> Those whom he justified he also glorified. (AT)

Verses 31–39 develop into an *amplificatio* filled with pathos and function as a *recipatulatio* that summarizes the essential elements of the argument.[38] As the first-person plural indicates, Paul includes himself among those who celebrate, creating a bond with his gentile readers—those who believe God raised Christ from the dead (cf. 4:24–25).[39] The gentiles have been brought into Israel's narrative, and now they await its conclusion in the triumph of God.

If the exordium (5:1–11) and peroratio (8:18–39) of chapters 5–8 invite the gentile community to experience hope as the outcome of the revelation of God's righteousness, the argument in 5:12–8:17 addresses the challenge of living between the turn of the ages (3:21) and the ultimate salvation, for the community lives with "the sufferings of this age" (8:18 AT; cf. 5:2–3) and the temptations of the flesh (6:1–23). Paul answers two critical questions that his doctrine of justification has raised. The question "Shall we continue in sin that grace may abound?" (6:1 AT) responds to a misrepresentation of

---

37. See Aletti, "Rhetoric of Romans 5–8," 297.
38. Aletti, "Rhetoric of Romans 5–8," 298.
39. On the use of the first-person plural to create a bond between speaker and audience, see Conley, "Philo of Alexandria," 698.

Paul's doctrine of grace (cf. 3:8), and the question "Is the law sin?" (7:7 AT) anticipates a false conclusion from Paul's argument associating the law with sin (cf. 4:15; 5:13–14; 7:1–7). Paul laid the foundation for the former question earlier with his conclusion that "all are under sin" (3:9 AT) and with his description of the invasion of sin into world history in 5:12–21. To "remain in sin" (6:1 AT) is to continue in the vices Paul has listed in 1:18–3:20, which characterized the previous existence of the believers (6:17, 19–20).

Paul's answers to these questions begin with a second exemplum from Scripture (cf. 4:1–23) and a premise that should be accepted by the audience: sin entered into the world by one man. As the example of the first human indicates in 5:12–21, sin (hamartia) is an invading power (5:12) that passed to all people (5:12), bringing death with it, a power that ruled (5:14, 17, 21) over humankind. In accordance with the ancient understanding of solidarity, according to which the destiny of the one determines the destiny of the many (cf. Heb. 7:4–10),[40] Paul appeals to assumptions presumably known to the community, contrasting the founder of the old humanity to the founder of the new humanity, whose destiny also determined the destiny of the many.

In Romans 5:12–21, Paul offers a doctrine of the human situation for which the righteousness of God is the answer, reiterating the claims made in 1:18–3:20. While Paul has repeatedly indicated that Christ died "for our sins" (cf. Gal. 1:4; 1 Cor. 15:3), in Romans, the problem is the singular *sin*, an enslaving and occupying power (cf. Rom. 3:9; 6:17–19) that Paul describes with particular frequency in chapters 5–8. He anticipated the argument in 1:18–3:20, arguing that no one—even those who have the law—is righteous, a view that is contrary to the Jewish tradition, and in the argument in 7:7–25, he portrays one who is powerless to do the good (cf. 8:7–8). Both gentiles and Jews are under the power of the passions (*epithymiai*; cf. 1:18–32; 7:5–25). While both

40. One rabbinic parable seeks to explain our situation. "Rabbi Levi said: 'What comparison can you make? It is like a pregnant woman who was put in prison. Then she bore a son. When the king entered, the son asked, "Why am I here?" The king said, "Because of the sins of your mother." Also Moses said: "Lord of the world, there are 26 commandments with the death penalty. Why must I die? What have I done?" He answered, "Because of the sin of the first man"'" (*Deut. Rab.* 9.206a). The writer of *4 Ezra* complains, "For the first Adam, burdened with an evil heart, transgressed and was overcome, as were also all who were descended from him. Thus the disease became permanent; the law was in the people's heart along with the evil root, but what was good departed, and the evil remained" (3:21–22). He adds, "O Adam, what have you done? For though it was you who sinned, the fall was not yours alone, but ours also who are your descendants. For what good is it to us, if an eternal age has been promised to us, but we have done deeds that bring death?" (7:118–20). The author of *2 Baruch* says, "For what did it profit Adam that he lived nine hundred and thirty years and transgressed that which he was commanded? Therefore, the multitude of time that he lived did not profit him, but it brought death and cut off the years of those who were born from him" (17:3).

Jewish and Christian writers describe the problem of overcoming the passions, Paul expresses an anthropological pessimism that is unprecedented: no one is able to do the good.[41] Perhaps, as E. P. Sanders has argued,[42] Paul begins with the answer—Christ died for our sins—and then reflects on the problem. This anthropological pessimism is central to the argument of 5:12–8:17. While enslavement to *epithymia* belongs to the past for believers (6:1, 17–19; 7:5–6), it remains a continuing temptation to be overcome (6:12–23). Paul provides the answer in this section. In 5:12–21, Paul presupposes the apocalyptic view that the end-time will restore the primordial state and the Jewish view that the destiny of the one determines the destiny of the many, providing the initial argument in describing the resolution to the problem of sin.

> One brings condemnation [*katakrima*], the other brings justification [*dikaiōma*]. (5:16 AT)

> Through one death ruled, but those who receive the gift of righteousness [*dikaiosynē*] rule in life through Jesus Christ. (5:17 AT)

> One man's trespass brought condemnation, but the righteous act [*dikaiōma*] of one leads to justification [*dikaiōsis*] of life. (5:18 AT)

> As sin ruled in death, so also grace rules through righteousness [*dikaiosynē*] leading to eternal life through Jesus Christ our Lord. (5:21 AT)

In this example in 5:12–21, Paul presents two competing powers. Basing his argument on the rabbinic argument from the lesser to the greater (5:15, 17),[43] Paul concludes that the power of the new age surpasses that of the old

41. For most philosophers, the answer to the problem of the passions was education and reason. According to Socrates, no one ever does wrong knowingly, for bad behavior is the result of misinformation (Plato, *Prot.* 345d–e). The Stoics maintained that reason can conquer the passions (cf. Diogenes Laertius, *Lives* 7.111). The writer of 4 Maccabees portrayed the martyrs as heroes who demonstrated that reason, inculcated through the law, overcomes the passion of fear. Paul probably encountered gentiles who saw the law as a means of gaining self-control. For Paul, however, the law is not the means for gaining self-mastery. Indeed, it provides the opportunity for sin to gain a foothold. Enslavement to the flesh and its passions is the result of the invasion of sin through the first man. Having declared that neither Jew nor Greek is righteous (Rom. 3:10) and that all are enslaved to the cravings (Rom. 1:24–26; 7:5), he reiterates this condition in Rom. 7:7–25, describing the story of all humanity apart from the saving grace of God. This portrayal is an elaboration of Paul's depiction of the believers' story in 7:5: once, "when we were in the flesh, the passions of sins worked in our members, bearing fruit to death" (AT). See Thompson, *Moral Formation according to Paul*, 136–41.

42. Sanders, *Paul and Palestinian Judaism*, 442–43.

43. Comparison is also a common argument in Greek rhetoric (see n. 36). According to Theon, *synkrisis* is "language setting the better or the worse side by side." He adds, "*Synkrises*

age (5:17, 20–21). Paul thus explains the righteousness that he announced in chapters 1–4, indicating that the righteousness of God is the power of the new age. Because of the solidarity between the one and the many, believers have been made righteous and liberated from the power of sin. Thus Paul's question "Shall we continue in sin that grace may abound?" (AT) is inseparable from the preceding description of the power of sin, suggesting that, despite the coming of the new aeon, the dominion of sin remains a reality and that believers may choose between the old and the new aeon, rejecting the righteousness that has been given to them.

Paul answers the question with a question: "We who died to sin, how shall we go on living in it?" (6:2 AT). He appeals to a premise that he assumes the readers will accept: "We died to sin." He also returns to the first-person plural that he employed in 4:23–5:11, indicating that the story of triumph over sin is our own story. While sin remains a ruling power in the world (5:12–21) and all humanity is under the power of sin (3:9), the community of believers "died to sin." The inclusio of 6:2 ("we who died to sin") and 6:11 ("Consider yourselves dead to sin") indicates that sin has lost its power over believers. At the heart of Paul's response to the charge that he encourages sin is the claim that believers have made an irrevocable step in leaving the power of sin.

Paul has consistently indicated that faith is the proper response to the righteousness of God revealed in the cross of Christ (1:16; cf. 3:22). When he wants to elaborate on our death to sin (6:2), he speaks not of faith, however, but of baptism, assuming that the readers will know that "we were baptized . . . into his death" (6:3 AT) and recognize the relationship between faith and baptism. Elsewhere, Paul describes believers' participation in the death of Jesus: "One died for all; therefore all have died" (2 Cor. 5:14 AT). To the Galatians, he says, "I have been crucified with Christ" (Gal. 2:19). Similarly, he describes the Lord's Supper as a "participation" (koinōnia) in the body and blood of Christ (1 Cor. 10:16). Paul apparently speaks of being "baptized into his death" because baptism provides a remarkable image for the crossing of a threshold from one existence to another. Although sin remains a reality in the world, believers have died to this power. No one who crosses this threshold wishes to return to the enslavement to sin that Paul describes in Romans 1:18–3:20.

The climax of the story of Jesus was that he was "raised from the dead through the glory of the Father" (Rom. 6:4 AT), a premise already accepted

---

are not comparisons of things having a great difference between them. . . . Comparisons should be of likes and where we are in doubt which should be preferred because of no evident superiority of one to the other." Cited in Kennedy, *Progymnasmata*, 53. On the use of comparison (*synkrisis*) in ancient rhetoric, see Kneepkens, "Comparatio," 2:293.

by the listeners. While believers share in the story of Jesus, Paul does not say here that we have been raised with him,[44] for we continue to wait on the fulfillment of God's promises. Indeed, Paul insists that we who died with Christ will one day live with him (6:8). Paul says that Christ has been raised "in order that we might walk in newness of life" (6:4 AT). Although we have not been raised with him, we are no longer enslaved by the power of sin that the first human brought. Nor are we enslaved to the destructive passions that Paul mentions in 1:18–31. The power of the resurrection enables us to walk in "newness of life" (6:4). Our baptism is not only a moment of leaving one domain for another but also the empowerment to live the ethical life. Those who receive this new power will never want to "continue in sin that grace may abound" (AT; cf. 6:1) but will turn to the new ethical existence. Indeed, the gospel is "the power of God to salvation" (AT; cf. 1:16) because it overcomes the enslaving power of sin.

Believers thus choose between two competing powers: either the power of sin that invaded the world or the power that God has made available at baptism. Five times in Romans 6:12–23 Paul describes the believers' choice with the word *paristēmi* ("to present," NRSV; "to place at someone's disposal"), suggesting that we are like slaves who place ourselves at the disposal of either the power of sin or the power of God's righteousness.

> Do not place your members at the disposal of unrighteousness to sin, but place yourselves at the disposal of God as living from the dead. (6:13 AT)

> Do you not know that if you present yourselves to anyone as obedient slaves, you are slaves of the one whom you obey? (6:16)

> As you once placed your members at the disposal of uncleanness and lawlessness, now place your members at the disposal of righteousness for sanctification. (6:19 AT)

With the imperatives, Paul argues from his own authority. The body becomes the battleground between the two powers. When Paul says, "Do not let sin reign in your mortal bodies" (6:12 AT), he undoubtedly recalls the past, when the listeners participated in sinful activities, "degrading . . . their bodies among themselves" (1:24) with sinful passions at work when they were "living in the flesh" (7:5). Paul has already described the previous time when the believers yielded their bodies to the slavery of the passions (cf. 1:24; 6:12).

---

44. Col. 2:12 indicates that "you have been raised with him" (AT). Because Paul in Romans insists that we live between the times, he chooses not to say that "we have been raised with him."

But because of the power of the gospel, the body is not compelled to be at the disposal of evil, for "the body of sin is destroyed" when the old person is crucified with Christ (6:6 AT). The imagery of slavery (cf. 6:16, 18) suggests that all humanity is enslaved and that we all place ourselves at the disposal of something. Those who have died with Christ may choose to be enslaved to righteousness (6:18–19) and to God (6:22). Rather than place their bodies at the disposal of sin, they may present their bodies as a living sacrifice to God (cf. 12:1).

Although God's righteousness (*dikaiosynē*) was revealed at the cross, it was not only the moment of acquittal for guilty people but also an invasion by the power to transform lives. Paul's statement that "whoever has died has been justified [*dikaiōtai*] from sin" (6:7 AT) associates God's righteousness with baptism, the transitional moment for believers. The fact that they may be enslaved to righteousness (6:18–19) indicates that God's righteousness continues to empower those who make themselves available to it.

However, Paul's doctrine of grace does not undermine ethics, as his critics have maintained (cf. 3:8). Nor is his doctrine of grace an invitation to moral relativity, as his friends have mistakenly claimed. God's gift is not cheap grace that leads to permissiveness but empowering grace that enables believers to obey the will of God (cf. 6:17). The body is not only the locus of uncontrollable passions but also, under God's power, the place of service to God.

Paul's claims require clarification. For many readers, the claim that "where sin abounded, grace abounded all the more" (5:20 AT) leads to the logical conclusion that believers should "continue in sin that grace may abound" (6:1 AT). Similarly, the logical conclusion to the claim that "we died to sin" (6:2 AT) and "died to the law" (7:4 AT) appears to be that "the law is sin" (7:7). Paul rejects both conclusions. After clarifying the first claim in 6:1–23, affirming that believers are no longer under the power of sin, in 7:7–25, he responds to the question "Is the law sin?" Once more he responds, "By no means!" (7:7; cf. 6:2). Speaking in the first-person singular, he employs the past tense in 7:7–13 and the present tense in 7:14–25.

As we follow the argument, we recognize that the context does not suggest that Paul is speaking of himself as he focuses on the question "Is the law sin?" He begins his response in Romans 7:7 with two parallel statements: "If it had not been for the law, I would not have known sin" and "I would not have known what it is to covet if the law had not said, 'You shall not covet' [Exod. 20:17]." The parallel passages suggest that Paul agrees with the traditional Jewish view that desire is the source of sin. Here he elaborates on the earlier statement that "through the law comes the knowledge of sin" (Rom. 3:20).

Paul did not arbitrarily choose the tenth commandment as the illustration of the relationship between sin and the law. He omits the direct object of the verb ("your neighbor's house . . . your neighbor's wife") in order to generalize the command. Furthermore, the Greek word *epithymein* (covet) is commonly rendered "desire," "crave," or "lust." Paul uses the noun (*epithymia*) for sexual lusts (Rom. 1:24; 6:12) that enslave those who are under the power of sin. Thus in 7:8, Paul speaks of the commandment that evokes the desire that leads to sin. By using the word *epithymia*, he places Jews and gentiles on the same level: gentiles without the law were enslaved to "desire" (1:24–26 AT), and those who knew the law were enslaved to the "passions" (7:5 AT). While the law is not sin, it provides the opportunity (*aphormē*, lit., "beachhead") for the invasion by sin.[45] Paul anticipated this comment in 4:15, where he said, "The law came in to increase the trespass" (AT).

That Paul is actually telling the story of humanity rather than his own story becomes clearer in his description of the incursion of sin. The statement "I was once alive apart from the law, but when the commandment came, sin revived and I died" (7:9) evokes the story of Adam, for the commandment that was meant for life resulted in death (7:11). Indeed, the statement that sin "deceived me and through it killed me" (7:11) echoes the description of Eve, who was "deceived" by the serpent (cf. Gen. 3:13). Thus Paul has told the story of humanity, indicating that "the law is not sin" (Rom. 7:7 AT) but is "good and just and holy" (7:12 AT). The problem is not with the law but with the way in which sin exploits the commandment.

As Paul moves to the present tense in 7:14–25, he continues to insist that the law is not sin, for it is "spiritual" (7:14). However, the power of sin to rule (cf. 6:21) and to enslave is nowhere more vividly stated than in the experience of the tortured speaker, who is "sold into slavery to sin" (7:14 AT). The nature of this slavery is evident in the repeated expressions of the conflict between willing and doing.

I do not do what I want to do, but I do what I hate. (7:15 AT)

If I do what I do not want to do, I agree that the law is good. (7:16 AT)

To want to do is at hand for me, but to do the good is not. (7:18 AT)

For I do not do the good I want, but the evil I hate is what I do. (7:19 AT)

But if I do what I do not want, it is not I that do it but sin living in me. (7:20 AT)

45. *Aphormē* was used for the basis of operations in an expedition. Cf. BDAG 158.

I agree with the law in my inner person, but I see another law in my members. (7:22–23 AT)

This description of the inner conflict between willing and doing echoes the conversations in the philosophical literature over the problem of doing the good when our passions drive us toward the evil. Euripides's *Medea* became the topic of discussion for those who wished to comprehend why we do not do the good we know. Driven by the passion of anger over being betrayed by Jason, Medea exacts revenge by killing her children, crying out:

> I know indeed what evil I intend to do,
> But stronger than all my afterthoughts is my fury,
> Fury that brings upon mortals the greatest evils.[46]

Ovid's Medea expresses the same view, describing her emotional state:

> I'd act more sanely, if only I could,
> but this new power overwhelms my will;
> reason advises this, and passion, that;
> I see the better way, and I approve it,
> while I pursue the worse.[47]

Critics of Paul's portrayal object that neither he nor countless others actually experienced the torture described in Romans 7:7–25. He himself was "blameless" (Phil. 3:6) before his conversion, and others are described in the New Testament as "righteous" (cf. Luke 1:6, 17; 2:25). However, Paul speaks as the liberated man who now looks back on the past, recognizing where he had been. Only in retrospect does he see his earlier incapacity to do the good. As we shall see in Romans 8:1–17, Paul provides a foil in chapter 7 for the depiction of the liberated person in chapter 8. Whereas the Spirit is not mentioned in 7:7–25, the Spirit becomes the dominant theme in Romans 8.

The missing dimension in the tortured person in Romans 7 is the Holy Spirit. The Spirit has been mentioned only in passing throughout Romans before chapter 8 (cf. 1:4; 2:29; 5:5; 7:6). In the introduction to this section on living between the times (chaps. 5–8), Paul acknowledges that, although we have been justified (5:1), we continue to live in hope for salvation in the midst of pain and suffering (5:2–4). God has "poured out his Spirit" (5:5 AT) as a guarantee that our hope is not in vain. In 7:6, Paul says that we now serve

---

46. Euripides, *Medea* 1078–80.
47. Ovid, *Metam.* 7.18–21.

"in the newness of the Spirit" (AT). Thus 7:7–25 is the elaboration of 7:5, and 8:1–17 is the elaboration of 7:6. After mentioning the Spirit only four times before chapter 8, Paul mentions the Spirit twenty times in chapter 8. The Spirit is the gift for those who live between the times.

"There is therefore now no condemnation [*katakrima*] to those who are in Christ" (8:1 AT) marks a radical transition from the description of the tortured person of chapter 7. Once more the word "now" emphasizes that believers live in the new era promised by the prophets (cf. 3:21, 26; 5:9, 11; 6:19, 21–22; 7:6). Paul has repeatedly distinguished the believers' former existence in slavery to sin from their new existence in Christ (cf. 6:17–23; 7:5–6). In baptism, they died to the old existence and arose to "newness of life" (6:4).

"Condemnation" (*katakrima*) continues the judicial metaphor, recalling the condemnation that accompanied Adam's sin (5:16). Consistent with the judicial images, "there is no condemnation" is the equivalent to "we have been justified" (AT; cf. 5:1). This new situation comes only to those who are "in Christ"—those who have died with him. Some may continue to live under the power of sin that came with Adam, but those who are "in Christ" have been justified. The power of sin expressed in the conflicted person of chapter 7 has been broken.

In 8:2–4, Paul elaborates on this new situation. "The law of sin and death" (8:2) is undoubtedly the law as it was experienced by the tortured person in chapter 7. Although it was "just and good and holy" (7:12 AT), it provided the beachhead for sin and death (7:11), resulting in the slavery described in 7:7–25. A greater power, "the law of the Spirit of life" (8:2), has liberated us from slavery to sin, as Paul has already indicated (6:18, 22).

What is "the law of the Spirit of life" that sets us free? Despite Paul's negative comments about "works of the law" (3:27–28; 4:2), he speaks positively of the liberating effect of "the law of the Spirit." He probably envisions the words of the exilic prophets who proclaimed the good news of the return from exile. According to the exilic prophets, Israel went into captivity because of its failure to keep the law (Ezek. 11:12). The prophets announced the time when God would cleanse Israel from its transgressions. Ezekiel says, "A new spirit I will put within you; and I will remove from your body the heart of stone and give you a heart of flesh. I will put my spirit within you, and make you follow my statutes and be careful to observe my ordinances" (Ezek. 36:26–27; cf. 11:19). Jeremiah laments that Israel did not keep God's covenant (Jer. 31:32) but looks forward to the time when God will make a new covenant and write it on the hearts of Israel so that Israel will keep the covenant after the exile (Jer. 31:33). "The law of the Spirit of life" (Rom.

8:2) is the new covenant announced by Ezekiel and Jeremiah. The power of the Spirit is the new dimension in the life of those who are "in Christ," for it liberates believers from their inability to keep the law.

Freedom is also the capacity to do the will of God, as Paul indicates in Romans 8:4. The result of the saving work of Christ is that "the just requirement of the law might be fulfilled in those who walk, not according to the flesh, but according to the Spirit" (AT). After describing humanity that does not fulfill God's just requirement (cf. 1:32), Paul now describes a community in which God's requirement is fulfilled. The passive voice ("might be fulfilled") suggests that believers do not keep God's commandments under their own power. Indeed, the power of the Spirit enables them to keep God's requirement. Believers are not, therefore, among those who say, "I can will what is right but cannot do it" (7:18 AT), for they are the returning exiles whom God empowers to keep the commandments.

Despite the victorious language of 8:1–4, Paul must acknowledge that sin and the flesh remain in the world and remain options for believers. Because God has poured out the Spirit (5:5; 8:4), the new possibility exists that "the just requirement of the law might be fulfilled in us" (8:4). We may observe the parallel between "in order that we may walk in newness of life" (6:4 AT) and "in order that the just requirement of the law might be fulfilled in us" (8:4 AT). That is, the wretched condition of chapter 7 is not an inevitability, for the new possibility exists to leave the power of sin introduced by Adam and to live within the new power of God's Spirit.

If slavery to sin is not an inevitability for believers, neither is their obedience to God's will, for sin remains in the world. Thus God has empowered believers to live in newness of life, but believers must choose between the competing powers. Indeed, as Paul indicated in 6:11–12, we may consider ourselves dead to sin, but we must nevertheless choose not to let "sin reign in [our] mortal body" (AT). Paul elaborates on this choice in 8:5–11, describing the alternative that believers now confront as they live between the time of the resurrection and the end of time. He depicts two alternative mind-sets. Using a term that is employed almost exclusively in Romans and Philippians,[48] Paul contrasts those who "set their minds" (*phronousin*) on the flesh and those who "set their minds" (*phronousin*) on the Spirit (Rom. 8:5), elaborating by contrasting the "mind" (*phronēma*) of the flesh and the "mind" (*phronēma*) of the Spirit (Rom. 8:6–7).[49] The word is used in the Septuagint to describe

48. See Phil. 1:7; 2:5; 3:15, 19; 4:10.
49. The NRSV translates both the verb and the noun as "set the mind on." The NIV maintains the distinction between the two forms.

alternative dispositions in which one chooses between two sides.[50] Similarly, Paul uses the verb in Philippians to describe alternatives on which one may set one's mind. One may either set one's mind on the higher calling Paul has described (*touto phroneite*) or "think otherwise" (*heterōs phroneite*, Phil. 3:15). He contrasts those who "set their mind on earthly things" (*hoi ta epigeia phronountes*) with those whose citizenship is in heaven (Phil. 3:19–20). In Romans 8:5, Paul describes the two different groups, who are distinguished by the power they have chosen to rule their lives.

Paul has already described the mind of the flesh in Romans 6 and 7, indicating that the readers were once enslaved to the flesh and its passions (6:17–22; 7:5) and that "the mind of the flesh is death, but the mind of the Spirit is life and peace" (8:6 AT; cf. 5:1, 12; 6:23). He has shown that the mind of the flesh is hostile to God and cannot please God (8:7–8; cf. 7:14–25). Thus as the earlier question "Shall we continue in sin?" suggests, the return to the flesh remains an option for believers, but the end result is death.

To return to the old world would be to reject the divine gift, as Paul indicates in 8:9–11. Having reiterated the negative consequences of this return in 8:5–8, Paul speaks of the believers' extraordinary entry into the power of the new aeon. Addressing the readers directly, he says, "But you are not in the flesh, but in the Spirit, if the Spirit of God dwells in you" (8:9 AT). This reassurance recalls the earlier statement "We were once in the flesh. . . . But now we are discharged from the law, dead to that which held us captive, so that we are slaves not under the old written code [lit., "letter"] but in the new life in the Spirit" (7:5–6). Although we still live in a time of suffering and temptation, God has "poured out his Spirit" (5:5 AT). Thus to continue in sin is to reject the power that enables us to overcome slavery to evil.

Paul describes the divine gift in a series of "if" clauses that may be more appropriately translated "since,"[51] suggesting that what God has already given is the basis for believers' new existence and hope for the future:

> You [plural] are not in the flesh, but in the Spirit, if the Spirit of God dwells in you. (8:9 AT)

> Anyone[52] who does not have the Spirit of God does not belong to him. (8:9)

> If Christ is in you [lit., "among you"], the body is dead because of sin but the Spirit is life because of righteousness. (8:10 AT)

---

50. Cf. 1 Macc. 10:20: "You are to take our side [*phronein ta hēmōn*] and keep friendship with us." Cf. 2 Macc. 14:26.

51. BDAG 279.

52. The Greek says, "if anyone."

> If the Spirit of the one who raised up Christ from the dead dwells among you, the one who raised Christ . . . will give life to you through the Spirit that is dwelling among you. (8:11 AT)

What distinguishes believers from others is the gift of the Spirit. Paul employs the imagery of a house, indicating that already the Spirit and Christ dwell (*oikei*) in the community. Whereas the tortured human cries out, "It is not I that do it but sin that dwells [*oikei*] in me" (7:17 AT), believers recognize that the Spirit dwells in them. Because of the Spirit, the body that was once enslaved to the passions is now dead (7:10; cf. 6:6, 12). It is no longer a slave to sin, for it has a new resident in the indwelling Spirit. Moreover, since Christ has been raised from the dead, he will ultimately give life to our mortal bodies at the resurrection (8:11). Because sin remains a power in the world, the return to the old existence remains a possibility. The challenge for believers is to choose which occupying power they will serve (cf. 6:15–17). Only those who are "in Christ" (8:1) are free to do the good, for only they have been empowered to set their minds on the Spirit.

While we live between the times, the Spirit is the guarantee that we are not merely children; we are heirs of God awaiting our inheritance. But we are more than heirs, for we are "joint heirs" with Jesus Christ (8:17). Indeed, as we have been "buried with him" (6:4), have "died with him" (6:8), and were "crucified with him" (6:6), we also "suffer with him in order that we may be glorified with him" (8:17 AT). Paul employs a remarkable array of compound words with the Greek *syn* (with) to express our total identification with Christ.[53] Believers have died with him but have not been raised with him. Although the victory has not yet come, because believers identify with Christ rather than with Adam, they receive God's grace with gratitude, not as permission to continue in sin but as the new power that enables them to live faithfully.

Paul's lyrical conclusion in 8:31–39 not only contains his most extensive treatment of major theological themes (anthropology and pneumatology) but also is an invitation for his readers to celebrate the victory in the midst of their suffering and temptation. Employing premises that he shares with his audience (cf. 5:1, 12; 6:2), he gives answers that are unprecedented in earlier letters, arguing from ethos (the first-person plural), pathos (cf. 8:31–39), and logos (cf. 5:9–11; 6:2–11) in order to persuade his readers.

---

53. *Synthaptomai* ("buried with him," Rom. 6:4), *syzao* ("live with him," 6:8), *sympaschō* ("suffer with him," 8:17), *syndoxazō* ("to glorify with," 8:17), *synklēronomos* ("joint heir," 8:17), *symmorphos* ("have the same form as," 8:29).

Is God Unjust? (9–11)

Those who join with Paul in the lyrical expression of God's triumph and their salvation "believe in the one who raised Jesus Christ from the dead" (4:24 AT), as the first-person plural in chapters 5–8 demonstrates. As the sudden change of tone in 9:1–5 indicates, those who celebrate in 8:31–39 are predominantly gentiles. The preaching of the gospel for "the Jew first and then the Greek" (1:16 AT) has resulted in a church in which the Jews are largely absent. Paul's doctrine of the impartial justice of God for all has resulted in a gentile church. This situation raised the question to which Paul responded earlier: "Is God unjust?" (3:3, 5 AT). The implicit charge that Paul answers, therefore, is that Israel's rejection of Jesus demonstrates that God's word has failed (cf. 9:6) and that God is unjust.

Paul introduces the new topic in 9:1–5, the exordium of this rhetorical unit.[54] He expresses his deep love for Israel, echoing Moses's earlier lament over disobedient Israel (9:2–3; cf. Exod. 32:30–34). In establishing his ethos and demonstrating his pathos, he indicates his deep investment in Israel's salvation and the fulfillment of his mission to "the Jew first and then the Greek." His persona plays an important role in the argument (cf. Rom. 10:1; 11:1–2).

The propositio that Paul will argue is that God's word has not failed (9:6a), a claim that recurs implicitly throughout the argument (cf. 9:14, 30; 11:1, 11). He builds his case in the probatio with suspense, employing three arguments (9:6b–29; 9:30–10:21; 11:1–32) that progress toward the resolution of the problem of Israel in 11:25–26. The first argument (9:6b–29) reviews God's word in the past, as it is revealed in Scripture,[55] while the second argument (9:30–10:21) addresses Israel's situation in the present, explaining via Scripture Israel's rejection (cf. 10:5–21). The final argument (11:1–32) describes God's action in the future that will resolve the issue of the justice of God. Just as Paul concludes chapters 5–8 with a lyrical peroratio, he ends this rhetorical unit with the doxology in 11:33–36, which functions as the peroratio of the argument. Thus chapters 9–11 compose a masterful rhetorical unit that begins with the exordium, a lament over Israel in the present (an argument from ethos and pathos), and concludes with the peroratio celebrating the salvation of Israel in the future (11:33–36), an argument from pathos.[56]

The claim that the word of God has not failed (9:6a) is the propositio for the first argument (9:6b–29) and the entire probatio. As the rhetorical question in

---

54. See Aletti, *God's Justice in Romans*, 172.

55. Mohrmann, "Paul's Use of Scripture in Romans 9–11," 133.

56. As a defense of God's justice, the argument may be characterized as forensic. It consists of the rebutting of charges (cf. Quintilian, *Inst.* 3.9.1). See J. Kim, *God, Israel and the Gentiles*, 120.

9:14 indicates, the issue is the justice of God, which Paul affirmed in 1:16–17, the propositio of the letter. The first argument continues the exemplum from chapter 4 based on Israel's narrative, at first focusing on God's action rather than the human response. The focal point of 9:6b–29 is the sovereignty of God, who elects a people. Having frequently communicated to his gentile readers in the earlier letters that they are the elect and the called (cf. 1 Cor. 1:9; Gal. 5:13; 1 Thess. 1:4; 4:7), Paul recalls Israel's narrative as the story of election. One may observe the prominence of election (*eklogē*, Rom. 9:11; cf. 11:5, 7) and calling (9:12, 24), as Paul recalls the stories of Abraham, Isaac, Jacob, and Moses. The focus on election continues in the final argument in 11:1–32 (cf. 11:5, 7, 28–29). God's calling was not based on works (9:11–12, 16; cf. 11:6). Contrary to the Jewish narrative, however, God has called both Jews and gentiles (9:24). Passages that, in their original context, referred to the election of Israel (cf. 9:24–26; cf. Hosea 2:25 LXX) now refer to the gentiles. If only a few physical descendants of Abraham are present in Paul's churches, the situation is no different from the one addressed by Isaiah, according to whom the remnant will be saved (Rom. 9:27; cf. Isa. 10:22). Thus Paul appeals to Israel's narrative and to Scripture to justify the current situation. God is just, calling both Jews and gentiles, but only the righteous remnant of Israel remains (Rom. 9:27–28). Thus God's word has not failed, for the result of Paul's mission is according to God's word.

Having answered the question of God's justice, Paul could have concluded in 9:29. However, he offers another argument in 9:30–10:21. While he focused on God's sovereign election in 9:6b–29, he now focuses on the human response. Israel, attempting to establish its own righteousness, did not submit to the principle of righteousness by faith enunciated in 1:16–17 (cf. 3:21–26) and exemplified by Abraham (chap. 4). The condition for salvation, according to 9:30–10:21, is faith, as Paul indicates in the propositio of this section,[57] for "Christ is the end of the law for everyone who believes" (10:4 AT; cf. 7:1–6). In the Scripture citation (10:5–8) and the commentary that follows (10:9–13), Paul illustrates this principle, indicating that Christ has taken the place of the Torah for those who believe. Whereas the reflections in Deuteronomy 30:11–14 described the commandment of the Torah as "not too hard for you" (30:11) and not far away—neither in heaven nor beyond the sea—Paul explains that it is the word of faith rather than the Torah that is near us (Rom. 10:8), explaining that "if you believe in your heart that God raised him from the dead, you will be saved" (10:9). He adds two Scripture references: "Everyone [*pas*] who believes in him will not be put to shame" (10:11 AT; cf. Isa. 28:16)

---

57. For 10:4 as the propositio of 9:30–10:21, see Aletti, *God's Justice in Romans*, 172.

and "Everyone [*pas*] who calls on the name of the Lord will be saved" (Rom. 10:13 AT; cf. Joel 3:5 LXX), in both instances applying to Christ the words originally used for God. Paul emphasizes *pas*, as in the earlier parts of the letter, to reiterate that "there is no distinction between Jew and Greek" (Rom. 10:12 AT; cf. 1:16; 2:10; 3:22). As Paul said in the propositio, the gospel is "for everyone who believes" (1:16 AT).

The current situation exists, however, because "not all [*pantes*] have obeyed the gospel" (10:16 AT). Paul associates himself with the herald of Deutero-Isaiah (Rom. 10:15; cf. Isa. 52:7), who proclaims the good news, and he also recalls the words of the servant, "Lord, who has believed what we have heard?" (Isa. 53:1 LXX). Using the words from Scripture, he concludes that Israel has both heard the message (Rom. 10:18) and known God's will (10:19). Consequently, because Israel did not meet the conditions for salvation, the church is primarily composed of gentiles. Paul concludes this section of the argument with the voice of God. Of the gentiles, God says, "I was found by those who did not seek me" (10:20 AT; Isa. 65:1), and of Israel, God says, "All day long I have held out my hands to a disobedient and contrary people" (Rom. 10:21; cf. Isa. 65:2). Thus Paul appeals to the prophets to argue that Jewish disbelief in the current situation is no different from Israel's disobedience in the past. This argument reaffirms the propositio (Rom. 9:6a) of Romans 9–11: God's word has not failed.

The response that Israel had not met the conditions for salvation (9:30–10:21) could lead to the conclusion that God has rejected his people.[58] However, although "Has God rejected his people?" is the logical response to the preceding argument, Paul answers, contrary to all logic, "By no means" (*mē genoito*, 11:1), introducing the concluding argument with the propositio. In 11:2–10, he answers the question by reiterating what he has introduced in earlier letters and in 9:6–29. Paul defends the results of his ministry by calling Scripture to witness against the Jews who have not believed his gospel. Paul explains why Israel has not received his gospel. Their present unfaithfulness corresponds to the unfaithfulness witnessed by the prophets. However, Paul must still answer two related questions: "What is the advantage of the Jew?" (cf. 3:1) and "Has God rejected his people?" (11:1–2). As the story of Elijah illustrates (Rom. 11:3–4; cf. 1 Kings 19:10, 14), a remnant of Israel still exists, as Isaiah prophesied (Rom. 11:5; cf. 9:11, 27; Isa. 10:22). Elijah's life explains Paul's situation, for Paul's experience is similar to that of Elijah.[59] This remnant was, like all of the faithful, chosen by the election of grace rather than

---

58. Hübner, *Theologie des Neuen Testaments*, 2:256.
59. Mohrmann, "Paul's Use of Scripture in Romans 9–11," 139.

works. Paul cites two passages to confirm that the present state of the majority of Israel is nothing new but was indicated already by the prophets.

In Romans 11:11, Paul asks the question in a new way: "Did they stumble in order that they may fall?" (AT). Again he gives the strong *mē genoito*, and once more developing a theme from the previous section, he maintains that the salvation of the gentiles is intended to make Israel jealous (11:11; cf. 10:19), recalling God's complaint about Israel in Deuteronomy 32:21, which is part of an extended indictment of Israel's disobedience. Consistent with the indictment in Deuteronomy and elsewhere in the prophetic literature, Paul concludes that Israel's disobedience is not final. Thus as in Deuteronomy, Israel is now being made jealous by foreigners. Paul anticipates the outcome with the question "If their trespass is salvation for the gentiles, how much more would be their fullness?" (Rom. 11:12 AT).

The rhetorical significance of this extended discussion of the justice of God is evident in Paul's address to gentiles in 11:13–26. Although he is a minister to the nations, his task is to make Israel jealous and save some of them (11:14). He is the herald who announces good news to the nations, and the collection he now brings to Jerusalem is probably intended to be the wealth of the nations coming into Zion (15:25–27; cf. Isa. 60:4–13). However, the pilgrimage of the nations to Zion did not involve the final failure of Israel. As the image of the wild olive tree suggests, the sovereign God who elected the gentiles (Rom. 9:26–29) can also elect Israel. Thus Paul, speaking as a prophetic seer, announces the mystery: "All Israel will be saved" (11:26). That is, God is not unjust, and it is not only the remnant that will be saved (cf. 9:27). Those over whom he has mourned (9:1–5) "will be saved." Having stated the conditions for those who "will be saved" (10:9, 13; cf. 10:10–11), Paul now concludes that Israel will meet the conditions for salvation and be included among "everyone who believes" (1:16; 3:21 AT). They will turn from disobedience to obedience (11:27–32). The grief that Paul expressed in 9:1–5 has now turned to joy, as the concluding doxology indicates (11:33–36). Paul begins this section with the pathos of grief and ends with the pathos of celebration.

Isaiah 40–66 undoubtedly frames Paul's approach. Isaiah 59:20, cited by Paul in Romans 11:27, appears near the end of the prophet's reflections about the future of Israel. The prophet has complained that Israel's transgressions have separated the people from God. They do not know justice (*dikaiosynē*, Isa. 59:9; cf. 59:14). They wait for justice and salvation (Isa. 59:11) until finally God puts on justice (*dikaiosynē*), punishes the enemies, and comes to Zion as Redeemer (Isa. 59:20). God's justice will ultimately mean salvation for Israel. Indeed, Paul, like the prophet, anticipates a day when "every knee will bow and every tongue confess that Jesus Christ is Lord" (Phil. 2:10–11 AT; cf. Isa. 45:23). This involves Israel, "for all the offspring of Israel shall triumph and glory" (Isa. 45:25; cf. 45:17).

Paul's resolution to the problem of Israel's disobedience is unanticipated in the earlier letters. According to 1 Thessalonians, "God's wrath has come upon [Israel] to the end" (1 Thess. 2:16 AT), and in 2 Corinthians, Paul speaks of the hardening of the minds and blindness of Israel in his own time (2 Cor. 3:14–15; cf. Rom. 11:25). The resolution in Romans 11:26 must be seen in the context of the rhetorical situation that he encounters. This assurance has a rhetorical function, as is indicated by Paul's warning against gentile boasting (Rom. 11:18) and against being "wiser than [they] are" (Rom. 11:25). As a defense of his own ministry to the nations, Paul assures Jewish readers that this ministry will not ultimately result in gentile salvation alone but will also benefit Israel. Faced with an ethnically divided church, with gentiles in the majority, Paul undermines potential boasting and anticipates the conflicts in 14:1–15:13.[60] As one whose theology was largely shaped by the reading of Deutero-Isaiah, Paul answers new questions about his ministry by returning to the prophet to answer this pressing question. His argument rests on both Scripture and his prophetic authority. His theology and rhetorical needs are inextricably bound together.

Living the Righteousness of God (12:1–15:13)

The fact that Paul proceeds from the advice for gentile readers not to be wise among themselves (11:25) to the instruction for readers "not to think more highly of [themselves] than they ought to think" (12:3 AT) indicates that Paul was building the case in chapters 9–11 for the moral advice in 12:1–15:13. The ethical section is not an appendix to the argument of Romans but the conclusion of the argument. Having described humanity under God's wrath because it does not do the will of God (1:18, 32; cf. 3:9), Paul challenges the community to do the will of God (12:2), indicating that the people who were formerly unable to do the will of God and were enslaved to the passions (cf. 7:5, 7–25) are now capable of doing God's will (cf. 8:4). Justification by faith is not only an initial event but also the entrance into the reality of the new aeon. The goal of the righteousness of God for those who believe is that they "be transformed by the renewing of the mind" (12:2 AT) because they no longer belong to the old aeon. Paul describes the specific conduct in 12:3–15:13.

60. Hübner, *Theologie des Neuen Testaments*, 2:257.

The instructions begin with the command "not to think more highly of [themselves] than [they] ought to think" (12:3) and concludes with the obligations "not to please [themselves]" (15:1) and to "welcome one another" (15:7). As 14:1–15:13 indicates, this advice is not for a homogeneous community but for those who have different opinions (14:1) based on their interpretation of the purity laws of Scripture. The argument of Romans lays the foundation for Jewish and gentile Christians, despite their differences, to "glorify God with one voice" (15:6 AT).

Paul offers ethical advice that reiterates the moral advice from previous letters, but he places it within the framework of the argument in Romans. Those who do not think too highly of themselves will live as parts of the body (cf. 1 Cor. 12:12–28) in a multiethnic community. The ethical advice in Romans 12:9–13:10 is framed by the command to love (12:9; 13:8–10), enclosing specific instructions on the practice of love. Indeed, those who are no longer under the law (Rom. 6:15) follow the love command (Lev. 19:18), knowing that all of the commands are fulfilled in it. This new humanity thus keeps "the just requirements of the law" (Rom. 8:4 AT). Thus those who are guilty of self-serving behavior are not conducting themselves with love (Rom. 14:15).

Conclusion: The Transforming Power of the Righteousness of God

In the only direct references to the readers of Romans, Paul addresses them as gentiles (1:13; 11:13). As in all of the letters, he places gentile readers within Israel's narrative world, offering a grand vision of the purpose of God, which extends from the creation to the new creation (8:18–39). Believers join with the entire creation, awaiting the ultimate outcome when the humanity that was overwhelmed by sin at the beginning will ultimately be "conformed to the image of [God's] Son" (8:29), the founder of the new humanity (5:12–21).

Paul's ultimate goal is to offer a sanctified people to God (15:15–16), but his work is incomplete as long as only the gentiles can join in the stirring claim of victory (8:31–39). He envisions a united people of faith in which "all Israel will be saved" (11:26) along with the gentiles. Although God's *dikaiosynē* has already been revealed in the saving death of Christ (1:17; 3:21), it is an ongoing power that will lead to sanctification (6:16–22) for those who obey. Indeed, the end result is a people in whom "the just requirement of the law is fulfilled" (8:4 AT). Living within Israel's narrative world, the church is the community of the new covenant with the law written on their hearts (Jer. 31:33; cf. Rom. 2:25–29). The ethical instructions in Romans 12:1–15:13 describe the united community of the new aeon that exists in sharp distinction from those who do not keep "the just requirement of the law" (8:4 AT; cf. 1:32). In its practice of love across ethnic boundaries, the community fulfills the law (13:8–10).

Paul's arguments in previous letters have called for elaboration. He has consistently claimed, either implicitly or explicitly, that the turn of the ages has come with the death of Christ, that the inclusion of the gentiles promised in Isaiah has become a reality, and that he is God's prophetic voice. Throughout his correspondence, he has insisted that the events promised by Jeremiah (Jer. 31:31–34), Ezekiel (Ezek. 11:19; 36:22–36), and Deutero-Isaiah (Isa. 40:1–8; 52:7; 53:4–7) have become a reality within the gentile church: the Spirit has been poured out (cf. Ezek. 11:19; 1 Thess. 4:8), and now the community keeps the commandments in the new covenant (cf. Jer. 31:31–34; 2 Cor. 3:6). The elaboration of these themes and the claim that God's righteousness will ultimately include Israel, which Paul has not argued previously, do not reflect a development in Paul's theology but his continuing response to new questions within his churches.

Paul demonstrates rhetorical competence in his invention and arrangement. The argument employs numerous features that were commended in the rhetorical handbooks, as I have demonstrated in this chapter, and the arrangement corresponds in some ways to ancient ideals for speech. He appeals to ethos (Rom. 1:11–12; 15:22–29) and pathos (8:31–39; 9:1–5) to persuade his readers to "be transformed" (12:2) and overcome slavery to sin by yielding to the righteousness of God. However, the fundamental premises, which he articulates in all of his letters, belong to the subculture of Israel and the early church: the gentile church exists within Israel's narrative world because of the saving event of the death of Christ, and Paul is the instrument for God's plan for the restoration of a united humanity. He argues as a prophetic figure, announcing God's revelation in Jesus Christ (1:17–18) and the mystery of God's purposes (cf. 11:25). He employs premises based on the witness of Scripture and on the traditions that he received from earlier believers (cf. 3:25; 4:25; 6:1–2; 8:32). He not only articulates theological ideas but also crafts them to fit his rhetorical and pastoral needs as he expands on the argument of Galatians. The new dimension of Romans is Paul's insistence that the revelation of God's righteousness in the death of Jesus Christ and the response of faith are not only events of the past but also the continuing power that is present among believers. Their faith is not merely their conversion but their total orientation to God's power to transform them into the image of the Son (8:29).

10

"Seek the Things That Are Above"

Persuasion in Colossians and Ephesians

Interpreters have long recognized that the literary features connecting Colossians and Ephesians to each other also distinguish them from the other Pauline letters. The victory of Christ over the cosmic forces, which Paul declares in Romans (8:35–39) and 1 Corinthians (15:23–28), becomes a major focus in Colossians and Ephesians. The verbatim agreements between these two letters, including stylistic features, a distinctive vocabulary, long, poetic sentences, and the household codes also distinguish them from the other letters. While the eschatological hope is present in the two letters, the emphasis has shifted from eschatology to cosmology. According to the traditional view, these changes reflect a later stage in Pauline writing: when the apostle writes from a Roman prison in the 60s to confront new issues. In modern times, the distinctive features have led to the conclusion that one or both of the letters were written by a disciple of Paul.

One of the major reasons for attributing Colossians and Ephesians to a Paulinist rather than to Paul himself is the apparent shift in theology in these two letters. The issues of gentile mission have long been settled, and the themes of justification by faith and the validity of the law are no longer topics for debate. While both the eschatological hope (cf. Eph. 1:18; 2:12; 4:4; Col. 1:5, 23, 27) and the meaning of the cross (Eph. 2:14–18; Col. 2:14–15) are mentioned, they remain undeveloped in both letters. In Ephesians and

Colossians, the church is now the universal body of Christ (Eph. 1:22; 3:10, 21; 5:27; Col. 1:18, 24), not merely the local congregation. Interpreters have maintained that the theology of baptism shifts from the writing of Romans (Rom. 6:1–11) to the writing of Colossians (Col. 2:12–13). While Colossians repeats the claim found in Romans that "you were buried with him in baptism" (Col. 2:12; cf. Rom. 6:4), only in Colossians does Paul say that we "were raised" by the divine power (Col. 2:12–13).

In this chapter, my concern is not to argue the authorship of Colossians and Ephesians[1] but to recognize the means of persuasion in the two letters, which becomes evident in the relationship between theology and persuasion. Indeed, the shape of the letters, with their move from theological vision to moral behavior, continues the focus on moral transformation that is evident in the undisputed letters. In the study of Ephesians and Colossians, scholars have treated the theological vision and rhetorical persuasion as separate disciplines. I shall demonstrate that Paul's theology corresponds to his rhetorical needs.

The Rhetorical Situation of Colossians and Ephesians

The frequent references in both Colossians and Ephesians to the principalities and powers indicate that cosmic powers have an important place in the readers' view of the world (Eph. 1:20–22; 2:2; 3:10; 6:12; Col. 1:18; 2:15). While Ephesians does not directly indicate the rhetorical situation, the argument of the letter suggests that it is addressed to gentile house churches in Asia Minor whose members need reassurance of their place in a world dominated by cosmic powers (cf. Eph. 2:11–22). The reference to the Ephesians' pre-Christian past (Eph. 2:1–11) suggests that enslavement to cosmic powers has determined their moral behavior (Eph. 2:2), while their present existence involves warfare against the principalities and powers (Eph. 6:10–15). The letter is an assurance that liberation from cosmic forces empowers the readers to conduct themselves worthily of the one who called them (Eph. 4:1).

Colossians gives more direct references to the rhetorical situation (Col. 2:8, 16, 18, 20–21), which has led to numerous attempts to define the Colossian heresy. Despite the references in Colossians 2, scholars have sought in vain for

---

1. I have chosen to refer to the author as Paul throughout this chapter because he is the implied, if not the actual, author of Colossians, Ephesians, and the Pastoral Epistles. I treat these letters as a second stage in the Pauline correspondence; thus my argument does not require a demarcation between the actual voice of Paul and that of his interpreters.

a coherent vision of the opponents, choosing highly speculative hypotheses. Indeed, the absence of the kind of heated polemic that appears in Galatians and 2 Corinthians suggests that the threat in Colossians is more a potential than a current crisis.[2] Of the four direct references to the false teaching (Col. 2:8, 16, 18, 20), only one suggests that it is a present reality (Col. 2:20). Nevertheless, while the identity of the opponents eludes us, we can conclude that the readers live in a world of principalities and powers and that their continuing faithfulness requires that they grasp the meaning of their Christian confession within this context.

As the shape of Ephesians and Colossians indicates, both focus primarily on the moral behavior of the readers. Both are persuasive documents intended to reinforce the behavior that will lead to transformation. Both letters lay the theological foundation for moral instruction before giving specific instructions for moral conduct. Inasmuch as the shape of Colossians is consistent with that of the undisputed letters, its rhetorical function is similar. It begins with a thanksgiving (Col. 1:3–12), offers theological instruction (1:15–20) and autobiographical reflection (1:24–2:5), and contains an extended ethical section marked by the use of the imperative (2:6–4:6). Similarly, Ephesians proceeds from praise (Eph. 1:3–23) to theological and autobiographical reflection (chaps. 2–3) to moral instruction (4:1–6:19). Both are also letters of persuasion about future conduct. While the letters contain epideictic elements, their focus on future conduct gives them features associated with deliberative rhetoric. In both letters, Paul presents a vision of a community that will be "blameless" before God (Eph. 1:4; 5:27; Col. 1:22) and encourages the moral conduct that will bring the community to that goal.

Theology and Rhetoric in Colossians

Scholarly attention to Colossians has focused primarily on the world behind the text: the origin and literary genre of Colossians 1:15–20, the Christology of the passage, and its relation to a Colossian heresy. Interpreters have also searched ancient texts to discover the elusive Colossian heresy as a background of the letter. A primary focus has also been the origin and function of the household code (3:18–4:1) and its relationship to a common literary form in antiquity. Less attention has been given to the world within the text and the relationship between theology and rhetoric in the letter itself.[3]

2. See Hooker, "Were There False Teachers in Colossae?"
3. Cf. Copenhaver, "Echoes of a Hymn in a Letter of Paul," 236.

The Exordium (1:3–23)

As with the other Pauline letters, Colossians begins with the identity and credentials of the author (1:1–2) and a thanksgiving for the recipients (1:3–8). The topic of the thanksgiving is the moral progress of the readers (cf. Rom. 1:8; 1 Cor. 1:4–8; Phil. 1:3–11; 1 Thess. 1:2–10; Philem. 4–5) in anticipation of the ethical exhortations that will follow.[4] Having heard from Epaphras about the Colossians' faith (Col. 1:7; cf. Rom. 1:8), Paul expresses gratitude for the Colossians' faith in Christ and love for the saints (Col. 1:4), based on the hope that is laid up in the heavens (Col. 1:5). While Paul mentions the triad of faith, hope, and love elsewhere (1 Cor. 13:10–13; 1 Thess. 1:3–4) and frequently mentions one or more from this triad in his exhortations, only here does he indicate that faith and love are derived from hope.[5] These topics are the central features of Pauline moral instruction in all of the letters. One may note the frequency of faith and love in Paul's thanksgiving and moral instruction (cf. Rom. 1:8; Gal. 5:6; Phil. 1:9–11; 1 Thess. 3:6; Philem. 3–5).

Paul's expression of thanks for the Colossians' faith in Christ Jesus and their love for the saints (Col. 1:4) based on their "hope laid up in the heavens" (1:5) introduces these themes in the letter and makes the audience favorably disposed. He writes to ensure that the readers remain unmoved from their hope (1:23) and confirmed in faith (2:8). He not only gives thanks for their love (1:4, 8) but also describes their status in "the kingdom of love" (1:13 AT) and encourages the Colossians to practice love because it is "the bond of perfection" (3:14 AT).

Faith in Christ and love for the saints are the two primary dimensions of Christian response to the hope that is revealed in the gospel. While faith is the orientation toward Christ, love is the orientation toward fellow believers.[6] Elsewhere in the letter, faith (*pistis*) is used without an object (1:7, 23; 2:7); here it refers to faith in Christ (*en Christō*), the equivalent of faith *eis christon* (2:5), the orientation that gives strength (*stereōma*, 2:5), deep roots (*errizōmenoi*, 2:6), and a solid foundation (*tethemeliōmenoi*, 1:23) that prevents the readers from being carried away by false teaching (cf. 2:6–8).

Hope is a constituent element in the preaching of the gospel (1:5, 23), for "Christ in you, the hope of glory" (1:27) is the mystery that has been revealed in the gospel. As in the other Pauline letters, Paul expresses "the hope of

4. Hans Hübner correctly observes that a division of the letter into separate theological and paraenetic sections is artificial, for the entire letter has a paraenetic focus. See Hübner, *Theologie des Neuen Testaments*, 2:348.

5. Dunn, *Colossians*, 58; cf. Rockwell, "Faith, Hope and Love," 38.

6. See Van der Watt, "Colossians 1:3–12 Considered as an Exordium," 34.

glory" (1:27; cf. Rom. 5:2), the expectation of the inheritance (Col. 3:24) for faithful people, and the coming wrath on the sons of disobedience (3:6, 8).

This moral progress is an indication of the power of the gospel, which is "bearing fruit and growing throughout the world" and among the Colossians (1:6 AT). The reference to progress throughout the world is a hyperbole, but it indicates to anxious readers that they are a part of a worldwide movement and anticipates the letter's theme of a worldwide church. The image of bearing fruit is a common expression for moral conduct, expressed particularly in love for others (cf. Rom. 7:4–5; Gal. 5:22; Eph. 5:9; Phil. 1:11; 4:17). Paul gives thanks that the Colossians are bearing fruit and growing but anticipates the petition that they will continue to bear fruit and grow (Col. 1:10).

Like the introductory thanksgiving in the undisputed letters of Paul, these opening words introduce the topic of the letter and make the audience favorably disposed to the message that follows. The words conform to the definition of the exordium of the speech, as indicated in the rhetorical handbooks. According to Aristotle, the task of the exordium is to provide a sample of what is to come (*Rhet.* 3.14.5) and to make the audience favorably disposed (*Rhet.* 3.14.7). The thanksgiving indicates what is fundamentally important for this discourse and for Pauline theology: the moral formation of the community expressed by faith in Christ and love for the community.

The exordium extends beyond 1:3–8, for Paul continues with a petition (1:9–11) and thanksgiving (1:12). The petition, that they "walk worthily of the Lord in everything that is pleasing, bearing fruit and growing" (1:10 AT), continues the focus on the moral progress and indicates that it is not complete. Thus it anticipates the exhortation that follows in 2:6–4:6. Paul is thankful that the Colossians are "bearing fruit and growing" (1:6), and he prays that they will continue to do so. This prayer recalls the consistent plea that his converts conduct themselves "worthy [*axios*] of the gospel" (Phil. 1:27) and "worthy [*axios*] of God" (1 Thess. 2:12) as they are "filled with the fruit of righteousness" (Phil. 1:11 AT).

In Colossians 1:13–23, Paul celebrates the saving events that brought the community into existence and then turns to the future in the exhortations that follow. Thus the exordium includes 1:3–23, which is a single syntactical unit.[7] The thanksgiving for the community's faith, hope, and love produced by the hope of the gospel (1:5) forms an inclusio with the words "If you remain grounded and firm in the faith and not being moved from the hope of the gospel" (1:23 AT). One may observe the chiastic structure of 1:13–23.[8]

---

7. Broekhoven, "Persuasion or Praise in Colossians," 72. See also Aletti, *Saint Paul: Épitre aux Colossiens.*

8. This structure adapts that of Wright, "Poetry and Theology in Colossians 1:15–20."

A Who [the Father] delivered us from the authority of darkness and transferred us to the kingdom of the Son of his love, in whom we have the
   redemption, the forgiveness of sins. (1:13–14 AT)

   B Who is [*hos estin*] the image of the invisible God, firstborn of all
      creation, for in him all things were created, in heaven and on earth,
      visible and invisible, whether thrones or dominions or principalities
      or authorities—all things were created through him and for him.
      (1:15–16 AT)

      C He is [*kai autos*] before all things, and in him all things hold
         together. (1:17 AT)

      C′ He is [*kai autos*] the head of the body, the church. (1:18a AT)

   B′ Who is the beginning [*archē*], the firstborn from the dead, that in
      everything he may be preeminent. For in him the fullness of God was
      pleased to dwell, through him to reconcile all things to him, making
      peace by the blood of the cross. (1:18b–20 AT)

A′ And you, being alienated and enemies . . . , but now he has reconciled
   in the body of his flesh. (1:22a AT)

In the second part of the exordium (1:13–23), Paul expresses gratitude
for the saving event of the past that made moral formation possible. God
has empowered the community (1:12) and delivered it from the authority of
darkness. This event is signified by the inclusio in 1:13–14 and 1:21–23: God
has delivered the community (1:13–14), and God has reconciled them in one
body (1:23). The end result, according to 1:22, is to be "holy and blameless [*amōmos*] and irreproachable [*anenklētos*]" (AT), the goal that Paul
regularly states in his letters (cf. 1 Cor. 1:8; 2 Cor. 1:14; Phil. 2:16; 1 Thess.
3:11–13).

Soteriological reflections form the inclusio in Colossians 1:13–14 and
1:20–23.[9] That "Christ delivered [*errysato*] us" (1:13 AT) recalls Paul's earlier
declaration that Christ is the deliverer (*ho rhyomenos*) from Zion (Rom. 11:26;
cf. Isa. 59:20), the one who "delivers us from the coming wrath" (1 Thess.
1:10 AT), and recalls the frequent references in the Old Testament to the
God who delivers[10] from enemies or from death. Thus the community now
belongs within Israel's narrative as people who have been delivered by God. As
with the undisputed letters, Paul envisions a world divided between light and
darkness (cf. Rom. 2:12; 13:12; 2 Cor. 4:6; 6:14; 1 Thess. 5:4–5), and believers

9. Cf. Wright, "Poetry and Theology in Colossians 1:15–20," 453–54.
10. Cf. Pss. 6:4; 7:1; 18:17, 19, 43, 48; 22:20; 25:20; 31:1, 15; 33:19; 34:4, 17, 19; 40:13; 43:1;
50:15; 54:7; 56:13; 60:5; 71:2, 4, 11; 79:9; 86:13; 89:48; 108:6.

have already been delivered from "the authority [*exousia*] of darkness" and "transferred to the kingdom of the Son of his love" (Col. 1:13 AT). This claim anticipates the theme of the subjugation of the cosmic powers by Christ and the believers' participation in that victory (Col. 2:12–13).

In Colossians 1:14, Paul indicates the consequences of the past act for the present: "In whom we have redemption, the forgiveness of sins." Deliverance (Col. 1:13) is redemption, a term with echoes of the exodus that Paul employs for the saving event (Rom. 3:24; 1 Cor. 1:30), the forgiveness of sins (Col. 1:14; cf. Eph. 1:7). One may compare the claim of Romans 3:23, "For all have sinned and fallen short of the glory of God" (AT), followed by the assurance of redemption. Paul elaborates in Colossians 1:20–23, declaring that Christ "reconciled all things, making peace by the blood of his cross" (Col. 1:20 AT), adding that "you, being alienated, have been reconciled in the body of his death through his death" (Col. 1:21–22 AT).

Redemption and reconciliation are familiar Pauline categories. Here Paul expands on the soteriology by indicating a cosmic dimension: at the cross, Christ delivered us from the authority of darkness (Col. 1:13) and reconciled the cosmos (*ta panta*). The church participates in the cosmic act of redemption and reconciliation at the cross, which involves not only the forgiveness of sins but also the victory over cosmic powers.

The Christ Hymn (1:15–20)

The appearance of the poetic narrative (1:15–20) within the inclusio of 1:13–14 and 1:21–23 indicates the poem's significance for Paul's persuasive task of ensuring that the Colossians are "holy and blameless and irreproachable" (1:22). The opening words, "He is" (*hos estin*, lit., "who is"), continues the series of declarations introduced by "who" (*hos*, 1:13) and "in whom" (*en hō*, 1:14), as Paul brings together soteriological, christological, and ecclesiological reflections to indicate the place of the church in the divine plan. That Christ "delivered us from the authority [*exousia*] of darkness and transferred us to the kingdom of light" (1:13 AT) anticipates the claim in the hymn that Christ is above the principalities and authorities (1:16). The claim that we have redemption (*apolytrōsis*) echoes the use of this image of rescue from slavery in the undisputed letters (cf. Rom. 3:24; 8:23; 1 Cor. 1:30)—from the past to the present tense. Here Paul turns from addressing the readers, writing in the second person in Colossians 1:9–14 and 1:21–23, to writing in the third person in 1:15–20, speaking in the exalted prose that is frequently identified with the hymn and celebrating the source of redemption in the present tense (1:15–18) before returning to the aorist (1:19–20).

The hymn is divided into two parts, each beginning with "he/who is" (1:15, 18). In 1:15–17, Paul celebrates the role of Christ in creation, while in 1:18–20, he celebrates Christ's role in redemption. Christ is the firstborn of the whole creation (1:15) and firstborn from the dead (1:18), "before all things" (1:17 AT) and "first among all things" (1:18 AT). *Ta panta* (and the synonym "creation," 1:15) is the thread running through the hymn (1:16 bis, 17, 20).

The first line, "Who is the image [*eikōn*] of the invisible God," continues the depiction of Christ as the image of God from the undisputed Pauline letters (2 Cor. 3:18 AT; 4:4; cf. "form [*morphē*] of God," Phil. 2:6). Christ has taken on the role of preexistent Wisdom (cf. Wis. 7:26; 9:1–10; Sir. 1:4; 24:9) and of the Logos (Philo, *Heir.* 230–31) and of the heavenly man of Philo (cf. *Alleg. Interp.* 1.31). The second line, "firstborn of the creation," recalls the role of Wisdom in Jewish literature (cf. Prov. 8:22; Wis. 9:9) and suggests preeminence rather than a sequential relationship. *Hoti* in 1:16 introduces the ways in which he is "the firstborn of the creation." *Ta panta* becomes the word for the creation. This recalls the confessional statement in 1 Corinthians 8:6 and the Wisdom tradition that one finds in John 1:1–3 and Hebrews 1:1–4. Paul specifically mentions the cosmic powers in Colossians 1:16 because they are the concerns of the readers.

That "all things hold together in him" is reminiscent of Hebrews 1:3 and the reflections of Hellenistic Judaism. The statement has a close parallel in Sirach's assertion that God's Logos holds the world together (Sir. 43:26) and Philo's view that God (*Creation* 46; *Spec. Laws* 1.224) or the Logos sustains the world (*Migration* 6; *Planting* 8; *Flight* 112; *Heir* 188).

In the second half of the hymn, Paul turns from celebration of the role of Christ in creation to his place in redemption, introducing the new theme: "He is head of the body, the church" (Col. 1:18). Because of the sudden change from creation to redemption, interpreters have suggested that Paul is adapting the phrase from an earlier source that spoke of "the head of the body, the cosmos." Here Paul suggests that Christ is head over the cosmos ("He is before all things," 1:17) and head of the church. Having introduced the image of the body in the earlier letters, for the first time he mentions the head of the body, the church. That is, the one who is above all things (1:17) is the head of the church, a universal body of the cosmic Lord. Furthermore, he is not only "firstborn of creation" (1:15) but also "firstborn from the dead" (1:18).

Just as creation and redemption are commonly connected in the Old Testament, they are brought together in 1:15–20. "In him the divine fullness was pleased to dwell" recalls Old Testament reflections on the relationship between the transcendent God and the creation. Although *plērōma* appears nowhere else in this sense, the claim echoes Old Testament references to the God who dwells on Mount Zion or in the temple. Solomon asks, "Will God dwell [*katoikēsei*] on the earth?" (1 Kings 8:27 AT). He replies that heaven and earth cannot contain God but prays that God might be present in the temple (1 Kings 8:27–29). One may compare the psalmist's declaration that "it pleased God to dwell [*katoikein*] on the holy mountain" (Ps. 67:17 LXX).

Cosmology and redemption are brought together clearly in the claim that it pleased God also "to reconcile all things, making peace through the blood of the cross" (Col. 1:20 AT). Whereas the Paul of the undisputed letters said that "in Christ God was reconciling the world" (2 Cor. 5:19), here he says that Christ has reconciled "all things" (*ta panta*) at the cross. Christ is not only the agent of creation but also the agent of reconciliation.

The Hymn and the Argument

The Christ hymn introduces the themes that play a role in the argument, as the graphic below indicates.

The Hymn (1:15–20)	Use in the Argument (1:21–4:5)
And through him to reconcile all things to himself, making peace by the blood of his cross. (1:20)	And you . . . he reconciled in the body of his flesh through death. (1:21–22)
And he is the head of the body, the church. (1:18)	On behalf of his body, the church. (1:24)
Because in him it pleased all the fullness to dwell. (1:19)	Because in him dwells all the fullness of deity bodily. (2:9)
	And you are in him being filled, who is the
The head. (1:18) Whether thrones or dominions. (1:16)	Head of every principality and dominion. (2:10)
He is the head of the body, the church. (1:18)	The body of Christ. (2:17) And not holding fast to the head, from whom all the body. (2:19)
Who is the image of the invisible God. (1:15) Because in him all things were created . . . all things were created through him and to him. (1:16)	According to the image of the one who created him. (3:10)

This graphic is based on Copenhaver, "Echoes of a Hymn in a Letter of Paul," 241–48.

Christ is victorious over the cosmic powers (2:10, 15) and head over the church, his body (1:18, 24), into which believers have been called (3:15). Christ is the head, "from whom the whole body . . . grows with a growth that is from God" (2:19). Christ is above the powers, and the community has been raised with him (3:1).

Not only the Christ hymn in 1:15–20 but also the entire exordium (1:3–23) introduces the themes that follow in the body of the letter.[11] The Christ who has reconciled the cosmos has also reconciled those who were under the threatening powers. The emphatic "you" (*hymas*) at the beginning of the Greek sentence (1:21) indicates the rhetorical significance of the hymn for the readers.[12] Both the periodic sentences and the hymn create an experience of gratitude and empowerment, declaring the community's identity in a world populated by threatening powers. With the ecclesiology of a universal and cosmic church, Paul assures the readers that they now participate in a movement of universal significance. Only those who are "delivered from the power of darkness" (1:13 AT) can ultimately be "holy and blameless" (1:22). The thanksgivings and petitions for moral progress are implicitly an exhortation to continue the moral formation that has already begun. In the exhortations that follow, Paul offers specific instructions for the continued growth.

The Narratio (1:24–2:5)

In 1:24–2:5, Paul argues from ethos and pathos, establishing his credibility and indicating his investment in the Colossians' outcome. As in the earlier Pauline letters, he offers autobiographical reflections to indicate his exemplary conduct (cf. 1 Cor. 1:18–2:17; 2 Cor. 1:12–2:13; Gal. 1:10–21; Phil. 1:12–26; 1 Thess. 2:1–12). He participates in the sufferings of Christ (Col. 1:24; cf. 2 Cor. 1:3–11; 4:7–10; Phil. 3:10) with a special calling to fulfill his mission: to present every person perfect in Christ (Col. 1:28). He echoes the hymn in his claim that he suffers on behalf of "his body, the church" (Col. 1:24 AT; cf. 1:18), and he struggles specifically for them (Col. 2:1), a community that he did not establish. He assures them that the cosmic Christ who is "among" them is "the hope of glory" (Col. 1:27), that Paul's ultimate goal is "to present everyone perfect in Christ" (Col. 1:28 AT), and that his hope for the Colossians is that they may be joined together in love (Col. 2:2) as he rejoices when he sees the strength of their faith (Col. 2:5). Thus his mission is the moral formation of the community, and he suffers on their behalf. He employs his own self-understanding as a participant in the sufferings of Christ as a means of persuasion, indicating that he suffers for their formation,[13] anticipating the specific instructions in 2:8–4:6.

---

11. For the hymn in Col. 1:15–20 as a part of the exordium, see Gordley, *Colossian Hymn in Context*, 231.

12. Longinus speaks of the "vivid you" that is designed to place the readers in the presence of the action. Cited in Copenhaver, "Echoes of a Hymn in a Letter of Paul," 242.

13. See Sumney, "Function of Ēthos in Colossians," 309–10.

The Propositio (2:6–7)

In 2:6–7, Paul begins the imperatives that dominate the remainder of the letter. Paul has made the case, prayed that they "walk worthily of the Lord" (1:10 AT), and now Paul instructs the readers to "walk in him" (2:6 AT), rooted in Christ and confirmed in the faith (2:7).[14] The turn from the indicative to the imperative marks the propositio of the letter. "As you have received Christ" (2:6 AT) is the transition to the exhortation that follows, an indication of the ethical implications of the exordium (1:3–23), which Paul will elaborate on in the rest of the letter. The purpose of Colossians, therefore, is that the readers be "rooted and grounded in faith" (2:7). Paul expresses gratitude for their faith, and he writes to ensure that the readers remain grounded in it.

The Probatio (2:8–4:6)

The exordium (1:3–23) provides the background for the imperatives that follow. The imperatives in 2:8–4:6 compose the probatio of Paul's argument. Paul recognizes the obstacles to Christian formation, as indicated in the warnings in 2:8–23. In the four warning passages, Paul presents the alternatives between the exalted Christ and the traditions of human beings, or *stoicheia* (2:8, 20), a term that is probably equivalent to the cosmic powers mentioned in 1:16. The probatio does not employ the traditional proofs of Greco-Roman rhetoric, for Paul speaks as one who has been granted the revelation of the divine mystery (1:25–27). Thus his imperatives are followed by reasons that are accessible only to those who have received the revelation from God (cf. 2:10–15, 17, 19; 3:1).

In the first of the imperatives (2:8–15), Paul's warning presents the exalted Christ as the alternative to the traditions of human beings and the *stoicheia*.[15] The reason is that "in him dwells the fullness of deity bodily" (2:9 AT).[16] This recalls the claims in the hymn that Christ is the image of the invisible God and that the fullness (*plērōma*) dwells (*katoikei*) in him (1:19), the one who is above the principalities and powers. *Plērōma*, a term later used in Gnostic literature, is also used in the Old Testament to refer most often to the earth and its fullness (Pss. 24:1 [23:1 LXX]; 50:12 [49:12 LXX]; 89:11 [88:12 LXX];

14. Dübbers, *Christologie und Existenz im Kolosserbrief*, 178–95.
15. See Sumney, "Argument of Colossians," 306–10: "Verse 8 opens the *refutatio* (2:18–15), which is an elaborate argument from the contrary."
16. Cf. Copenhaver, "Echoes of a Hymn in a Letter of Paul," 245, who points out the syllogism in Paul's reason. Major premise: "All the fullness of deity dwells in him bodily" (2:9 AT). Minor premise: "You have been filled with Christ, who is the head of all rulers and authorities" (2:10 AT). Conclusion: "Therefore, watch out lest someone should take you captive through the philosophy and empty deceit that is not according to Christ" (2:8 AT).

Jer. 8:16; 47:2). Old Testament passages also speak of God, whose "glory fills the earth" (Ps. 72:19; cf. Jer. 23:24; Wis. 1:7). The verb *plēroun* is employed in Isaiah, according to which "the hem of [the Lord's] garment filled the temple" (Isa. 6:1 AT), and "seraphs called to each other, 'The whole earth is full of his glory'" (Isa. 6:3 AT).

This is not an abstract idea, however, for the focus is on the implications of the divine status of Christ for the Colossians' capacity to "walk in him" (Col. 2:6 AT). They are, in fact, "being filled with him" (2:10 AT). Just as the fullness of God dwells in the exalted Christ (1:19), the community is "being filled" with Christ. That is, his victory over the powers includes them. They are a part of the cosmic body, of which Christ is the head (1:18). To be "filled with him" is to be "filled with the full knowledge of his will in all wisdom and spiritual understanding" (1:9 AT) and to be "empowered according to the strength of his glorious power" (1:11 AT). Believers share in the divine victory over the powers, enabling them to overcome the obstacles to moral formation. This claim is the major premise for heeding his warning about the traditions of human beings (2:7).[17]

This continuing status is made possible by the singular event of the past, as indicated by the aorist tenses that follow. The Colossians are not only "in him" being filled, but also "in him" they were circumcised with a circumcision not made by hands. As in the undisputed letters, believers are the true circumcision (cf. Rom. 2:25–29; Phil. 3:2). In contrast to the earlier letters, however, baptism is here the occasion when the believers received the circumcision not made with hands. Believers have been "buried with him in baptism," "raised with him through faith in the power of God to raise the dead" (Col. 2:12), and "made alive with him," having their trespasses forgiven (Col. 2:12–13 AT). Scholars have observed in these verses both the echoes of the theology of Romans and the departure from it. While Colossians, like Romans, has "we were buried with him," only Colossians adds, "we were raised with him." This departure fits the rhetorical needs of the argument, becoming the premise for the exhortations. Paul has argued that believers are "in him," the cosmic victor, and are liberated from the cosmic powers, which were both "created in him" (Col. 1:16 AT) and vanquished by him at the cross (Col. 2:14–15). The rhetorical point is that they, having a place that is not subject to the powers, are empowered to "walk in him" and to become "blameless" at the end.

The exordium anticipated the claim that Christ made us alive, "forgiving our transgressions" (2:13 AT; cf. 1:14), which Paul develops with the image of the blotting out (*exaleipsas*) of a record of debts (*cheirographon*), which

17. Copenhaver, "Echoes of a Hymn in a Letter of Paul," 246.

Christ nailed to the cross (2:14). He does not mention the law here but assumes with the earlier letters of Paul that all humanity falls short of the glory of God and is thus forgiven at the cross. The triumph of Christ occurred not only at the exaltation (cf. Rom. 8:34–39) but also at the cross. Paul insists that believers who die with Christ also share in the victory over sin.

The description of the Christ event in Colossians 2:14–15 reflects both continuity and discontinuity with the depictions of the relationship between soteriology and the law in the undisputed letters. Since the law is not an issue, unlike in Galatians and Romans, Paul does not repeat the earlier arguments but employs language that is intelligible to his gentile audience. The vivid metaphor for the forgiveness of sins—a record of debts nailed to the cross—is never used in the undisputed letters, but Paul adapts the image for the audience. That the death of Christ is a conquest of the powers is also a new dimension in Colossians, but it is an image that addresses a community threatened by the powers.

The alternative between Christ and the powers is evident in each of the warnings, as Paul develops what he mentioned first in the exordium. In the second alternative, he contrasts the shadows—the regulations, new moon, and Sabbaths—with the body of Christ (2:16–17; cf. 1:18, 22, 24), again recalling the Christ hymn in 1:15–20. In the third warning (2:18–19), he presents the alternative in a new way, contrasting those who engage in the worship of angels with those who hold to the head, Christ (2:19), from whom the body, nourished and held together by its ligaments, grows with a growth that is from God (2:19). This growth, as Paul has suggested earlier, is the moral formation, which he goes on to describe in 3:1–4:5.

Paul then concludes the warnings against false teaching (2:20–23), once more contrasting Christ with human traditions. If the listeners have been raised with Christ, they should no longer obey regulations that are the commandments of people (2:20). In the rhetorical question, he draws the implications of their baptism: "If you have been raised with Christ, why are you, as people living in the world, obedient to human rules, 'Do not touch, do not taste, according to the commandments and teachings of people'?" (AT). That is, believers have been raised with Christ and have shared in his death and resurrection. As people who share in the triumph over the powers, they have risen above human commandments.

While the moral instructions in chapter 3 echo earlier Pauline paraenesis, with vices to "put to death" (3:5) and "take off" (3:8 AT) and virtues to "put on" (3:10, 12 AT), they emerge from the specific theological instruction of Colossians. "If you have been raised with Christ, seek the things that are above" (3:1) is the foundation for the new behavior. Christ is at the right hand of God. The cosmic dimension gives a new *phronēsis*: set your affections on things that are above. The people now "put to death the things that are on the earth" (3:5 AT).

Readers are instructed not to follow the ascetic practices that are the teachings of people (cf. 2:16, 21) but to put on "the new person who is being renewed into the full knowledge according to the image of the one who created him" (3:10 AT), a humanity in which "there is neither Jew nor Greek, circumcision or uncircumcision, barbarian, Scythian, slave or free" (3:11 AT). They put on the new person, who is being renewed in the image of the one who created him (cf. 2 Cor. 3:18).

This claim echoes both the Christ hymn and Paul's undisputed letters. According to the hymn in Colossians 1:15–20, Christ "is the image of God" in whom all things were created (1:16 AT), while in 3:10, the "new person" is being renewed into the image of Christ, who created it. The renewal into the image of Christ echoes the claim that the "new person" is "being renewed" (2 Cor. 4:16) and that all believers are being transformed into the image of Christ (2 Cor. 3:18; cf. Rom. 12:1–2). This transformation is a present experience as believers anticipate the ultimate transformation at the end (cf. Rom. 8:29; Phil. 3:21). The "new person" is a corporate reality, the equivalent of the body of Christ, as the description of the new humanity in 3:11 indicates. This description recalls Paul's claim in Galatians 3:27 that believers have "put on" Christ, the corporate person, in a community where there is no longer Jew or Greek, slave or free, male and female (Gal. 3:28). Now the body is being renewed as believers adopt behavior that Paul commends in Colossians 3:12–4:6.

Whereas the earlier Pauline letters have presented the sharp alternatives between Christ and the law (Gal. 2:19–21; Phil. 3:7–11) or Christ and human wisdom (1 Cor. 1:18–25; 2:6–17), the cosmic Christology of Colossians stands in sharp contrast to the *stoicheia* of the world and human traditions. In Colossians, as in the earlier letters, the ultimate goal for the church is moral formation that becomes possible through the triumph of Christ and the divine empowerment. Paul presents a community that has been reconciled in the past and continues to grow toward the perfect man.

Conclusion

The focal point of Colossians is the transformation of the behavior of people who have converted from paganism. For a people who were anxious that their moral life was controlled by cosmic powers, Paul persuades them that they now participate in the cosmic victory over these forces. The hymnic christological confession is the premise for the persuasive argument that follows. Thus theology is the foundation for the moral persuasion, but it is adapted to confront the challenges facing the readers.

Moral Persuasion in Ephesians

Ephesians shares with Colossians and earlier Pauline letters an arrangement that proceeds from theological argument (Eph. 1–3) to ethical exhortation (4–6). Since Ephesians, unlike most of the undisputed letters of Paul, offers little indication of the rhetorical situation, the purpose of the letter is a matter of continuing debate.[18] However, the shape of the letter, with its progression toward ethical instructions (4:1–6:20), suggests that the letter is intended to shape the behavior of the readers. The alternation of prayer (1:3–23; 3:14–21) and theological instruction (2:1–3:10) introduces the themes that Paul develops in chapters 4–6. Within the context of the liturgy, Paul describes the ultimate purpose of God, "a community that is holy and blameless in [God's] sight" (1:4 AT), and prays that God will give them a spirit of wisdom and revelation in full knowledge (1:17), that they will grasp the nature of the divine power among believers (1:19), and that they will grasp the extent of the love of God and be filled with the divine fullness (3:19). The divine action empowers the community to grow together (2:20–22) so that they may "grow up in him" (4:15 AT) by conducting themselves worthily of their calling (4:1). The purpose of the letter, therefore, is to persuade readers who consider themselves powerless, threatened by principalities and powers (cf. 2:3; 6:10), that they have become empowered to become "holy and blameless" (1:4) in their moral conduct. Indeed, they are not only empowered but also fill a vital role in God's eternal plan.

The Exordium (1:3–23)

Paul begins the persuasive task by leading the readers in worship in the form of a eulogy.[19] The opening words, "Blessed [*eulogētos*] is the God and Father of our Lord Jesus Christ, who . . ." (AT), echo the Jewish liturgy (cf. Pss. 65:20 LXX; 71:18 LXX; 123:6 LXX; 134:21 LXX; 143:1 LXX; 1 Macc. 4:30; Luke 1:68), a form that Paul employed in place of the traditional thanksgiving in 2 Corinthians 1:3–7 (cf. 1 Pet. 1:3). Both the repetition

18. See the summary of attempts to determine the purpose in Jeal, "Rhetorical Argumentation in the Letter to the Ephesians," 310.
19. See Berger, *Formen und Gattungen im Neuen Testament*, 303, for the designation as eulogy.

of *eulog-* in the opening line (*eulogētos* = "blessed"; *eulogēsas* = "having blessed"; *eulogia* = "blessing") and the extended heaping up of multiple clauses in a single sentence create a positive effect on the readers. The themes discussed later in the theological and ethical sections are introduced in the context of praise, inviting the readers to celebrate the values that will be the focus of theological and ethical reflection in the context of worship and praise.[20] As Andrew Lincoln has observed, "The heaping up of words and phrases in this profuse style are [*sic*] a deliberate attempt to express the riches of which he speaks in an appropriate way. This is the language of prayer and worship."[21] Thus by introducing the themes that follow and making the audience favorably disposed, the opening blessing functions as the exordium of Ephesians.

Paul praises God for all of the spiritual blessings in the heavenly places (*en tois epouraniois*), elaborating on these spiritual blessings in Ephesians 1:3–14 and developing that theme in chapters 2–3. The reference to the heavenly places anticipates the argument of the book (cf. 1:20; 2:6; 3:10; 6:12), with its focus on the exaltation of Christ and the triumph of Christ over cosmic forces (cf. 1:19–23; 2:6; 4:10). With the first-person plural ("who blessed us") that dominates 1:3–12 (cf. 1:5 bis, 7, 10, 11–12), Paul includes himself along with the gentile listeners, participating with them in worship and praise and establishing ethos and pathos for the argument that follows. Indeed, the first-person plural establishes the identity of the readers, reassuring them that they are not powerless in a world of cosmic forces.[22] This identification is vital for Paul's persuasive task, for people "are generally receptive only to things that provoke their interest or are significant for their lives."[23] Paul reassures the community of its place in the divine plan while establishing their identity as the basis for the exhortations that follow.

Despite the rhetorical power of the lengthy sentence in 1:3–14, scholars have reached no consensus on the structure of the passage. The unit offers multiple structural signals (the repetition of aorist participles in 1:5, 9, 13; the refrain "to the praise of his glory" in 1:6, 12, 14; the repetition of "in whom" in 1:7, 11, 13), but interpreters do not agree on how they come together into a coherent thought. Nevertheless, this hymnic celebration has a movement of thought and a dominant theological message. Verse 3 is the main clause, and all that follows is an elaboration indicating the nature of the blessing,

20. See Selby, *Not with Wisdom of Words*, 106.
21. Lincoln, *Ephesians*, 22.
22. Beginning in 1:13, the collective identity of the readers is expressed with the second-person plural.
23. Jeal, "Rhetorical Argumentation in the Letter to the Ephesians," 316.

syntactically linked to 1:3, as *kathōs* ("just as") indicates.[24] While Paul does not mention the *ekklēsia* until 1:23, the constant use of the first-person plural is a window into his ecclesiology.

In Ephesians 1:3–6, he describes the spiritual blessings as the election of the community; then in 1:7–14, he elaborates with a series of passages introduced by "in whom we." This blessing assures the readers that they are participants in Israel's narrative, the plan of God (cf. 1:9–10) that extends from "the foundation of the world" (1:4 AT) to "the fullness of the times" (1:10 AT). Indeed, this community has been elected and foreordained to adoption. Paul continues the victorious claim, further indicating the participation of the community in the divine triumph: "In whom *we* have gained an inheritance" (1:11 AT) so that *we* "may be to the praise of his glory" (1:12 AT).

Twice the blessing elaborates on election, referring to the community as "foreordained" (*proorisas*, 1:5; *prooristhentes*, 1:11) according to the favor (*eudokia*, 1:5) and purpose (*prothesis*, 1:11) of the divine will. The claim echoes Romans, according to which God "foreordained" (*proōrisen*) and "called" (*ekalesen*) the community composed of Jews and gentiles (Rom. 8:29–30) according to the divine purpose (*prothesis*, Rom. 8:28). As in the undisputed letters, the community of gentiles has received adoption (*huiothesia*) as children of God (cf. Rom. 8:15, 23; 9:4; Gal. 4:5); thus they are saints (Eph. 1:1) now living in continuity with ancient Israel.

This claim also echoes other earlier letters, according to which the gentile community, at its conversion, was "called" by God (1 Cor. 1:9; 7:17–18, 20–21; Gal. 5:13; 1 Thess. 2:12; 4:7) and "elected" (Rom. 8:33; 9:11; 11:5, 7, 28; Col. 3:12; 1 Thess. 1:4). Indeed, the church shares in Israel's identity (cf. Eph. 2:11–22), which is reflected in the Deuteronomist's reminder that God chose Israel, "the fewest of all peoples" (Deut. 7:7), separating the people from "out of all the peoples" (Deut. 14:2; cf. 1:8, 10, 15; 12:5, 11, 18, 21; 16:6, 7, 11, 15–16). The belief in God's election was basic to Israel's existence, becoming particularly prominent in Deutero-Isaiah, which insists that, despite Israel's humiliation, the people remain God's elect (Isa. 42:1; 43:20; 45:4; 65:9). Other New Testament writers consistently employ the image of election to describe the new community that includes gentiles (cf. Mark 13:20; 13:22; Luke 18:7; 23:35; 1 Pet. 1:2; 2:4, 9), transforming the ancient understanding of election.

The goal of the divine election is indicated in the purpose clauses that accompany the claim of election. The ultimate outcome of election, according to Ephesians 1:4, is a community that is "holy and blameless in his sight in love" (Eph. 1:4), the result that Paul consistently expresses for his churches.

24. Talbert, *Ephesians and Colossians*, 43.

"Blameless" (*amōmos*) is the term for the unblemished animal (cf. Exod. 29:1, 38 LXX), but it is also the term for people who are morally upright (Pss. 15:2; 18:23; 19:13; 37:18; 64:4; 101:2, 6; 119:1; Prov. 11:5, 20; 20:7; Dan. 1:4 LXX).

The related purpose of election, according to Ephesians 1:11–12, is that "we may be to the praise of his glory," which is also a refrain in 1:3–14 (cf. 1:6, 12, 14). That is, God's ultimate plan is the moral formation of a new humanity, a theme that Paul develops in the ethical exhortation in chapters 4–6. As Paul indicates in the instructions to husbands, Christ gave himself in order that he "might present to himself a glorious church, . . . in order that it may be holy and blameless" (5:27 AT).

In the series of passages that begin with "in whom" (1:7–14), Paul elaborates on the spiritual blessings in Christ and the significance of election, indicating the past, present, and future of the community's existence. As the elect people, "we have redemption through his blood, the forgiveness of trespasses according to the riches of his grace" (1:7 AT). Paul develops the theme of the death of Christ in the letter (2:14–18) as the foundation for the believers' behavior (cf. 5:1–2, 25). This claim echoes earlier confessional statements in the Pauline literature, including the near-identical claim in Colossians 1:14. Additionally, "Redemption [*apolytrōsis*] through his blood" (Eph. 1:7) recalls the image in Romans 3:24 and the common hope for the "redemption" of Israel (cf. Luke 21:28), which probably alludes to the redemption of Israel from Egypt (cf. Deut. 7:8; 9:26; 13:5; 15:15; Pss. 74:2; 77:15) and the hope expressed in Deutero-Isaiah that God would "redeem" his people (Isa. 41:14; 43:1, 14; 44:22–24; 52:3; 54:5). For Paul, *apolytrōsis* is both a past event (Rom. 3:24) and a future hope (Rom. 8:23). Here Paul shares the view that the long-awaited redemption has taken place at the cross, "by his blood" (cf. Rom. 3:25; 5:9; Col. 1:20).

In other words, the series of statements introduced by "in whom" (Eph. 1:7, 11, 13) describes the nature of God's election.[25] As the first-person plural ("we have," 1:7) indicates, the focus of the soteriological statement is the participation of the community in God's saving event. God's grace abounded *to us* (1:8) as he made known *to us* the mystery of God's plan (*oikonomia*, 1:10) for the fullness of the times. That is, the spiritual blessings (1:3) given to the community include the revelation of God's ultimate plan: to sum up (*anakephalaiōsasthai*, 1:10) all things in Christ. Christ has both eschatological

25. See Jeal, "Rhetorical Argumentation in Ephesians," 318: "When an audience is confronted with word patterns the tendency is to collaborate with the pattern to make a complete utterance. . . . The resultant rhetorical effect is the tendency of the audience to assent to the praise of God and to the proposition that God is the one who blessed them 'in every spiritual blessing in the heavenlies in Christ.'"

and cosmological significance, for he is the culmination of God's plan in history and the head of the universe (*ta panta*). This anticipates the claim that God has put all things under his feet (1:22). Christ both shed his blood (1:7) and now reigns over all things. This mystery is known only to the church. As the second "in whom" clause indicates (1:11), the divine election occurred in the cross, the ultimate expression of God's grace.

In the final clause introduced by "in whom," Paul reminds the readers of the past event that points to a future consummation: in its response to the divine grace, the community was "sealed" (*esphragisthēte*, 1:13) by the promised Holy Spirit, the deposit of the inheritance. The church thus stands in the middle of the divine narrative. The culmination of the divine plan is the transformed community. This sets the stage for the exhortations that follow.

The thanksgiving (1:15–23) then extends the exordium, further introducing the goal of the letter. Paul's focus on moral formation is evident in his thanksgiving for the Ephesians' faith in Christ and love for the saints, anticipating the emphasis on faith (4:5, 13, 29) and love (1:4; 3:17, 19; 4:2; 6:23) later in the letter. The emphasis of the letter is not on the readers' progress thus far but on their subsequent formation, as chapters 4–6 indicate. Thus the thanksgiving becomes a petition (1:17–23) on behalf of the community's welfare. With the transition from the first-person plural (1:3–14) to the second-person plural (1:17–23), Paul continues to demonstrate his concern for the readers, an expression of both ethos and pathos. The emphasis is on their cognition: that God may give the spirit of wisdom and revelation in full knowledge (1:17), that they may know the hope of their calling (1:18) and the power among those who believe (1:19). The focal point of the petition is the power among those who believe. The powerless community needs to recognize that it is the recipient of the supreme power. Paul expands on this power, declaring that it raised Christ from the dead and sat him down at God's right hand in the heavenly places, echoing the early Christian creed, according to which God "raised him from the dead and seated him at the right hand of God" (1:20 AT). However, he does not mention the death and resurrection but rather the resurrection and exaltation, echoing Psalm 110:1, which is consistently interpreted as a reference to the exalted Christ (Rom. 8:34; 1 Cor. 15:25; cf. Matt. 22:44; 26:64; Eph. 1:22; Heb. 1:3, 13; 8:1; 10:12). That the exaltation involves the victory over cosmic powers is anticipated in the undisputed letters of Paul (1 Cor. 15:25–27; cf. Phil. 2:11). Indeed, both Ephesians (1:20–22) and 1 Corinthians (15:25–27) link Psalms 110:1 and 8:5–7 to describe the cosmic victory of Christ (cf. also Heb. 1:3–2:10). In Ephesians, however, the victory over the cosmic powers occurs with the exaltation of Christ (cf. 1 Pet. 3:22). In two parallel statements, Paul says that God (1) has placed all things (*ta panta*) under Christ's feet and (2) has made Christ head over all things (*ta panta*) with respect to the church, a claim that also appears in Colossians, where the exalted Christ is both "head of his body, the church" (Col. 1:18 AT), and "head of every power and authority" (Col. 2:10 AT). That is, he is not only the head over the universe (*ta panta*) but also the head of the church (*ekklēsia*), a theme that Paul reiterates in the argument that follows (Eph. 4:15; 5:23). Thus the *ekklēsia* is not, as in the undisputed letters, limited to the local house church, for the local house church is part of a cosmic reality. The *ekklēsia* is the equivalent of the first- and second-person plural that has been used throughout chapter 1. Similarly, the image of the church as the body of Christ recalls the undisputed letters (Rom. 12; 1 Cor. 12), yet here in Ephesians, it is not the local body but a universal reality, as in Colossians (Col. 1:18, 24). The readers' participation in the universal *ekklēsia* establishes their corporate self-esteem and lays the foundation for the behavior that Paul commends in Ephesians 4–6.

The description of the body as Christ's fullness (*plērōma*) further defines the church as the body of Christ. *Plērōma*, a term that is used almost exclusively in Ephesians and Colossians, has a variety of meanings but a dominant meaning in these letters, as suggested by the phrase "the one who fills all things" (Eph. 1:23 AT). Paul prays that the readers may be "filled with all the fullness of God" (3:19), and he encourages them to "grow into the fullness of Christ" (4:13 AT) and to "grow up in every way to the one who is the head, Christ" (4:15 AT). Thus in a dynamic process, the church is being filled by the one who fills the cosmos and is empowered to grow into the head (4:16). The *plērōma* is the divine power that fills the church, making moral formation possible. "One may speak metaphorically of two concentric circles in which the inner one is the church and the outer one is the cosmos, both ruled by Christ. . . . The church increases in size and grows in love."[26]

Paul prays that the Ephesians will grasp that they participate in something of cosmic importance. Having celebrated their place in the divine plan (1:3–14), he now prays that they understand the cosmic significance of their status. Because Jesus Christ stands above threatening powers, the same power that raised Christ from the dead is present in those who believe, empowering them for the challenges facing the church. While in 1 Corinthians the victory over cosmic powers is not complete, in Ephesians, the victory has taken place already. The two hymnic statements in Ephesians 1 not only indicate the theological reality but also prepare the way for the exhortations that follow. They function together as the exordium of the persuasion that follows. The church

---

26. Schnackenburg, *Der Brief an die Epheser*, 83.

is the heir not only of Israel but also of the cosmic church. The struggling house churches participate in the cosmic victory.

Ephesians echoes earlier Pauline letters, indicating the early Christian understanding of a church that lives between the "now" and the "not yet": the view that the community is God's elect; that God's grace has been made known in the death, resurrection, and exaltation of Christ; and that the church is the body of Christ. The new dimension, which was first introduced in Colossians, is that Christ is the head of the body, the universal church, and even the head over the cosmos.

By introducing these topics in the context of praise and worship, Paul invites the readers to share in the celebration of God's saving deeds. They are not an insignificant house church but participants in a community that is both the culmination of Israel's story and the victory of Christ over cosmic powers. Paul does not begin the presentation by lecturing on these themes but by leading the readers in worship, expecting them not only to know these theological truths but also to experience them. The developments from the earlier Pauline letters are evoked by the issues facing the readers, who remain convinced that they are threatened by cosmic powers. Paul has reshaped theological themes to reassure the readers of their identity, celebrating their victory over these powers. By praising God, he takes the readers into his own faith in order to lead them to further reflection and to inner renewal (cf. Eph. 4:23–24).[27] In the prayer that introduces the ethical section, Paul mentions "the power at work in us" (Eph. 3:20 AT).

The Narratio (2:1–3:13)

While 1:3–23 establishes the identity of the readers, 2:1–3:13 recalls the prior narrative of the community's existence; thus it functions as the narratio of the argument. In 2:1–22, Paul recalls the events that made the community a part of the divine plan, while in 3:1–14, he describes his own ministry, which called the universal church into existence. In two distinct descriptions of the community's identity (2:1–10, 11–22), Paul contrasts the "once" and the "now" of their existence, building the foundation of the instructions for future conduct in chapters 4–6. Paul continues the second-person plural in 2:1–22, indicating that he does not speak in abstractions but continues to remind the readers of their shared narrative. This contrast between "once" and "now" is commonplace in the undisputed letters (Rom. 6:17–18; 1 Cor. 6:11; Gal. 4:8–9; 1 Thess. 1:9; cf. Col. 3:7–8). In Ephesians, the twofold contrast

27. Schnackenburg, *Der Brief an die Epheser*, 67–68.

between "once" and "now" (Eph. 2:1–10, 11–22) elicits gratitude among the readers and reminds them who they are.

Paul focuses first on the community's past and present moral condition, contrasting how they once lived (*periepatēsate*, 2:2) with how they are now empowered to live (*peripatēsōmen*, 2:10). Having been once under the power of the authority (*exousia*) of the air (2:2), they have been "made alive" (*synezōopoiēsen*) with Christ (2:5) and "raised with him" (*synēgeiren*) and have been "made to sit with him" (*synekathisen*), the exalted Christ, in the heavenly places (2:6), demonstrating to the coming ages the wealth of God's grace. That is, they participate in the exaltation of Christ to God's right hand (cf. 1:20); thus they are above the powers that enslave people into immoral practices. This claim has no precedent in the undisputed letters of Paul, but it is anticipated in the affirmation in Colossians 2:12 that believers have been "raised with [Christ]" in baptism.[28] To sit with Christ in the heavenly places is to live above "the ruler of the power of the air" (Eph. 2:2), who enslaved them into immoral practices. While the imagery differs from that of Romans, the statement is consistent with the earlier description of sin as the invading power (cf. Rom. 5:12–21) that is now overcome by the power of the Spirit in the lives of believers (Rom. 8:1–11).

Echoing the distinction between faith and works outlined in Galatians (Gal. 2:16; 3:2) and Romans (Rom. 3:20, 27; 4:2, 6; 9:12, 32), Paul declares that their present situation is not a result of their own works but of the grace of God (Eph. 2:8–9). Inasmuch as the issues that evoked Paul's earlier distinction between faith and works are no longer current, these categories no longer address arguments about the admission of the gentiles into the church but expand on the meaning of grace to establish the identity and conduct of the believers.[29] The result of grace is that "we are created for good works, . . . in order that we may walk in them" (Eph. 2:10 AT). The community that is no longer under the control of cosmic forces is now empowered for moral formation. This dramatic contrast between "once" and "now" reaffirms the identity of the readers and evokes the emotion of gratitude for the possibility of transformed behavior. This new possibility is the basis for

28. While Col. 2:12–13 adapts the baptismal instruction of Rom. 6:1–11, Eph. 2:5–6 adapts Col. 2:12–13. While all three passages employ the prefix *syn-* to describe participation in the destiny of Christ, the three *syn-* verbs in Eph. 2:5–6 do not mention being buried with Christ, as in Rom. 6:4 and Col. 2:12, but focus on the believers' participation in the resurrection of Christ. See Gese, *Das Vermächtnis des Apostels*, 149–50.

29. Cf. Matera, *New Testament Theology*, 232: "In some ways, Ephesians 2 is a synopsis of Paul's theology in Romans. Ephesians 2:1–10 summarizes Paul's soteriology as presented in Romans 1–8. . . . Ephesians, however, is not so much a summary of Paul's theology as it is a restatement of that theology for a new day."

the exhortations in chapters 4–6, the concrete description of what it means to "walk in them."

While the image changes in 2:11–22, the contrast between "once" and "now" continues. The image now is that of citizenship as Paul addresses gentiles who were once "alienated from the commonwealth of Israel" (2:12 AT), "foreigners" (*xenoi*) and "strangers" (*paroikoi*) to the covenant of Israel, and "far away" (2:13 AT). Now they are "near," "fellow citizens" (*sympolitai*), and "members of the household [*oikeioi*] of God" (2:19). Their previous status stands in sharp contrast to the Israelites, who had "the adoption and the glory and the covenants and the legislation and the worship and the promises" (Rom. 9:4 AT). Having earlier indicated that "we have redemption through his blood" (Eph. 1:7 AT), Paul now declares that "those who were once far away have been brought near by the blood of Christ" (Eph. 2:13 AT), elaborating on the grace of God mentioned in 2:8–9. The image of those "far" and "near" echoes prophetic traditions (cf. Isa. 49:1; 66:19; Jer. 31:10), especially the promise of "peace, peace to the far and the near" in Isaiah 57:19.[30]

In Ephesians 2:14–18, Paul elaborates on the effect of the blood of Christ in creating a new status for believers in a section that interrupts the "once-now" theme and the direct address to the readers (2:11–13, 19–22) with a description of the saving event. "He is our peace" (2:14) forms an inclusio with the claim "Through him we both have access in one spirit to the Father" (2:18 AT). In three parallel aorist participial phrases, Paul describes how Jesus has become "our peace": "having made [*poiēsas*] the two one" (2:14b AT), "having torn [*lysas*] down the dividing wall of partition" (2:14b AT), and "having abolished [*katargēsas*] the law with its commandments and ordinances" (2:15a AT). These parallel expressions point to a singular event and its implications for Paul's understanding of both the law and the church.

Only in 2:14b–15 does Paul address the topic of Christ and the law, a subject that plays a major role in two of the undisputed letters, describing it here as the "dividing wall [*mesotoichon*] of the partition [*phragmos*]" (2:14 AT) and the law of commandments consisting in ordinances (*en dogmasin*). The description recalls the numerous statements in Jewish literature that the law is a wall or a fence to protect Israel. According to the *Letter of Aristeas*, Moses, "being endowed by God . . . , surrounded us with unbroken palisades and iron walls to prevent our mixing with any other peoples" (139).[31] The author of the *Letter of Aristeas* adds, "To prevent our being perverted by contact with others or by mixing with bad influences, he hedges us in on all

---

30. Schnackenburg, *Der Brief an die Epheser*, 111.
31. Translation by R. J. H. Shutt in *OTP* 2:22.

sides with strict observances" (142). While the law as the partition between Jews and gentiles is implicit in the undisputed letters (cf. Gal. 3), it becomes the singular focus in Ephesians.

The view of the law as a barrier is the background for the declaration that Christ abolished the law at the cross, an interpretation that is probably anticipated in the claim in Colossians 2:14 that Christ "blotted out the record of debts" (AT) at the cross. This is an understanding of both the death on the cross and the law that is unprecedented in the undisputed letters. Nowhere in the undisputed letters does Paul declare that Christ abolished the law, although he did say that believers have "died to the law" (Rom. 7:4; cf. Gal. 2:19; Phil. 3:1–10), that Christ is the end of the law for those who believe (Rom. 10:4), and that it is no longer in force (2 Cor. 3:11, 14). However, Paul also insists that he affirms the law (Rom. 3:31), which is "just and good and holy" (Rom. 7:12 AT).[32]

Consistent with the cosmological focus of the letter, the exaltation of Christ is the primary focus of the saving event (cf. Eph. 1:19–22; 2:6; 4:10–16). However, in the exordium (1:7) Paul mentions redemption through the blood of Christ and the forgiveness of our trespasses and later appeals to the death of Christ as the example of self-giving love (4:32; 5:1–2, 25–27). While this interpretation of the death of Christ is a common theme in the undisputed letters, the new dimension in Ephesians 2:14 is the interpretation of the death of Christ as the tearing down of the partition between Jews and gentiles.

The result of the abolition of the law as a partition is the end of the separation between the peoples and the creation of the "new person," the church composed of Jews and gentiles. The "new person" is the church, the body of Christ (1:22; 4:15; 5:22–23). As Paul established in the opening blessing, the gentile readers have been elected and foreordained to be members of the people of God (1:4–6). This understanding is a development of the view that Christ is the inclusive person in the undisputed letters (cf. Gal. 3).

This narrative of "once" and "now" is not complete, however, for Paul changes the image to declare that "you are no longer strangers and outsiders, but fellow citizens and members of the household of God" (Eph. 2:19 AT). The image has changed from the body to the building (*oikodomē*, 2:21), recalling the imagery of 1 Corinthians 3:10–17. The community is being built on the foundation of the apostles and prophets, with Christ as the cornerstone. In this instance, the foundation is not Christ, as in 1 Corinthians 3:11, but

---

32. While Eph. 2:14–15 declares that Christ abolished the law, Paul later appeals to the law as the warrant for moral instructions (cf. Eph. 5:31; 6:2).

the apostles and prophets (Eph. 3:20). This foundation "will grow into a holy temple" (2:21 AT) and is being built into a dwelling place. Thus the church is not only being filled (1:23) but also being formed, as Paul will explain in 4:7–16.

In the excursus in 3:1–13, Paul declares his investment in the community in an argument from both ethos and pathos, as the inclusio "on your behalf" (*hyper hymōn*) indicates (3:1, 13). By God's grace (3:2, 7–8) he is a minister "on behalf of you gentiles" (3:1 AT), and he suffers "for you" (3:13 AT). He has received a revelation from God, and his mission is that the readers know the mystery that has been revealed (3:5, 8–9), the divine purpose that the gentiles (cf. 1:3–10) are joint heirs (*synklēronoma*) and joined together in the same body (*syssōma*) and share in the same promises with Israel (3:6). The church, which is above the powers, may proclaim God's wisdom to the powers (3:10).

Paul prays for the divine empowerment to be grasped in the inner human (3:14–19), that Christ may live in their hearts through faith, that they may be rooted in love, based on the love of Christ. He ends the section with a doxology. Paul's prayer in 3:14–21 reinforces the purpose of the letter and resumes the prayers of 1:3–23, turning from the past to the future and anticipating the moral instructions. Having declared earlier that his readers are empowered by the one who raised Jesus from the dead (1:19–20), he now prays that they will be empowered through the Spirit, that Christ will take up residence in their hearts through faith, and that they will be rooted in love (3:17). Thus the prayer for the transformation of the community precedes the specific instructions for the appropriate conduct of the transformed people.

The basis for Paul's persuasion is the grand picture of the church's place in the cosmos. House churches scattered in Asia Minor are given a glimpse of their significance in the eternal plan of God. They are also given a glimpse of a work that is incomplete. This is performative speech, for in declaring that God has created the "new person," Paul is encouraging his readers to become the new person (4:25).

The Propositio (4:1–6)

The establishment of the identity of the empowered people lays the foundation for the exhortations that follow. Having begun the letter with the reminder that his readers were "chosen from the foundation of the world to be holy and blameless" (1:4 AT), Paul turns from the declaration of God's primordial action to the community's response: "to walk worthily of the calling with which [they] were called" (4:1 AT). The exhortations in 4:1–6 function as the propositio, indicating how their heavenly identity shapes their conduct. The community's task, articulated in chapters 4–6, is to "keep the spirit of unity in the bond of peace" (4:3 AT), maintaining what God has provided—"one Lord, one faith, one baptism" (4:4–6), which includes peoples who were once hostile to each other (cf. 2:11–22). Consistent with the focus on ecclesiology in chapters 1–3, Paul describes an ecclesial ethic. To "maintain the unity" of a universal body (4:3 AT), one must practice the qualities that Paul describes in 4:7–6:9.

The Probatio (4:7–6:9)

In the probatio in 4:7–6:9, Paul indicates how the empowered people may fulfill God's purpose of a transformed people, developing the theme of empowerment in 4:7–16 before indicating the specific conduct in 4:17–6:9. The introduction "to each was given the grace" (4:7 AT) recalls the emphasis in Ephesians 1–3 on empowerment from the God who fills all things (cf. *charis* in 1:6–7; 2:5, 8–9), and it anticipates the reflection on Psalm 68:18, according to which the exalted Christ "gave gifts to people" (AT). Thus Paul introduces the first proof with an argument from Scripture, which he interprets.

The original Psalm 68:18 celebrates the triumph of Yahweh over Israel's enemies and his ascent to Mount Zion, where he "received gifts from people." Paul's reading, "he gave gifts to people"—whether his own alteration or one that preceded him—prepares the way for the reflections that follow. In the christological reading that follows, it is Christ who ascended, not to Mount Zion but into heaven, a claim that Paul made earlier in Ephesians 1:22–23. This exaltation implies an earlier descent, recalling the theme of descent and ascent in the undisputed letters. Echoing earlier Pauline tradition (cf. 1 Cor. 12:12–28), Paul speaks of the gifts that the exalted one gives. Consistent with the focus of Ephesians, however, the exalted Christ gives the gifts. The purpose of the gifts was "for the building up of the body of Christ" (Eph. 4:12 AT). As Paul has already indicated, the cosmic body is growing as the people are being built up (Eph. 2:19–20). The church is thus incomplete until it attains the unity of the body of Christ that Paul has already declared to be a reality (cf. 2:14–18; 4:1–6). Thus Paul encourages the community, "Let us grow into him in every way [*ta panta*], who is the head, Jesus Christ" (4:15 AT). The community has received the power and now grows into the head. Twice Paul indicates that love is the criterion for growth (4:15–16). This growth into the head, Jesus Christ, corresponds to the consistent Pauline theme of moral formation. In Ephesians, however, moral formation is specifically associated with the empowerment from the exalted Lord.

Paul introduces the second proof (4:17–6:9) with an argument from his authoritative ethos (4:17), the ethical instructions that echo the lists of vices to "take off" (*apotithēmi*, 4:22, 25; cf. Rom. 13:12; Col. 3:8) and virtues to "put on" (*endyein*, Eph. 4:23–24; cf. Rom. 13:12–14; Gal. 3:27) in the undisputed letters of Paul. These instructions are framed in a way that is consistent with the rhetorical vision of the letter. Having once "walked . . . according to the ruler of the authority of the world" (Eph. 2:2 AT), the community is instructed now no longer to "walk" as the gentiles do (4:17), with the vices that Paul enumerates, but to "put on the new person, who is being created in righteousness" (4:25 AT). The community that is being filled with Christ is now growing up into him. To put on the new person is to abandon self-serving behavior and live in love (3:17; 4:2; 5:2, 25, 28). Having focused throughout the letter on the church as the culmination of God's plan, Paul insists on an ecclesial ethic that is expressed as the community grows in love toward one another (4:17–5:20) and includes also the family (5:21–6:9) in Christ.

The Peroratio (6:10–20)

Having declared the triumph over the principalities and powers (Eph. 1:21–23) that once determined the destiny of the readers (2:2–3), Paul concludes the letter with the recognition that the believers are still engaged in a battle against the rulers, the authorities, and "the cosmic forces of darkness" (6:12 AT). The military imagery echoes the language of the undisputed letters (cf. 2 Cor. 6:7; 10:2–7; 1 Thess. 5:8). In Ephesians, as in Romans (8:35), the exaltation of Christ is the victory over the cosmic forces, but these powers continue to be a threatening reality for believers. The series of imperatives ("be strong," Eph. 6:10; "put on the armor of God," 6:11; "stand," 6:14) describes the believers' response to the cosmic powers. They are not, however, defenseless against an overwhelming force, for the cosmic victory of Christ (cf. 1:20–23) ensures that they may "be strong in the Lord and in the power of his strength" (6:10 AT). Their weapons include righteousness (6:14), faith (6:16), and the word of God (6:17), and they find a continuing resource in prayer (6:18).

Ephesians 6:10–20 is an appropriate peroratio in a message to a community that is anxious about its place in a world populated by threatening powers, for it summarizes with pathos the consequences of the letter's central message. Living as a minority group in scattered house churches, the readers have received a vision of participation in a universal triumph. They now, like a military force, can engage these forces in battle because of the empowerment that they receive from the exalted Christ. Paul adds to the pathos with the reminder that he is an ambassador in chains (6:20) and in need of their prayers.

Conclusion: Colossians and Ephesians as Theology and Rhetoric

Like the undisputed letters of Paul, both Colossians and Ephesians are intended to shape moral communities among gentile converts, who now participate in Israel's incomplete narrative (cf. Eph. 2:11–21). The readers live in "the hope of glory" (Col. 1:27; cf. Eph. 1:18; 2:12; 4:1; Col. 1:5, 23), and Paul's ambition is that they be "holy and blameless" (Col. 1:22; cf. Eph. 1:4). He writes to ensure that they reach that goal.

The new dimensions in Pauline theology—the cosmic Christ and the cosmic church—must be read as both theology and rhetoric. The new rhetorical situation has undoubtedly required new answers. Communities that are powerless before cosmic forces can make moral progress only if these powers have been overcome. Paul does not offer a thoroughgoing Christology, but he focuses on the dimension that empowers the community to "seek the things that are above" (Col. 3:1). Similarly, the cosmic ecclesiology provides an anxious people with their identity and place in the cosmos, assuring them of the power that transforms them into the divine image (cf. Col. 3:10). Paul not only offers theological answers but also creates an experience among his readers with the hymns (cf. Col. 1:15–20) and liturgical language (Eph. 1:3–14). Thus the rhetorical dimension cannot be separated from the theology of Ephesians and Colossians.

11

Pauline Theology and Rhetoric in the Pastoral Epistles

To read the Pastoral Epistles is to enter a world that is different from that of both the undisputed and the disputed letters to the churches, as interpreters in the last two centuries have established. These letters are written to men who are envoys in the undisputed letters and speak to the churches on Paul's behalf. While all three of the Pastoral Epistles have the epistolary form, they are unlike the other letters, for they speak primarily in the imperative and without extended argumentation. First Timothy and Titus resemble letters from officials to subordinates in the empire.[1] Second Timothy has features of the familiar last will and testament and is a fitting conclusion to the Pauline corpus.[2]

In the letters to Timothy and Titus, Paul's envoys serve in the role that they had in the undisputed letters. According to 1 Corinthians 4:17, Paul is sending Timothy to Corinth to "remind [the church] of [his] ways" (AT). Timothy is entrusted to speak for Paul, representing the apostle with visits to the churches (cf. 1 Cor. 16:10–11; Phil. 2:19–24; 1 Thess. 3:2, 6), and joins Paul in writing to the churches (cf. 2 Cor. 1:1; Phil. 1:1; Col. 1:1; 1 Thess. 1:1). Titus is Paul's representative in 2 Corinthians (cf. 2 Cor. 2:13; 7:5–16; 8:6, 16) and companion

---

1. On 1 Timothy and Titus as a *mandata principis*, a public document from a ruler to an appointed official, see Johnson, *First and Second Letters to Timothy and Titus*, 137–42; Wolter, *Die Pastoralbriefe*, 161–77; Fiore, *Function of Personal Example*, 79–82.
2. See Wolter, *Die Pastoralbriefe*, 222–41, for 2 Timothy as a last will and testament.

in the apostle's second visit to Jerusalem (cf. Gal. 2:1–10). In the Pastoral
Epistles, Timothy and Titus continue as Paul's representatives, speaking with
the apostle's authoritative voice as they give instructions to the churches.

Since Friedrich Schleiermacher, scholars have maintained that the Pastoral
Epistles are pseudonymous,[3] concluding that both the author and the setting
in the epistles are literary fictions. One of the reasons for the denial of Pauline
authorship is the absence of familiar Pauline themes and the presence of a new
theological discourse and vocabulary. All three Pastoral Epistles speak of the
coming of Christ as an epiphany; he "appeared" (*epiphanē*, Titus 2:11; 3:4)
already, and the church now awaits his appearance (*epiphaneia*, 1 Tim. 6:14;
2 Tim. 1:10; Titus 2:13). Additionally, the phrase "God our Savior" appears only
in the Pastoral Epistles (1 Tim. 1:1; 2:3; 4:10; Titus 1:3; 2:10, 13; 3:4; cf. 2 Tim.
1:8–9).[4] Indeed, *sotēr* has a predominance in the Pastoral Epistles that is unprecedented in the Pauline correspondence.[5] Only the Pastorals have the repeated
references to "sound teaching" (1 Tim. 1:10; 2 Tim. 4:3; Titus 1:9; 2:1; cf. 1:13;
2:2), although the content of the sound teaching remains largely undefined.[6]

In this chapter, I will not engage in the argument over pseudonymity but
will analyze the letters at the level of the implied author and implied reader.
While the actual historical situation remains uncertain, the letters present a
rhetorical situation as a background to this correspondence.[7] I shall examine
the rhetorical situation and the intersection of rhetoric and theology in the
letters to determine their place in the Pauline tradition. Thus I will speak of
the implied author as Paul and the implied audience as Timothy and Titus.

Rhetoric and Theology in the Epistle to Titus

The Rhetorical Situation

Paul writes to his envoy Titus, having left him in Crete to "set in order
what remains" in the churches there (Titus 1:5 AT). This task is necessary

3. Friedrich Schleiermacher questioned the Pauline authorship of the Pastorals in 1807. See
the discussion in Johnson, "First Timothy 1:1–20," 221.

4. In 2 Tim. 1:10, Christ is the *sotēr*.

5. The term *sotēr* is used elsewhere, as in Eph. 5:23; Phil. 3:20.

6. Cf. Schnelle, *Theology of the New Testament*, 600: "In modern discussions of the history of early Christian theology the Pastoral Epistles have mostly been interpreted within the
framework of a decadent theory of church history: Paul stands at the beginning, then follow
Colossians and Ephesians (and 2 Thessalonians), until finally the Pastoral Epistles completely
dissolve Pauline theology into contemporary moral and bourgeois social standards."

7. The rhetorical situation is the problem as perceived by the implied author, to which the
discourse is the answer.

because aspects of the Cretan reputation now threaten the church (cf. 1:12). Some within the church are "disorderly [*anypotaktai*], idle talkers [*mataiologoi*], and deceivers [*phrenapatai*], especially those of the circumcision" (1:10 AT), who disturb entire households, teaching for shameful gain (1:11). Such people are incapable of good works (1:16). The concluding warnings against stupid controversies, genealogies, dissensions, and quarrels (3:9) suggest that these issues are current in the churches of Crete. These descriptions offer little insight into possible doctrinal issues but focus on the behavior of people who are incapable of good works. Titus's task of setting in order what remains involves rescuing the church from those who ought to be stopped. Paul's persuasive task is to equip Titus to speak to this situation on his behalf.

Rhetoric and Theology

Interpreters have commented on the disproportion between the lengthy prescript (1:1–4) and the brief letter. Among Paul's letters, only the prescripts in Romans and Galatians compare to Titus's in length. As in the other letters, Paul gives his credentials at the beginning of the letter, establishing the nature of the persuasion. He speaks as a slave (*doulos*) and apostle of Jesus Christ, indicating his prophetic voice; his identification of himself as *doulos*, a term that is traditionally associated with Moses and the prophets,[8] establishes his authority and prepares readers for the dominance of the imperatives in the letter that will shape the nature of the persuasion. His ministry "for the faith of God's elect" (1:1) is consistent with the undisputed letters; the gentile churches are God's elect, living in continuity with ancient Israel. Their participation in Israel's narrative is further indicated in the reference to "the hope of eternal life," promised "before the ages" but now manifest in his own time (1:2–3) in the message that Paul preaches. Participation is defined by faith (*pistis*), as Paul indicates throughout the letter (1:4, 13; 2:2, 10; 3:15). In each instance, the object of faith is not mentioned.[9] Thus Paul signifies a narrative in which the church participates, which extends from ancient times until the end, consistent with the earlier letters. By reminding the readers of their participation in a narrative that is eternal, he undoubtedly intends to make them favorably disposed to his message.

What is at stake in the letter is "the full knowledge of the truth in accordance with godliness" (*eusebeia*, 1:1 AT). "Knowledge of the truth" anticipates the

---

8. See Classen, "Rhetorical Reading of the Epistle to Titus," 430.

9. While the object of *pistis/pisteuō* is common in Paul's undisputed letters, he also refers to faith without an object, as in the Pastoral Epistles. Cf. Rom. 1:8, 12; 1 Cor. 16:13; 2 Cor. 1:24; Gal. 1:23; 1 Thess. 1:3; 3:2, 6.

discussion in 1:10–16, where truth, the gospel message, stands in contrast to the error, specifically the "Jewish myths" (1:14). *Eusebeia*, a term used in the Pauline corpus only in the Pastoral Epistles, refers to dutiful conduct (cf. 1 Tim. 2:2; 3:16; 4:7–8; 6:3, 5–6; 2 Tim. 3:5).[10] The teaching that accords with piety (*eusebeia*) indicates the close relationship between the moral life (cf. Titus 2:1–2) and the message of the gospel. Failure to acknowledge the truth results in immoral behavior, and the knowledge of the truth leads to *eusebeia*. In Titus, *eusebeia* is a "cipher" for the Christian behavior that the letter commends.[11]

This truth is the equivalent of Paul's preaching (*kērygma*, 1:3) and stands in relation to the teaching (*didaskalia*) that is emphasized in the letter: "sound teaching" (2:1; cf. 1:13), "the teaching of God our Savior" (cf. 2:10). This preaching has been entrusted to Paul (1:3; cf. 1 Tim. 1:11). Thus the persuasion begins with a prophetic voice of one who has been entrusted by God (cf. 1 Thess. 2:4).

The epistolary prescript in Titus 1:1–4 establishes Paul's ethos and introduces the major theme of the letter: the truth of the gospel and the pattern of life that results from it. Thus it functions as the exordium of the letter.[12] The goal of the persuasion is to instill in Paul's communities the moral transformation that accompanies the reception of the gospel and to address those issues that prevent transformation.

In 1:5–12, Paul recalls recent events in Crete and states the issue at hand by referring to the past. Because of the presence of those who are disturbing the church (1:10–12), Paul left Timothy in Crete to "set right what remains" (*epidiorthōsē ta leiponta*) and appoint elders (*presbyteroi*) in every city (1:5). These elders were to exhibit a life in accordance with piety, for the list of their moral qualities stands in sharp contrast to the conduct of the opposition. Whereas the opposition is disorderly (*anypotaktoi*, 1:10), the elders should not be disorderly (1:6). Unlike the opponents who teach "for sordid gain" (1:11), the elders should not be "greedy for gain" (1:7). Whereas the opponents are incapable of good works (1:16), the elders exemplify good deeds. Indeed, the elders should exemplify the impact of sound teaching on the moral life and teach others by word and by example. This recollection of the events leading to the writing of the letter functions as the narratio, preparing the way for the argument of the letter.

10. See Thompson, *Moral Formation according to Paul*, 203: "*Eusebeia* is the most comprehensive term for moral conduct; . . . it also includes reverence for parents, ancestors, rulers, and the social order" in classical literature.
11. Collins, "Theology of the Epistle to Titus," 59.
12. Collins, "Theology of the Epistle to Titus," 62.

Titus's task is not only to appoint elders to silence the opposition but also to instruct the church himself. Beginning at 1:13, Paul speaks in the imperative, the dominant mode of speech in the remainder of the letter. The imperatives in 1:13 and 2:1 serve as the propositio of the argument. The task of Titus is to refute the opposition (1:13–16) and to teach the entire church to live in accordance with sound teaching (2:1), exhibiting the same qualities as the elders. Titus himself will be the model of teaching and good conduct (2:7).

The argument (probatio) consists of two series of imperatives (1:13–2:10; 3:1–2), each followed with a theological foundation (2:11–14; 3:3–7). Thus the foundation for the argument is the authoritative voice of Paul and the message that he has taught already. As in the undisputed letters (cf. 1 Cor. 8:6; 2 Cor. 5:14–15), the Christian tradition is the premise for the persuasion.

The first argument (Titus 2:1–15) is marked by an inclusio in 2:1, 15: Titus's commission is to teach on Paul's behalf, giving behavioral norms to the entire community that are consistent with the ethical norms of the elders and the alternative to the behavior of the false teachers. The sequence of purpose clauses introduced by "in order that" (hina, 2:5, 8, 10) focuses on the impact of Christian behavior on outsiders, indicating the countercultural nature of their moral life. As in the undisputed letters, the moral advice assumes a demarcation between insiders and outsiders (cf. 1 Cor. 5:1–11; 6:1–11; 1 Thess. 4:9–12).

The inclusio also declares the theological foundation of the moral life. The moral life is "in accordance with sound teaching" (Titus 2:1); Titus 2:11–14 gives a summary of sound teaching, which is the message that has been entrusted to Paul (cf. Titus 1:3). As in the undisputed letters, believers live "worthily of the gospel" (Phil. 1:27 AT). While the heretics' moral bankruptcy corresponds to their false teaching (Titus 1:10), the believers' moral behavior is "fitting" (prepei, Titus 2:1) to sound teaching.

The theological foundation for the moral life is given in 2:11–14, introduced by gar. As in the undisputed Pauline letters, Paul builds ethics on the grace of God (Titus 2:11; cf. Rom. 3:24; 5:1; 2 Cor. 6:2; 8:9) in Christ. The new dimension of the formulation in Titus is the reference to "God our Savior," a phrase that is common in the Pastoral Epistles but never appears in the undisputed letters of Paul. Another new dimension is the statement that God's grace "appeared" (epiphanē, Titus 2:11) to all people, a reference to the incarnation.[13] This term was employed in antiquity for the epiphany of the gods;[14] in the

13. The word appears in 2 Thess. 2:8 in reference to the parousia.
14. See Spicq, "ἐπιφαίνω, ἐπιφάνεια, ἐπιφανής," TLNT 2:66.

Old Testament, it is used for an epiphany of God or for heavenly manifesta-
tions.[15] The word is used again in Titus 3:4 but nowhere else in the Pastoral
Epistles. This is comparable to Paul's appeal to the incarnation as a basis for
the moral life in the undisputed letters (2 Cor. 8:9; Phil. 2:6; cf. Rom. 15:3).
This appearance is the turn of the ages, for the church now awaits a second
epiphany (Titus 2:13). Thus the church lives between the times, and its task
is to live "soberly [*sōphronōs*], righteously [*dikaiōs*], and godly [*eusebōs*] in
this present age" (Titus 2:12 AT), a summary of the moral advice in 2:1–10.

This moral vision has only faint echoes of Pauline moral instruction.
Sōphrōn- is a significant part of the moral instruction in the Pastoral Epistles.
The task of Titus is to ensure that the older women encourage (*sōphronizein*,
i.e., "instruct in prudence")[16] the young women (Titus 2:3–5) and that younger
men be sensible (*sōphronein*, Titus 2:6). This recalls Paul's advice to the church
in Rome to "think with sober judgment" (*eis to sōphronein*, Rom. 12:3). To
live "righteously" (*dikaiōs*) recalls his inclusion of items that the community
should think about in Philippians ("whatever is . . . *dikaia*," Phil. 4:8). While
Paul employs common terms from Greek ethics, he shapes them to include
the qualities of character that are consistent with life in the community.

The moral response of the community is based not only on the incarnation but also on the death of Christ (Titus 2:14). That he gave himself "for
us" (*hyper hēmōn*) recalls the frequent appeal to the death of Christ "for us"
and "for our sins" in the undisputed letters of Paul. Paul expands the phrase
with the purpose clause indicating the result of Jesus's saving death: "in
order to (1) redeem [*lytrōsētai*] us from lawlessness [*anomia*] and (2) purify
for himself [*katharisē*] a chosen [*periousin*] people" (AT). The imagery suggests that the community is the heir of ancient Israel, which looked back to
the redemption from slavery (cf. Exod. 6:6; 15:13, 16) and looked to Israel's
redemption from captivity (cf. Isa. 35:9; 41:14; 43:1, 14; 44:22–24; 51:11;
52:3; Luke 1:68; 2:38; 24:21). In purifying a chosen people through the cross,
Christ has brought the gentile community into Israel's narrative, for Israel
was God's chosen people (cf. Exod. 19:5; 23:22; Deut. 7:6; 14:2; 26:18). Living in a covenant with God, the chosen people separate themselves from the
mores of the surrounding world.

In the second cycle of the argument, Paul begins with moral instructions
(Titus 3:1–2) under the heading of being prepared for every good work (3:1),
once more contrasting the community with the false teachers (cf. 1:16). The
instruction to submit to authorities (3:1) repeats the instructions of Romans

15. Spicq, "ἐπιφαίνω," *TLNT* 2:65.
16. BDAG 986.

13:1–7. The imperative not to blaspheme appears elsewhere only in Colossians (3:8) and Ephesians (4:31), and the instruction to be peaceable (*amachos*) appears elsewhere only in the qualification for bishops in 1 Timothy 3:3. The instruction to demonstrate kindness (*epieikēs*) and meekness (*prautēs*) also appears in the Pauline tradition (1 Cor. 4:21; 2 Cor. 10:1; Gal. 5:23; 6:1; Eph. 4:2; Phil. 4:5; Col. 3:12). Titus's challenge is to remind the church of conduct that further exemplifies the life in accordance with godliness. Paul supports the argument with the familiar "once [*pote*] . . . when [*hote*]" (Titus 3:3–4), recalling the radical break and the corporate journey of all believers.[17] The radical change came with the initiative of God. Having spoken in 2:11 of the grace of God that appeared, he now speaks of the kindness (*chrēstotēs*) and loving-kindness (*philanthrōpia*) of God our Savior that appeared (3:4), once more pointing to the incarnation. This is the equivalent of the mercy (*eleos*) of God (3:5). The divine initiative is emphasized with the phrase "not of works done in righteousness that we did ourselves" (AT), a clear echo of Galatians and Romans.

"He saved us" indicates that the turn of the ages has come. Paul apparently assumes the message of the cross, but he does not elaborate. Instead, he indicates that "[God] saved us through the washing of regeneration and renewal of the Holy Spirit," apparently collapsing the incarnation and the crucifixion into one event (3:5 AT). "He saved us" echoes Paul in the undisputed letters, where he also speaks of salvation in the past (aorist) tense (cf. Rom. 8:24). The alternative to "works that we did" is the washing of regeneration. This echoes Paul's comment to the Corinthians, "You were washed, you were sanctified, you were justified" (1 Cor. 6:11; cf. Eph. 5:26), and a Christian tradition that associates baptism with washing (cf. 1 Pet. 3:21). This "washing of regeneration" employs terminology that is not used elsewhere in Paul. It is obviously a passive act, the opposite of works done in righteousness, and the language is parallel to the "newness of life" in Romans 6:4 (cf. 2 Cor. 5:17).

The parallel between "washing of regeneration" and "renewal of the Spirit" indicates the close association between baptism and the Holy Spirit that was characteristic of the undisputed Pauline letters (cf. 1 Cor. 12:12–13). The Holy Spirit was "poured out" (cf. Rom. 5:5). The community lives between the times: between "having been justified" and becoming heirs of eternal life. The present, therefore, is the time for moral change under the power of the Holy Spirit. The Christian creed is thus the foundation of Paul's argument for the behavior of those who live between the times.

17. Cf. Rom. 6:17–18, 20–22; 7:5–6; 1 Cor. 6:11; Gal. 4:8–9; Eph. 5:8; Col. 3:7–8. See Thompson, *Church according to Paul*, 105–6.

The final advice in Titus 3:8–11 serves as the peroratio. Paul summarizes the letter, indicating that the believers should pay attention to good works (3:8; cf. 1:16; 2:7, 14) and avoid heretical teachers (3:9–11). In contrast to false teachers, who are incapable of good works (1:16), believers are zealous of good works (2:7, 14). Having presented instructions for a moral life that is appropriate to sound teaching (2:1), Paul concludes the body of the letter with a warning against false teachers, recapitulating the subject that he introduced near the beginning of the letter (1:10–13). The foundation of the argument is his role as God's prophetic voice and the Christian *kerygma* that he preaches.

Persuasion in 1 Timothy

First Timothy shares with Titus both the basic literary form and a parallel setting. As a letter from the apostle to a subordinate, it contains the authoritative voice of Paul, who speaks predominantly in the imperative with the instructions that Timothy is commissioned to deliver. Titus is left in Crete to ensure that false teachers are silenced and sound teaching is maintained, and Timothy is left in Ephesus for the same reason. Both letters envision churches that will exist in the absence of Paul and his envoys; thus they have a focus on local leadership that distinguishes them from the undisputed letters of Paul.

The Rhetorical Situation

Contrary to the popular image of the Pastoral Epistles, their concern is not the leadership structure of the church but a response to the opposition to which Paul alludes. Although the actual historical situation and the identity of the opponents have been major topics of research in the past two centuries, the letters offer insufficient details for determining the identity of the opponents. Furthermore, the description of them is the standard material in philosophical polemics, in which opponents are commonly accused of moral bankruptcy.[18] We can, however, determine the rhetorical situation that drives the argument. Some have already "gone astray" from the faith (1 Tim. 1:6, 19; 6:21), and other dangers lie on the horizon (4:1–6). Those who do not hold to sound teaching are known by the vices that are mentioned near the beginning (1:8–11) and end (6:3–6) of the letter. They miss "the goal of our instruction," which is "love from a pure heart, a good conscience, and sincere faith" (1:5 AT). This response to the gospel is consistent with the qualities of the moral life that Paul encourages throughout the undisputed letters and

---

18. See Karris, "Polemic of the Pastoral Epistles."

is a thread throughout the Pastoral Epistles (cf. 1 Tim. 1:14; 2:15; 4:12; 6:11; 2 Tim. 1:13; 2:22; 3:10; Titus 2:2, 10). Paul writes to ensure that Timothy (as well as the church) knows how to behave in the house of God (1 Tim. 3:15) and is faithful to sound teaching. The focus of the letter on moral behavior indicates that sound instruction will result in proper conduct.

The Argument

First Timothy is not, as some have argued, a loose collection of imperatives[19] but a coherent argument intended to address the crisis caused by false teaching. In recent years, scholars have identified the features that make 1 Timothy a coherent argument.[20] Peter Bush, for example, observes the symmetry between 1:3–20 and 6:11–21.[21] Other scholars appropriately describe 1:3–20 and 6:3–21 as the bookends of the argument.[22] Paul expresses the concern that some "teach otherwise" (*heterodidaskalein*, 1:3; 6:3), knowing that some have deviated (*astochēsantes*, 1:6; 6:21) from the truth into empty speech (1:6; 6:20). Timothy's task is to guard the deposit (*parathēkē*, 6:20) that Paul commits (*paratithemai*) to him (1:18) and to fight the good fight (1:18; 6:12). The argument consists of a series of instructions to Timothy, each prefaced by *parakalō* (2:1; cf. *boulomai*, 2:8), *dei* (3:2), or an imperative (cf. 4:11; 5:1, 9, 17, 23; 6:1, 2a).

Before the imperatives, Paul establishes the foundation of his argument with a view of recent events (1:3–7), a description of the opposition (1:8–11), and a statement of his credentials (1:12–17). He has left Timothy to ensure that no one teaches anything that is contrary to sound teaching (1:3, 10). Sound teaching coheres with the gospel that was entrusted to Paul (1:11), a theme that Paul develops in the undisputed letters (1 Thess. 2:4; cf. 1 Cor. 4:1) and Titus (Titus 1:3). Paul explains this trust in 1 Timothy 1:12–17, an autobiographical section that is reminiscent of the autobiographical sections in the undisputed letters in which Paul establishes his ethos. The familiar contrast between the believers' past and present is also Paul's own story, as he contrasts what he was formerly (*proteron*, 1:13) to what he is now. He describes himself in the past in unusually harsh terms as a blasphemer (*blasphēmos*), a persecutor (*diōktēs*), and a violent person (*hybristēs*), using

19. For the argument that all three Pastoral Epistles are loose collections of paraenetic material, see especially Dibelius and Conzelmann, *Pastoral Epistles*, 5.
20. See Van Neste, *Cohesion and Structure in the Pastoral Epistles*, 1–145; Gibson, "Literary and Theological Coherence of 1 Timothy"; O'Donnell, "Rhetorical Strategy of 1 Timothy."
21. Bush, "Note on the Structure of 1 Timothy."
22. Cf. Yarbrough, *Paul's Utilization of Preformed Traditions in 1 Timothy*, 150.

terms that he uses elsewhere only rarely (cf. Rom. 1:30; 2 Tim. 3:2). Indeed, he once had some of the characteristics that he attributes to the opposition. Like the opponents who are "without knowledge" (1 Tim. 1:7 AT), Paul once acted "in ignorance" (1:13 AT). His former life as a blasphemer is parallel to the practices of the opponents (1:20). His life as a violent man corresponds to the conduct of those who kill fathers and mothers (1:9). His radical break from persecutor to faithful witness is paradigmatic for others who make a radical change. Twice he says, "I received mercy" (1:13, 16), and mentions the grace that "abounded" to him (1:14; cf. Rom. 5:20).

At the center of his reflection is the creedal statement "Faithful is the saying, and worthy of all acceptance, that Christ came into the world to save sinners" (1 Tim. 1:15 AT). The saying recalls Paul's references to the saving effects of the incarnation. "Christ came into the world" recalls Paul's statements that "God sent his Son" (Rom. 8:3; Gal. 4:6 AT) and that the preexistent Christ "became poor" for our sakes (2 Cor. 8:9; cf. Phil. 2:6–7). This event is parallel to the references elsewhere to the event in the past when God's grace "appeared" (Titus 2:11; 3:4) and when he "was manifest in the flesh" (1 Tim. 3:16 AT). Thus the incarnation plays a significant role in the Pastoral Epistles. That Christ came "to save sinners" is the first of the creedal statements of 1 Timothy that summarize the basic proclamation and provide a window into Paul's soteriology. Salvation is universal in scope, for God desires that "all people be saved and come to a knowledge of the truth" (1 Tim. 2:4 AT). Paul elaborates on salvation with the creedal statements that follow throughout the argument (cf. 1 Tim. 2:4; 3:16; 4:10; cf. 2 Tim. 1:9; 4:18; Titus 3:5). This creed is a variant form of the most basic creed that "Christ died for our sins according to the Scriptures" (1 Cor. 15:3 AT).

With his radical change from being "the first of sinners" (1 Tim. 1:15 AT), Paul became the prototype and embodiment of the transforming effect of the gospel for Christian behavior (1 Tim. 1:16).[23] As he indicates throughout the Pastoral Epistles, he is the model for Timothy, and Timothy is the model for others (1 Tim. 4:11–16; 2 Tim. 3:10–15). Indeed, the goal for believers is "love from a pure heart, a good conscience, and sincere faith" (1 Tim. 1:5 AT). Consequently, the imperatives that follow focus largely on the conduct of believers who follow the examples of Paul and Timothy.

This section (1 Tim. 1:3–17) functions as both the exordium and the narratio of the letter. The antithetical examples of Paul and the opponents are similar to antithetical examples in ancient philosophical literature;[24] argu-

---

23. See Lohfink, "Paulinische Theologie," 80. See also Johnson, "1 Timothy 1:1–20," 31.
24. See Fiore, *Function of Personal Example*, 67.

ments from personal example are commonplace as means of persuasion in both rhetorical and epistolary literature.[25] Paul introduces the major themes of the letter—the moral formation that the gospel produces as the alternative to the ethical bankruptcy of those who do not adhere to sound instruction. Paul left Timothy to fight the good fight on his behalf (1:18) in the past, and he writes to Timothy to ensure the community's faithfulness in the future. Paul's indication of the transforming effect of the gospel on his life (1:12–17) establishes the foundation for the ethical instructions that follow. Paul thus introduces the argument with an appeal both to his ethos and to the Christian tradition, of which he is the trustee (1:11).

The first imperative of the letter appears in 1:18–20 as Paul turns from the past to the future. In the face of the threats to the faith, Timothy's task is to fight the fight. This is the heading for the argument in 2:1–6:2 and the propositio of the argument, which consists of imperatives detailing Timothy's task. With "faith and a good conscience" (1:19), Timothy is also the model of the transforming effect of the gospel (cf. 1:5) and the opposite of those who have made a shipwreck of the faith.

According to 2:1–6:2, Timothy fights the good fight by communicating the instructions from Paul. The argument consists of two major sections. In 2:1–3:13, Paul, having established his ethos (1:12–17), gives instructions for worship and leadership in the church, while in 4:1–15, he describes the dangers facing the church (cf. 1:3–11) before instructing Timothy to establish his own ethos (4:6–16) in order to give instructions concerning other members of the church: older people (5:1–2), widows (5:3–16), elders (5:17–22), Timothy himself (5:23–25), and slaves (6:1–2). At the center of the letter is the creedal statement (3:14–16), which both concludes the first section (2:1–3:13) and forms a bridge to the second section (4:1–6:2).

Paul initiates the instructions in 1 Timothy with the familiar "I urge" (*parakalō*, 2:1) and "I desire" (*boulomai*, 2:8) and continues with the third-person imperative (2:11, "Let the women learn in quietness," AT) and "it is necessary that" (3:2 AT) before speaking directly in the imperative to Timothy in chapters 4–6. In the argument (probatio, 2:1–6:2), Paul gives instructions involving the conduct of various members of the community, expanding on the household codes of Colossians (Col. 3:18–4:1) and Ephesians (Eph. 5:21–6:9) to include the house church.

---

25. Cf. Quintilian, *Inst.* 2.2.8: "For however many models for imitation he may give them from the authors they are reading, it will still be found that fuller nourishment is provided by the living voice, as we call it, more especially when it proceeds from the teacher himself, who, if his pupils are rightly instructed, should be the object of their affection and respect. And it is scarcely possible to say how much more readily we imitate those whom we like" (LCL).

As 1 Timothy 2:1–15 indicates, Timothy's first task is to ensure order in the assembly as the church fulfills its mission. In the opening line, Paul instructs Timothy to ensure that prayers are made "for all" (2:1), including kings and rulers—those who are outside the church. The focus on "all people" is indicated in the claim that God wants "all people to be saved and come to a knowledge of the truth" (2:4 AT). Paul supports his mandate for prayer for rulers and the desire to live a quiet and peaceful life with the creed. "There is one God" (2:5 AT) echoes 1 Corinthians 8:6, recalling the Shema. Paul elaborates on the Shema with the confession that Jesus Christ is the one mediator (*mesitēs*, cf. Gal. 3:19; Heb. 8:6). That he gave himself as a ransom (*antilytron*, 1 Tim. 2:6) recalls early soteriological claims, including the statement of Jesus (Mark 10:45) that the Son of Man came to give himself as "a ransom [*lytron*] for many." "For all" recalls 2 Corinthians 5:14–15 and connects with the will of God that all will be saved (1 Tim. 2:4). Thus Paul's appeal to the creed as the foundation of the argument is consistent with his argumentation in the undisputed letters. God's will that all will be saved is the foundation for the argument on the behavior of men and women and is programmatic for the entire letter.[26] The advice for men and women (1 Tim. 2:8–13) is supported also by an appeal to Scripture (1 Tim. 2:13–15), recalling the appeal to Scripture in a similar context (1 Cor. 14:34).

Timothy's task is also to ensure that pastoral roles are filled by those who have the qualities of character. Unlike the instructions given to Titus (Titus 1:5), the instructions on church offices in 1 Timothy 3 do not involve the establishment of a church order but of ensuring that the existing offices are held by people who have the appropriate qualities of character that are consistent with the gospel. These qualities are parallel, for the most part, to the attributes listed in Titus but unlike the ethical attributes commonly listed in the undisputed Pauline letters. Consistent with the theme of the church's separation from outsiders (cf. 1 Tim. 2:1–2; 5:14), these qualities have the approval of the surrounding world, giving the leaders a good reputation among outsiders (1 Tim. 3:7).

Although the moral qualities listed in 3:1–13 are consistent with the values of the larger environment, Christian conduct has a distinctive theological foundation, as Paul indicates in 3:14–16, appealing to a creedal statement as the foundation of the argument. Indeed, the purpose of the letter, as Paul has indicated earlier, is to teach the church how to act in his absence (1:3) and how to behave in the household of God, "the pillar and ground of the truth" (3:15). That is, like the undisputed letters of Paul, this letter is an appeal

26. Gibson, "Literary Coherence of 1 Timothy," 65.

for behavior that is consistent with the gospel. It is the theological center of 1 Timothy, for it is the foundation of both the instructions that precede it and those that come afterward.[27] This behavior has both an ecclesiological and a christological dimension.

1. Paul describes behavior in "the household of God, . . . the church" (1 Tim. 3:15). The image of the church as God's household (*oikos*) recalls Paul's frequent use of the language of the building as an image of the church (cf. 1 Cor. 3:9–17; 8:1; 14:1–5), especially his association of the church as the temple of the Holy Spirit (1 Cor. 3:16; 2 Cor. 6:16) and of the church as a building (*oikodomē*). This image is greatly expanded in Ephesians (2:19–21; 4:16). In contrast to the building metaphor in 1 Corinthians and Ephesians, the church is not built on a foundation but is the foundation—the pillar (*stylos*) and foundation (*edraiōma*)—of the truth. This truth is at the center of concern throughout the Pastoral Epistles. God's will is that "all people come to a knowledge of the truth" (1 Tim. 2:4; 2 Tim. 2:25 AT; cf. Titus 1:1), but some have missed out on the truth (1 Tim. 6:5; cf. 2 Tim. 3:8; Titus 1:14). The church is the bearer of the truth, which is the apparent equivalent of sound instruction. It is important to know how to behave in the household of God because of the surpassing greatness of God's house as "the pillar and ground of the truth" (1 Tim. 3:15 AT) that Paul wishes to preserve.

2. The truth that the church bears is evident in the confession that Paul recites in 1 Timothy 3:16. The community agrees (*homologoumenōs*) on the greatness of the mystery (3:16) of piety (*eusebeia*). This mystery is apparently the equivalent of "the mystery of faith" that church leaders hold (3:9). "The mystery of piety" in 3:16a (AT) is the mystery that leads to piety,[28] the comprehensive term in the Pastoral Epistles for the manner of life that characterizes believers (cf. 1 Tim. 2:2; 4:7–8; 6:3, 5–6; 2 Tim. 3:5; 5:4; Titus 1:1; 2:12). It is probably the umbrella term for the instructions that appear in the Pastoral Epistles. The mystery that leads to godliness is parallel to the instruction that is appropriate to sound teaching (Titus 2:1).

The fundamental proof for the moral life—and what the community agrees on—is the mystery that Paul recalls in 1 Timothy 3:16b. While the church is "the pillar and ground of the truth" (3:15), the christological confession in 3:16 is the mystery that constitutes the church. The hymn, the climactic part of the argument, is arranged in three couplets introduced by "who" as a reference to the Christ event. The three couplets all contain the aorist passive, with the

---

27. Roloff, *Der erste Brief an Timotheus*, 190.

28. The genitive *tēs eusebeias* is a genitive of direction (cf. BDF 166). Roloff, *Der erste Brief an Timotheus*, 201.

first and third pointing to the acts of God.[29] In contrast to the other hymns (cf. Phil. 2:6–11; Col. 1:15–20), this confession does not tell the story of Jesus in a strictly linear way but presents three contrasts between two spheres of reality—flesh and spirit (first strophe), angels (in heaven) and nations (on earth, second strophe), the world and glory (third strophe). Together they describe the universal impact of Christ. The contrast in the first strophe between flesh and Spirit recalls the confessional statement that Christ was born of the seed of David according to the flesh and was designated Son of God in power according to the Spirit of holiness (Rom. 1:3–4). The manifestation in the flesh is probably a reference to the initial appearance of Christ in the flesh (cf. 2 Tim. 1:10; Titus 2:11), while the vindication in the Spirit is the triumph over death and recalls the suffering servant's vindication after his suffering (Isa. 53:11).

The claim in the second strophe that Jesus "appeared to angels" may be a reference to the exaltation, while he was preached among the nations on earth. In the third strophe, preaching is followed by "he was believed" in the world and taken up in glory. This claim recalls the focus on descent and ascent among Paul and his predecessors (Phil. 2:6–11; cf. John 1:1–18; Heb. 1:1–4).

The hymnic confession is the centerpiece of 1 Timothy, the proof for the instructions in 2:1–3:13 and for the instructions that follow in 4:1–6:2. The christological message leads to piety, the religious practice that Paul inculcates. As with the undisputed letters, the concern of 1 Timothy is the moral formation of the community, which is based on the christological narrative.

Although the conclusion in 6:3–21 introduces new instructions (cf. 6:17–20), it also recapitulates much of the argument of the letter, functioning as the peroratio. The numerous points of correspondence between 1:3–20 and 6:3–21 indicate the significance of this section as the conclusion of the argument. In addition, the moral qualities Paul urges Timothy to emulate (righteousness, piety, faith, love, endurance, humility, 6:11) reiterate the earlier encouragement for Timothy to be an example of moral formation (cf. 4:11).

While differences in terminology distinguish 1 Timothy from the undisputed letters of Paul, the goal of the letter is consistent with them. First Timothy is a cohesive letter intended to instruct the readers how to behave in the house of God (3:15). As in the undisputed letters, this letter appeals to creedal formulations—the assumptions shared by the readers—as a foundation for the exhortation. With its focus on persuasion and dissuasion, it has affinities to deliberative rhetoric,[30] but it differs from ancient rhetoric in its appeal to convictions that are shared only within this subculture.

---

29. Roloff, *Der erste Brief an Timotheus*, 204.
30. Harding, *Tradition and Rhetoric*, 189.

Persuasion in 2 Timothy

In contrast to 1 Timothy and Titus, 2 Timothy is not a letter of instruction that Paul gives to a church through an emissary, and it contains instructions for neither church order nor specific groups within the church. Of the three Pastoral Epistles, only 2 Timothy is written from a Roman prison (cf. 2 Tim. 2:16–17) as Paul anticipates his death (2 Tim. 4:6–8). The focus is on Timothy's role in Paul's absence. Thus the letter resembles the familiar last will and testament in which a dying person gives instructions to successors. This genre frequently offers moral advice to those who remain after the author's death.

The Rhetorical Situation

The letter reflects a critical time in the life of the church, for in Paul's absence, threatening forces are already at work. Some have turned away (cf. 2 Tim. 1:15), and others have abandoned Paul's mission (2 Tim. 4:10). As in 1 Timothy and Titus, we receive only scattered descriptions of the opposition (cf. 2 Tim. 2:17–18; 4:3–4), which is known also in 2 Timothy for its moral degeneration (cf. 2 Tim. 3:1–9). As the repeated "but you" indicates (2 Tim. 3:10; 4:5; cf. 2:1), the internal opposition serves as a foil for the conduct that Paul encourages Timothy to maintain.

The Argument

Second Timothy is an exercise in persuasion characterized by the sequence of imperatives (2 Tim. 1:6, 8; 2:1–3, 14, 22; 3:10; 4:5). Both the salutation (1:1–2) and the thanksgiving (1:3–5) lay the foundation for the argument. The credentials in 1:1 ("Paul an apostle of Jesus Christ through the will of God," AT) indicate the prophetic voice that stands behind the imperatives to Timothy. Like the undisputed letters, 2 Timothy begins with a thanksgiving, a report of Paul's prayers (cf. Rom. 1:9; Phil. 1:3; 1 Thess. 1:2). He appeals to pathos in his expression of his desire to see Timothy and his memory of the latter's tears (2 Tim. 1:4).[31] Just as Paul's thanksgiving in earlier letters involved "remembering" (mnēmoneuein) the good qualities of the recipients (cf. Rom. 1:9; Phil. 1:3; 1 Thess. 1:3), Paul now remembers Timothy's legacy of faith. The confidence in Timothy's current faith (pistis) and the expression of affection build goodwill for the recipient. The reference to Timothy's pistis anticipates Paul's continuing focus on one of the essential characteristics of Christian formation

---

31. The assurance of desiring to see the addressee was commonplace in letters of friendship and in the Pauline literature (cf. Rom. 15:23; Phil. 1:8). See the relevant texts in Wolter, *Die Pastoralbriefe*, 206–7.

(cf. 2 Tim. 2:22; 3:8, 10), which is consistent with the undisputed letters. As in the undisputed letters, the thanksgiving functions as a *captatio benevolentiae*, the exordium that creates goodwill and introduces the subject that follows.

This legacy is the background for the purpose of the letter, which Paul states in 1:6–8. Paul writes to "rekindle the gift [*charisma*] . . . that is in [Timothy] through the laying on of hands" (2 Tim. 1:6 AT; cf. 1 Tim. 4:14). Before he speaks in the imperative, he recalls the gift of power, love, and self-control, indicating that these moral qualities are a gift of the Spirit (cf. Rom. 8:1–11; Gal. 5:22–25). By the power of God, Timothy will suffer along with Paul (2 Tim. 1:8). While love (*agapē*) is a gift, it is also a moral quality that Paul encourages Timothy to pursue (cf. 2 Tim. 2:22; 3:10). Self-discipline (*sōphronismos*) is also a gift of the Spirit that enables Timothy to fulfill his mission.

The gift is the presupposition for the imperatives that follow. The first ones appear in 1:8: "Do not be ashamed of the witness and of me his prisoner" and "suffer with me in the gospel according to the power of God" (AT). This first imperative is the *propositio* of the letter, which consistently describes the suffering in the gospel (cf. 2:3, 9; 4:5), following the example of Paul (cf. 1:12; 3:11–12). To suffer in the gospel echoes the undisputed Pauline letters (cf. Phil. 1:7; 4:3). The summary of the gospel (2 Tim. 1:9–11; cf. 1 Tim. 1:15; Titus 2:11–14; 3:3–7) also echoes the undisputed letters (cf. Rom. 5:7–8; 1 Cor. 15:3; 2 Cor. 5:14–15). He repeats the familiar Pauline theme that salvation is by grace and the sovereignty of God apart from works, and he declares that the community lives at the turn of the ages.

In 2 Timothy 1:11–18, Paul offers examples for the conduct that Timothy should adopt as he suffers for the message. Having instructed Timothy not to be ashamed of the message, Paul declares that he is not ashamed as he suffers for the gospel (1:12). He insists that God is able to guard his "deposit" (1:12), and he encourages Timothy to "guard the deposit" as well (1:14 AT). Indeed, Paul is the model (*hypotyōsis*) of sound words and behavior characterized by faith and love (1:13; cf. 3:10). He offers further positive and negative examples of this conduct, recalling that some have left him, including Phygelus and Hermogenes, but that the household of Onesiphorus was not ashamed of his bonds. Thus Paul argues from *exempla* for the moral conduct that he encourages Timothy to maintain.

In 2:1–3:17, Paul turns from past examples to Timothy's future conduct in a sequence of imperatives punctuated with "you, therefore" (2:1; 3:10, 14), which present a contrast between Timothy and the negative examples as Paul elaborates on the commands he gave in 1:6–8. The challenge to "be strong" (*endynamou*, 2:1) echoes the charge given in the Old Testament to one who is given a mission to perform (cf. Exod. 4:12–13; 1 Chron. 9:13;

1 QSa 1.17–18), suggesting that God's power is present with the individual.[32] This opening charge resonates especially with the commissioning of Joshua by Moses (cf. Deut. 31:7, 23; Josh. 1:6–7, 18). Having been told to "guard the deposit" (2 Tim. 1:14 AT), Timothy is now to commit the deposit to others (2:1–2) and suffer with Paul (2:3–7), a command that Paul reinforces with exempla from several areas of life—the military, athletics, and agriculture.

The next imperative, "Remember Jesus Christ" (2:8), is accompanied by the creedal statement "Jesus Christ, raised from the dead, of the seed of David" (AT), followed by the exemplum of Paul's own suffering (2:9–10) and the faithful saying (2:11–13) that is apparently common knowledge within the community.

In 2:14–26, Paul further elaborates on the qualities of character expected of his emissary in contrast to the negative behavior of the false teachers. Timothy's challenge is to avoid what they embody and to follow the ideal of formation that is described in 2:22–26. The qualities of character are also common in the undisputed Pauline letters. Timothy's task to "pursue [*diōke*] righteousness" (2:22; cf. 1 Tim. 6:11) recalls Paul's pursuit of Christ (Phil. 3:12) and his instructions to pursue other moral qualities (cf. Rom. 12:13; 14:19). Righteousness (*dikaiosynē*), faith (*pistis*), love, and peace (2 Tim. 2:22) are also the moral qualities that Paul inculcates for his communities in the undisputed letters (cf. Gal. 5:22–25). Paul further encourages Timothy to teach with humility (*prautēs*, 2 Tim. 2:25). Thus Timothy is to embody the moral formation that characterizes the whole church—those who call on the Lord (2:22). This conduct is consistent with the ideal of moral formation in the undisputed letters.

In 3:1–17, Paul presents the contrast between the moral bankruptcy of the false teachers (3:1–9) and the conduct of Timothy (3:10–17), whose task is to follow the example of Paul, who has demonstrated the moral qualities of teaching, conduct, faith, patience, love, and endurance as he suffers for the gospel. Paul concludes with a peroratio in 4:1–5, repeating the contrast between the others and Timothy ("but you," 4:5; cf. 3:10, 14). The concluding words "suffer evil" reiterate a common theme in the letter (4:5 AT).

Conclusion: Persuasion in the Pastoral Epistles and the Pauline Tradition

Scholars have frequently observed the unique theological vocabulary that the Pastoral Epistles share with each other that distinguishes them from the

32. Wolter, *Die Pastoralbriefe*, 217.

undisputed letters. Moreover, while the Pastoral Epistles share with all of
Paul's other works the epistolary genre, they are unlike the others. Indeed,
the parallels between 1 Timothy and Titus and the *mandata principis* shape
the nature of the persuasion, and the adaptation of the familiar last will and
testament in 2 Timothy also distinguishes it from the other letters. Thus with
the predominance of the imperative and the absence of extended argumentation in the Pastoral Epistles, much of the argumentative texture of the other
letters disappears.

Despite these differences from the earlier writings, the Pastoral Epistles exhibit considerable continuity with the letters to the churches. In all three letters,
Paul indicates that gentile converts have now entered Israel's narrative world,
which began "before the ages" (2 Tim. 1:9; Titus 1:2) and will come to an end
with the future epiphany of the Lord (1 Tim. 6:14; 2 Tim. 4:1, 8; Titus 2:13).
The church now lives between the times—between the first epiphany (Titus
2:11; cf. 1 Tim. 3:16; 2 Tim. 2:10) of the Lord and his second epiphany (Titus
2:13). Paul anticipates the second epiphany as the time of judgment (2 Tim.
4:1), which will be on the basis of works (1 Tim. 5:24–25; cf. 2 Tim. 4:8; Titus
2:13). He gives no indication of the time of the event, but he assures his readers that it will be "in [God's] own time" (1 Tim. 6:15 AT). These themes are
consistent with the undisputed letters, according to which "each will receive
recompense for what has been done in the body, whether good or evil" (2 Cor.
5:10 AT; cf. Rom. 14:12). While the Pastoral Epistles give no indication of the
imminence of the end, the undisputed letters also give no uniform perspective on the time of the end; 2 Corinthians, Galatians, and Philippians do not
indicate an expectation that the return of Christ is imminent.

As in the earlier letters, the turn of the ages is the coming of Christ and
the salvation that brought gentile converts into the narrative of Israel. The
creedal statements reflect the understanding of the Christology and soteriology of the Pastoral Epistles. Christ is the preexistent one who "came into the
world" (1 Tim. 1:15)—that is, "was manifest in the flesh" (1 Tim. 3:16 AT) as
a descendant of David (2 Tim. 2:8). He saved us, "giving himself as a ransom
for all" (1 Tim. 2:6 AT; cf. Titus 2:14) as an expression of the kindness, good-
ness (*philanthrōpia*), and mercy of God (Titus 3:3, 5). He was then raised
from the dead (2 Tim. 2:8), "vindicated in the Spirit" (1 Tim. 3:16 AT), and
"taken up in glory" (1 Tim. 3:16). These are the premises of the argument of
the Pastoral Epistles. While the vocabulary differs from that of the undisputed
letters of Paul, the Christian tradition known to Paul is also central to the
argument of the Pastoral Epistles.

While the vocabulary of moral formation in the Pastoral Epistles differs
from that of the undisputed letters, the concern in all three letters is the ethical

life of Paul's emissaries and his churches. The statement "the goal [*telos*] of our instruction is love from a pure heart, a good conscience, and sincere faith" (1 Tim. 1:5 AT) is programmatic for the three Pastoral Epistles. Faith and love remain the central categories of the moral life (cf. 1 Tim. 1:14; 2:15; 2 Tim. 1:13). Paul has been the model of faith, patience, love, and steadfastness (2 Tim. 3:10), and he encourages Timothy to be a model to others of "love, faith, and purity" (1 Tim. 4:12) and to pursue "righteousness, godliness, faith, love, endurance, gentleness" (1 Tim. 6:11). His challenge for Timothy to "keep the commandment without spot or blemish until the epiphany of our Lord Jesus Christ" (1 Tim. 6:14 AT) echoes the consistent theme in the undisputed letters—and Colossians and Ephesians—of the goal of a blameless people at the end. Thus the Pastoral Epistles maintain the Pauline theology of transformation.

The argument from example is fundamental to both the Pastoral Epistles and the undisputed letters. As one whose existence has been transformed, Paul is an example (*hypotypōsis*) for future believers (1 Tim. 1:16) of a way of life (2 Tim. 3:10); and especially an example of suffering (cf. 2 Tim. 1:8, 12; 2:3, 9; 3:11–12). Even where Paul does not specifically mention his example, he serves that function, particularly in 2 Timothy 4:1–8, where he is the paradigmatic martyr. Paul is an example to Timothy, who, along with Titus (cf. Titus 2:7), is an example for others. This theme continues the frequent appeal to Paul's example in the undisputed letters (cf. 1 Cor. 11:1; Phil. 3:17) and autobiographical reflections (cf. 2 Cor. 4:10–11; Phil. 1:12–26; 3:2–21).[33]

As in the undisputed letters, Paul's argument for moral formation is based also on premises drawn from the Christian tradition. He rarely appeals to authoritative Scripture (cf. 1 Tim. 2:13–15), but his argument is commonly based on creedal statements (cf. 1 Tim. 1:15; 2:5–6; 3:16; 2 Tim. 1:9–10; 2:11–13; Titus 2:11–14; 3:3–7) and the common assumptions of the community—the faithful sayings (cf. 1 Tim. 1:15; 3:1; 4:9; 2 Tim. 2:11; Titus 3:8). Thus the argument of the Pastoral Epistles, like that of the undisputed letters, is based on premises that would have been persuasive only to those who acknowledged the validity of the Christian confession.

33. See Lohfink, "Paulinische Theologie," 79–83.

Conclusion

Paul's Pastoral Theology

Despite Paul's frequent claims that he does not, like the rhetoricians, persuade others (cf. 1 Cor. 2:4; Gal. 1:10; 1 Thess. 2:4), all of his letters are exercises in persuasion. Although he employs some of the conventions of letter writing, he "destroys arguments" (2 Cor. 10:4 AT) in a way that was unparalleled in both Jewish and Greco-Roman letters. While one can classify his arguments according to the categories established for orators (ethos, pathos, logos), his arguments are primarily based on premises that are intelligible only within the subculture of believers. In other words, argumentation for Paul involves theologizing.

While one may analyze both Paul's theology and his rhetoric, both must be seen within Paul's larger aim. As his letters consistently indicate, his primary aim is to present a transformed people to Christ at the end, and he writes letters to ensure that his work is not in vain (cf. 2 Cor. 6:2; Gal. 4:11; Phil. 2:16; 1 Thess. 2:1, 4; 3:5). Theology and persuasion are the means toward that goal, for the ultimate outcome of the churches remains in doubt in the midst of both internal and external challenges.

Paul's Basic Convictions

All of Paul's letters presuppose basic convictions that provide the foundation for his arguments. He maintains the inherited beliefs and categories from Pharisaic Judaism, according to which the church lives in continuity with Israel's narrative as God's elect (cf. 1 Thess. 1:4) and holy (cf. 1 Thess. 3:11–13) people, worshiping Israel's God, keeping the commandments (1 Cor. 7:19; cf. 1 Thess. 4:1–8), and awaiting the conclusion of the narrative.

From Jesus and the early church, Paul has inherited the convictions that both reiterate and transform traditional beliefs. The new age of Pharisaic expectation has arrived, and the messiah of their expectation is Jesus, who is Christ, Son of God, and Lord. God has poured out the Spirit, and the community now reads Scripture through the lenses of the Christ event. Thus the death of Christ was "for our sins in accordance with the scriptures" (1 Cor. 15:3), and the Pharisaic hope for the resurrection has become a reality in Jesus, who is now the exalted Lord at God's right hand. Paul has also inherited the conviction that "the day of the Lord" of Jewish expectation is now "the day of Christ," when the exalted one returns.

Paul's basic convictions are also shaped by his call and conversion. Living out the narrative of Scripture, he envisions the era when the good news goes out to the nations (Isa. 49:6; 52:7), and he is its messenger (Isa. 49:6). The death of Christ "for our sins" includes not only Israel in exile but also all of the nations. From his letters, we know only of his work among gentile churches, which have been brought within Israel's narrative. Paul hopes that his ministry through visits and letters will result in the formation of communities into the image of Christ (2 Cor. 3:18; Gal. 4:19). His theologizing involves his own prophetic consciousness and the working out of the implications of the basic premises that he inherited.

Paul consistently presupposes that the gentile church not only lives in continuity with Israel but also is the restored people who have returned from exile. His echoes of the exilic prophets—Deutero-Isaiah, Jeremiah, and Ezekiel—indicate that the community now lives in the new era that these promised earlier. He consistently assumes that the eschatological outpouring of the Spirit has taken place (cf. Ezek. 11:19; 36:25–26) and that the new covenant promised by Jeremiah is a reality (cf. Isa. 55:3; 61:8; Jer. 31:31–34; cf. 1 Cor. 11:25; 2 Cor. 3:6). Consequently, Paul expects that the people of the new covenant, unlike preexilic Israel, will now be empowered to do the will of God, as both Jeremiah and Ezekiel promised (cf. Jer. 31:31; Ezek. 11:20; 36:27). The focus on the behavior of the people in the paraenetic sections of all of the letters presupposes that the renewed people will not be enslaved to sin but will keep the commandments (1 Cor. 7:19). The claim in Romans that "the just requirement of the law might be fulfilled in us" (Rom. 8:4) assumes that the community is the renewed people of God envisioned by the exilic prophets. Indeed, despite Paul's negative comments about the law (cf. Rom. 4:15; 7:7–25; Gal. 3:10–14), he envisions a community that is faithful to the renewed covenant, which does not include the common Jewish boundary markers (circumcision, Sabbath, food laws) but is "fulfilled" in the love commandment (cf. Rom. 13:8–10; Gal. 5:14). The moral instructions that Paul gives in the paraeneses depict the renewed covenant, which includes precepts from the Jewish moral tradition that can be practiced in a multiethnic community.[1]

While Paul does not elaborate on Christology, he assumes throughout his letters that the exalted Lord is also the inclusive person and that believers exist "in him" (cf. Gal. 3:28–29; Phil. 2:5) and share a destiny "with him" (cf. Rom. 6:3–4, 6, 8; 8:17, 29; 2 Cor. 4:14; 13:4; Gal. 2:19; Phil. 3:10, 21; 1 Thess. 4:14, 17).[2] Consequently, loyalty to the risen Christ is exclusive. Whether to Corinthians who boast of human wisdom (cf. 1 Cor. 3:18–21) or to Roman readers who boast in the law (Rom. 2:17), Paul insists that one may boast "only in the Lord" (1 Cor. 1:31; 2 Cor. 10:17). Paul's claim that he died to the law in order to live for the Lord is paradigmatic for other believers (Gal. 2:19; cf. Rom. 14:7–8; 2 Cor. 5:15). Believers not only keep the commandments but also participate in the suffering and triumph of Christ. Those who are being transformed (2 Cor. 3:18) into the image of the crucified Lord in the present will ultimately be transformed (Rom. 8:29; Phil. 3:21) and sanctified (1 Thess. 3:13; cf. Rom. 15:16). Paul's persuasive task is to ensure the ultimate transformation.

Paul's Theology and Rhetoric

Theology plays a vital role in Paul's persuasive task. Indeed, in one instance, after he comments "We persuade others" (2 Cor. 5:11 AT), he indicates the importance of theological competence by his readers: "So that you may be able to boast on our behalf to those who boast in outward appearance" (2 Cor. 5:12 AT). What follows is a dense theological defense of Paul's ministry and a window into the place of theology in Paul's persuasive task (2 Cor. 5:11–6:2). He appeals both to his prophetic call and to the community's traditions (2 Cor. 5:14, 18–19, 21) as the basis for his persuasion.

In 1 Thessalonians, which is probably his earliest letter, Paul employs theological categories as he continues his earlier encouragement for readers to be transformed and sanctified before the end (cf. 1 Thess. 2:12; 3:11–13). He places the exalted Lord alongside God (1 Thess. 1:1, 9–10; 3:11–13) without elaborating on his Christology. He speaks of their election (1:4), holiness (3:11–13), and possession of the Holy Spirit (4:8) without elaborating on these themes. He also initiates them into Israel's narrative world, which will

---

1. See Thompson, *Moral Formation according to Paul*, 207–13. Paul is also familiar, to some extent, with the Greek moral tradition, which may have come to him from Hellenistic Jewish sources.

2. See Gorman, *Cruciformity*, 45–46.

end with the day of the Lord (5:2). Writing both to comfort and to encourage the Thessalonians, he offers a vision of the end that should sustain them as their faith is tested (4:13–5:11). In subsequent letters, he expands on these themes in response to the issues that emerge. Since the major themes of his theology are introduced in 1 Thessalonians, one can scarcely describe 1 Thessalonians as an example of early Pauline theology. Even the themes that are absent from 1 Thessalonians, including justification by faith, are implicit in the letter. It was in response to the issues in his churches that he worked out the implications of his basic convictions.

In other words, Paul's theology serves a rhetorical purpose. In his description of the end, for example, he does not lay out a plan for the sequence of events but first invites the Thessalonians to enter into a vision of God's ultimate triumph. Consequently, one cannot trace the development in Paul's eschatology, for in each case, he develops a vision for rhetorical effect, drawing on a storehouse of Jewish apocalyptic images. While he maintains the inherited conviction of the ultimate triumph of God, he describes it in various ways for persuasive effect. Thus theology and rhetoric are intertwined in Paul's eschatological statements.

While Paul inherited the conviction that "Christ died for our sins," he expresses his theology of the cross in different ways. Against the Corinthians' understanding of community, which was shaped by Greco-Roman culture, the cross is the basis for a new epistemology (1 Cor. 2:6–16) that turns worldly values upside down. As the symbol of self-denial, the cross becomes the foundation for ethics (cf. 1 Cor. 8:11; 11:17–34) and the reality in which believers participate (cf. 1 Cor. 4:9–12; 2 Cor. 1:3–11; 4:7–15; 5:11–21). While Paul employs the language of participation in the cross, especially in 2 Corinthians, he employs the forensic images of justification in Galatians (2:16–21) and Romans (cf. 3:21–26) in describing the meaning of the cross. Faced with new circumstances in Galatians and Romans—the admission of gentiles into the community—Paul appeals to the cross as God's means of creating a united church. The death of Christ "for us" now includes both Jews and gentiles.

Paul's puzzling claim that "all Israel will be saved" (Rom. 11:26), which appears to be in conflict with Paul's statements elsewhere (1 Thess. 2:15–16; cf. Gal. 4:21–31), addresses gentile arrogance (Rom. 11:13–24), offering a reason the gentiles should not be "wise among themselves" (Rom. 11:25 AT; cf. 12:3, 16). Beginning with the premise that the narrative of Deutero-Isaiah is being fulfilled in the mission to the gentiles, he also returns to the prophet's announcement that the redeemer will turn disobedience away from Israel (Rom. 11:26; cf. Isa. 59:20). The rhetorical situation in Rome—the boasting of the gentiles (Rom. 11:18)—has led Paul to explore new dimensions of his reading of Isaiah.

To interpret Paul is to acknowledge both the theological and the rhetorical layers of his communication, which exist in a dialectical relationship to each other. Inasmuch as he has firm convictions, one cannot reduce his theologizing to mere strategy. Nor is he a theologian whose ideas develop apart from the dialogue with his churches. Starting with his basic convictions, he both makes theological arguments and speaks for rhetorical effect with the larger aim of ensuring the transformation of his churches into the image of Christ.

Bibliography

Adams, Sean A. "Paul's Letter Opening and Greek Epistolography: A Matter of Re-lationship." In *Paul and the Ancient Letter Form*, edited by Stanley E. Porter and Sean A. Adams, 33–56. Pauline Studies 6. Leiden: Brill, 2010.

Aletti, Jean-Noël. *God's Justice in Romans: Keys for Interpreting the Epistle to the Romans*. Translated by Peggy Manning Meyer. Rome: Gregorian and Biblical Press, 2010.

———. "The Rhetoric of Romans 5–8." In *The Rhetorical Analysis of Scripture: Essays from the 1995 London Conference*, edited by Stanley E. Porter and Thomas H. Olbricht, 294–308. Journal for the Study of the New Testament Supplement Series 146. Sheffield: Sheffield Academic, 1997.

———. *Saint Paul: Épitre aux Colossiens*. Études Biblique 2/30. Paris: Gabaldi, 1993.

Allison, Dale. *Constructing Jesus: Memory, Imagination, and History*. Grand Rapids: Baker Academic, 2010.

Anderson, R. Dean. *Ancient Rhetorical Theory and Paul*. Rev. ed. Leuven: Peeters, 1998.

———. *Glossary of Greek Rhetorical Terms Connected to Methods of Argumentation, Figures and Tropes from Anaximenes to Quintilian*. Leiden: Brill, 2000.

Arzt, Peter. "The 'Epistolary Introductory Thanksgiving' in the Papyri and in Paul." *Novum Testamentum* 36 (1994): 29–46.

Arzt-Grabner, Peter. "Paul's Letter Thanksgiving." In *Paul and the Ancient Letter Form*, edited by Stanley E. Porter and Sean A. Adams, 129–58. Pauline Studies 6. Leiden: Brill, 2010.

Aune, David E. "*Ēthos*." In *The Westminster Dictionary of the New Testament and Early Christian Rhetoric*, 169–73. Louisville: Westminster John Knox, 2002.

———. *The New Testament in Its Literary Environment*. Philadelphia: Westminster, 1987.

———. *The Westminster Dictionary of the New Testament and Early Christian Rhetoric*. Louisville: Westminster John Knox, 2003.

Balz, Horst, and Gerhard Schneider, eds. *Exegetical Dictionary of the New Testament*. Eng. trans. 3 vols. Grand Rapids: Eerdmans, 1990–93.

Barclay, John M. G. "Believer and the 'Last Judgment' in Paul: Rethinking Grace and Recompense." In *Eschatologie/Eschatology: The Sixth Durham-Tübingen Research Symposium; Eschatology in Old Testament, Ancient Judaism and Early Christianity (Tübingen, September 2009)*, edited by Hans-Joachim Eckstein, Christof Landmesser, Hermann Lichtenberger, Jens Adam, and Martin Bauspiess, 195–208. Wissenschaftliche Untersuchungen zum Neuen Testament 272. Tübingen: Mohr Siebeck, 2011.

———. *Jews in the Mediterranean Diaspora: From Alexander to Trajan (323 BCE–117 CE)*. Berkeley: University of California Press, 1996.

———. "Mirror Reading a Polemical Letter: Galatians as a Test Case." *Journal for the Study of the New Testament* 31 (1987): 73–93.

———. *Paul and the Gift*. Grand Rapids: Eerdmans, 2015.

Bauckham, Richard. "The Worship of Jesus in Philippians 2:9–11." In *Where Christology Began: Essays on Philippians 2*, edited by Ralph P. Martin and Brian J. Dodd, 128–39. Louisville: Westminster John Knox, 1998.

Bauer, W., F. W. Danker, W. F. Arndt, and F. W. Gingrich, eds. *A Greek-English Lexicon of the New Testament and Other Early Christian Literature*. 3rd ed. Chicago: University of Chicago Press, 2000.

Beale, Gregory K. "The Old Testament Background of Reconciliation in 2 Corinthians 5–7 and Its Bearing on the Literary Problem of 2 Corinthians." *New Testament Studies* 35 (1989): 550–81.

Becker, Jürgen. *Paul: Apostle to the Gentiles*. Louisville: Westminster John Knox, 1993.

Beker, J. Christiaan. *Paul the Apostle: The Triumph of God in Life and Thought*. Philadelphia: Fortress, 1980.

———. "Paul's Theology: Consistent or Inconsistent?" *New Testament Studies* 34 (1988): 364–77.

Berger, Klaus. "Apostelbrief and apostolische Rede." *Zeitschrift für die neutestamentliche Wissenschaft* 65 (1974): 193–227.

———. *Formen und Gattungen im Neuen Testament*. Uni-Taschenbücher 2532. Tübingen: Francke, 2005.

Betz, Hans Dieter. *Galatians: A Commentary on Paul's Letter to the Galatians*. Hermeneia. Philadelphia: Fortress, 1979.

———. "The Problem of Rhetoric and Theology according to the Apostle Paul." In *L'Apôtre Paul: Personalité, Style et Conception du Ministère*, edited by A. Vanhoye, 16–38. Leuven: Leuven University Press, 1986.

Bieringer, Reimund. "Dying and Being Raised For: Shifts in the Meaning of ὑπέρ in 2 Cor 5:14–15." In *Theologizing in the Corinthian Conflict: Studies in the Exegesis and Theology of 2 Corinthians*, edited by Reimund Bieringer, Ma Marilou S. Ibita, Dominika A. Kurek-Chomycz, and Thomas A. Vollmer, 163–76. Biblical Tools and Studies 16. Leuven: Peeters, 2013.

———. "Sünde und Gerechtigkeit 2 Korinther 5,21." In Bieringer and Lambrecht, *Studies on 2 Corinthians*, 461–514.

———. "2 Korinther 5,14a und die Versöhnung der Welt." In Bieringer and Lambrecht, *Studies on 2 Corinthians*, 429–59.

Bieringer, Reimund, and J. Lambrecht, eds. *Studies on 2 Corinthians*. Bibliotheca Ephemeridum Theologicarum Lovaniensium 112. Leuven: Leuven University Press, 1994.

Bird, Michael F. *An Anomalous Jew: Paul among Jews, Greeks, and Romans*. Grand Rapids: Eerdmans, 2016.

Blass, F., A. Debrunner, and R. W. Funk. *A Greek Grammar of the New Testament and Other Early Christian Literature*. Chicago: University of Chicago Press, 1961.

Boccaccini, Gabriele, Carlos A. Segovia, and Cameron J. Doody, eds. *Paul the Jew: Rereading the Apostle as a Figure of Second Temple Judaism*. Minneapolis: Fortress, 2016.

Bousset, Wilhelm. *Kyrios Christos: A History of the Belief in Christ from the Beginning of Christianity to Irenaeus*. Translated by John E. Steely. New York: Abingdon, 1970.

Broekhoven, Harold Van. "Persuasion or Praise in Colossians." *Proceedings of the 1995 Conference of the Eastern Great Lakes and Midwest Biblical Societies* 15 (1995): 65–78.

Brown, Alexandra. *The Cross and Human Transformation: Paul's Apocalyptic Word in 1 Corinthians*. Minneapolis: Fortress, 1995.

Bultmann, Rudolf. *Der Stil der paulinischen Predigt und die kynisch-stoische Diatribe*. Göttingen: Vandenhoeck & Ruprecht, 1910.

——— *Theology of the New Testament*. Translated by Kendrick Grobel. Vol. 1. London: SCM, 1952.

Bush, Peter. "A Note on the Structure of 1 Timothy." *New Testament Studies* 36 (1990): 152–56.

Chadwick, Henry. "St. Paul and Philo of Alexandria." *Bulletin of the John Rylands Library* 48 (1965–66): 286–308.

Charlesworth, James H., ed. *Old Testament Pseudepigrapha*. 2 vols. New York: Doubleday, 1983–85.

———. "Paul, the Jewish Apocalypses, and Apocalyptic Eschatology." In *Paul the Jew*, edited by Gabriele Boccaccini, Carlos A. Segovia, and Cameron J. Doody, 83–106. Minneapolis: Fortress, 2016.

Chester, Andrew. *Future Hope and Present Reality*. Vol. 1, *Eschatology and Transformation in the Hebrew Bible*. Wissenschaftliche Untersuchungen zum Neuen Testament 293. Tübingen: J. C. B. Mohr, 2012.

Ciampa, Roy E. "Paul's Theology of the Gospel." In *Paul as Missionary: Identity, Activity, Theology, and Practice*, edited by Trevor J. Burke and Brian S. Rosner, 180–92. The Library of New Testament Studies 420. London: T&T Clark, 2011.

Classen, Carl Joachim. "Can the Theory of Rhetoric Help Us to Understand the New Testament, and in Particular the Letters of Paul?" In *Paul and Ancient Rhetoric: Theory and Practice in the Hellenistic Context*, edited by Stanley E. Porter and Bryan R. Dyer, 13–39. Cambridge: Cambridge University Press, 2016.

———. *Rhetorical Criticism of the New Testament*. Wissenschaftliche Untersuchungen zum Neuen Testament 128. Tübingen: Mohr Siebeck, 1992.

———. "A Rhetorical Reading of the Epistle to Titus." In *The Rhetorical Analysis of Scripture: Essays from the 1995 London Conference*, edited by Stanley E. Porter and Thomas H. Olbricht, 427–44. Journal for the Study of the New Testament Supplement Series 146. Sheffield: Sheffield Academic, 1997.

Collins, Raymond F. "The Theology of the Epistle to Titus." *Ephemerides theologicae Lovanienses* 76 (2000): 56–72.

Conley, Thomas M. "Philo of Alexandria." In *Handbook of Classical Rhetoric in the Hellenistic Period, 330 B.C.–A.D. 400*, edited by Stanley E. Porter, 695–713. Leiden: Brill, 1997.

Copenhaver, Adam. "Echoes of a Hymn in a Letter of Paul: The Rhetorical Function of the Christ-Hymn in the Letter to the Colossians." *Journal of Paul and His Letters* 4 (2014): 235–55.

Cosby, Michael R. "Galatians: Red-Hot Rhetoric." In *Rhetorical Argumentation in Biblical Texts: Essays from the Lund 2000 Conference*, edited by Anders Eriksson, Thomas H. Olbricht, and Walter Übelacker, 296–309. Emory Studies in Early Christianity 8. Harrisburg, PA: Trinity Press International, 2002.

Cousar, Charles B. "The Theological Task of 1 Corinthians: A Conversation with Gordon D. Fee and Victor Paul Furnish." In *Pauline Theology*. Vol. 2, *1 and 2 Corinthians*, 90–102. Minneapolis: Fortress, 1993.

Deines, R. "The Pharisees between 'Judaisms' and 'Common Judaism.'" In *Justification and Variegated Nomism*. Vol. 1, *The Complexities of Second Temple Judaism*, 443–504. Grand Rapids: Baker Academic, 2001.

Deissmann, Adolf. *Bible Studies*. Edinburgh: T&T Clark, 1901.

———. *Light from the Ancient East: The New Testament Illustrated by Recently Discovered Texts of the Graeco-Roman World*. 4th ed. London: Hodder & Stoughton, 1927.

Dibelius, Martin, and Hans Conzelmann. *The Pastoral Epistles*. Hermeneia. Philadelphia: Fortress, 1972.

DiCicco, Mario M. *Paul's Use of Ēthos, Pathos, and Logos in 2 Corinthians 10–13.* Mellen Biblical Press Series 31. Lewiston, NY: Mellen, 1995.

Dodd, Brian. *Paul's Paradigmatic "I": Personal Example as Literary Strategy.* Journal for the Study of the New Testament Supplement Series 177. Sheffield: Sheffield Academic, 1999.

Dodd, C. H. *The Apostolic Preaching and Its Developments.* New York: Harper & Row, 1964.

Dübbers, Michael. *Christologie und Existenz im Kolosserbrief: Exegetische und semantische Untersuchugen zur Intention des Kolosserbriefes.* Wissenschaftliche Untersuchungen zum Neuen Testament 2/191. Tübingen: Mohr Siebeck, 2005.

Dunn, James D. G. *Beginning from Jerusalem.* Grand Rapids: Eerdmans, 2009.

———. *Did the First Christians Worship Jesus? The New Testament Evidence.* Louisville: Westminster John Knox, 2010.

———. *The Epistles to the Colossians and to Philemon.* New International Greek Testament Commentary. Grand Rapids: Eerdmans, 1996.

———. *The Theology of Paul the Apostle.* Grand Rapids: Eerdmans, 1998.

Eckstein, Peter. *Gemeinde, Brief und Heilsbotschaft: Ein phänomenologischer Vergleich zwischen Paulus und Epikur.* Herders biblische Studien. Freiburg: Herder, 2004.

Ehrensperger, Kathy. *That We May Be Mutually Encouraged: Feminism and the New Perspective in Pauline Studies.* London: T&T Clark, 2004.

Eriksson, Anders. *Traditions as Rhetorical Proof: Pauline Argumentation in 1 Corinthians.* Coniectanea Biblica New Testament Series 29. Stockholm: Almqvist & Wiksell International, 1998.

Euripides. *Medea.* In *Euripides I: Alcestis, The Medea, The Heracleidae, Hippolytus.* Translated by Rex Warner. The Complete Greek Tragedies 5. Chicago: University of Chicago Press, 1955.

Fairweather, Janet. "The Epistle to the Galatians and Classical Rhetoric: Part 3." *Tyndale Bulletin* 45 (1994): 213–43.

Fee, Gordon. *Pauline Christology: An Exegetical-Theological Study.* Peabody, MA: Hendrickson, 2007.

Fenske, Wolfgang. *Die Argumentation des Paulus in ethischen Herausforderung.* Göttingen: V&R Unipress, 2004.

Fiore, Benjamin. *The Function of Personal Example in the Socratic and Pastoral Epistles.* Analecta Biblica 105. Rome: Biblical Institute Press, 1986.

Fitzmyer, Joseph. *Romans: A New Translation with Introduction and Commentary.* Anchor Bible 33. New York: Doubleday, 1992.

Forbes, Christopher. "Ancient Rhetoric and Ancient Letters." In *Paul and Rhetoric,* edited by J. Paul Sampley and Peter Lampe, 143–60. New York: T&T Clark, 2010.

Fortna, Robert. "Philippians: Paul's Most Egocentric Letter." In *The Conversation Continues,* edited by Robert Fortna and Beverly Gaventa. Nashville: Abingdon, 1990.

Frey, Jörg. "The Jewishness of Paul." In *Paul: Life, Setting, Work, Letters*, edited by Oda Wischmeyer, translated by Helen S. Heron with Dieter T. Roth, 57–96. London: T&T Clark, 2012.

Gathercole, Simon J. *Where Is Boasting? Early Jewish Soteriology and Paul's Response in Romans 1–5.* Grand Rapids: Eerdmans, 2002.

Gaventa, Beverly Roberts. "Galatians 1 and 2: Autobiography as Paradigm." *Novum Testamentum* 28 (1986): 309–26.

Gese, Michael. *Das Vermächtnis des Apostels: Die Rezeption der paulinischen Theologie im Epheserbrief.* Wissenschaftliche Untersuchungen zum Neuen Testament 2/99. Tübingen: Mohr Siebeck, 1997.

Gibson, Richard J. "The Literary and Theological Coherence of 1 Timothy." Thesis. Kingsford, NSW: Australian College of Theology, 1995.

———. "The Literary Coherence of 1 Timothy." *Reformed Theological Review* 55 (1996): 53–66.

———. "Paul the Missionary in Priestly Service (Romans 15:16)." In *Paul as Missionary: Identity, Activity, Theology, and Practice*, edited by Trevor J. Burke and Brian S. Rosner, 51–62. The Library of New Testament Studies 420. London: T&T Clark, 2011.

Gordley, Matthew E. *The Colossian Hymn in Context: An Exegesis in Light of Jewish and Greco-Roman Hymnic and Epistolary Conventions.* Wissenschaftliche Untersuchungen zum Neuen Testament 2/28. Tübingen: Mohr Siebeck, 2007.

Gorman, Michael J. *Cruciformity: Paul's Narrative Spirituality of the Cross.* Grand Rapids: Eerdmans, 2001.

Grabner-Haider, Anton. *Paraklese und Eschatologie in Paulus.* Münster: Aschendorff, 1985.

Guthrie, W. C. K. *The Sophists.* Cambridge: Cambridge University Press, 1971.

Hahn, Ferdinand. *Theologie des Neuen Testaments.* 2nd ed. Tübingen: Mohr Siebeck, 2002.

Hardin, Justin K. "Galatians 1 and 2 without a Mirror." *Tyndale Bulletin* 65 (2014): 275–303.

Harding, Mark. *Tradition and Rhetoric in the Pastoral Epistles.* Studies in Biblical Literature 3. New York: Lang, 1998.

Harnack, Adolf von. *What Is Christianity?* New York: Harper & Row, 1957.

Hartman, Lars. "Galatians 3:15–4:11 as Part of a Theological Argument on a Practical Issue." In *The Truth of the Gospel (Gal. 1:1–4:11)*, edited by J. Lambrecht, 127–58. Rome: Benedicta, 1993.

Häußer, Detlef. *Christusbekenntnis und Jesusüberlieferung bei Paulus.* Tübingen: Francke, 2006.

Hays, Richard B. *The Faith of Jesus Christ: An Investigation of the Narrative Substructure of Galatians 3:1–4:11.* Society of Biblical Literature Dissertation Series 56. Chico, CA: Scholars Press, 1983.

Hengel, Martin. *The Atonement: The Origins of the Doctrine in the New Testament.* Translated by John Bowden. Philadelphia: Fortress, 1981.

———. "The Attitude of Paul to the Law in the Unknown Years between Damascus and Antioch." In *Paul and the Mosaic Law*, edited by James D. G. Dunn, 25–51. Grand Rapids: Eerdmans, 2001.

———. *Between Jesus and Paul: Studies in the Early History of Christianity.* Philadelphia: Fortress, 1983.

———. "Die Stellung des Apostels Paulus zum Gesetz in den unbekannten Jahren zwischen Damascus und Antiochien." In *Paulus und Jakobus*, 213–39. Kleine Schriften 3. Wissenschaftliche Untersuchungen zum Neuen Testament 141. Tübingen: Mohr Siebeck, 2002.

———. *Studies in Early Christology.* Edinburgh: T&T Clark, 1995.

Hengel, Martin, and Anna Maria Schwemer. *Paul between Damascus and Antioch: The Unknown Years.* Louisville: Westminster John Knox, 1997.

Hester, James D. "Creating the Future: Apocalyptic Rhetoric in 1 Thessalonians." *Religion and Theology* 7 (2000): 192–212.

Hock, Ronald. *The Social Context of Paul's Ministry: Tentmaking and Apostleship.* Philadelphia: Fortress, 1980.

Hodge, Caroline E. Johnson. *If Sons, Then Heirs: A Study of Kinship and Ethnicity in the Letters of Paul.* Oxford: Oxford University Press, 2007.

Hofius, Otfried. *Der Christushymnus Philipper 2,6–11: Untersuchungen zu Gestalt und Aussage eines urchristlichen Psalms.* 2nd ed. Wissenschaftliche Untersuchungen zum Neuen Testament 17. Tübingen: Mohr Siebeck, 1991.

Holtz, Gudrun. "Von Alexandrien nach Jerusalem: Überlegungen zum Vermittlung philonish-alexandrinisches Tradition an Paulus." *Zeitschrift für die neutestamentliche Wissenschaft* 105 (2014): 228–63.

Holtz, Traugott. *Der erste Brief an die Thessalonicher.* 3rd ed. Evangelisch-Katholischer Kommentar zum Neuen Testament. Neukirchen-Vluyn: Neukirchener Verlag, 1998.

Hooker, Morna D. "Interchange in Christ and Ethics." *Journal for the Study of the New Testament* 25 (1985): 3–17.

———. "Were There False Teachers in Colossae?" In *Christ and Spirit in the New Testament: Essays in Honour of C. F. D. Moule*, edited by Barnabas Lindars and S. S. Smalley, 315–31. Cambridge: Cambridge University Press, 1973.

Hoover, Roy W. "The *Harpagmos* Enigma: A Philological Solution." *Harvard Theological Review* 64 (1971): 95–119.

Horsley, Richard. *Paul and Empire: Religion and Power in Roman Imperial Society.* Harrisburg, PA: Trinity Press International, 1997.

Hübner, Hans. *Biblische Theologie des Neuen Testaments.* Vol. 2, *Die Theologie des Paulus und ihre neutestamentliche Wirkungsgeschichte.* Göttingen: Vandenhoeck & Ruprecht, 1993.

————. "Der Galaterbrief und das Verhältnis von antiker Rhetorik und Epistolographie." *Theologische Literaturzeitung* 109 (1984): 242–50.

————. "Die Rhetorik und die Theologie: Der Römerbrief und die rhetorische Kompetenz des Paulus." In *Die Macht des Wortes: Aspekte gegenwärtiger Rhetorikforschung*, edited by Carl Joachim Classen and Heinz-Joachim Müllenbrock, 165–79. Ars rhetorica 4. Marburg: Hitzeroth, 1992.

Hultgren, Stephen. "The Origin of the Doctrine of the Two Adams in 1 Cor. 15:45–49." *Journal for the Study of the New Testament* 25 (2003): 343–70.

Hunn, Debbie. "Pleasing God or Pleasing People? Defending the Gospel in Galatians 1–2." *Biblica* 91 (2010): 24–49.

Hurtado, Larry. "Paul's Messianic Christology." In *Paul the Jew*, edited by Gabriele Boccaccini, Carlos A. Segovia, and Cameron J. Doody, 107–32. Minneapolis: Fortress, 2016.

Jeal, Roy R. "Rhetorical Argumentation in the Letter to the Ephesians." In *Rhetorical Argumentation in Biblical Texts: Essays from the Lund 2000 Conference*, edited by Anders Eriksson, Thomas H. Olbricht, and Walter Übelacker, 310–24. Emory Studies in Early Christianity 8. Harrisburg, PA: Trinity Press International, 2002.

Jewett, Robert. *The Thessalonian Correspondence: Pauline Rhetoric and Millenarian Piety*. Philadelphia: Fortress, 1986.

Johnson, Luke Timothy. *The First and Second Letters to Timothy: A New Translation with Introduction and Commentary*. Anchor Bible 35A. New York: Doubleday, 2000.

————. "First Timothy 1:1–20: The Shape of the Struggle." In *1 Timothy Reconsidered*, edited by Karl Paul Donfried, 19–40. Colloquium Oecumenicum Paulinum. Leuven: Peeters, 2008.

————. "The Paul of the Letters: A Catholic Perspective." In *Four Views of the Apostle Paul*, edited by Michael F. Bird, 65–96. Grand Rapids: Zondervan, 2012.

Judge, E. A. "Paul's Boasting in Relation to Contemporary Professional Practice." *Australian Biblical Review* 10 (1968): 37–50.

Karris, Robert J. "The Background and Significance of the Polemic of the Pastoral Epistles." *Journal of Biblical Literature* 92 (1973): 549–64.

————. "Romans 14:1–15:13 and the Occasion of Romans." In *The Romans Debate*, edited by Karl P. Donfried, 65–84. Revised and expanded. Peabody, MA: Hendrickson, 1971.

Kennedy, George A. *New Testament Interpretation through Rhetorical Criticism*. Chapel Hill: University of North Carolina Press, 1984.

————, trans. and ed. *Progymnasmata: Greek Textbooks of Prose Composition and Rhetoric*. Writings from the Greco-Roman World. Atlanta: Society of Biblical Literature, 2003.

Kim, Johann. *God, Israel and the Gentiles: Rhetoric and Situation in Romans 9–11.* Society of Biblical Literature Dissertation Series 176. Atlanta: Society of Biblical Literature, 2000.

Kim, Seyoon. *Paul and the New Perspective: Second Thoughts on the Origin of Paul's Gospel.* Grand Rapids: Eerdmans, 2002.

————. "Paul as an Eschatological Herald." In *Paul as Missionary: Identity, Activity, Theology, and Practice*, edited by Trevor J. Burke and Brian S. Rosner, 9–24. Library of New Testament Studies 420. London: T&T Clark, 2011.

Kittel, Gerhard, and Gerhard Friedrich, eds. *Theological Dictionary of the New Testament.* 10 vols. Grand Rapids: Eerdmans, 1964–76.

Kneepkens, C. H., Gregor Kalivoda, Heike Mayer, and Franz-Hubert Robling. "Comparatio." In *Historisches Wörterbuch der Rhetorik*, edited by Gert Ueding, 2:293–99. Tübingen: Niemeyer, 1994.

Koch, Dietrich-Alex. *Die Schrift als Zeuge des Evangeliums: Zur Verwendung und zum Verständnis der Schrift bei Paulus.* Beiträge zur historischen Theologie. Tübingen: Mohr Siebeck, 1986.

Koester, Helmut. "1 Thessalonians—Experiment in Christian Writing." In *Continuity and Discontinuity in Church History: Essays Presented to G. H. Williams*, edited by F. F. Church and T. George, 33–44. Leiden: Brill, 1979.

Koestler, Arthur. *Arrival and Departure.* London: Macmillan, 1943.

Krentz, Edgar. "*Logos* or *Sophia*: The Pauline Use of the Ancient Dispute between Rhetoric and Philosophy." In *Early Christianity and Classical Culture: Comparative Studies in Honor of Abraham J. Malherbe*, edited by John T. Fitzgerald, Thomas H. Olbricht, and L. Michael White, 277–90. Supplements to Novum Testamentum 110. Leiden: Brill, 2003.

Kümmel, W. G. *Die Theologie des Neuen Testaments nach seinen Hauptzeugen.* Das Neue Testament Deutsch Ergänzungsreihe 3. Göttingen: Vandenhoeck & Ruprecht, 1987.

Lampe, Peter. "The Roman Christians of Romans 16." In *The Romans Debate*, edited by Karl P. Donfried, 203–15. Revised and expanded. Peabody, MA: Hendrickson, 1971.

————. "Theology and Rhetoric: Redefining the Relationship between *Res* and *Verba*." *Acta Theologica* 33 (2013): 90–112.

Landmesser, Christoph. "Die Entwicklung der paulinischen Theologie und die Frage nach der Eschatologie." In *Eschatologie/Eschatology: The Sixth Durham-Tübingen Research Symposium; Eschatology in Old Testament, Ancient Judaism and Early Christianity (Tübingen, September 2009)*, edited by Hans-Joachim Eckstein, Christof Landmesser, Hermann Lichtenberger, Jens Adam, and Martin Bauspiess, 173–94. Wissenschaftliche Untersuchungen zum Neuen Testament 272. Tübingen: Mohr Siebeck, 2011.

Lausberg, Heinrich. *Handbook of Literary Rhetoric: A Foundation for Literary Study*. Edited by David E. Orton and R. Dean Anderson. Translated by Matthew T. Bliss, Annemiek Jansen, and David E. Orton. Leiden: Brill, 1998.

Lincoln, Andrew T. *Ephesians*. Word Biblical Commentary. Dallas: Word, 1990.

———. "The Theology of Ephesians." In *The Theology of the Later Pauline Letters*, 75–166. New Testament Theology. Cambridge: Cambridge University Press, 1993.

Litfin, Duane. *Paul's Theology of Preaching: The Apostle's Challenge to the Art of Persuasion in Ancient Corinth*. Downers Grove, IL: IVP Academic, 2015.

Lohfink, Gerhard. "Paulinische Theologie in der Rezeption der Pastoralbriefe." In *Paulus in den neutestamentlichen Spätschriften: Zur Paulusrezeption im Neuen Testament*, edited by Karl Kertelge and Gerhard Lohfink, 70–121. Freiburg: Herder, 1981.

Lohmeyer, Ernst. *Der Brief an die Philipper*. Kritisch-exegetischer Kommentar über das Neue Testament 9. Göttingen: Vandenhoeck & Ruprecht, 1961.

———. *Kyrios Jesus: Eine Untersuchung zu Phil. 2.5–11*. Darmstadt: Wissenschaftliche Buchgesellschaft, 1961. First published 1928.

Long, Frederick J. *Ancient Rhetoric and Paul's Apology: The Compositional Unity of 2 Corinthians*. Cambridge: Cambridge University Press, 2004.

Lührmann, Dieter. "Paul and the Pharisaic Tradition." *Journal for the Study of the New Testament* 36 (1989): 75–94.

Mack, Burton. *Rhetoric and the New Testament*. Minneapolis: Fortress, 1990.

Malherbe, Abraham J. *Ancient Epistolary Theorists*. SBL Sources for Biblical Study 19. Atlanta: Scholars Press, 1988.

———. "Antisthenes and Paul at War." *Harvard Theological Review* 76 (1983): 143–73.

———. *The Letters to the Thessalonians*. Anchor Bible 32B. New York: Doubleday, 2000.

Marshall, Peter. *Enmity at Corinth: Social Conventions in Paul's Relations with the Corinthians*. Tübingen: Mohr Siebeck, 1987.

Martens, John W. "Romans 2:14–16: A Stoic Reading." *New Testament Studies* 40 (1994): 55–67.

Martin, Troy W. "Invention and Arrangement in Recent Pauline Studies." In *Paul and Rhetoric*, edited by J. Paul Sampley and Peter Lampe, 48–118. New York: T&T Clark, 2010.

———. "Investigating the Pauline Letter Body: Issues, Methods, and Approaches." In *Paul and the Ancient Letter Form*, edited by Stanley E. Porter and Sean A. Adams, 185–212. Pauline Studies 6. Leiden: Brill, 2010.

Matera, Frank J. *New Testament Theology: Exploring Diversity and Unity*. Louisville: Westminster John Knox, 2007.

Meeks, Wayne A. "The Christian Proteus." In *The Writings of St. Paul*, edited by Wayne A. Meeks, 435–44. 2nd ed. New York: Norton, 1972.

————. "Judgment and the Brother: Romans 14:1–15:13." In *Tradition and Interpretation in the New Testament: Essays in Honor of E. Earle Ellis for His Sixtieth Birthday*, edited by Gerald F. Hawthorne and Otto Betz, 290–300. Grand Rapids: Eerdmans, 1987.

Minear, Paul S. *The Obedience of Faith: The Purposes of Paul in the Epistle to the Romans*. Naperville, IL: Allenson, 1971.

Mitchell, Margaret. *Paul and the Rhetoric of Reconciliation: An Exegetical Investigation of the Language and Composition of 1 Corinthians*. Louisville: Westminster John Knox, 1991.

————. "Rhetorical Shorthand in Pauline Argumentation: The Function of 'the Gospel' in the Corinthian Correspondence." In *Gospel in Paul: Studies in Corinthians, Galatians, and Romans for Richard Longenecker*, edited by L. Ann Jervis and Peter Richardson, 63–88. Journal for the Study of the New Testament Supplement Series 108. Sheffield: Sheffield Academic, 1994.

Mohrmann, Douglas C. "Paul's Use of Scripture in Romans 9–11 as Palimpsest: Literature in the Second Degree." In *The Crucified Apostle: Essays on Peter and Paul*, edited by Todd A. Wilson and Paul R. House, 129–50. Wissenschaftliche Untersuchungen zum Neuen Testament 2/450. Tübingen: Mohr Siebeck, 2017.

Morgan, Teresa. *Roman Faith and Christian Faith: Pistis and Fides in the Early Roman Empire and the Early Churches*. Oxford: Oxford University Press, 2015.

Nanos, Mark D. "Paul and the Jewish Tradition: The Ideology of the *Shema*." In *Celebrating Paul: Festschrift in Honor of Jerome Murphy-O'Connor, O.P., and Joseph A. Fitzmyer, S.J.*, edited by Peter Spitaler, 62–80. Catholic Biblical Quarterly Monograph Series 48. Washington, DC: The Catholic Biblical Association of America, 2011.

Neusner, Jacob. "From Judaism to Judaisms: My Approach to the History of Judaism." In *Ancient Judaism: Debates and Disputes; Second Series*, 181–221. South Florida Studies in the History of Judaism 5. Atlanta: Scholars Press, 1990.

————. "The Rabbinic Traditions about the Pharisees before 70 CE: An Overview." In *In Quest of the Historical Pharisees*, edited by Jacob Neusner and Bruce D. Chilton, 297–311. Waco: Baylor University Press, 2007.

Noack, Christian. "Haben oder Empfangen: Antiethische Charakterisierungen von Torheit und Weisheit bei Philo und bei Paulus." In *Philo und das Neue Testament*, edited by Roland Deines and Karl-Wilhelm Niebuhr, 283–307. Wissenschaftliche Untersuchungen zum Neuen Testament 172. Tübingen: Mohr Siebeck, 2004.

Norden, Eduard. *Die antike Kunstprosa*. Leipzig: Teubner, 1909.

O'Donnell, Tim. "The Rhetorical Strategy of 1 Timothy." *Catholic Biblical Quarterly* 79 (2017): 455–75.

Olbricht, Thomas H. "An Aristotelian Rhetorical Analysis of 1 Thessalonians." In *Greeks, Romans, Christians: Essays in Honor of Abraham J. Malherbe*, edited by David L. Balch, Everett Ferguson, and Wayne Meeks, 216–36. Minneapolis: Fortress, 1990.

———. "The Foundations of the Ēthos in Paul and the Classical Rhetoricians." In *Rhetoric, Ethic, and Moral Persuasion in Biblical Discourse: Essays from the 2002 Heidelberg Conference*, edited by Thomas H. Olbricht and Anders Eriksson, 138–59. Emory Studies in Early Christianity 11. London: T&T Clark, 2005.

Pao, David W. "Gospel within the Constraints of an Epistolary Form." In *Paul and the Ancient Letter Form*, edited by Stanley E. Porter and Sean A. Adams, 101–28. Pauline Studies 6. Leiden: Brill, 2010.

Peterson, Jeffrey. "Christ Our Pasch: Shaping Christian Identity in Corinth." In *Renewing Tradition: Studies in Texts and Contexts in Honor of James W. Thompson*, edited by Mark W. Hamilton, Thomas H. Olbricht, and Jeffrey Peterson, 133–44. Princeton Monograph Series 65. Eugene, OR: Pickwick, 2007.

Pitts, Andrew W. "Philosophical and Epistolary Contexts for Pauline Paraenesis." In *Paul and the Ancient Letter Form*, edited by Stanley E. Porter and Sean A. Adams, 269–306. Pauline Studies 6. Leiden: Brill, 2010.

Plank, Karl A. *Paul and the Irony of Affliction*. Atlanta: Scholars Press, 1987.

Pogoloff, Stephen M. *Logos and Sophia: The Rhetorical Situation of 1 Corinthians*. Atlanta: Scholars Press, 1992.

Porter, Stanley E. "Ancient Literate Culture and Popular Rhetorical Knowledge." In *Paul and Ancient Rhetoric: Theory and Practice in the Hellenistic Context*, edited by Stanley E. Porter and Bryan R. Dyer, 96–116. Cambridge: Cambridge University Press, 2016.

———. "Paul of Tarsus and His Letters." In *Handbook of Classical Rhetoric in the Hellenistic Period, 330 B.C.–A.D. 400*, edited by Stanley E. Porter, 578–83. Leiden: Brill, 1997.

Räisänen, Heikki. *Paul and the Law*. 2nd ed. Wissenschaftliche Untersuchungen zum Neuen Testament 29. Tübingen: Mohr Siebeck, 1987.

Ramsaran, Rollin A. "Living and Dying, Living Is Dying (Philippians 1:21): Paul's Maxim and Exemplary Argumentation in Philippians." In *Rhetorical Argumentation in Biblical Texts: Essays from the Lund 2000 Conference*, edited by Anders Eriksson, Thomas H. Olbricht, and Walter Übelacker, 325–38. Emory Studies in Early Christianity 8. Harrisburg, PA: Trinity Press International, 2002.

Riesner, Rainer. "Paulus und die Jesus-Überlieferung." In *Evangelium, Schriftauslegung, Kirche: Festschrift für Peter Stuhlmacher zum 65. Geburtstag*, edited by Jostein Ådna, Scott J. Hafemann, and Otfried Hofius, 347–65. Göttingen: Vandenhoeck & Ruprecht, 1997.

Rockwell, Stephen. "Faith, Hope and Love in the Colossian Epistle." *Reformed Theological Review* 72 (2013): 36–52.

Roloff, Jürgen. *Der erste Brief an Timotheus*. Evangelisch-katholischer Kommentar zum Neuen Testament 15. Zurich: Benziger, 1988.

Sakenfeld, Katharine Doob, ed. *New Interpreters Dictionary of the Bible*. 5 vols. Nashville: Abingdon, 2006–9.

Sanders, E. P. *Paul and Palestinian Judaism*. Minneapolis: Fortress, 1977.

———. *Paul, the Law, and the Jewish People*. Philadelphia: Fortress, 1985.

Saw, Insawn. *Paul's Rhetoric in 1 Corinthians 15: An Analysis Utilizing the Themes of Classical Rhetoric*. Lewiston, NY: Mellen, 1995.

Schellenberg, Ryan S. *Rethinking Paul's Rhetorical Education: Comparative Rhetoric and 2 Corinthians 10–13*. Atlanta: Society of Biblical Literature, 2013.

Schiffman, Lawrence H. "Shema." In *New Interpreters Dictionary of the Bible*, edited by Katharine Doob Sakenfeld, 5:224–25. Nashville: Abingdon, 2006–9.

Schließer, Benjamin. "Paulustheologien im Vergleich." In *Die Theologie des Paulus in der Diskussion: Reflexionen im Anschluss an Michael Wolters Grundriss*, edited by Jörg Frey and Benjamin Schließer, 1–80. Neukirchen-Vluyn: Neukirchener Verlag, 2013.

Schmeller, Thomas. *Der zweite Brief an die Korinther (2 Kor 1:1–7:4)*. Evangelisch-Katholischer Kommentar zum Neuen Testament 8/1. Neukirchen-Vluyn: Patmos, 2010.

Schnackenburg, Rudolf. *Der Brief an die Epheser*. Evangelisch-Katholischer Kommentar zum Neuen Testament 10. Neukirchen-Vluyn: Neukirchener Verlag, 1982.

Schnelle, Udo. *Apostle Paul: His Life and Theology*. Translated by M. Eugene Boring. Grand Rapids: Baker Academic, 2005.

———. "Gibt es eine Entwicklung in der Rechtfertigungslehre vom Galater- zum Römerbrief?" In *Paulus—Werk und Wirkung: Festschrift für Andreas Lindemann zum 70. Geburtstag*, edited by Paul-Gerhard Klumbies and David S. Du Toit, 289–309. Tübingen: Mohr Siebeck, 2013.

———. *Theology of the New Testament*. Grand Rapids: Baker Academic, 2009.

———. *Wandlungen im paulinischen Denken*. Stuttgarter Bibelstudien 137. Stuttgart: Katholisches Bibelwerk, 1989.

Schrage, Wolfgang. *Der erste Brief an die Korinther*. Evangelisch-Katholischer Kommentar zum Neuen Testament 7. 4 vols. Neukirchen-Vluyn: Neukirchener Verlag, 1991–2001.

———. "Heiligung als Prozess bei Paulus." In *Kreuzestheologie und Ethik im Neuen Testament: Gesammelte Schriften*, 203–15. Göttingen: Vandenhoeck & Ruprecht, 2004.

Schreiner, Thomas. "Did Paul Believe in Justification by Works? Another Look at Romans 2." *Bulletin for Biblical Research* 3 (1993): 131–58.

Schubert, Paul. *Form and Function of the Pauline Thanksgivings*. Beihefte zur Zeitschrift für die neutestamentliche Wissenschaft 20. Berlin: Topelmann, 1939.

Schweitzer, Albert. *The Mysticism of Paul the Apostle*. London: A. & C. Black, 1931.

Selby, Gary S. *Not with Wisdom of Words: Nonrational Persuasion in the New Testament*. Grand Rapids: Eerdmans, 2016.

———. "Paul the Seer: The Rhetorical Persona in 1 Corinthians 2.1–16." In *The Rhetorical Analysis of Scripture: Essays from the 1995 London Conference*, edited by Stanley E. Porter and Thomas H. Olbricht, 351–73. Sheffield: Sheffield Academic, 1997.

Sherwood, Alan. *Paul and the Restoration of Humanity in Light of Jewish Traditions*. Ancient Judaism and Early Christianity. Leiden: Brill, 2013.

Silva, Moisés. "Faith versus Works of the Law in Galatians." In *The Paradoxes of Paul*, 217–48. Vol. 2 of *Justification and Variegated Nomism*, edited by D. A. Carson, Peter T. O'Brien, and Mark A. Seifrid. Wissenschaftliche Untersuchungen zum Neuen Testament 2/181. Grand Rapids: Baker Academic, 2004.

Smit, J. "The Letter of Paul to the Galatians: A Deliberative Speech." *New Testament Studies* 35 (1989): 1–26.

Söding, Thomas. "Der erste Thessalonicherbrief und die frühe paulinische Evangeliumsverkündigung: Zur Frage einer Entwicklung der paulinischen Theologie." In *Texts and Contexts: Biblical Texts in Their Textual and Situational Contexts; Essays in Honor of Lars Hartman*, edited by Tord Fornberg and David Hellholm, 180–201. Oslo: Scandinavian University Press, 1995.

Spicq, C. *Theological Lexicon of the New Testament*. Translated and edited by J. D. Ernest. 3 vols. Peabody, MA: Hendrickson, 1994.

Stamps, Dennis L. "Rethinking the Rhetorical Situation: The Entextualization of the Situation in New Testament Epistles." In *Rhetoric and the New Testament: Essays from the 1992 Heidelberg Conference*, edited by Stanley E. Porter and Thomas H. Olbricht, 193–210. Journal for the Study of the New Testament Supplement Series 90. Sheffield: JSOT Press, 1993.

Stegemann, Wolfgang. "Wie wörtlich müssen wir die Worte des Apostel Paulus nehmen?" In *Die Theologie des Paulus in der Diskussion: Reflexionen im Anschluss an Michael Wolters Grundriss*, edited by Jörg Frey and Benjamin Schließer, 185–212. Neukirchen-Vluyn: Neukirchener Verlag, 2013.

Stendahl, Krister. *Final Account: Paul's Letter to the Romans*. Minneapolis: Fortress, 1993.

———. *Paul among Jews and Gentiles, and Other Essays*. Philadelphia: Fortress, 1976.

Stirewalt, M. Luther. *Paul, the Letter Writer*. Grand Rapids: Eerdmans, 2003.

Stowers, Stanley K. *Letter Writing in Greco-Roman Antiquity*. Library of Early Christianity. Philadelphia: Westminster, 1986.

Strecker, G., and Torsten Nolting. "Der vorchristliche Paulus: Überlegungen zum biographischen Kontext biblischer Überlieferung—zugleich eine Antwort an Martin Hengel." In *Texts and Contexts: Biblical Texts in Their Textual and Situational Contexts; Essays in Honor of Lars Hartman*, edited by Tord Fornberg and David Hellholm, 713–41. Oslo: Scandinavian University Press, 1995.

Stuhlmacher, Peter. *Biblische Theologie des Neuen Testaments*. Vol. 1, *Grundlegung von Jesus zu Paulus*. Göttingen: Vandenhoeck & Ruprecht, 1992.

Sumney, Jerry L. "The Argument of Colossians." In *Rhetorical Argumentation in Biblical Texts: Essays from the Lund 2000 Conference*, edited by Anders Eriksson, Thomas H. Olbricht, and Walter Übelacker, 339–52. Emory Studies in Early Christianity 8. Harrisburg, PA: Trinity Press International, 2002.

———. "The Function of Ēthos in Colossians." In *Rhetoric, Ethic, and Moral Persuasion in Biblical Discourse*, edited by Thomas H. Olbricht and Anders Eriksson, 301–15. Emory Studies in Early Christianity. London: T&T Clark, 2005.

Taatz, Irene. *Frühjüdische Briefe: Die paulinischen Briefe im Rahmen der offiziellen religiösen Briefe des Frühjudentum*. Novum Testamentum et Orbis Antiqua. Göttingen: Vandenhoeck & Ruprecht, 1991.

Talbert, Charles. *Ephesians and Colossians*. Paideia. Grand Rapids: Baker Academic, 2007.

Theissen, Gerd. *The Social Setting of Pauline Christianity: Essays on Corinth*. Philadelphia: Fortress, 1982.

Thompson, James W. *The Church according to Paul: Rediscovering the Community Conformed to Christ*. Grand Rapids: Baker Academic, 2014.

———. *Moral Formation according to Paul*. Grand Rapids: Baker Academic, 2011.

———. "Reading the Letters as Narrative." In *Narrative Reading, Narrative Preaching: Reuniting New Testament Interpretation and Proclamation*, edited by Joel B. Green and Michael Pasquarello III. Grand Rapids: Baker Academic, 2003.

Thompson, James W., and Bruce W. Longenecker. *Philippians and Philemon*. Paideia. Grand Rapids: Baker Academic, 2016.

Thurén, Lauri. *Derhetorizing Paul: A Dynamic Perspective on Pauline Theology and the Law*. Harrisburg, PA: Trinity Press International, 2000.

———. "On Studying Ethical Argumentation and Persuasion in the New Testament." In *Rhetoric and the New Testament: Essays from the 1992 Heidelberg Conference*, edited by Stanley E. Porter and Thomas H. Olbricht, 464–78. Journal for the Study of the New Testament Supplement Series 90. Sheffield. JSOT Press, 1993.

———. "Rhetoric and Epistolography: Case Not Closed." In *Paul and Ancient Rhetoric: Theory and Practice in the Hellenistic Context*, edited by Stanley E. Porter and Bryan R. Dyer, 141–60. Cambridge: Cambridge University Press, 2016.

Tite, Philip L. "How to Begin, and Why?" In *Paul and the Ancient Letter Form*, edited by Stanley E. Porter and Sean A. Adams, 57–100. Pauline Studies 6. Leiden: Brill, 2010.

Tobin, Thomas. *Paul's Rhetoric in Its Contexts: The Argument of Romans*. Peabody, MA: Hendrickson, 2004.

Tolmie, D. François. *Persuading the Galatians: A Text-Centred Rhetorical Analysis of a Pauline Letter*. Wissenschaftliche Untersuchungen zum Neuen Testament 2/190. Tübingen: Mohr Siebeck, 2005.

Trebilco, Paul. "Why Did the Early Christians Call Themselves ἡ ἐκκλησία?" *New Testament Studies* 57 (2011): 440–60.

Van der Watt, J. G. "Colossians 1:3–12 Considered as an Exordium." *Journal of Theology for Southern Africa* 57 (1986): 32–42.

Van Neste, Ray. *Cohesion and Structure in the Pastoral Epistles*. Journal for the Study of the New Testament Supplement Series 280. London: T&T Clark, 2004.

Vegge, T. *Paulus und das antike Schulwesen*. Beihefte zur Zeitschrift für die neutestamentliche Wissenschaft 13. Berlin: de Gruyter, 2006.

Vos, Johann S. "Rhetoric and Theology in the Letters of Paul." In *Paul and Rhetoric*, edited by J. Paul Sampley and Peter Lampe, 161–79. New York: T&T Clark, 2010.

Vouga, Francois. "Zur rhetorischen Gattung des Galaterbriefes." *Zeitschrift für die neutestamentliche Wissenschaft* 79 (1988): 291–92.

Wagner, J. Ross. *Heralds of the Good News: Isaiah and Paul "in Concert" in the Letter to the Romans*. Supplements to Novum Testamentum 101. Leiden: Brill, 2002.

Watson, Duane F. "Paul's Appropriation of Apocalyptic Discourse: The Rhetorical Strategy of 1 Thessalonians." In *Vision and Persuasion: Rhetorical Dimensions of Apocalyptic Discourse*, edited by Greg Carey and L. Gregory Bloomquist, 61–80. St. Louis: Chalice, 1999.

———. "Paul's Rhetorical Strategy in 1 Corinthians 15." In *Rhetoric and the New Testament: Essays from the 1992 Heidelberg Conference*, edited by Stanley E. Porter and Thomas H. Olbricht, 231–49. Journal for the Study of the New Testament Supplement Series 90. Sheffield: JSOT Press, 1993.

———. "The Role of Style in the Pauline Epistles: From Ornamentation to Argumentative Strategies." In *Paul and Rhetoric*, edited by J. Paul Sampley and Peter Lampe, 119–39. London: T&T Clark, 2010.

Watson, Francis. *Paul, Judaism, and the Gentiles: A Sociological Approach*. Society for New Testament Studies Monograph Series 56. Cambridge: Cambridge University Press, 1986.

Wegener, L. "The Rhetorical Strategy of 1 Corinthians 15." *Currents in Theology and Mission* 31 (2004): 438–55.

Weiss, Johannes. *Beiträge zur paulinische Rhetorik*. Göttingen: Vandenhoeck & Ruprecht, 1897.

White, John L. *The Form and Function of the Body of the Greek Letter: A Study of the Letter-Body in the Non-literary Papyri and in Paul the Apostle*. 2nd ed. Society of Biblical Literature Dissertation Series 2. Missoula, MT: Scholars Press, 1972.

Wilckens, Ulrich. *Rechtfertigung als Freiheit*. Neukirchen-Vluyn: Neukirchener Verlag, 1974.

Wilder, Amos. *Early Christian Rhetoric: The Language of the Gospel*. London: SCM, 1964.

Winter, Bruce. *After Paul Left Corinth: The Influence of Secular Ethics and Social Change*. Grand Rapids: Eerdmans, 2001.

Wischmeyer, Oda. "Das Gebot der Nächstenliebe bei Paulus: Eine traditionsgeschichtliche Untersuchung." *Biblische Zeitschrift*. Neue Folge 30 (1986): 161–87.

———. "Themes in Pauline Theology." In *Paul: Life, Setting, Work, Letters*, edited by Oda Wischmeyer, translated by Helen S. Heron with Dieter T. Roth, 277–304. London: T&T Clark, 2012.

Wolter, Michael. *Die Pastoralbriefe als Paulustradition*. Göttingen: Vandenhoeck & Ruprecht, 1988.

———. *Paul: An Outline of His Theology*. Waco: Baylor University Press, 2015.

Wrede, William. *Paul*. Boston: American Unitarian Association, 1909.

———. *Paulus*. 2nd ed. Tübingen: Mohr Siebeck, 1907.

Wright, N. T. "4QMMT and Paul: Justification, 'Works' and Eschatology." In *Pauline Perspectives: Essays on Paul, 1978–2013*, 332–43. Minneapolis: Fortress, 2013.

———. "Israel's Scriptures in Paul's Narrative Theology." In *Pauline Perspectives: Essays on Paul, 1978–2003*, 547–53. Minneapolis: Fortress, 2013.

———. "Jesus Christ Is Lord: Phil. 2:5–11." In *The Climax of the Covenant: Christ and the Law in Pauline Theology*, 56–98. Minneapolis: Fortress, 1999.

———. "The Law in Romans 2." In *Paul and the Mosaic Law*, edited by James D. G. Dunn, 131–50. Grand Rapids: Eerdmans, 1996.

———. *The New Testament and the People of God*. Minneapolis: Fortress, 1992.

———. *Paul and His Recent Interpreters*. Minneapolis: Fortress, 2015.

———. *Paul and the Faithfulness of God*. 2 vols. Minneapolis: Fortress, 2013.

———. "Poetry and Theology in Colossians 1:15–20." *New Testament Studies* 36 (1990): 444–68.

———. *The Resurrection of the Son of God*. Minneapolis: Fortress, 2003.

———. *What St. Paul Really Said: Was Paul of Tarsus the Real Founder of Christianity?* Oxford: Lion, 1997.

Wuellner, Wilhelm. "The Argumentative Structure of 1 Thessalonians as a Paradoxical Encomium." In *The Thessalonian Correspondence*, edited by Raymond F. Collins, 117–36. Bibliotheca Ephemeridum Theologicarum Lovaniensium 87. Leuven: Leuven University Press, 1990.

———. "Paul's Rhetoric of Argumentation in Romans: An Alternative to the Donfried-Karris Debate over Romans." *Catholic Biblical Quarterly* 38 (1976): 330–51.

Yarbrough, Mark M. *Paul's Utilization of Preformed Traditions in 1 Timothy: An Evaluation of the Apostle's Literary, Rhetorical, and Theological Tactics*. The Library of New Testament Studies 417. London: T&T Clark, 2009.

Zetterholm, Magnus. *Approaches to Paul: A Student's Guide to Recent Scholarship*. Minneapolis: Fortress, 2009.

Name Index

Schnelle, Udo, 4, 5, 38, 58, 61, 64, 66, 83, 101, 120, 122, 123, 185, 186, 248
Schrage, Wolfgang, 80, 88, 115, 135, 136, 139, 147, 153
Schreiner, Thomas, 50, 52
Schubert, Paul, 11, 20
Schweitzer, Albert, 6
Schwemer, Anna Maria, 57, 59, 66, 131
Selby, Gary S., 34, 104, 111, 134, 158, 234
Sherwood, Alan, 43
Silva, Moisés, 181
Söding, Thomas, 5, 101, 112
Spicq, C., xii, 29, 153, 157, 251, 252
Stamps, Dennis L., 102
Stegemann, Wolfgang, 5, 6
Stendahl, Krister, 6, 187
Stirewalt, M. Luther, 21
Stowers, Stanley K., 20
Strecker, G., 1, 46
Stuhlmacher, Peter, 65, 66, 284
Sumney, Jerry L., 228, 229

Taatz, Irene, 32
Talbert, Charles, 235
Theissen, Gerd, 146
Thompson, James W., 69, 95, 105, 106, 154, 202, 250, 253, 269
Thurén, Lauri, 2, 8, 9, 16, 23
Tite, Philip L., 22
Tobin, Thomas, 186

Tolmie, D. François, 173, 180
Trebilco, Paul, 69

Van der Watt, J. G., 222
Van Neste, Ray, 255
Vegge, T., 8
Vos, Johann S., 10

Wagner, J. Ross, 82, 83
Watson, Duane F., 26, 104, 105, 121
Watson, Francis, 6, 7, 179
Wegener, L., 121
Weiss, Johannes, 8, 24, 26
White, John L., 20
Wilckens, Ulrich, 37
Wilder, Amos, 35
Winter, Bruce, 145, 155
Wischmeyer, Oda, 17, 63
Wolter, Michael, 4, 5, 57, 58, 59, 61, 72, 83, 98, 107, 111, 113, 114, 120, 121, 124, 144, 152, 170, 179, 197, 247, 261, 263
Wrede, William, 2, 6, 59
Wright, N. T., 1, 2, 6, 38, 40, 41, 42, 43, 44, 45, 46, 47, 53, 132, 141, 178, 223, 224
Wuellner, Wilhelm, 101, 189, 192

Yarbrough, Mark M., 255

Zeller, D., 51
Zetterholm, Magnus, 6

Scripture and Ancient Sources Index

Subject Index